D1408149

PHP
Advanced
and Object-Oriented
Programming

LARRY ULLMAN

Peachpit Press

Visual QuickPro Guide
PHP Advanced and Object-Oriented Programming
Larry Ullman

Peachpit Press
1249 Eighth Street
Berkeley, CA 94710

Find us on the Web at: www.peachpit.com
To report errors, please send a note to: errata@peachpit.com
Peachpit Press is a division of Pearson Education.

Acquisitions Editor: Rebecca Gulick
Production Coordinator: Myrna Vladic
Copy Editor: Liz Welch
Technical Reviewer: Alan Solis
Compositor: Danielle Foster
Proofreader: Patricia Pane
Indexer: Valerie Haynes Perry
Cover Design: RHDG / Riezebos Holzbaur Design Group, Peachpit Press
Interior Design: Peachpit Press
Logo Design: MINE™ www.minesf.com

13-digit ISBN: 978-0-321-83218-4
10-digit ISBN: 0-321-83218-3

9 8 7 6 5 4 3 2 1

Printed and bound in the United States of America

Dedication

To my good friend Michael K. and his family: I cannot thank you all enough for your continuing friendship, generosity, and kindness over these many years.

My utmost thanks to...

Jessica, the love of my life, for just about everything.

Zoe and Sam, for making my world a better place.

Everyone at Peachpit Press for their support, for their dedication to putting out quality books, and for everything else they do to make all this happen.

The most excellent editor, Rebecca Gulick, for so many reasons.

Liz Welch, for her spot-on copyediting and attention to detail.

The production coordinator, Myrna Vladic, the compositor, Danielle Foster, the proofreader, Patricia Pane, and the indexer, Valerie Haynes Perry, who turn my mess of files into an actual book.

Alan Solis, for his very, very helpful technical review.

Thomas Larsson, for his input on the design patterns chapter. Always helpful to get even one more extra set of eyes!

Tjobbe Andrews (**http://tawd.co.uk**), for volunteering to create a new HTML5 design for the example chapter. And for doing so on such short notice!

Sara, for entertaining the kids so that I can get some work done, even if I'd rather not.

The readers, the readers, the readers!

Table of Contents

Introduction

In this humble author's (or not-so-humble author's) opinion, "advanced PHP" is about continuing to learn: you already know how to use PHP, and presumably MySQL, for all the standard stuff, and now it's time to expand that knowledge. This new knowledge can range from how to do different things, how to improve on the basic things, and how other technologies intersect with PHP. In short, you know how to make a dynamic Web site with PHP, but you'd like to know how to make a *better* Web site, with every possible meaning of "better."

This is the approach I've taken in writing this book. I haven't set out to blow your mind discussing esoteric idiosyncrasies the language has; rewriting the PHP, MySQL, or Apache source code; or making theoretically interesting but practically useless code. In short, I present to you several hundred pages of beyond-the-norm but still absolutely necessary (and often cool) tips and techniques.

About This Book

Simply put, I've tried to make this book's content accessible and useful for every PHP intermediate-level programmer out there. As I suggest in the introductory paragraphs, I believe that "advanced" PHP is mostly a matter of extended topics. You already possess all the basic knowledge—you retrieve database query results in your sleep—but want to go further. This may mean learning object-oriented programming (OOP), using PEAR (PHP Extension and Application Repository), invoking PHP on the command line, picking up eXtensible Markup Language (XML), or fine-tuning aspects of your existing skill set.

My definition of advanced PHP programming covers three loosely grouped areas:

- Doing what you already do better, faster, and more securely

- Learning OOP

- Doing standard things using PHP and other technologies (like networking, unit testing, or XML)

This book can be loosely divided into three sections. The first three chapters cover advanced PHP knowledge in general: programming techniques, Web applications, and databases. Those chapters all cover information that the average PHP programmer may not be familiar with but should be able to comprehend. In the process, you'll pick up lots of useful code, too.

The next six chapters focus on object-oriented programming. This section constitutes about half of the book. OOP is explained starting with the fundamentals, then going into lots of advanced topics, and ending with plenty of real-world examples.

The final five chapters are all "PHP and..." chapters:

- Communicating with networked servers
- Communicating with the host server
- Using the command-line interface
- XML
- Debugging, testing, and performance

Most examples used in this book are intended to be applicable in the real world, omitting the frivolous code you might see in other books, tutorials, and manuals. I focus almost equally on the philosophies involved as on the coding itself so that, in the end, you will come away with not just how to do this or that but also how to apply the new skills and ideas to your own projects.

Unlike with most of my other books, I do not expect that you'll necessarily read this book in sequential order, for the most part. Some chapters do assume that you've read others, like the object-oriented ones, which have a progression to them. Some later chapters also reference examples completed in earlier ones. If you read the later ones first, you'll just need to skip back over to the earlier ones to generate whatever database or scripts the later chapter requires.

Finally, I'll be using HTML5 in my scripts instead of HTML. I'll also use some CSS, as warranted. I do not discuss either of these subjects in this book (and, to be frank, may not adhere to them perfectly). If you are not already familiar with the subjects, you should look at some online resources or good books (such as Elizabeth Castro's excellent Visual QuickStart Guides) for more information.

What's new in this edition

I had three goals in writing this new edition:

- Greatly expanding the coverage of OOP

- Introducing new, more current topics, such as unit testing and debugging

- Cutting content that is outdated or has since been better covered in my other books

In terms of additional new material, by far the biggest change has been the additional coverage of object-oriented programming, including a chapter on design patterns. There's also a new example chapter that uses objects instead of procedural code.

Of course, all of the code and writing has been refreshed, edited, and improved as needed. This could mean just switching to HTML5 and better use of CSS, or my doing a better job of explaining complex ideas and examples.

How this book compares to my others

Those readers who have come to this book from my *PHP for the Web: Visual Quick-Start Guide* (Peachpit Press, 2011) may find themselves in a bit over their heads. This book does assume complete comfort with standard PHP programming, in particular debugging your own scripts. I'm not suggesting you put this book down, but if you find it goes too fast for you or assumes knowledge you don't currently possess, you may want to check out my *PHP and MySQL for Dynamic Web Sites: Visual QuickPro Guide* (Peachpit Press, 2011) instead.

If you have read the *PHP and MySQL* book, or a previous edition of this one, I'm hoping that you'll find this to be a wonderful addition to your library and skill set.

What You'll Need

Just as this book assumes that you already possess the fundamental skills to program in PHP (and, more important, to debug it when things go awry), it also assumes that you already have everything you need to follow along with the material. For starters, this means a PHP-enabled server. As of this writing, the latest version of PHP was 5.4, and much of the book depends on your using at least PHP 5.3.

Along with PHP, you'll often need a database application. I use MySQL for the examples, but you can use anything. And, for the scripts in some of the chapters to work—particularly the last five—your PHP installation will have to include support for the corresponding technology, and that technology's library may need to be installed, too. Fortunately, PHP 5 comes with built-in support for many advanced features. If the scripts in a particular chapter require special extensions, that will be referenced in the chapter's introduction. This includes the few times where I make use of a PEAR or PECL class. Nowhere in this book will I discuss installation of PHP, MySQL, and a Web server, though, as I expect you should already know or have accomplished that.

Should you have questions or problems, you can always search the Web or post a message in my support forums (**www.Larry Ullman.com/forums/**) for assistance.

Beyond PHP, you need the things you should already have: a text editor or IDE, an FTP application (if using a remote server), and a Web browser. All of the code in this book has been tested on both Windows XP and Mac OS X; you'll see screen shots in both operating systems.

Support Web Site

I have developed a Web site to support this book, available at **www.LarryUllman.com**. This site:

- Has every script available for download

- Has the SQL commands available for download

- Has extra files, as necessary, available for download

- Lists errors that have been found in the book

- Features a support forum where you can get help or assist others

- Provides a way to contact me directly

I'll also post at the site articles that extend some of the information covered in this book.

When using this site, please make sure you've gone to the correct URL (the book's title and edition are plastered everywhere). Each book I've written has its own support area; if you go to the wrong one, the downloadable files won't match those in the book.

Advanced PHP Techniques

One thing the advanced PHP programmer does better than the beginner is learn to take advantage of the obscure or hard-to-comprehend features of the language. For example, though you already know how to use arrays, you may not have mastered *multidimensional arrays*: creating them, sorting them, and so on. You have written your own functions by this point but may not understand how to use *recursion* and *static variables*. In this chapter, issues like these will be discussed, as well as other beyond-the-basics concepts, like the *heredoc* syntax and the **printf()**/ **sprintf()** family of functions.

In This Chapter

Multidimensional Arrays

Because of their power and flexibility, arrays are widely used in all PHP programming. In advanced situations, the multidimensional array often solves problems where other variable types just won't do.

For the first of the two examples, you'll see how to sort a multidimensional array. It's a common question users have and it isn't as hard as you might think. For the second example, you'll create a database-driven to-do list **A**.

Sorting multidimensional arrays

Sorting arrays is easy in PHP, thanks to the **sort()**, **ksort()**, and related functions. Using them, you can sort a one-dimensional array by key, by value, in reverse order, and so forth. But these functions will not work on multidimensional arrays (not as you'd probably like, at least).

Say you have an array defined like so:

```
$a = array(
array('key1' => 940, 'key2' => 'blah'),
array('key1' => 23, 'key2' => 'this'),
array('key1' => 894, 'key2' => 'that')
);
```

Current To-Do List

1. Must Do This!
2. Another Task
   1. Subtask 1
   2. Subtask 2
      1. Subsubtask1
   3. Subtask 3
3. My New Task

A One use of multidimensional arrays will be to create a nested to-do list.

The Short Array Syntax

New in PHP 5.4 is the *short array syntax*, which is simply an alternative way of creating an array. To use the short array syntax, replace calls to the **array()** function with the square array brackets:

```
// Old way:
$a = array(); // Empty
$b = array('this' => 'that');
// New way:
$a = []; // Empty
$b = ['this' => 'that'];
```

```
Array
(
    [0] => Array
        (
            [key1] => 23
            [key2] => this
        )

    [1] => Array
        (
            [key1] => 894
            [key2] => that
        )

    [2] => Array
        (
            [key1] => 940
            [key2] => blah
        )

)
```

B The multidimensional array sorted by numeric value (**key1**).

```
Iteration 1: 23 vs. 940

Iteration 2: 894 vs. 23

Iteration 3: 940 vs. 23

Iteration 4: 894 vs. 940

Array
(
    [0] => Array
        (
            [key1] => 23
            [key2] => this
        )
```

C By printing out the values of **$x['key1']** and **$y['key1']**, you can see how the user-defined sorting function is invoked.

This is a simple two-dimensional array (an array whose elements are also arrays) that you might need to sort using **key1** (a numeric sort) or **key2** (an alphabetical sort). To sort a multidimensional array, you define your own sort function and then tell PHP to use that function by invoking the built-in **usort()**, **uasort()**, or **uksort()** function.

The function you define must take exactly two parameters and return a value indicating which parameter should be first in the sorted list. A negative or false value means that the first parameter should be listed before the second. A positive or true value means the second parameter should come first. A value of 0 indicates the parameters have the same value.

To sort the preceding array on the first key, the sorting function would be defined as

```
function asc_number_sort($x, $y) {
    if ($x['key1'] > $y['key1']) {
        return true;
    } elseif ($x['key1'] < $y['key1']) {
        return false;
    } else {
        return 0;
    }
}
```

Then the PHP code would use this function **B**:

```
usort($a, 'asc_number_sort');
```

PHP will continue sending the inner arrays to this function so that they may be sorted. If you want to see this in detail, print the values being compared in the function **C**.

The **usort()** function sorts by values but does not maintain the keys (for the outermost array). When you use **uasort()**, the keys will be maintained. When you use **uksort()**, the sort is based on the keys.

To sort on the second key in the preceding example, you would want to compare two strings. That code would be **D**

```
function string_sort($x, $y) {
    return strcasecmp($x['key2'],
      $y['key2']);
}
usort($a, 'string_sort');
```

Or you could just use **strcmp()** to perform a case-sensitive sort. (In case you're not clear as to how **strcasecmp()** works, it will be explained in the following steps.)

To see this in action for yourself, let's run through an example.

To sort a multidimensional array:

1. Create a new PHP script in your text editor or IDE, to be named **sort.php**, starting with the HTML code (**Script 1.1**):

```
<!doctype html>
<html lang="en">
<head>
    <meta charset="utf-8">
    <title>Sorting
      Multidimensional
      Arrays</title>
    <link rel="stylesheet"
      href="style.css">
</head>
<body>
<?php # Script 1.1 - sort.php
```

continues on page 6

```
Array
(
    [0] => Array
        (
            [key1] => 940
            [key2] => blah
        )

    [1] => Array
        (
            [key1] => 894
            [key2] => that
        )

    [2] => Array
        (
            [key1] => 23
            [key2] => this
        )
)
```

D An alphabetical sort on the example array using **key2**.

Script 1.1 This script defines a two-dimensional array, which is then sorted based upon the inner array values.

```
1   <!doctype html>
2   <html lang="en">
3   <head>
4      <meta charset="utf-8">
5      <title>Sorting Multidimensional Arrays</title>
6      <link rel="stylesheet" href="style.css">
7   </head>
8   <body>
9   <?php # Script 1.1 - sort.php
10
11  /* This page creates a multidimensional array
12   * of names and grades.
13   * The array is then sorted twice:
14   * once by name and once by grade.
15   */
16
17  // Create the array...
18  // Array structure:
19  // studentID => array('name' => 'Name', 'grade' => XX.X)
20  $students = array(
21     256 => array('name' => 'Jon', 'grade' => 98.5),
22     2 => array('name' => 'Vance', 'grade' => 85.1),
23     9 => array('name' => 'Stephen', 'grade' => 94.0),
24     364 => array('name' => 'Steve', 'grade' => 85.1),
25     68 => array('name' => 'Rob', 'grade' => 74.6)
26  );
27
28  // Name sorting function:
29  function name_sort($x, $y) {
30     return strcasecmp($x['name'], $y['name']);
31  }
32
33  // Grade sorting function:
34  // Sort in DESCENDING order!
35  function grade_sort($x, $y) {
36     return ($x['grade'] < $y['grade']);
37  }
38
39  // Print the array as is:
40  echo '<h2>Array As Is</h2><pre>' . print_r($students, 1) . '</pre>';
41
42  // Sort by name:
43  uasort($students, 'name_sort');
44  echo '<h2>Array Sorted By Name</h2><pre>' . print_r($students, 1) . '</pre>';
45
46  // Sort by grade:
47  uasort($students, 'grade_sort');
48  echo '<h2>Array Sorted By Grade</h2><pre>' . print_r($students, 1) . '</pre>';
49
50  ?>
51  </body>
52  </html>
```

You'll note that I'm using HTML5 for all of the examples in this book, although that won't have an impact on any of the PHP code. I'm also using a simple style sheet from the HTML5 Boilerplate (**http://html5boilerplate.com/**).

You can download all of the book's code from **LarryUllman.com**.

2. Define a multidimensional array:

```
$students = array(
    256 => array('name' => 'Jon',
    → 'grade' => 98.5),
    2 => array('name' => 'Vance',
    → 'grade' => 85.1),
    9 => array('name' => 'Stephen',
    → 'grade' => 94.0),
    364 => array('name' => 'Steve',
    → 'grade' => 85.1),
    68 => array('name' => 'Rob',
    → 'grade' => 74.6)
);
```

The outer array, **$students**, has five elements, each of which is also an array. The inner arrays use the student's ID for the key (a made-up value) and store two pieces of data: the student's name and their grade.

3. Define the name-sorting function:

```
function name_sort($x, $y) {
    return strcasecmp($x['name'],
    → $y['name']);
}
```

The **strcasecmp()** function returns a number—negative, 0, or positive—indicating how similar two strings are. If a negative value is returned, the first string comes before the second alphabetically; if a positive value is returned, the second string comes first. If 0 is returned, the strings are the same.

Array Sorted By Name

```
Array
(
    [256] => Array
        (
            [name] => Jon
            [grade] => 98.5
        )

    [68] => Array
        (
            [name] => Rob
            [grade] => 74.6
        )

    [9] => Array
        (
            [name] => Stephen
            [grade] => 94
        )

    [364] => Array
        (
            [name] => Steve
            [grade] => 85.1
        )

    [2] => Array
        (
            [name] => Vance
            [grade] => 85.1
        )
)
```

E The array sorted by name.

Array Sorted By Name

```
Array
(
    [0] => Array
        (
            [name] => Jon
            [grade] => 98.5
        )

    [1] => Array
        (
            [name] => Rob
            [grade] => 74.6
        )

    [2] => Array
        (
            [name] => Stephen
            [grade] => 94
        )
```

F Failure to use **uasort()** would cause the keys, which store meaningful values (see Script 1.1), to be lost.

4. Define the grade sorting function:

```
function grade_sort($x, $y) {
    return ($x['grade'] <
    ⟶ $y['grade']);
}
```

This example is like the demo in the introduction to these steps, but in its shortest format. One significant difference is that this example should perform a *descending* sort, listing the highest grades first. This is easily accomplished: change the comparison operator from greater than to less than. Thus, if the first argument is less than the second, the value true is returned, which indicates the second argument should come first in the ordered list.

5. Print the array as it's initially defined:

```
echo '<h2>Array As Is</h2><pre>' .
⟶ print_r($students, 1) . '</pre>';
```

To quickly print out the array's contents, use the **print_r()** function. The output will be wrapped within **<pre>** tags for improved legibility.

6. Sort the array by name and print the results:

```
uasort($students, 'name_sort');
```

```
echo '<h2>Array Sorted By
⟶ Name</h2><pre>' . print_r
⟶ ($students, 1) . '</pre>';
```

Here the **uasort()** function is used so that the keys—the student IDs—are not lost **E**. If just **usort()** was invoked, the sorting would drop those keys **F**.

continues on next page

7. Sort the array by grade and print the results **G**:

```
uasort($students, 'grade_sort');
echo '<h2>Array Sorted By
→ Grade</h2><pre>' . print_r
→ ($students, 1) . '</pre>';
```

8. Complete the page:

```
?>
</body>
</html>
```

9. Save the file as **sort.php**, place it in your Web directory, and test in your Web browser.

Database-driven arrays

If you think about it, most database queries return a multidimensional array **H**. When the query results are fetched one record at a time, the multidimensional structure doesn't add any complication to your code. However, if you need to do something more elaborate with the results, you'll need a way to comprehend and manage the nested structure.

Array Sorted By Grade

```
Array
(
    [256] => Array
        (
            [name] => Jon
            [grade] => 98.5
        )

    [9] => Array
        (
            [name] => Stephen
            [grade] => 94
        )

    [2] => Array
        (
            [name] => Vance
            [grade] => 85.1
        )

    [364] => Array
        (
            [name] => Steve
            [grade] => 85.1
        )

    [68] => Array
        (
            [name] => Rob
            [grade] => 74.6
        )

)
```

G The array sorted by grade, in descending order.

```
 ● ● ○                    🏠 larryullman — PHP Advanced
mysql> SELECT * FROM tasks;
+---------+-----------+-------------+---------------------+---------------------+
| task_id | parent_id | task        | date_added          | date_completed      |
+---------+-----------+-------------+---------------------+---------------------+
|       1 |         0 | Must Do This!| 2012-04-22 16:06:42 | 0000-00-00 00:00:00 |
|       2 |         0 | Another Task | 2012-04-22 16:06:42 | 0000-00-00 00:00:00 |
|       3 |         0 | My New Task  | 2012-04-22 16:06:42 | 0000-00-00 00:00:00 |
|       4 |         2 | Subtask 1    | 2012-04-22 16:06:42 | 0000-00-00 00:00:00 |
|       5 |         2 | Subtask 2    | 2012-04-22 16:06:42 | 0000-00-00 00:00:00 |
|       6 |         2 | Subtask 3    | 2012-04-22 16:06:42 | 0000-00-00 00:00:00 |
|       7 |         5 | Subsubtask1  | 2012-04-22 16:07:12 | 0000-00-00 00:00:00 |
+---------+-----------+-------------+---------------------+---------------------+
7 rows in set (0.00 sec)

mysql>
```

H Selecting multiple columns from multiple rows in a database results in a multidimensional array.

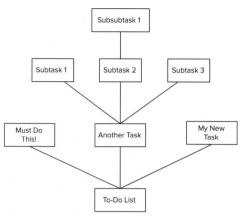

 How a nested to-do list looks as a tree.

task__id	parent_id	task
1	0	Must Do This!
2	0	Another Task
3	0	My New Task
4	2	Subtask 1
5	2	Subtask 2
6	2	Subtask 3
7	5	Subsubtask 1

This table represents the same data as in and . There will be a pseudo-foreign key-primary key relationship between the **task_id** and the **parent_id** columns.

To demonstrate this, the next example will create a database-driven, Web-based to-do list system. If the to-do list were one-dimensional, this wouldn't be that hard. But this list needs to be nestable, where each item can have multiple steps. The result will be a tree-like structure, where each branch can have its own offshoots.

The database table required to accomplish this is surprisingly simple:

```
CREATE TABLE tasks (
task_id INT UNSIGNED NOT NULL
→ AUTO_INCREMENT,
parent_id INT UNSIGNED NOT NULL
→ DEFAULT 0,
task VARCHAR(100) NOT NULL,
date_added TIMESTAMP NOT NULL,
date_completed TIMESTAMP,
PRIMARY KEY (task_id),
INDEX parent (parent_id),
INDEX added (date_added),
INDEX completed (date_completed)
);
```

The **task_id** is an automatically incremented primary key. The value will also be used as the **parent_id** if a task is a substep. The task itself goes into a **VARCHAR(100)** column, which you could also define as a text type if you wanted to allow for longer descriptions. Two time-stamp columns round out the table, one documenting when the task was added and another to indicate its completion. Three standard indexes are placed on columns that might be used in queries.

The trick to this application is that each item has a **parent_id** attribute. If an item is a substep, its **parent_id** would be the task number of the item that it falls under.

If an item is not a substep, its **parent_id** would be 0. It's a very simple setup that allows for the flexible, nested structure, but handling this in PHP will take some effort.

You're reading an advanced book on PHP, so I'm going to assume that you're fully capable of creating this database table for yourself. The next few pages will walk through the PHP script that adds new tasks to this table. In the upcoming sections of the chapter, you'll see how to use recursive functions to handle the multidimensional array.

To add tasks to the database:

1. Begin a new PHP script in your text editor or IDE, to be named **add_task.php**, starting with the HTML (**Script 1.2**):

```
<!doctype html>
<html lang="en">
<head>
    <meta charset="utf-8">
    <title>Add a Task</title>
    <link rel="stylesheet"
    → href="style.css">
</head>
<body>
<?php # Script 1.2 - add_task.php
```

2. Connect to the database:

```
$dbc = mysqli_connect('localhost',
→ 'username', 'password', 'test');
```

I'll be using MySQL and the Improved MySQL functions in this script. You'll need to change the particulars—username, password, and database name—to match what's correct for your setup.

For simplicity's sake, no error handling is involved, although you would certainly add that in a real-world application.

continues on page 13

Script 1.2 Tasks are added to the database using this script. Tasks can even be filed under other tasks using the drop-down menu.

```php
1    <!doctype html>
2    <html lang="en">
3    <head>
4        <meta charset="utf-8">
5        <title>Add a Task</title>
6        <link rel="stylesheet" href="style.css">
7    </head>
8    <body>
9    <?php # Script 1.2 - add_task.php
10
11   /* This page adds tasks to the tasks table.
12    * The page both displays and handles the form.
13    */
14
15   // Connect to the database:
16   $dbc = mysqli_connect('localhost', 'username', 'password', 'test');
17
18   // Check if the form has been submitted:
19   if (($_SERVER['REQUEST_METHOD'] == 'POST') && !empty($_POST['task'])) {
20
21       // Sanctify the input...
22
23       // The parent_id must be an integer:
24       if (isset($_POST['parent_id']) &&
25       filter_var($_POST['parent_id'], FILTER_VALIDATE_INT, array('min_range' => 1)) ) {
26           $parent_id = $_POST['parent_id'];
27       } else {
28           $parent_id = 0;
29       }
30
31       // Escape the task:
32       $task = mysqli_real_escape_string($dbc, strip_tags($_POST['task']));
33
34       // Add the task to the database.
35       $q = "INSERT INTO tasks (parent_id, task) VALUES ($parent_id, '$task')";
36       $r = mysqli_query($dbc, $q);
37
38       // Report on the results:
39       if (mysqli_affected_rows($dbc) == 1) {
40           echo '<p>The task has been added!</p>';
41       } else {
42           echo '<p>The task could not be added!</p>';
43       }
44
45   } // End of submission IF.
46
47   // Display the form:
48   echo '<form action="add_task.php" method="post">
```

script continues on next page

```
49   <fieldset>
50      <legend>Add a Task</legend>
51      <p>Task: <input name="task" type="text" size="60" maxlength="100" required></p>
52      <p>Parent Task: <select name="parent_id"><option value="0">None</option>';
53
54   // Retrieve all the uncompleted tasks:
55   $q = 'SELECT task_id, parent_id, task FROM tasks WHERE date_completed="0000-00-00 00:00:00"
     → ORDER BY date_added ASC';
56   $r = mysqli_query($dbc, $q);
57
58   // Also store the tasks in an array for use later:
59   $tasks = array();
60
61   // Fetch the records:
62   while (list($task_id, $parent_id, $task) = mysqli_fetch_array($r, MYSQLI_NUM)) {
63
64      // Add to the select menu:
65      echo "<option value=\"$task_id\">$task</option>\n";
66
67      // Add to the array:
68      $tasks[] = array('task_id' => $task_id, 'parent_id' => $parent_id, 'task' => $task);
69
70   }
71
72   // Complete the form:
73   echo '</select></p>
74   <input name="submit" type="submit" value="Add This Task">
75   </fieldset>
76   </form>';
77
78   // Sort the tasks by parent_id:
79   function parent_sort($x, $y) {
80      return ($x['parent_id'] > $y['parent_id']);
81   }
82   usort($tasks, 'parent_sort');
83
84   // Display all the tasks:
85   echo '<h2>Current To-Do List</h2><ul>';
86   foreach ($tasks as $task) {
87      echo "<li>{$task['task']}</li>\n";
88   }
89   echo '</ul>';
90   ?>
91   </body>
92   </html>
```

Add a Task
Task:
Parent Task ✓ None
Must Do This!
Add This T Another Task
My New Task

K The HTML form for adding tasks.

3. Check if the form has been submitted:

```
if (($_SERVER['REQUEST_METHOD'] ==
→'POST') && !empty($_POST['task'])) {
```

The form has one main text box and a drop-down menu **K**. To test for the form's submission, the conditional checks that the request method is POST and that the text box (named *task*) isn't empty. Certainly a more well-rounded script would do better, but that's sufficient for now.

4. Ensure that the **parent_id** value is an integer:

```
if (isset($_POST['parent_id']) &&
filter_var($_POST['parent_id'],
→FILTER_VALIDATE_INT, array
→('min_range' => 1)) ) {
    $parent_id =
    →$_POST['parent_id'];
} else {
    $parent_id = 0;
}
```

The **parent_id** value is another task's **task_id**. It will come from the drop-down menu, which means that it should be an integer. But you shouldn't make assumptions (because if someone hacked the form to send text as the **parent_id**, it would break the query), so the Filter extension is used to guarantee that the value is an integer greater than 1. If that's not the case, for whatever reason, 0 will be used instead.

The Filter extension was added to core PHP as of version 5.2. If you're not familiar with it, see the PHP manual.

continues on next page

5. Secure the task value:

```
$task = mysqli_real_escape_
→ string($dbc, strip_tags
→ ($_POST['task']));
```

The `mysqli_real_escape_string()` function will make whatever submitted task value safe to use in the query. To prevent Cross-Site Scripting (XSS) attacks, the task is also run through `strip_tags()`.

6. Add the task to the database:

```
$q = "INSERT INTO tasks
→ (parent_id, task) VALUES
→ ($parent_id, '$task')";

$r = mysqli_query($dbc, $q);
```

7. Report on the query results:

```
if (mysqli_affected_rows($dbc) ==
→ 1) {

    echo '<p>The task has been
    → added!</p>';

} else {

    echo '<p>The task could not be
    → added!</p>';

}
```

8. Complete the submission conditional and start the form:

```
} // End of submission IF.

echo '<form action="add_task.php"
→ method="post">

<fieldset>

    <legend>Add a Task</legend>

    <p>Task: <input name="task"
    → type="text" size="60"
    → maxlength="100" required></p>

    <p>Parent Task: <select
    → name="parent_id"><option
    → value="0">None</option>';
```

The form has one text input and one drop-down menu. The menu will be populated from the list of existing tasks. The first possible value will be 0, for tasks that are not subservient to other tasks.

9. Retrieve all the *uncompleted* tasks:

```
$q = 'SELECT task_id, parent_id,
→ task FROM tasks WHERE date_
→ completed="0000-00-00 00:00:00"
→ ORDER BY date_added ASC';

$r = mysqli_query($dbc, $q);
```

The query returns three pieces of information for every uncompleted task (once a task has been completed, its `date_completed` column would have a nonzero value). I'm only selecting uncompleted tasks because it would not make sense to add a subtask to a task that has been completed.

The `task_id` and the `task` itself will be used in the drop-down menu. The `parent_id` will be used later to nest the tasks.

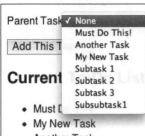

- Must D
- My New Task
- Another Task
- Subtask 3
- Subtask 1
- Subtask 2
- Subsubtask1

L The page contains the list of tasks two times.

```
          <p>Parent Task: <select name="parent_id">
<option value="2">Another Task</option>
<option value="3">My New Task</option>
<option value="4">Subtask 1</option>
<option value="5">Subtask 2</option>
<option value="6">Subtask 3</option>
<option value="7">Subsubtask1</option>
</select></p>
```

M The PHP-generated HTML source code for the drop-down menu.

Type Hinting Function Parameters

PHP5 quietly added the ability to perform *type hinting* of a function's parameters. Type hinting is the act of indicating what type a variable needs to be. For example, this code insists that the function's single parameter is an array:

```
function f(array $input) {}
```

If the function is called without providing an array, an error will be triggered.

As of this writing, there are limitations as to what types of values you can hint. You can hint arrays and objects, but not scalar types such as strings and integers. As you'll see later in the book, type hinting is most useful in object-oriented programming. The topic will be fully covered in Chapter 6, "More Advanced OOP."

10. Create an array for storing the tasks:

    ```
    $tasks = array();
    ```

    This script will list all the tasks twice: once in the drop-down menu and once after the form **L**. This array will store the tasks to be used in the second list.

11. Retrieve each database record and use it accordingly:

    ```
    while (list($task_id, $parent_id,
    → $task) = mysqli_fetch_array
    → ($r, MYSQLI_NUM)) {
        echo "<option value=
        → \"$task_id\">$task</option>\n";
        → $tasks[] = array('task_id' =>
        → $task_id, 'parent_id' =>
        → $parent_id, 'task' => $task);
    }
    ```

    Within the **while** loop the retrieved record is used to populate the drop-down menu **M** and is also stored in the **$tasks** array. This array will be multidimensional.

12. Complete the form:

    ```
    echo '</select></p>
    <input name="submit" type="submit"
    → value="Add This Task">
    </fieldset>
    </form>';
    ```

    continues on next page

13. Sort the tasks by `parent_id`:

```php
function parent_sort($x, $y) {
  return ($x['parent_id'] >
  ⇥ $y['parent_id']);
}
usort($tasks, 'parent_sort');
```

The `parent_id` value is what separates primary tasks from secondary ones, so working with this value in the PHP script is important. Using the information discussed earlier in the chapter, a user-defined function will sort the multidimensional array.

14. Display the full list of uncompleted tasks:

```php
echo '<h2>Current To-Do List</
h2><ul>';
foreach ($tasks as $task) {
  echo "<li>{$task['task']}
  ⇥ </li>\n";
}
echo '</ul>';
```

This loop will display each task in order of its `parent_id`. This is the first step toward making the list shown in **Ⓐ**, although as you can see in **Ⓛ**, the list isn't displayed quite as it should be yet. This will be solved later in the chapter.

15. Complete the page:

```php
?>
</body>
</html>
```

16. Save the file as **add_task.php**, place it in your Web directory, and test in your Web browser **Ⓝ**.

Add a Task

Task: `This is a new subtask!`

Parent Task: `This is a new task!` ⬍

`Add This Task`

Ⓝ Adding a task that's a subset of an existing task.

Advanced Function Definitions

Being able to define and use your own functions is integral to any programming language. After gaining even a modicum of PHP experience, you've no doubt created many. But there are four potential features of user-defined functions that arise in more advanced programming. These are:

- Recursive functions
- Static variables
- Accepting values by reference
- Anonymous functions

While not often used, sometimes these concepts are indispensable. In discussing and demonstrating these first two concepts, I'll continue to build on the tasks example just begun in the chapter.

Recursive functions

Recursion is the act of a function calling itself:

```
function somefunction() {
    // Some code.
    somefunction();
    // Possible other code.
}
```

The end result of a recursion is that the function's code is executed repeatedly, as if called from within a loop.

Recursive functions are necessary when you have a process that would be followed to an unknown depth. For example, a script that searches through a directory may have to search through any number of subdirectories. That can easily be accomplished using recursion:

```
function list_dir($start) {
    $contents = scandir($start);
    foreach ($contents as $item) {
        if (is_dir("$start/$item") &&
        ↪ (substr($item, 0, 1) != '.') ) {
            // Use $item.
            list_dir("$start/$item");
        } else {
            // Use $item.
        } // End of if-else.
    } // End of foreach.
} // End of function.
list_dir('.');
```

The function call—the last line—invokes the **list_dir('.');** function, providing the current directory as the starting point. Within the function, **scandir()** gets the directory's contents, and a **foreach** goes through each item. If an item is a directory, the function will be called again, using that new directory as the starting point. Recursion will continue down through all the subdirectories.

You need to be aware of two things when using recursion. The first is that, as with any loop, you need to ensure that there's an "out": a point at which the function will stop calling itself. In the above example, the function stops calling itself when it stops finding directories to iterate through.

The second issue is that recursion can be quite expensive in terms of server resources. Keep in mind that each function call requires memory and processing, and the very first call is not completed until they all are. Recursion that goes deeper than, say, 100 iterations could crash the server (depending on the server). Simply put, sometimes recursion is the only solution, but often the same need can be more efficiently addressed using a loop.

With the **tasks** table created earlier in the chapter, retrieving and displaying all the tasks is not hard (see ⓛ in the previous section). However, the method used in **add_task.php** (Script 1.2) does not properly nest the tasks like that in Ⓐ (in the first section). To help you accomplish that desired end, this next new script requires a multidimensional array and a recursive function.

To use recursion:

1. Begin a new PHP script in your text editor or IDE, to be named **view_tasks.php**, starting with the HTML (**Script 1.3**):

```
<!doctype html>
<html lang="en">
<head>
    <meta charset="utf-8">
    <title>View Tasks</title>
    <link rel="stylesheet" href="style.css">
</head>
<body>
<h2>Current To-Do List</h2>
<?php # Script 1.3 - view_tasks.php
```

2. Begin defining a recursive function:

```
function make_list($parent) {
    global $tasks;
    echo '<ol>';
```

The purpose of the function will be to convert an array of items into an ordered list:

```
<ol>
<li>Item 1</li>
<li>Item 2</li>
<li>Item 3</li>
</ol>
```

This function will take one argument, which will always be an array. Within the function, the **$tasks** array (the main array) needs to be available—you'll soon see why. Then the ordered list is begun.

I will add that, generally speaking, it's best not to use global variables, and so I'll discuss alternative solutions later in the chapter.

continues on page 21

Script 1.3 One recursive function and a multidimensional array will properly display the nested list of tasks.

```
1    <!doctype html>
2    <html lang="en">
3    <head>
4       <meta charset="utf-8">
5       <title>View Tasks</title>
6       <link rel="stylesheet" href="style.css">
7    </head>
8    <body>
9    <h2>Current To-Do List</h2>
10   <?php # Script 1.3 - view_tasks.php
11
12   /*  This page shows all existing tasks.
13    *  A recursive function is used to show the
14    *  tasks as nested lists, as applicable.
15    */
16
17   // Function for displaying a list.
18   // Receives one argument: an array.
19   function make_list($parent) {
20
21      // Need the main $tasks array:
22      global $tasks;
23
24      echo '<ol>'; // Start an ordered list.
25
26      // Loop through each subarray:
27      foreach ($parent as $task_id => $todo) {
28
29         // Display the item:
30         echo "<li>$todo";
31
32         // Check for subtasks:
33         if (isset($tasks[$task_id])) {
34            // Call this function again:
35            make_list($tasks[$task_id]);
36         }
37
38         echo '</li>'; // Complete the list item.
39
40      } // End of FOREACH loop.
41
42      echo '</ol>'; // Close the ordered list.
43
44   } // End of make_list() function.
45
46   // Connect to the database:
47   $dbc = mysqli_connect('localhost', 'username', 'password', 'test');
48
```

script continues on next page

```
49    // Retrieve all the uncompleted tasks:
50    $q = 'SELECT task_id, parent_id, task FROM tasks WHERE date_completed="0000-00-00 00:00:00"
      → ORDER BY parent_id, date_added ASC';
51    $r = mysqli_query($dbc, $q);
52
53    // Initialize the storage array:
54    $tasks = array();
55
56    // Loop through the results:
57    while (list($task_id, $parent_id, $task) = mysqli_fetch_array($r, MYSQLI_NUM)) {
58
59        // Add to the array:
60        $tasks[$parent_id][$task_id] =  $task;
61
62    }
63
64    // For debugging:
65    //echo '<pre>' . print_r($tasks,1) . '</pre>';
66
67    // Send the first array element
68    // to the make_list() function:
69    make_list($tasks[0]);
70
71    ?>
72    </body>
73    </html>
```

```
Array
(
    [0] => Array
        (
            [1] => Must Do This!
            [2] => Another Task
            [3] => My New Task
            [8] => This is a new task!
        )

    [2] => Array
        (
            [4] => Subtask 1
            [5] => Subtask 2
            [6] => Subtask 3
        )

    [5] => Array
        (
            [7] => Subsubtask1
        )

)
```

A The PHP script takes the tasks from the database and creates this multidimensional array.

3. Loop through the array, printing each item:

```
foreach ($parent as $task_id =>
→ $todo) {
    echo "<li>$todo";
```

A **foreach** loop will go through the array, printing each item within **<li>** tags. Those tags are begun here.

4. Call this function again if any subtasks exist:

```
if (isset($tasks[$task_id])) {
    make_list($tasks[$task_id]);
}
```

This is the most important part of the script. The tasks retrieved from the database will be tossed into a multidimensional array A. For the main array, each key is a **parent_id**. The value for each key is an array of tasks that fall under that **parent_id**. Thus, after printing the initial **<li>** and task, the function needs to check if this task has any subtasks (i.e., is this task a parent?); in other words: is there an array element in **$tasks** whose key is this task ID? If so, then the current task has subtasks and this function should be called again, sending that other part of the array (the element whose key is this **task_id** and whose value is an array of subtasks) as the argument.

continues on next page

The end results will be code like

```
<ol>
<li>Item 1</li>
<li>Item 2
  <ol>
  <li>Subitem 1</li>
  <li>Subitem 2</li>
  </ol>
</li>
<li>Item 3</li>
</ol>
```

5. Complete the **foreach** loop and the function:

```
    echo '</li>';
  } // End of FOREACH loop.
  echo '</ol>';
} // End of make_list() function.
```

6. Connect to the database:

```
$dbc = mysqli_connect('localhost',
→ 'username', 'password', 'test');
```

With the recursive function defined, the rest of the script needs to retrieve all the tasks, organize them in an array, and then call the **make_list()** function once.

7. Define and execute the query:

```
$q = 'SELECT task_id, parent_id,
→ task FROM tasks WHERE date_
→ completed="0000-00-00 00:00:00"
→ ORDER BY parent_id, date_added
→ ASC';
```

```
$r = mysqli_query($dbc, $q);
```

The query retrieves three pieces of information for each task: its ID, its **parent_id**, and the task itself. The conditional means that only noncompleted tasks are selected. The results are also ordered by the **parent_id** so that every top-level task (with a **parent_id** of 0) is returned first. A secondary ordering by **date_added** returns the tasks in the order they were added (an assumption being that's how they are prioritized).

8. Add each task to an array:

```
$tasks = array();
while (list($task_id, $parent_id,
→ $task) = mysqli_fetch_array($r,
→ MYSQLI_NUM)) {
  $tasks[$parent_id][$task_id] =
  → $task;
}
```

The **$tasks** array will store every task in a two-dimensional array Ⓐ. As described in Step 4, the outermost array uses the **parent_id** values from the table for its keys. The values of this outermost array's elements are arrays of the tasks that have that **parent_id**.

Current To-Do List

1. Must Do This!
2. Another Task
   1. Subtask 1
   2. Subtask 2
      1. Subsubtask1
   3. Subtask 3
3. My New Task
4. This is a new task!

B The page of tasks, as a bunch of nested lists.

Current To-Do List

1. Must Do This!
2. Another Task
   1. Subtask 1
   2. Subtask 2
      1. Subsubtask1
      2. Subsubtask 2
         1. Sub-cubed task 1
         2. Sub-cubed task 2
         3. Sub-cubed task 3
   3. Subtask 3
3. My New Task
4. This is a new task!

C There is no limit to the number of subtasks that this system supports.

9. Add a debugging line, if desired:

```
echo '<pre>' . print_r($tasks,1) .
→ '</pre>';
```

When dealing with multidimensional arrays, it's vitally important to confirm and understand the structure with which you're working. When you uncomment this line (by removing the two slashes), the script will print out the array for debugging purposes, as in **A**.

10. Call the `make_list()` function, sending it the array of top-level tasks:

```
make_list($tasks[0]);
```

Although the **$tasks** variable is a multidimensional array, the `make_list()` function needs to be called only once, sending it the first array element. This element's value is an array of tasks whose **parent_id** is 0. Within the function, for each of these tasks, a check will see if there are subtasks. In the end, the function will end up accessing every task thanks to its recursive nature.

11. Complete the page:

```
?>
</body>
</html>
```

12. Save the file as **view_tasks.php**, place it in your Web directory, and test in your Web browser **B**.

13. Add some more subtasks using **add_task.php** and retest this script in your Web browser **C**.

TIP This page does assume that some tasks were returned by the database. You could add a conditional checking that $tasks isn't empty prior to calling the `make_list()` function.

Using static variables

When working with recursion or, in fact, any script in which the same function may be called multiple times, you might want to consider using the **static** statement. **static** forces the function to remember the value of a variable from function call to function call, without using global variables. For example, the **make_list()** function could be rewritten to take the full tasks list as an optional second argument and assign this to a static local variable:

```
function make_list($parent, $all =
→ null) {
   static $tasks;
   if (isset($all)) {
      $tasks = $all;
   }
```

Now the function can be called initially using

```
make_list($tasks[0], $tasks);
```

Within the function, subsequent calls would just be

```
make_list($tasks[$task_id]);
```

Thanks to the use of a static variable and a little function redesign, no global variable would be required.

As a simple example of this, the very astute reader may have wondered how I achieved the result shown in ⓒ under "Sorting Multidimensional Arrays." Showing the values being compared is not hard, but counting the iterations requires the use of **static**. To demonstrate, **sort.php** will be modified in the following steps.

To use static variables:

1. Open **sort.php** (Script 1.1) in your text editor or IDE.

2. Modify the **name_sort()** function to read as follows (**Script 1.4**):

```
function name_sort ($x, $y) {
   static $count = 1;
   echo "<p>Iteration $count:
   → {$x['name']} vs. {$y['name']}
   → </p>\n";
   $count++;
   return strcasecmp($x['name'],
   → $y['name']);
}
```

continues on page 26

Script 1.4 This modified version of the sorting script reveals how many times each sorting function is invoked, thanks to a static variable.

```
1    <!doctype html>
2    <html lang="en">
3    <head>
4       <meta charset="utf-8">
5       <title>Sorting Multidimensional Arrays</title>
6       <link rel="stylesheet" href="style.css">
7    </head>
8    <body>
9    <?php # Script 1.4 - sort2.php
10
```

script continues on next page

```
11    /*  This page creates a multidimensional array
12     *  of names and grades.
13     *  The array is then sorted twice:
14     *  once by name and once by grade.
15     *  A static variable has been added to both
16     *  functions to see how many times they are called.
17     */
18
19    // Create the array...
20    // Array structure:
21    // studentID => array('name' => 'Name', 'grade' => XX.X)
22    $students = array(
23       256 => array('name' => 'Jon', 'grade' => 98.5),
24       2 => array('name' => 'Vance', 'grade' => 85.1),
25       9 => array('name' => 'Stephen', 'grade' => 94.0),
26       364 => array('name' => 'Steve', 'grade' => 85.1),
27       68 => array('name' => 'Rob', 'grade' => 74.6)
28    );
29
30    // Name sorting function:
31    function name_sort($x, $y) {
32       // Show iterations using a static variable:
33       static $count = 1;
34       echo "<p>Iteration $count: {$x['name']} vs. {$y['name']}</p>\n";
35       $count++;
36       return strcasecmp($x['name'], $y['name']);
37    }
38
39    // Grade sorting function:
40    // Sort in DESCENDING order!
41    function grade_sort($x, $y) {
42       // Show iterations using a static variable:
43       static $count = 1;
44       echo "<p>Iteration $count: {$x['grade']} vs. {$y['grade']}</p>\n";
45       $count++;
46       return ($x['grade'] < $y['grade']);
47    }
48
49    // Sort by name:
50    uasort($students, 'name_sort');
51    echo '<h2>Array Sorted By Name</h2><pre>' . print_r($students, 1) . '</pre>';
52
53    // Sort by grade:
54    uasort($students, 'grade_sort');
55    echo '<h2>Array Sorted By Grade</h2><pre>' . print_r($students, 1) . '</pre>';
56
57    ?>
58    </body>
59    </html>
```

Three lines of code have been added to the function. The first is the declaration of the static variable **$count**. It's initially set to 1, but that assignment only applies the first time this function is called (because it's a static variable). Then the iteration number is printed (how many times this function has been called in this execution of the script), along with the values being compared. Finally, the **$count** variable is incremented.

3. Modify the **grade_sort()** function to read

```
function grade_sort($x, $y) {
    static $count = 1;
    echo "<p>Iteration $count:
    ↪ {$x['grade']} vs. {$y['grade']}
    ↪ </p>\n";
    $count++;
    return ($x['grade'] <
    ↪ $y['grade']);
}
```

The same three lines of code that were added to **name_sort()** are added to **grade_sort()**, except the key being compared here is *grade*, not *name*.

4. Save the file as **sort2.php**, place it in your Web directory, and test in your Web browser **D**.

(I've also removed from the script the line that prints the array's original structure.)

5. Add more items to the **$students** array and rerun the script **E**.

Iteration 1: Stephen vs. Vance

Iteration 2: Rob vs. Stephen

Iteration 3: Stephen vs. Jon

Iteration 4: Steve vs. Stephen

Iteration 5: Rob vs. Jon

Iteration 6: Vance vs. Steve

Array Sorted By Name

```
Array
(
    [256] => Array
        (
            [name] => Jon
            [grade] => 98.5
        )

    [68] => Array
        (
            [name] => Rob
            [grade] => 74.6
        )
```

D Sorting the original five-element array by name requires six calls of the sorting function.

Iteration 10: Stephen vs. Jon

Iteration 11: Stephen vs. Rob

Iteration 12: Ed vs. Stephen

Iteration 13: Samantha vs. John

Iteration 14: Samantha vs. Ed

Iteration 15: Samantha vs. Jon

Iteration 16: Rob vs. Samantha

Iteration 17: John vs. Rob

Iteration 18: Jon vs. John

Iteration 19: Ed vs. John

Iteration 20: Jon vs. Rob

Array Sorted By Name

E After adding three more elements to the main array, the name sort now requires 20 iterations.

Anonymous functions

A final more advanced topic that I'd like to cover is the use of *anonymous functions*, also called *lambdas*. Simply put, an anonymous function is a function without a name. The ability to create an anonymous function was added in PHP 5.3 and expanded in version 5.4.

Anonymous functions are created by defining a function as you would any other, but without a name. However, in order to be able to later reference that function (e.g., call it), the unnamed definition needs to be assigned to a variable:

```
$hello = function($who) {
    echo "<p>Hello, $who</p>";
};
```

This might seem like utter madness, but the premise is simply this: instead of assigning a string or number to the variable, you assign a function definition. For this reason, a semicolon is required at the end to complete the assignment statement.

Speaking of madness, to invoke this function (after it's been defined), add parentheses to the variable's name. Because this function takes an argument, put that within the parentheses **F**:

```
$hello('World!');
```

```
$hello('Universe!');
```

This particular use of anonymous functions has its benefits, but there's a more obvious and easier use of them we need to discuss. Several functions in PHP take a function as an argument. For example,

Hello, World!

Hello, Universe!

F The anonymous function is called through the variable.

the `array_map()` function takes a function as its first argument and an array whose elements will be run through that function as its second:

```
function format_names($value) {
    // Do whatever with $value.
}
array_map('format_names', $names);
```

As in the above, historically the name of the function was provided. If you don't need a reusable `format_names()` function, you could just use an anonymous function by defining it inline:

```
array_map(function($value) {
    // Do whatever with $value.
}, $names);
```

The benefits of this approach are:

- Related code—the function definition and its implied invocation—is kept tightly together.

- PHP will only need to maintain the anonymous function's definition while the function is being directly used.

The major downside to using anonymous functions is that it's easy to create parse errors. If you find yourself having that problem, define the anonymous function separately and then move the entire definition into place (i.e., within the other function call).

If you're paying close attention to this chapter, you've already seen another situation in which you could use anonymous functions: when sorting multidimensional arrays. In the following steps, you'll update **sort.php** one last time to use anonymous functions. Note that you'll only be able to execute this script if you're using PHP 5.3 or later.

To use anonymous functions:

1. Open **sort.php** (Script 1.4) in your text editor or IDE, if it is not already.

2. Remove the current definitions of the **name_sort()** and **grade_sort()** functions (**Script 1.5**).

   These two functions will be defined anonymously, and therefore are no longer needed.

3. Modify the first invocation of **uasort()** to use an anonymous function:

```
uasort($students, function($x, $y) {
    return strcasecmp($x['name'],
     → $y['name']);
});
```

   The anonymous function definition is the same as in the original script. It takes two arguments and returns the case-sensitive comparison of the two strings.

4. Modify the second invocation of **uasort()** to use an anonymous function:

```
uasort($students, function
 → ($x, $y) {
    return ($x['grade'] <
     → $y['grade']);
});
```

   Again, I'm returning to the original sorting function definition.

5. Save the file as **sort3.php**, place it in your Web directory, and test in your Web browser **G**.

TIP Prior to version 5.3, you could create anonymous-like functions in PHP using **create_function()**.

TIP Anonymous functions can be used as *closures*, a fairly advanced concept. Closures are less common in PHP but are used frequently in JavaScript.

Array Sorted By Name

```
Array
(
    [256] => Array
        (
            [name] => Jon
            [grade] => 98.5
        )

    [68] => Array
        (
            [name] => Rob
            [grade] => 74.6
        )
```

G The end result is not affected by the use of anonymous functions.

Script 1.5 This new take on sorting multidimensional arrays makes use of inline anonymous functions.

```php
1   <!doctype html>
2   <html lang="en">
3   <head>
4      <meta charset="utf-8">
5      <title>Sorting Multidimensional Arrays</title>
6      <link rel="stylesheet" href="style.css">
7   </head>
8   <body>
9   <?php # Script 1.5 - sort3.php
10
11  /*  This page creates a multidimensional array
12   *  of names and grades.
13   *  The array is then sorted twice:
14   *  once by name and once by grade.
15   *  This version uses anonymous functions!
16   */
17
18  // Create the array...
19  // Array structure:
20  // studentID => array('name' => 'Name', 'grade' => XX.X)
21  $students = array(
22      256 => array('name' => 'Jon', 'grade' => 98.5),
23      2 => array('name' => 'Vance', 'grade' => 85.1),
24      9 => array('name' => 'Stephen', 'grade' => 94.0),
25      364 => array('name' => 'Steve', 'grade' => 85.1),
26      68 => array('name' => 'Rob', 'grade' => 74.6)
27  );
28
29  // Sort by name:
30  uasort($students, function($x, $y) {
31      return strcasecmp($x['name'], $y['name']);
32  });
33  echo '<h2>Array Sorted By Name</h2><pre>' . print_r($students, 1) . '</pre>';
34
35  // Sort by grade:
36  uasort($students, function ($x, $y) {
37      return ($x['grade'] < $y['grade']);
38  });
39  echo '<h2>Array Sorted By Grade</h2><pre>' . print_r($students, 1) . '</pre>';
40
41  ?>
42  </body>
43  </html>
```

References and Functions

As a default, function parameters are *passed by value*. This means that a function receives the value of a variable, not the actual variable itself. The function can also be described as *making a copy* of the variable. One result of this behavior is that changing the value within the function has no impact on the original variable outside of it:

```
function increment($var) {

    $var++;

}

$num = 2;

increment($num);

echo $num; // Still 2!
```

The alternative to this default behavior is to have a function's parameters be *passed by reference*, instead of by value. There are two benefits to doing so. The first is it allows you to change an external variable within a function without making that variable global. The second benefit is one of performance. In situations where the data being passed is large, passing by reference means that PHP will not need to make a duplicate of that data. For strings and numbers, the duplication is not an issue, but for a large data set as in the tasks example, it would be better if PHP did not have to make that copy.

To pass a variable by reference instead of by value, precede the variable in the parameter list with the ampersand (**&**):

```
function increment(&$var) {

    $var++;

}

$num = 2;

increment($num);

echo $num; // 3
```

Alternatively, the function definition can stay the same and how the function is called would change:

```
function increment($var) {

    $var++;

}

$num = 2;

increment(&$num);

echo $num; // 3
```

You probably won't (or shouldn't) find yourself passing values by reference often, but like the other techniques in this chapter, it's often the perfect solution to an advanced problem.

The Heredoc Syntax

Heredoc is an alternative way for encapsulating strings. It's used and seen much less often than the standard single or double quotes, but it fulfills the same role. Heredoc is like putting peanut butter on bananas: you either grow up doing it or you don't.

The heredoc approach works just like a double quote in that the values of variables will be printed but you can define your own delimiter. Heredoc is a particularly nice alternative to using double quotation marks when you are printing oodles of HTML (which normally has its own double quotation marks). The only catch to heredoc is that its syntax is very particular!

The heredoc syntax starts with <<<, immediately followed by an identifier. The identifier is normally a word in all caps. It can only contain alphanumeric characters plus the underscore (no spaces), and it cannot begin with a number. There should be nothing on the same line after the initial identifier, not even a space! Use of heredoc might begin like

echo <<<EOT

blah...

or

$string = <<<EOD

blah...

At the end of the string, use the same identifier without the <<<. The closing identifier has to be the very first item on the line (it cannot be indented at all) and can only be followed by a semicolon!

Examples **A**:

```php
$var = 23;

$that ='test';

echo <<<EOT

Somevar $var

Thisvar $that

EOT;

$string = <<<EOD

string with $var \n

EOD;

echo $string;
```

Using **EOD** and **EOT** as delimiters is common (they're unlikely to show up in the string) but not required. The heredoc syntax is a nice option but—and I'm trying to drive this point home—it's very particular. Failure to get the syntax 100 percent correct—even an errant space—results in a parse error.

To illustrate, let's write a new version of the **view_tasks.php** page that allows for marking tasks as updated **B**.

To use the heredoc syntax:

1. Open **view_tasks.php** (Script 1.3) in your text editor or IDE.

2. Within the **make_list()** function, change the printing of the task to (**Script 1.6**):

```php
echo <<<EOT

<li><input type="checkbox"
→ name="tasks[$task_id]"
→ value="done"> $todo

EOT;
```

Somevar 23 Thisvar teststring with 23

A As you can see from this output, the heredoc syntax has the same end result as using double quotation marks.

Current To-Do List

Check the box next to a task and click "Update" to mark a task as completed (it, and any subtasks, will no longer appear in this list).

1. ☑ Must Do This!
2. ☐ Another Task
   1. ☑ Subtask 1
   2. ☐ Subtask 2
      1. ☐ Subsubtask1
      2. ☐ Subsubtask 2
         1. ☐ Sub-cubed task 1
         2. ☐ Sub-cubed task 2
         3. ☑ Sub-cubed task 3
   3. ☐ Subtask 3
3. ☐ My New Task
4. ☐ This is a new task!

Update

B The page for viewing tasks will now have check boxes to mark tasks as complete.

continues on page 35

Script 1.6 The original `view_tasks.php` listing (Script 1.3) has been modified as a form so that tasks can be checked off. The heredoc syntax aids in the creation of some of the HTML.

```php
1    <!doctype html>
2    <html lang="en">
3    <head>
4       <meta charset="utf-8">
5       <title>View Tasks</title>
6       <link rel="stylesheet" href="style.css">
7    </head>
8    <body>
9    <h2>Current To-Do List</h2>
10   <?php # Script 1.6 - view_tasks2.php
11
12   /*  This page shows all existing tasks.
13    *  A recursive function is used to show the
14    *  tasks as nested lists, as applicable.
15    *  Tasks can now be marked as completed.
16    */
17
18   // Function for displaying a list.
19   // Receives one argument: an array.
20   function make_list ($parent) {
21       global $tasks;
22       echo '<ol>'; // Start an ordered list.
23       foreach ($parent as $task_id => $todo) {
24
25           // Start with a checkbox!
26           echo <<<EOT
27   <li><input type="checkbox" name="tasks[$task_id]" value="done"> $todo
28   EOT;
29
30           // Check for subtasks:
31           if (isset($tasks[$task_id])) {
32               make_list($tasks[$task_id]);
33           }
34           echo '</li>'; // Complete the list item.
35       } // End of FOREACH loop.
36       echo '</ol>'; // Close the ordered list.
37   } // End of make_list() function.
38
39   // Connect to the database:
40   $dbc = mysqli_connect('localhost', 'username', 'password', 'test');
41
42   // Check if the form has been submitted:
43   if (($_SERVER['REQUEST_METHOD'] == 'POST')
44       && isset($_POST['tasks'])
45       && is_array($_POST['tasks'])
46       && !empty($_POST['tasks'])) {
47
48       // Define the query:
```

script continues on next page

```
49      $q = 'UPDATE tasks SET date_completed=NOW() WHERE task_id IN (';
50
51      // Add each task ID:
52      foreach ($_POST['tasks'] as $task_id => $v) {
53          $q .= $task_id . ', ';
54      }
55
56      // Complete the query and execute:
57      $q = substr($q, 0, -2) . ')';
58      $r = mysqli_query($dbc, $q);
59
60      // Report on the results:
61      if (mysqli_affected_rows($dbc) == count($_POST['tasks'])) {
62          echo '<p>The task(s) have been marked as completed!</p>';
63      } else {
64          echo '<p>Not all tasks could be marked as completed!</p>';
65      }
66
67  } // End of submission IF.
68
69  // Retrieve all the uncompleted tasks:
70  $q = 'SELECT task_id, parent_id, task FROM tasks WHERE date_completed="0000-00-00 00:00:00"
    → ORDER BY parent_id, date_added ASC';
71  $r = mysqli_query($dbc, $q);
72  $tasks = array();
73  while (list($task_id, $parent_id, $task) = mysqli_fetch_array($r, MYSQLI_NUM)) {
74      $tasks[$parent_id][$task_id] = $task;
75  }
76
77  // Make a form:
78  echo <<<EOT
79  <p>Check the box next to a task and click "Update" to mark a task as completed
    → (it, and any subtasks, will no longer appear in this list).</p>
80  <form action="view_tasks2.php" method="post">
81  EOT;
82
83  make_list($tasks[0]);
84
85  // Complete the form:
86  echo <<<EOT
87  <input name="submit" type="submit" value="Update" />
88  </form>
89  EOT;
90
91  ?>
92  </body>
93  </html>
```

This is a good use of the heredoc syntax, as it's an alternative to:

```
echo "<li><input type=\"checkbox\"
→ name=\"tasks[$task_id]\"
→ value=\"done\">$todo";
```

That syntax, in my opinion, has way too many double quotation marks to escape. The single quotation mark example isn't as bad but requires concatenation:

```
echo '<li><input type="checkbox"
→ name="tasks['. $task_id . ']"
→ value="done"> ' . $todo;
```

With the heredoc code, be absolutely certain that nothing follows the opening identifier (**EOT**) except a return (a carriage return or newline) and that the closing identifier starts as the very first thing on its own line.

3. After connecting to the database, begin a conditional that checks for the form submission:

```
if (($_SERVER['REQUEST_METHOD'] ==
→ 'POST')
   && isset($_POST['tasks'])
   && is_array($_POST['tasks'])
   && !empty($_POST['tasks'])) {
```

The database update (marking the tasks as complete) will only occur if the form has been submitted, **$_POST['tasks']** has a value, and it is a non-empty array. Even if only one check box is selected, **$_POST['tasks']** would still be an array.

4. Dynamically generate the query:

```
$q = 'UPDATE tasks SET date_
→ completed=NOW() WHERE task_id
→ IN (';
foreach ($_POST['tasks'] as
→ $task_id => $v) {
   $q .= $task_id . ', ';
}
$q = substr($q, 0, -2) . ')';
$r = mysqli_query($dbc, $q);
```

The update query will be something like

```
UPDATE tasks SET date_completed=
→ NOW() WHERE task_id IN (X, Y, Z)
```

This will set each applicable task's **date_completed** column to the current date and time so that it will no longer show up in the view list (because that query checks for an empty **date_completed** value).

5. Report on the results and complete the submission conditional:

```
   if (mysqli_affected_rows($dbc)
→ == count($_POST['tasks'])) {
      echo '<p>The task(s) have been
→ marked as completed!</p>';
   } else {
      echo '<p>Not all tasks could
→ be marked as completed!</p>';
   }
} // End of submission IF.
```

continues on next page

6. Before calling the `make_list()` function, add the initial form tag:

```
echo <<<EOT

<p>Check the box next to a task
→ and click "Update" to mark a
→ task as completed (it, and any
→ subtasks, will no longer appear
→ in this list).</p>

<form action="view_tasks2.php"
→ method="post">

EOT;
```

Because of the way the `make_list()` function works, if a parent task is marked as completed, its subtasks will never be shown. A comment indicating such is added to the form.

I'm using heredoc syntax again here, mostly because that's the focus of this particular example.

7. After calling the `make_list()` function, complete the form:

```
echo <<<EOT

<input name="submit" type="submit"
→ value="Update" />

</form>

EOT;
```

8. Save the file as `view_tasks2.php`, place it in your Web directory, and test in your Web browser by checking tasks to be marked as completed Ⓑ and submitting the form Ⓒ.

Current To-Do List

The task(s) have been marked as completed!

Check the box next to a task and click "Update" to mark a task as completed (it, and any subtasks, will no longer appear in this list).

1. ☐ Another Task
    1. ☐ Subtask 2
        1. ☐ Subsubtask1
        2. ☐ Subsubtask 2
            1. ☐ Sub-cubed task 1
            2. ☐ Sub-cubed task 2
    2. ☐ Subtask 3
2. ☐ My New Task
3. ☐ This is a new task!
    [Update]

Ⓒ The updated tasks list.

The Nowdoc Syntax

Added in PHP 5.3 is the *nowdoc* syntax. Nowdoc is to heredoc as single quotes are to double quotes. This is to say that nowdoc provides another way to encapsulate a string, but any variables within the nowdoc syntax will not be replaced with their values.

In terms of syntax, nowdoc uses the same rules as heredoc except that the delimiting string needs to be placed within single quotes on the first line:

```
$var = 23;

$string = <<<'EOD'

string with $var

EOD;
```

To be clear, **$string** now has the literal value of *string with $var*, not *string with 23*.

TABLE 1.1 Type Specifiers

Character	Meaning
b	Binary integer
c	ASCII integer
d	Standard integer
e	Scientific notation
u	Unsigned decimal integer
f	Floating-point number
o	Octal integer
s	String
x	Hexadecimal integer

Using `printf()` and `sprintf()`

For most PHP programmers, the **print()** and **echo()** functions are all they need for printing text and variables. The advanced PHP programmer might occasionally use the more sophisticated **printf()** function. This function also prints text but has the added ability to format the output. The PHP manual definition of this function is

```
printf(string format [, mixed
→ arguments]);
```

The *format* is a combination of literal text and special formatting parameters, beginning with the percent sign (%). After that, you may have any combination of the following (in order):

- A sign specifier (+/-) to force a positive number to show the plus sign.

- A padding specifier that indicates the character used for right-padding (space is the default, but you might want to use 0 for numbers).

- An alignment specifier (default is right-justified, use - to force left-justification).

- A number indicating the minimum width to be used.

- A precision specifier for how many decimal digits should be shown for floating-point numbers (or how many characters in a string).

- The type specifier; see **Table 1.1**.

This all may seem complicated, and well, it kind of is. You can start practicing by playing with a number **A**:

```
printf('b: %b <br>c: %c <br>d:
→%d <br>f: %f', 80, 80, 80, 80);
```

That's four different representations of the same number. The first format will print 80 as a binary number, the second as 80's corresponding ASCII character (the capital letter *P*), the third as an integer, and the fourth as a floating-point number.

From there, take the two most common number types—*d* and *f*—and add some formatting **B**:

```
printf('%0.2f <br>%+d <br>%0.2f <br>',
→ 8, 8, 1235.456);
```

First, the number 8 is printed as a floating-point number, with two digits after the decimal and padded with zeros. Next, the number 8 is printed as a signed integer. Finally, the number 1235.456 is printed as a floating-point number with two digits after the decimal (resulting in the rounding of the number).

Taking this idea further, mix in the string type **C**:

```
printf('The cost of %d %s at $%0.2f
→ each is $%0.2f.', 4, 'brooms', 8.50,
→ (4*8.50));
```

The **sprintf()** function works exactly like **printf()**, but instead of printing the formatted string, it returns it. This function is great for generating database queries, without an ugly mixing of SQL and variables (and potentially function calls).

```
b: 1010000
c: P
d: 80
f: 80.000000
```

A The same number printed using four different type specifiers.

```
8.00
+8
1235.46
```

B Using **printf()** to format how numbers are printed.

```
The cost of 4 brooms at $8.50 each is $34.00.
```

C Printing a mix of numbers and strings.

To use sprintf():

1. Open **add_task.php** (Script 1.2) in your text editor or IDE.

2. Delete the call to the `mysqli_real_escape_string()` function (**Script 1.7**).

   I'll now call this function in the line that defines the query (Step 3).

3. Change the line that defines the **INSERT** query to read

   ```
   $q = sprintf("INSERT INTO tasks
   (parent_id, task) VALUES
   (%d, '%s')", $parent_id,
   mysqli_real_escape_string($dbc,
   strip_tags($_POST['task'])));
   ```

   When you use the **sprintf()** function, the query can be created without interspersing SQL and variables. While doing so wasn't too ugly in the original script, in more complex queries the result can be hideous (lots of `{$var['index']}` and such), prone to errors, and hard to debug.

   This syntax separates the query from the data being used and is still able to incorporate a function call, all without using concatenation or other techniques.

continues on page 41

Script 1.7 A minor modification to the **add_task.php** page (Script 1.1) shows an alternative way to create a database query.

```
1    <!doctype html>
2    <html lang="en">
3    <head>
4        <meta charset="utf-8">
5        <title>Add a Task</title>
6        <link rel="stylesheet" href="style.css">
7    </head>
8    <body>
9    <?php # Script 1.7 - add_task2.php
10
```

script continues on next page

```
11   /* This page adds tasks to the tasks table.
12    * The page both displays and handles the form.
13    *
14    */
15
16   $dbc = mysqli_connect('localhost', 'username', 'password', 'test');
17
18   if (($_SERVER['REQUEST_METHOD'] == 'POST') && !empty($_POST['task'])) {
19       if (isset($_POST['parent_id']) &&
20       filter_var($_POST['parent_id'], FILTER_VALIDATE_INT, array('min_range' => 1)) ) {
21           $parent_id = $_POST['parent_id'];
22       } else {
23           $parent_id = 0;
24       }
25
26       // Add the task to the database.
27       $q = sprintf("INSERT INTO tasks (parent_id, task) VALUES (%d, '%s')", $parent_id,
         → mysqli_real_escape_string($dbc, strip_tags($_POST['task'])));
28       $r = mysqli_query($dbc, $q);
29
30       if (mysqli_affected_rows($dbc) == 1) {
31           echo '<p>The task has been added!</p>';
32       } else {
33           echo '<p>The task could not be added!</p>';
34       }
35
36   } // End of submission IF.
37
38   // Display the form:
39   echo '<form action="add_task2.php" method="post">
40   <fieldset>
41       <legend>Add a Task</legend>
42       <p>Task: <input name="task" type="text" size="60" maxlength="100"></p>
43       <p>Parent Task: <select name="parent_id"><option value="0">None</option>';
44   $q = 'SELECT task_id, parent_id, task FROM tasks WHERE date_completed="0000-00-00 00:00:00"
       → ORDER BY date_added ASC';
45   $r = mysqli_query($dbc, $q);
46   $tasks = array();
47   while (list($task_id, $parent_id, $task) = mysqli_fetch_array($r, MYSQLI_NUM)) {
48       echo "<option value=\"$task_id\">$task</option>\n";
49       $tasks[] = array('task_id' => $task_id, 'parent_id' => $parent_id, 'task' => $task);
50   }
51   echo '</select></p>
52   <input name="submit" type="submit" value="Add This Task">
53   </fieldset>
54   </form>';
55   ?>
56   </body>
57   </html>
```

The task has been added!

Add a Task
Task: [   ]

Parent Task: [None   ▼]

[Add This Task]

D The page should still work exactly as it had before.

4. Change the action attribute of the form to **add_task2.php**.

   This script will be renamed to differentiate it from the original, and so the action attribute's value must be changed to match.

5. If you want, remove all the lines required to view the list of tasks.

   The **view_tasks.php** page (and its second version) both do this much better, so there's no need to still include that code here.

6. Save the file as **add_task2.php**, place it in your Web directory, and test in your Web browser **D**.

TIP To use a literal percent sign in a string, escape it with another percent sign:

```
printf('The tax rate is %0.2f%%',
→ $tax);
```

TIP The vprintf() function works exactly like printf() but takes only two arguments: the format and an array of values.

TIP The scanf() and fscanf() functions also work exactly like printf() and sprintf() in terms of formatting parameters. The scanf() function is used for reading input; fscanf() is used to read data from a file.

Review and Pursue

New in this edition of the book, each chapter ends with a "Review and Pursue" section. In these sections, you'll find questions regarding the material just covered and prompts for ways to expand your knowledge and experience on your own.

If you have any problems with these sections, either in answering the questions or pursuing your own endeavors, turn to the book's supporting forum (**www.Larry Ullman.com/forums/**). I've also provided page references below in case you cannot remember a particular answer off the top off your head.

Review

- What PHP function is used to sort a multidimensional array by value? To sort the multidimensional array while maintaining the keys? To sort the multidimensional array by key? (See page 3.)

- When writing a function to be used to sort a multidimensional array, what values should it return? (See page 3.)

- What is a *recursive* function? In what situations are they useful? What are the two things to be careful of when using them? (See page 17.)

- What is a *static* variable? In what situations are static variables helpful? (See page 24.)

- What is an *anonymous* function? When were anonymous functions added to PHP? (See page 27.)

- What are the rules for using the heredoc syntax? What advantages does heredoc have over alternative approaches? (See page 31.)

- How do you use the **printf()** and **sprintf()** functions? What benefits do they offer? (See page 37.)

Pursue

- Modify **sort.php** to use a custom function to generate the output in a more attractive manner.

- Round out **add_task.php** so that it includes proper error reporting.

- Implement the recursive directory function example to list the contents of a directory using nested unordered lists.

- Using one of the suggestions in the chapter, such as passing by reference or using static variables, update **make_list()** so that it does not require a global variable.

- If you're curious, modify one of the function definitions in this chapter to require an array as an argument using type hinting.

- Search online for more examples of anonymous functions in PHP, if you're curious.

- Update **view_tasks.php** to display both completed and to-be-completed tasks, formatting each differently.

- Add a link to **view_tasks.php** that passes a value in the URL indicating whether all tasks should be displayed, or just the incomplete ones. Change the SQL query based on this value.

- Modify **add_task.php** so that the drop-down menu reflects the hierarchy of tasks, too.

- Look into other uses of **printf()** and **sprintf()**. Hint: A good place to start is the PHP manual pages for these functions.

Developing
Web Applications

The career of a PHP programmer normally starts with writing individual scripts, each dedicated to a single purpose. From there you begin using more and more files, building up Web applications. Eventually you might develop sites on your own server and, if you're lucky, balanced over multiple servers. No matter how large your projects are, learning new and improved ways to develop Web applications is an important part of the life of the PHP programmer.

In this chapter, the focus is on developing Web applications beyond the beginner or intermediate level. We begin with an explanation of how to *modularize* a Web site. Then you'll learn a bit about the Apache Web server, including using its `mod_rewrite` feature that makes Search Engine Optimization (SEO)-friendly URLs. The chapter ends with a discussion of controlling the browser caching.

Modularizing a Web Site

In my experience, the arc of a programmer's development starts with writing one-page applications that do just a single thing. Over time, the work will evolve into multipage sites, involving templates and state management. After more and more experience, some seasoned PHP developers start doing the same amount of work in *fewer* pages, such as having the same script both display and handle a form instead of using two separate files. Or, conversely, the advanced PHP programmer may start generating *exponentially more scripts*, each of which doing far less, by focusing each script on a particular task. This last approach is the premise behind *modularizing* a Web site.

For an example of modularizing a site, I'll create a dummy Web site (i.e., it won't do much) that's broken into its individual components. The new knowledge here will be how those components are separated, organized, and put back together. Instead of having individual pages (`contact.php`, `about.php`, `index.php`, etc.), the entire application will also be run through one index page. That page will include the appropriate content module based on values passed in the URL.

Creating the Database File

I have not, for this application, created a database configuration file, because the dummy site does not use a database. But if a database were required, I would write a **mysql.inc.php** (or **postgresql. inc.php** or **db.inc.php** or whatever) file that establishes the database connection. Such a file should also define any functions that involve the database application.

This file could also be stored in the **includes** directory but would preferably be stored outside of the Web directory. The **config.inc.php** file has a constant named **DB** that should be an absolute path to this file on the server.

Any page that needs a database connection could then include it by just using

```
require(DB);
```

Because **DB** represents an absolute path to that file, it wouldn't matter if the including script was in the main folder or a subdirectory.

Creating the configuration file

Every Web application I build begins with a configuration file. Configuration files serve several purposes, the four most important being:

- Defining constants
- Establishing sitewide settings
- Creating user functions
- Managing errors

Basically, any piece of information that every page in a site might need to access should be stored in a configuration file. (As a side note, if a function would not likely be used by the *majority* of site pages, I would put it in a separate file, thereby avoiding the extra overhead of defining it on pages where it won't be called.)

To create the configuration file:

1. Begin a new PHP script in your text editor or IDE, to be named **config.inc.php** (Script 2.1):

   ```
   <?php # Script 2.1 - config.inc.php
   ```

continues on page 48

Script 2.1 The configuration file is the key back-end script. It defines sitewide constants and dictates how errors are handled.

```
1   <?php # Script 2.1 - config.inc.php
2
3   /*
4    * File name: config.inc.php
5    * Created by: Larry E. Ullman
6    * Contact: Larry@LarryUllman.com, LarryUllman.com
7    * Last modified: June 5, 2012
8    *
9    * Configuration file does the following things:
10   * - Has site settings in one location.
11   * - Stores URLs and URIs as constants.
12   * - Sets how errors will be handled.
13   */
14
```

script continues on next page

```
15  # ******************** #
16  # ***** SETTINGS ***** #
17
18  // Errors are emailed here:
19  $contact_email = 'address@example.com';
20
21  // Determine whether we're working on a local server
22  // or on the real server:
23  $host = substr($_SERVER['HTTP_HOST'], 0, 5);
24  if (in_array($host, array('local', '127.0', '192.1'))) {
25      $local = TRUE;
26  } else {
27      $local = FALSE;
28  }
29
30  // Determine location of files and the URL of the site:
31  // Allow for development on different servers.
32  if ($local) {
33
34      // Always debug when running locally:
35      $debug = TRUE;
36
37      // Define the constants:
38      define('BASE_URI', '/path/to/html/folder/');
39      define('BASE_URL', 'http://localhost/directory/');
40      define('DB', '/path/to/mysql.inc.php');
41
42  } else {
43
44      define('BASE_URI', '/path/to/live/html/folder/');
45      define('BASE_URL', 'http://www.example.com/');
46      define('DB', '/path/to/live/mysql.inc.php');
47
48  }
49
50  /*
51   *  Most important setting!
52   *  The $debug variable is used to set error management.
53   *  To debug a specific page, add this to the index.php page:
54
55  if ($p == 'thismodule') $debug = TRUE;
56  require('./includes/config.inc.php');
57
58   *  To debug the entire site, do
59
60  $debug = TRUE;
61
62   *  before this next conditional.
63   */
```

script continues on next page

```php
64
65    // Assume debugging is off.
66    if (!isset($debug)) {
67        $debug = FALSE;
68    }
69
70    # ***** SETTINGS ***** #
71    # ******************** #
72
73
74    # **************************** #
75    # ***** ERROR MANAGEMENT ***** #
76
77    // Create the error handler:
78    function my_error_handler($e_number, $e_message, $e_file, $e_line, $e_vars) {
79
80        global $debug, $contact_email;
81
82        // Build the error message:
83        $message = "An error occurred in script '$e_file' on line $e_line: $e_message";
84
85        // Append $e_vars to the $message:
86        $message .= print_r($e_vars, 1);
87
88        if ($debug) { // Show the error.
89
90            echo '<div class="error">' . $message . '</div>';
91            debug_print_backtrace();
92
93        } else {
94
95            // Log the error:
96            error_log ($message, 1, $contact_email); // Send email.
97
98            // Only print an error message if the error isn't a notice or strict.
99            if ( ($e_number != E_NOTICE) && ($e_number < 2048)) {
100               echo '<div class="error">A system error occurred. We apologize for the
                  → inconvenience.</div>';
101           }
102
103       } // End of $debug IF.
104
105   } // End of my_error_handler() definition.
106
107   // Use my error handler:
108   set_error_handler('my_error_handler');
109
110   # ***** ERROR MANAGEMENT ***** #
111   # **************************** #
```

2. Add some comments discussing the nature and purpose of this page:

```
/*
*File name: config.inc.php
*Created by: Larry E. Ullman
*Contact: Larry@LarryUllman.com,
→LarryUllman.com
*Last modified: June 5, 2012
*
*Configuration file does the
→following things:
*- Has site settings in one
→location.
*- Stores URLs and URIs as
→constants.
*- Sets how errors will be
→handled.
*/
```

Because the configuration file is a common file, it ought to be one of the best-documented scripts in a site.

3. Set the email address to be used for errors:

```
$contact_email =
→'address@example.com';
```

For live sites, I prefer to be emailed when errors occur. To that end, I declare a variable with the "to" email address for any general communications. This may be my address while developing a site but a client's once the site goes live.

4. Determine whether the script is running on the live server or a test server:

```
$host = substr($_SERVER
→['HTTP_HOST'], 0, 5);
if (in_array($host, array('local',
→'127.0', '192.1'))) {
    $local = TRUE;
} else {
    $local = FALSE;
}
```

I almost always develop on a local server and then upload the completed site to the live server. The two different environments will each have its own server-specific settings. Ideally, the configuration file ought to automatically switch the server-specific settings based on the environment.

To test if the site is running locally, I first grab a reference to the opening five characters in **$_SERVER['HTTP_HOST']**. I then check if that value is one of a number of possible combinations:

▸ The word *local* (as in **http://localhost**)

▸ The start of an IP address, 192.1, or 127.0, both of which indicate local networks

You'll need to adjust this list to values that work best for your local environment.

Whether that conditional is true or not, a **$local** variable is assigned a Boolean value, for reference later in the script.

5. Set the server-specific constants:

```
if ($local) {
    $debug = TRUE;
    define('BASE_URI',
    →'/path/to/html/folder/');
    define('BASE_URL',
    →'http://localhost/directory/');
    define('DB',
    →'/path/to/mysql.inc.php');
} else {
    define('BASE_URI',
    →'/path/to/live/html/folder/');
    define('BASE_URL',
    →'http://www.example.com/');
    define('DB',
    →'/path/to/live/mysql.inc.php');
}
```

I often use these three constants in my Web applications. The **BASE_URI** is the absolute file system path to where the site's root folder is on the server. This constant makes it easy to use absolute references when any script includes a file. If you're using, for example, XAMPP on Windows, this value might be *C:\xampp\htdocs\ch02*.

The **BASE_URL** constant is the hostname and directory (if applicable). On a test server, that might be just **http://localhost/ch02/**.

Finally, the **DB** constant is the absolute path to the file that contains the database connectivity information. For security purposes, it's best to keep this stored outside of the Web directory.

Note that each constant is represented twice: once for a test server and once for the live server. If this is a test server (if **$local** is **TRUE**), I also turn on debugging, which will mean more to you shortly.

6. Set the debugging level:

```
if (!isset($debug)) {
    $debug = FALSE;
}
```

I use a **$debug** variable to indicate how errors should be handled. If the site is being run locally, **$debug** will be **TRUE** by this point. Otherwise, debugging is disabled by default.

To debug a live site, a page would need to use the line

```
$debug = TRUE;
```

prior to including the configuration file.

7. Begin a function for handling errors:

```
function my_error_handler
→($e_number, $e_message,
→$e_file, $e_line, $e_vars) {
    global $debug, $contact_email;
```

PHP allows you to define your own function for handling errors, rather than using the built-in behavior. For more information on this process or the syntax, see the PHP manual or my *PHP and MySQL for Dynamic Web Sites: Visual QuickStart Guide* book (Peachpit Press, 2012).

Two global variables will be used in this function.

continues on next page

8. Build up the error message:

```
$message = "An error occurred in
→ script '$e_file' on line
→ $e_line: $e_message";

$message .= print_r($e_vars, 1);
```

For debugging purposes, the error message should be as informative as possible. To start, it will include the name of the file where the error occurred and on what line. Then, every existing variable is added. This can be a lot of data , but that's a good thing when you need to find and fix a problem.

9. If debugging is turned on, print the error and a backtrace:

```
if ($debug) { // Show the error.
    echo '<div class="error">' .
    → $message . '</div>';

    debug_print_backtrace();
```

If debugging is turned on, then the full message will appear in the Web browser . This is great when developing a site but a huge security flaw on a live site. This specific code will show that information within a **DIV** that has a class value of *error*, which presumably matches the corresponding CSS. You can edit this code to fit into your site's design, whether that means creating a special **DIV** or whatnot.

Along with the custom error message, a *backtrace* is printed. A backtrace is a hierarchy of function calls to that point in the program.

10. If debugging is turned off, send the message in an email and print a default message:

```
} else {
    error_log ($message, 1,
    → $contact_email);
```

An error occurred in script 'C:\xampp\htdocs\ch02\modules\main.inc.php' on line 20: Division by zeroArray ([GLOBALS] => Array "RECURSION" [_POST] => Array ( ) [_GET] => Array ( ) [_COOKIE] => Array ([PHPSESSID] => c4ve3mjfv1to0d0116mblcl6h1) [_FILES] => Array ( ) [_SERVER] => Array ([MIBDIRS] => C:/xampp/php/extras/mibs [MYSQL_HOME] => \xampp\mysql\bin [OPENSSL_CONF] => C:/xampp/apache/bin/openssl.cnf [PHP_PEAR_SYSCONF_DIR] => \xampp\php [PHPRC] => \xampp \php [TMP] => \xampp\tmp [HTTP_USER_AGENT] => Opera/9.80 (Windows NT 6.1; U; Edition United States Local; en) Presto/2.10.229 Version/11.61 [HTTP_HOST] => localhost [HTTP_ACCEPT] => text/html, application/xml;q=0.9, application/xhtml+xml, image/png, image/webp, image/jpeg, image/gif, image/x-xbitmap, */*;q=0.1 [HTTP_ACCEPT_LANGUAGE] => en-US,en;q=0.9 [HTTP_ACCEPT_ENCODING] => gzip, deflate [HTTP_REFERER] => http://localhost/ch02/index.php?

A How errors appear when debugging a page.

Site Structure

Much like your code structure and documentation, another overarching issue when developing larger Web applications is that of site structure: how the files are organized and stored on the server. Proper site structure is intended to improve security and administration of a site, as well as promote scalability, portability, and ease of modifications.

The key to site structure is to break up your code and applications into different pages and directories according to use, purpose, and function. Within the primary Web documents folder, which I'll call **html**, you would have one directory for images (almost everyone does this, at least), another for classes (if using object-oriented programming), another for functions, and so forth. Further, I suggest that you use your own personalized folder names for security purposes. Any time that a malicious user is blind to the names of folders and documents, the better. If you use the name *admin* for the administration section of a site, you're not doing yourself any favors, security-wise.

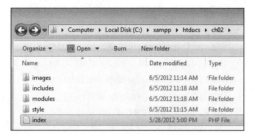

A On a live site, errors are handled more modestly (and securely).

C The root folder is where the site's index page may be found. Within the root folder, other subfolders—such as **images**, **includes**, and **modules**—would be used.

```
if ( ($e_number != E_NOTICE) &&
→(($e_number < 2048)) {
    echo '<div class="error">
    →A system error occurred.
    →We apologize for the
    →inconvenience.</div>';
}
} // End of $debug IF.
```

For a live site, the detailed error message should not be shown (unless debugging is temporarily enabled for that page) but should be emailed instead. The **error_log()** function will do this, if provided with the number 1 as its second argument. But the user probably needs to know that something didn't go right, so a generic message is displayed B. If the error happens to be a notice or a strict error (having a value of 2048), no message should be printed, as the error is likely not interfering with the operation of the page.

11. Complete the function, tell PHP to use this error handler, and complete the page:

```
} // End of my_error_handler()
→definition.

set_error_handler('my_error_
→handler');
```

12. Save the file as **config.inc.php** and place it in your Web directory (in an **includes** subfolder).

See C for the directory layout I'll use for this site. Note that I'm not using a closing PHP tag. This is acceptable in PHP and recommended for any file that is to be included by other scripts (because it helps to prevent *headers already sent* errors, for starters).

Creating the HTML template

Using an HTML template is a virtual certainty with any larger-scale application. You can use Smarty (**http://www.smarty.net**) or any other templating systems, but I often use just two simple files: a header that contains everything in a page up until the page-specific content, and a footer that contains the rest of the page. The style sheet handles all of the cosmetics and layout, of course.

For this template, I'll use the Colour Blue HTML5 design created by HTML5 Web Templates (**www.html5webtemplates.co.uk**), and gratefully used with their kind permission.

To create the template pages:

1. Design an HTML page in your text or WYSIWYG editor.

   To start creating a template for a Web site, design the layout like a standard HTML page, independent of any PHP code. For this example, as I already said, I'll be using the Colour Blue design **D**.

   Note: In order to save space, the CSS file for this example (which controls the layout) is not included in the book. You can download the file through the book's supporting Web site (**www.LarryUllman.com**, see the downloads page for this book).

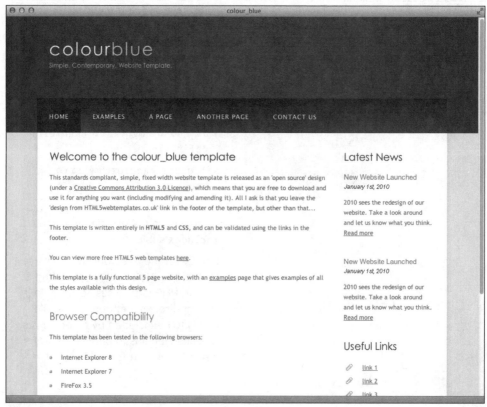

D The template this site will use for all its pages.

2. Copy everything from the first line of the layout's source to just before the page-specific content and paste it in a new document (**Script 2.2**). That is, start from

`<!DOCTYPE HTML>`

and continue through

`<div id="content">`

This first file will contain the initial HTML tags (from **DOCTYPE** through the head and into the beginning of the page body). It also has the code that makes the column of links on the top of the browser window and the sidebar on the right (see **D**). I've omitted a good chunk of the HTML from this step. For the complete code, see Script 2.2 or just download the file from the book's Web site.

3. Change the page's title line to read:

`<title><?php echo $page_title;`
`→ ?></title>`

I'll want the page title (which appears at the top of the Web browser; *colour_ blue* in **D** to be changeable on a page-by-page basis. To do so, I set this as a variable that will be printed out by PHP.

continues on page 55

Script 2.2 The header file begins the HTML template. It also includes the CSS file and uses a PHP variable for the browser window's title.

```
1   <?php # Script 2.2 - header.html
2   // This page begins the HTML header for the site.
3
4   // Check for a $page_title value:
5   if (!isset($page_title)) $page_title = 'Default Page Title';
6   ?><!DOCTYPE HTML>
7   <html>
8
9   <head>
```

script continues on next page

Script 2.2 *continued*

```
10      <title><?php echo $page_title; ?></title>
11      <link rel="stylesheet" type="text/css" href="style/style.css" title="style" />
12    </head>
13
14    <body>
15      <div id="main">
16        <div id="header">
17          <div id="logo">
18            <div id="logo_text">
19              <h1><a href="index.html">colour<span class="logo_colour">blue</span></a></h1>
20              <h2>Simple. Contemporary. Website Template.</h2>
21            </div>
22          </div>
23          <div id="menubar">
24            <ul id="menu">
25              <li><a href="index.php">Home</a></li>
26              <li><a href="index.php?p=about">About</a></li>
27              <li><a href="index.php?p=this">This</a></li>
28              <li><a href="index.php?p=that">That</a></li>
29              <li><a href="index.php?p=contact">Contact</a></li>
30            </ul>
31          </div>
32        </div>
33        <div id="site_content">
34          <div class="sidebar">
35            <h3>Latest News</h3>
36            <h4>New Website Launched</h4>
37            <h5>January 1st, 2010</h5>
38            <p>2010 sees the redesign of our website. Take a look around and let us know what you
                 → think.<br /><a href="#">Read more</a></p>
39            <h3>Useful Links</h3>
40            <ul>
41              <li><a href="#">link 1</a></li>
42              <li><a href="#">link 2</a></li>
43            </ul>
44            <h3>Search</h3>
45            <form method="get" action="index.php" id="search_form">
46              <p>
47                <input type="hidden" name="p" value="search" />
48                <input class="search" type="text" name="terms" value="Search..." />
49                <input name="search" type="image" style="border: 0; margin: 0 0 -9px 5px;"
                     → src="style/search.png" alt="Search" title="Search" />
50              </p>
51            </form>
52          </div>
53          <div id="content">
54        <!-- End of header. -->
```

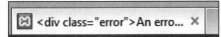

E Make sure that a **$page_title** value is set, or else the error reporting system will end up printing a detailed error message in the browser title area instead.

4. Before any HTML, create a PHP section that checks for a **$page_title**:

```
<?php # Script 2.2 - header.html
if (!isset($page_title))
→ $page_title = 'Default Page
→ Title'; ?>
```

Just in case a PHP script includes the header file without having set a **$page_title** first, this PHP code declares a default page title (which you'll likely want to make more meaningful). If you don't do this and error reporting is turned on, the browser title could get messy **E**.

5. Save the file as **header.html**.

Included files can use just about any extension for the filename. Some programmers like to use **.inc** to indicate that a file is used as an include. In this case, you could also use **.inc.html**, which would indicate that it's both an include and an HTML file (to distinguish it from includes full of PHP code).

continues on next page

6. Copy everything in the original template from the end of the page-specific content to the end of the page and paste it in a new file (**Script 2.3**):

```
<!-- # Script 2.3 - footer.html -->
    </div>
  </div>
  <div id="content_footer"></div>
  <div id="footer">
    Copyright &copy; colour_blue |
    → <a href="http://validator.
    → w3.org/check?uri=referer">
    → HTML5</a> | <a href="http://
    → jigsaw.w3.org/css-validator/
    → check/referer">CSS</a> |
    → <a href="http://www.html
    → 5webtemplates.co.uk">design
    → from HTML5webtemplates.
    → co.uk</a>
  </div>
</div>
</body>
</html>
```

The footer file contains the remaining formatting for the page body, including the page's footer, and then closes the HTML document.

7. Save the file as **footer.html**.

8. Place both files in the Web server's **includes** directory.

Script 2.3 The footer file completes the HTML template.

```
1    <!-- # Script 2.3 - footer.html -->
2        </div>
3      </div>
4      <div id="content_footer"></div>
5      <div id="footer">
6        Copyright &copy; colour_blue |
         → <a href="http://validator.
         → w3.org/check?uri=referer">
         → HTML5</a> | <a href="http://
         → jigsaw.w3.org/css-validator/
         → check/referer">CSS</a> |
         → <a href="http://www.
         → html5webtemplates.co.uk">design
         → from HTML5webtemplates.co.uk</a>
7      </div>
8    </div>
9    </body>
10   </html>
```

Creating the index page

The index page is the main script in the modularized application. In fact, it's the only page that should ever be loaded in the Web browser. The technical term for this construct is a ***bootstrap file***, and it's also the common approach in framework-based sites.

The index page has but a single purpose: to assemble all the proper pieces to make the complete Web page. Accomplishing this might involve:

- Including a configuration file
- Including a database connectivity file
- Incorporating an HTML template
- Determining and including the proper content module

Bootstrap files do not, conventionally, contain any HTML at all, because the requisite HTML will be placed in included files.

To create the main page:

1. Begin a new PHP script in your text editor or IDE, to be named **index.php** (**Script 2.4**):

   `<?php # Script 2.4 - index.php`

2. Include the configuration file:

   `require('./includes/config.inc.php');`

   The configuration file defines many important things, so it should be included first.

continues on page 59

Script 2.4 The index page is the script through which everything happens. It determines what module should be included, requires the configuration file, and pulls together the HTML template.

```
1    <?php # Script 2.4 - index.php
2
3    /*
4     *  This is the main page.
5     *  This page includes the configuration file,
6     *  the templates, and any content-specific modules.
7     */
8
9    // Require the configuration file before any PHP code:
10   require('./includes/config.inc.php');
11
12   // Validate what page to show:
13   if (isset($_GET['p'])) {
14       $p = $_GET['p'];
15   } elseif (isset($_POST['p'])) { // Forms
16       $p = $_POST['p'];
17   } else {
18       $p = NULL;
19   }
20
21   // Determine what page to display:
22   switch ($p) {
23
```

script continues on next page

```php
24      case 'about':
25          $page = 'about.inc.php';
26          $page_title = 'About This Site';
27          break;
28
29      case 'contact':
30          $page = 'contact.inc.php';
31          $page_title = 'Contact Us';
32          break;
33
34      case 'search':
35          $page = 'search.inc.php';
36          $page_title = 'Search Results';
37          break;
38
39      // Default is to include the main page.
40      default:
41          $page = 'main.inc.php';
42          $page_title = 'Site Home Page';
43          break;
44
45  } // End of main switch.
46
47  // Make sure the file exists:
48  if (!file_exists('./modules/' . $page)) {
49      $page = 'main.inc.php';
50      $page_title = 'Site Home Page';
51  }
52
53  // Include the header file:
54  include('./includes/header.html');
55
56  // Include the content-specific module:
57  // $page is determined from the above switch.
58  include('./modules/' . $page);
59
60  // Include the footer file to complete the template:
61  include('./includes/footer.html');
62
63  ?>
```

3. Validate the page being shown:

```php
if (isset($_GET['p'])) {
    $p = $_GET['p'];
} elseif (isset($_POST['p'])) {
    $p = $_POST['p'];
} else {
    $p = NULL;
}
```

The specific content being shown will be based on a value received by this page. When the user clicks links, the value will be passed in the URL. When most forms are submitted, the value will be sent in **$_POST**. If neither is the case, **$p** is set to **NULL**.

4. Begin a **switch** conditional that determines the page title and the file to include:

```php
switch ($p) {
    case 'about':
        $page = 'about.inc.php';
        $page_title =
        'About This Site';
        break;
```

Each module has a name of *something.inc.php*, which is my way of indicating that it's both a PHP script and also an included file. Due to the way computers handle extensions, only the final extension really matters (i.e., if you were to run the file directly, it would be treated as a PHP script).

For each module, the page's title (which will appear in the browser window) is also set.

5. Complete the **switch**:

```php
    case 'contact':
        $page = 'contact.inc.php';
        $page_title = 'Contact Us';
        break;
    case 'search':
        $page = 'search.inc.php';
        $page_title =
        'Search Results';
        break;
    default:
        $page = 'main.inc.php';
        $page_title =
        'Site Home Page';
        break;
} // End of main switch.
```

For each possible content module, another **switch** case is provided. For security purposes, the default case is critical. If **$p** does not have any value or does not have a *valid* value—one of the specific cases—then the **main.inc.php** file will be used. This is a necessary security step because some ill-intended person will see that your site has a URL like **index.php?p=contact** and will attempt to do something like **index.php?p=/path/to/secret/file**. In such a case, the page's main content will be included, and not the bad thing the hacker was trying to see.

continues on next page

6. Confirm that the module file exists:

```php
if (!file_exists('./modules/' .
→ $page)) {
    $page = 'main.inc.php';
    $page_title = 'Site Home Page';
}
```

This isn't absolutely necessary as long as the right module file exists for each case in the **switch**. However, including this code provides an extra layer of security.

7. Include the header file:

```php
include('./includes/header.html');
```

This is the start of the HTML template.

8. Include the module:

```php
include('./modules/' . $page);
```

This brings in all the specific content.

9. Include the footer file:

```php
include('./includes/footer.html');
```

This completes the HTML template.

10. Complete the page:

```php
?>
```

11. Save the file as **index.php** and place it in your Web directory.

You can't test this script until you've created some of the content modules (at least **main.inc.php**).

TIP The **switch** conditional that validates proper $p values is an important security measure. Another is using a separate variable for the name of the included file (i.e., $page). The following code would be *highly* insecure:

```php
include($_GET['p']);
```

F Content modules shouldn't be accessed directly through a URL, since they would then lack the HTML template (among other things).

Creating content modules

Now that all the legwork has been done and the configuration, template, and index files have been written, it's time to start creating the actual content modules. With this bootstrap system, a content module is stunningly simple to implement. The content files do not need to include the configuration or the template files, because the main script already does that. And since all the content files are includes, they can contain literal HTML or PHP code.

There is one catch: the modules should not be loadable directly. If you were to directly access **main.inc.php** (or any other module) in your Web browser, you'd see the result without the HTML template **F**, without the proper error management, and possibly without the database connectivity. To prevent this, every module should have some code that redirects the user to the proper page, if accessed directly. (Later in this chapter, you'll learn how to prevent direct access using the Web server itself.)

To create the main module:

1. Begin a new PHP script in your text editor or IDE, to be named **main.inc.php** (**Script 2.5**):

   `<?php # Script 2.5 - main.inc.php`

2. Check that this page has not been accessed directly:

   `if (!defined('BASE_URL')) {`

   There are any number of things you could check for to test if the module is being accessed directly, like whether **$page** or **$p** is set. Instead, I'll see if a constant is defined. This constant is created in the configuration file, which should be included first thing in the index file, prior to including this page.

continues on page 63

Script 2.5 The first content module has the HTML for the main page. Some PHP code redirects the Web browser if this script was accessed directly.

```php
1    <?php # Script 2.5 - main.inc.php
2
3    /*
4     *  This is the main content module.
5     *  This page is included by index.php.
6     */
7
8    // Redirect if this page was accessed directly:
9    if (!defined('BASE_URL')) {
10
11       // Need the BASE_URL, defined in the config file:
12       require('../includes/config.inc.php');
13
14       // Redirect to the index page:
15       $url = BASE_URL . 'index.php';
16       header ("Location: $url");
17       exit;
18
19   } // End of defined() IF.
20   ?>
21   <h1>Welcome to the colour_blue template</h1>
22   <p>This standards compliant, simple, fixed width website template is released as an 'open
     → source' design (under a <a href="http://creativecommons.org/licenses/by/3.0">Creative Commons
     → Attribution 3.0 Licence</a>), which means that you are free to download and use it for
     → anything you want (including modifying and amending it). All I ask is that you leave the
     → 'design from HTML5webtemplates.co.uk' link in the footer of the template, but other than
     → that...</p>
23   <p>This template is written entirely in <strong>HTML5</strong> and <strong>CSS</strong>, and can
     → be validated using the links in the footer.</p>
24   <p>You can view more free HTML5 web templates <a href="http://www.html5webtemplates.
     → co.uk">here</a>.</p>
25   <p>This template is a fully functional 5 page website, with an <a href="examples.html">
     → examples</a> page that gives examples of all the styles available with this design.</p>
26   <h2>Browser Compatibility</h2>
27   <p>This template has been tested in the following browsers:</p>
28   <ul>
29     <li>Internet Explorer 8</li>
30     <li>Internet Explorer 7</li>
31     <li>FireFox 3.5</li>
32     <li>Google Chrome 6</li>
33     <li>Safari 4</li>
34   </ul>
```

The complete, modularized, template-driven site home page.

3. Redirect the user:

```
$url = BASE_URL . 'index.php';
header ("Location: $url");
exit;
```

If this page is being accessed directly, then the user should be redirected to the index page. Because an absolute URL redirection is desired (which is best), the configuration file must be included to get the **BASE_URL** value.

4. Complete the PHP section:

```
} // End of defined() IF.
?>
```

5. Add your content:

```
<h1>Welcome to the colour_blue
→ template</h1>

<p>This standards compliant,
→ simple, fixed width website
→ template...
```

This can be any combination of HTML and PHP, just like any other PHP page. I'm omitting some of the content from this step, but you can find it in the downloadable version of the script.

6. Save the file as **main.inc.php**, place it in your Web directory (in the **modules** folder, Ⓐ), and test by going to **index. php** in your Web browser Ⓖ.

Creating the search module

As a demonstration of a PHP-driven module, I'll sketch out a search feature. Keep in mind that, having no real content and no database back end, this example makes it impossible to implement a real search. But that's not important in this case anyway. The focus here is on how you would use PHP to handle forms within the modular structure. Once again, I think you'll be surprised by how uncomplicated it is.

For this specific template, the search form is already present in the sidebar, created by **header.html**:

```
<form method="get" action=
→ "index.php" id="search_form">
  <p>
    <input type="hidden"
    → name="p" value="search" />
    <input class="search"
    → type="text" name="terms"
    → value="Search..." />
    <input name="search"
    → type="image" src="style/
    → search.png" alt="Search"
    → title="Search" />
  </p>
</form>
```

As you can see, the form uses the GET method, which is common for search forms. The **action** attribute points to **index.php**, because all page requests go through the bootstrap file. But to work within the modularized system, the **hidden** input is required, with a name of *p* and a value of *search*. This one line effectively tells the bootstrap file to load the search module when the form is submitted.

If you had a different form that used POST, such as a contact form, a **hidden** input with the proper value would work just the same.

To create the search module:

1. Begin a new PHP script in your text editor or IDE, to be named **search.inc.php** (Script 2.6):

   ```
   <?php # Script 2.6 - search.inc.php
   ```

2. Redirect the browser if the page has been accessed directly:

   ```
   if (!defined('BASE_URL')) {
     require('../includes/config.
     → inc.php');
     $url = BASE_URL .
     → 'index.php?p=search';
     if (isset($_GET['terms'])) {
       $url .= '&terms=' .
       → urlencode($_GET['terms']);
     }
     header ("Location: $url");
     exit;
   } // End of defined() IF.
   ```

The bulk of the code here is like that in **main.inc.php**, with two changes. First, the redirection URL is changed to **BASE_URL** plus **index.php?p=search**. This technique, which can be used for any module, allows the user to be immediately redirected to the page they want—via **index.php**. Second, if for some inexplicable reason the user arrived on this page while submitting a form, then the search terms will be present in the URL. If so, those terms will be passed along as well. The end result will be that going directly to **www.example.com/modules/search.inc.php?terms=blah** still results in a valid search.

continues on page 66

Script 2.6 The search module pretends to return some results as a way of demonstrating how easy it is to handle forms, even in a modularized structure.

```php
1   <?php # Script 2.6 - search.inc.php
2
3   /*
4    *  This is the search content module.
5    *  This page is included by index.php.
6    *  This page expects to receive $_GET['terms'].
7    */
8
9   // Redirect if this page was accessed directly:
10  if (!defined('BASE_URL')) {
11
12     // Need the BASE_URL, defined in the config file:
13     require('../includes/config.inc.php');
14
15     // Redirect to the index page:
16     $url = BASE_URL . 'index.php?p=search';
17
18     // Pass along search terms?
19     if (isset($_GET['terms'])) {
20        $url .= '&terms=' . urlencode($_GET['terms']);
21     }
22
23     header ("Location: $url");
24     exit;
25
26  } // End of defined() IF.
27
28  // Print a caption:
29  echo '<h1>Search Results</h1>';
30
31  // Display the search results if the form
32  // has been submitted.
33  if (isset($_GET['terms']) && ($_GET['terms'] != 'Search...') ) {
34
35     // Query the database.
36     // Fetch the results.
37     // Print the results:
38     for ($i = 1; $i <= 10; $i++) {
39        echo <<<EOT
40  <h4><a href="#">Search Result #$i</a></h4>
41  <p>This is some description. This is some description. This is some description.
   → This is some description.</p>\n
42  EOT;
43     }
44
45  } else { // Tell them to use the search form.
46     echo '<p class="error">Please use the search form to search this site.</p>';
47  }
```

3. Print a caption:

```
echo '<h1>Search Results</h1>';
```

4. Check for a proper search term:

```
if (isset($_GET['terms']) && ($_GET
→['terms'] != 'Search...') ) {
```

The database search would only take place if a search term were passed along in the URL. The search box uses *Search...* as the default value, so that needs to be ruled out, too.

5. Print the search results:

```
for ($i = 1; $i <= 10; $i++) {
    echo <<<EOT
<h4><a href="#">Search Result
→#$i</a></h4>
<p>This is some description. This
→is some description. This is
→some description. This is some
→description.</p>\n
EOT;
}
```

Since there's no database to search, I'll just use a **for** loop to print 10 search results. I'm using the heredoc syntax here, as described in Chapter 1, "Advanced PHP Techniques."

6. Complete the page:

```
} else {
    echo '<p class="error">Please
→use the search form to search
→this site.</p>';
}
```

This conditional applies if no valid search terms were entered 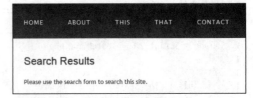.

7. Save the file as **search.inc.php**, place it in your Web directory (in the **modules** folder), and test by submitting the form 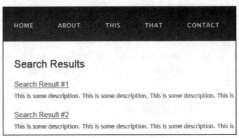.

H No search is performed without a term being submitted.

I Any search term will turn up these dummy results.

Improved SEO with mod_rewrite

The modularized site as written has a number of benefits, starting with the fact that it will be easier to maintain and expand as needed. One downside is that the URLs required by this approach are awkward and unappealing:

- `index.php?p=about`
- `index.php?p=contact`
- `index.php?p=this`

The standard solution in these situations is to use the Apache Web server's `mod_rewrite` module to allow for "prettier" URLs. `mod_rewrite` is a tool that lets you instruct the server that when the user goes to one URL, the server should provide another resource. `mod_rewrite` makes use of regular expressions, so the matching pattern and resulting actual URL can be as complex as needed.

These, and other changes to Apache's behavior, can be made in two ways: by editing the primary Apache configuration file or by creating directory-specific files. The primary configuration file is `httpd.conf`, found within a `conf` directory, and it dictates how the entire Apache Web server runs (where the `httpd.conf` file is on your system will depend on many things). An `.htaccess` file (pronounced "H-T access") is placed within a Web directory and is used to affect how Apache behaves within just that folder and subfolders.

Generally speaking, it's preferable to make changes in the `httpd.conf` file, since this file needs to be read only by the Web server each time the server is started. Conversely, `.htaccess` files must be read by the Web server once for every request to which an `.htaccess` file might apply. For example, if you have **www.example.com/somedir/.htaccess**, any request to **www.example.com/somedir/*whatever*** requires reading the `.htaccess` file, as well as reading an `.htaccess` file that might exist in **www.example.com/**. On the other hand, in shared hosting environments, individual users are not allowed to customize the entire Apache configuration, but they may be allowed to use `.htaccess` to make changes that only affect their sites. And changes to the primary configuration file do require restarting Apache to take effect.

TIP To be safe, I'd recommend making a backup copy of your original Apache configuration file before pursuing any of the subsequent edits.

Allowing for .htaccess overrides

As already stated, all Apache configuration can actually be accomplished within the `httpd.conf` file. In fact, doing so is preferred. But the configuration file is not always available for you to edit, so it's worth also knowing how to use `.htaccess` files to change how a site functions.

An `.htaccess` file is just a plain-text file, with the name `.htaccess`. Like `.htconf`, there is no file extension, and the initial period makes this a hidden file on the system. When placed within a Web directory, the directives defined in the `.htaccess` file will apply to that directory and its subdirectories.

A common hang-up when using **.htaccess** files is that permission has to be granted to allow **.htaccess** to make server behavior changes. Depending on the installation and configuration, Apache, on the strictest level of security, will not allow **.htaccess** files to change Apache behavior. This is accomplished with code like the following, in **httpd.conf**:

```
<Directory />
AllowOverride None
</Directory>
```

The **Directory** directive is used within **httpd.conf** to modify Apache's behavior within a specific directory. In the previous code, the root directory (**/**) is the target, meaning that Apache will not allow overrides—changes—made within any directories on the computer at all. Prior to creating **.htaccess** files, then, the main configuration file must be set to allow overrides in the applicable Web directory (or directories).

The **AllowOverride** directive takes one or more flags indicating what, specifically, can be overridden:

- *AuthConfig*, for using authorization and authentication
- *FileInfo*, for performing redirects and URL rewriting
- *Indexes*, for listing directory contents
- *Limit*, for restricting access to the directory
- *Options*, for setting directory behavior, such as the ability to execute CGI scripts or to index folder contents
- *All*
- *None*

For example, to allow *AuthConfig* and *FileInfo* to be overridden within the **site** directory, the **httpd.conf** file should include:

```
<Directory /path/to/site>
AllowOverride AuthConfig FileInfo
</Directory>
```

As long as this code comes after any **AllowOverride None** block, an **.htaccess** file in the **site** directory will be able to make some changes to Apache's behavior when serving files from that directory (and its subdirectories).

To allow .htaccess overrides:

1. Open **httpd.conf** in any text editor or IDE.

   If you're using XAMPP on Windows, the file to open is **C:\xampp\apache\conf\httpd.conf** (assuming XAMPP is installed in the root of the C drive). If you're using MAMP on Mac OS X, the file to open is **/Applications/MAMP/conf/apache/httpd.conf**.

   If you aren't using either of these but are using Apache, you'll need to hunt around for your **httpd.conf** file.

2. At the end of the file, add

   ```
   <Directory "/path/to/directory">
   </Directory>
   ```

   The **Directory** tag is how you customize Apache behavior for a specific directory or its subdirectories. Within the opening tag, provide an absolute path to the directory in question, such as **C:\xampp\htdocs*somedir*** or **/Applications/MAMP/htdocs/*somedir***.

   If your configuration file has a **VirtualHost** tag for the site in question, you'd want to add the **Directory** within that.

```
<Directory "C:/xampp/htdocs/ch02">
    AllowOverride All
</Directory>
```

A The modified configuration file should now allow for `.htaccess` overrides within the site's directory.

3. Within the **Directory** tags, add **A**:

   AllowOverride All

   This is a heavy-handed solution but will do the trick. On a live, publicly available server, you'd want to be more specific about what exact settings can be overridden, but on your home computer, this won't be a problem.

4. Save the configuration file.

5. Restart Apache.

   TIP If a directory has an `.htaccess` file but is not allowed to override a setting, the `.htaccess` file will just be ignored.

   TIP Anything accomplished within an `.htaccess` file can also be achieved using a `Directory` tag within `httpd.conf`.

   TIP Apache will not display `.htaccess` files in the Web browser by default, which is a smart security approach.

   TIP When creating `.htaccess` files, make sure your text editor or IDE is not secretly adding a `.txt` extension. Notepad, for example, will do this. You can confirm this has happened if you can load `www.example.com/.htaccess.txt` in your Web browser. In Notepad, you can prevent the added extension by quoting the file name and saving it as type "All files."

Protecting Directories

Another common use of an **.htaccess** file is to protect the contents of a directory. There are two possible scenarios:

- Denying all access
- Restricting access to authorized users

Strange as it may initially sound, there are plenty of situations in which files and folders placed in the Web directory should be made unavailable. For example, the **modules** directory in this site could reasonably be blocked, as could any directory you use to store sensitive PHP scripts or uploaded files. In all of these cases, the contents of the directory would not be meant for direct access, but rather PHP scripts in other directories would reference that content as needed.

To deny all access to a directory's contents, place this code in an **.htaccess** file in that folder (comments indicate what each line does):

```
# Disable directory browsing:
Options All -Indexes
# Prevent folder listing:
IndexIgnore *
# Prevent access to any file:
<FilesMatch "^.*$">
Order Allow,Deny
Deny from all
</FilesMatch>
```

Again, this code just prevents direct access to that directory's contents via a Web browser. A PHP script could still use **include()**, **require()**, **readfile()**, and other functions to access that content.

There are a couple of ways of restricting access to authorized users, with the **mod_auth** module being the most basic and common. It's not hard to use **mod_auth**, but you have to invoke a secondary Apache tool to create the credentials file. If you want to pursue this route, just do a search online for Apache **mod_auth**.

Enabling URL Rewriting

Finally we get to our destination: implementing URL rewriting. URL rewriting has gained attention as part of the overbearing focus on *search engine optimization* (SEO), but URL rewriting has been a useful tool for years. With a dynamically driven site, such as an e-commerce project, a value will often be passed to a page in the URL to indicate what products to display, resulting in URLs such as **www.example.com/category.php?id=23**. The PHP script, **category.php**, would then use the value of **$_GET['id']** to know what products to pull from the database and show.

With URL rewriting applied, the URL shown in the browser, visible to the end user and referenced in search engine results, can be transformed into something more obviously meaningful, such as **www.example.com/category/23/** or, better yet, **www.example.com/category/garden+gnomes/**. Apache, via URL rewriting, takes the more user-friendly URL and parses it into something usable by the PHP scripts. This is made possible by the Apache **mod_rewrite** module. To use it, the **.htaccess** file must first check for the module and turn on the rewrite engine:

```
<IfModule mod_rewrite.c>

RewriteEngine on

</IfModule>
```

After enabling the engine, and before the closing **IfModule** tag, you add rules dictating the rewrites. The syntax is

```
RewriteRule match rewrite
```

For example, you could do the following:

```
RewriteRule somepage.php otherpage.php
```

With that code, any time a user goes to **somepage.php**, the user will be shown the contents of **otherpage.php**, although the browser will still display **somepage.php** in the address bar.

To be clear, that's not actually a good use of **mod_rewrite**, as a literal redirection could be accomplished with the less complex **mod_alias** module instead. However, a line like that does represent an easy way to test that **mod_rewrite** is working.

Part of the complication with performing URL rewrites is that Perl-Compatible Regular Expressions (PCRE) are needed to most flexibly find matches. For example, to treat **www.example.com/category/23** as if it were **www.example.com/category.php?id=23**, you would have the following rule:

```
RewriteRule ^category/([0-9]+)/?$
category.php?id=$1
```

The initial caret (^) says that the expression must match the beginning of the string. After that should be the word *category*, followed by a slash. Then, any quantity of digits follows, concluding with an optional slash (allowing for both *category/23* and *category/23/*). The dollar sign closes the match, meaning that nothing can follow the optional slash. That's the pattern for the example match (and it's a simple pattern at that, really).

The rewrite part is what will actually be executed, unbeknownst to the Web browser and the end user. In this line, that's **category.php?id=$1**. The *$1* is a *backreference* to the first parenthetical grouping in the match (e.g., 23). Thus, **www.example.com/category/23** is treated by the server as if the URL was actually **www.example.com/category.php?id=23**.

With all of this in mind, in the particular case of this modularized site, the goal is to use, say, **www.example.com/about/** instead of **www.example.com/index.php?p=about**. Not only is this aesthetically better, but there can be an SEO benefit, considering the impact that URLs have on SEO rankings: an apparent directory name—**about**—is more significant than the **index.php** script being passed an argument of **p** with a value of *about*.

As you'll see in the following series of steps, the fact that the URL will appear to reference a subdirectory will have other implications that you'll need to address. But having identified the specific syntax to be addressed, you can configure Apache to make those dynamic changes.

To implement mod_rewrite:

1. Create a new file, to be named **.htaccess**, in your text editor or IDE (**Script 2.7**):

   # Script 2.7 - .htaccess

   Be certain to create the file without any extension, and watch that your text editor or IDE does not secretly create one.

   Alternatively, you can edit a **Directory** element within the main **httpd.conf** file, if you'd rather.

   The pound sign (or number sign, or hash) can be used to create comments within this file.

2. Add the following:

   <IfModule mod_rewrite.c>

   </IfModule>

   The **IfModule** tag is how you add rules that would apply only if a named module has been loaded. In this case, that's the **mod_rewrite** module.

Script 2.7 The redirection rules set within this **.htaccess** file will allow the site to use nicer URLs.

```
1   # Script 2.7 - .htaccess
2   <IfModule mod_rewrite.c>
3
4   # Turn on the engine:
5   RewriteEngine on
6
7   # Set the base to this directory:
8   RewriteBase /ch02/
9
10  # Redirect certain paths to index.php:
11  RewriteRule ^(about|contact|this|that|
    → search)/?$ index.php?p=$1
12
13  </IfModule>
```

3. Within the **IfModule** tags, add

   RewriteEngine on

   RewriteBase /ch02/

   The first line turns the rewrite engine on, if it is not already. The second identifies the URL base to which redirection matches should apply. This is a useful setting when redirections are taking place within a subdirectory (e.g., if you're using **http://localhost/ch02/** as the URL).

4. On the next line, but before the closing **IfModule** tag, add

   RewriteRule ^(about|contact|this|
   ↪ that|search)/?$ index.php?p=$1

   The goal is to rewrite certain URLs back to **index.php**, passing along the specific page requested. Rather than redirect everything—because other valid directories may exist, I'm only redirecting certain values: *about*, *contact*, *this*, *that*, and *search*.

   In case you're not terribly familiar with PCRE, the caret (^) indicates that this pattern must match the beginning of the URL, starting after the **RewriteBase** value. Then, within the parentheses, literal strings are enumerated using the pipe character (|). In other words, match something that begins with *about* or *contact* or...

   Then the slash is optional, but if present, can only exist once, as dictated by the question mark. This will provide matches for either **www.example.com/about** or **www.example.com/about/**. The dollar sign after the question mark indicates the end of the match.

   continues on next page

Matches will be redirected to **index. php?p=X**, where *X* is whatever matched the strings within the parentheses (i.e., this is a backreference to a grouping).

5. Save the configuration file in your Web site's directory.

6. Test in your Web browser **B**.

    Note that in order to test other pages, such as an about page, you'll need to create the corresponding module script.

TIP Once you adopt this system, you'd want to change the URLs for the links (in the HTML), and the **action** attribute of the search form.

TIP Because it will appear as if some URLs reference subdirectories (e.g., **www.example. com/about/**), you'll need to change references to external resources in your HTML to be absolute, instead of relative **C**:

```
<link rel="stylesheet" type="text/css"
→ href="/style/style.css"
→ title="style" />
```

B The new about page, being accessed through a nicer-looking URL.

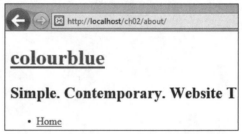

C Because the browser thinks it's within the **about** directory, it cannot find the referenced CSS file until I change the reference to it.

Affecting the Browser Cache

Web browsers and *proxy servers* (something ISPs and other corporations create to improve network efficiency) habitually cache Web pages. Caching a page is a matter of storing its content (or part of its content, like an image or video) and then providing that stored version, rather than the version on the server, when a request is made.

For most end users, this is not a problem. In fact, if done properly, the users will not be aware that they are receiving a cached version of a page or image. But if while developing a site you've struggled to get your Web browser (let's face it: the likely culprit is Internet Explorer) to recognize changes you know you've made in a page, then you've seen the dark side of caching. With your dynamic, PHP-driven sites, sometimes you want to make certain that end users are getting the most up-to-date version of your pages.

TABLE 2.1 Cache-Control Directives

Directive	Meaning
public	Can be cached anywhere
private	Only cacheable by browsers
no-cache	Cannot be cached anywhere
must-revalidate	Caches must check for newer versions
proxy-revalidate	Proxy caches must check for newer versions
max-age	A duration, in seconds, that the content is cacheable
s-maxage	Overrides the max-age value for shared caches

Caching—both in Web browsers and proxy servers—can be affected using PHP's `header()` function. Four header types are involved:

- Last-Modified
- Expires
- Pragma
- Cache-Control

The first three header types are part of the HTTP 1.0 standard. The *Last-Modified* header uses a UTC (Coordinated Universal Time) date-time value. If a caching system sees that the Last-Modified value is more recent than the date on the cached version of the page, it knows to use the new version from the server.

Expires is used as an indicator as to when a cached version of the page should no longer be used (in Greenwich Mean Time). Setting an Expires value in the past should always force the page from the server to be used:

```
header("Expires: Mon, 26 Jul 1997
    05:00:00 GMT");
```

Pragma is just a declaration for how the page data should be handled. To avoid caching of a page, use

```
header("Pragma: no-cache");
```

The *Cache-Control* header was added in HTTP 1.1 and is a more finely tuned option. (You should still use the HTTP 1.0 headers as well.) There are numerous Cache-Control settings (**Table 2.1**).

Putting all this information together, to keep all systems from caching a page, you would use these headers:

```
header("Last-Modified: Thu, 5 Jun
→ 2012 14:26:00 GMT"); // Right now!
```

```
header("Expires: Mon, 26 Jul 1997
→ 05:00:00 GMT"); // Way back when!
```

```
header("Pragma: no-cache");
```

```
header("Cache-Control: no-cache");
```

While all too common, this is a heavy-handed approach. Certainly not every PHP script you use is uncacheable. Even the most active site could cache some of its scripts for a minute or more (and a very active site would get many requests within a minute; the cached version would save the server all those hits). As a more focused and proper use of these concepts, let's rewrite the **view_tasks.php** page (Script 1.3) from Chapter 1.

To affect caching:

1. Open **view_tasks.php** in your text editor or IDE.

2. Before anything is sent to the Web browser, add the initial PHP tag (Script 2.8):

   `<?php # Script 2.8 - view_tasks.php`

   As you hopefully know, the **header()** function can only be called before anything is sent to the Web browser, including plain text, HTML, or even a blank space.

3. Connect to the database:

   `$dbc = mysqli_connect('localhost', → 'username', 'password', 'test');`

   To accurately determine when this page was last modified, the script will look at the database it uses.

continues on page 78

Script 2.8 This modified version of Chapter 1's **view_tasks.php** page (Script 1.3) uses the **header()** function to make caching recommendations.

```
1    <?php # Script 2.8 - view_tasks.php
2
3    // Connect to the database:
4    $dbc = mysqli_connect('localhost', 'username', 'password', 'test');
5
6    // Get the latest dates as timestamps:
7    $q = 'SELECT UNIX_TIMESTAMP(MAX(date_added)), UNIX_TIMESTAMP(MAX(date_completed)) FROM tasks';
8    $r = mysqli_query($dbc, $q);
9    list($max_a, $max_c) = mysqli_fetch_array($r, MYSQLI_NUM);
10
11   // Determine the greater timestamp:
12   $max = ($max_a > $max_c) ? $max_a : $max_c;
13
14   // Create a cache interval in seconds:
15   $interval = 60 * 60 * 6; // 6 hours
16
17   // Send the headers:
```

script continues on next page

```php
18    header("Last-Modified: " . gmdate ('r', $max));
19    header("Expires: " . gmdate ("r", ($max + $interval)));
20    header("Cache-Control: max-age=$interval");
21    ?><!doctype html>
22    <html lang="en">
23    <head>
24        <meta charset="utf-8">
25        <title>View Tasks</title>
26        <link rel="stylesheet" href="style.css">
27    </head>
28    <body>
29    <h2>Current To-Do List</h2>
30    <?php
31    function make_list($parent) {
32        global $tasks;
33        echo '<ol>'; // Start an ordered list.
34        foreach ($parent as $task_id => $todo) {
35            echo "<li>$todo";
36            if (isset($tasks[$task_id])) {
37                // Call this function again:
38                make_list($tasks[$task_id]);
39            }
40            echo '</li>'; // Complete the list item.
41        } // End of FOREACH loop.
42        echo '</ol>'; // Close the ordered list.
43    } // End of make_list() function.
44    $q = 'SELECT task_id, parent_id, task FROM tasks WHERE date_completed="0000-00-00 00:00:00"
      ⟶ ORDER BY parent_id, date_added ASC';
45    $r = mysqli_query($dbc, $q);
46    $tasks = array();
47    while (list($task_id, $parent_id, $task) = mysqli_fetch_array($r, MYSQLI_NUM)) {
48        $tasks[$parent_id][$task_id] =  $task;
49    }
50    make_list($tasks[0]);
51    ?>
52    </body>
53    </html>
```

4. Get the latest date values from the table:

```
$q = 'SELECT UNIX_TIMESTAMP
→ (MAX(date_added)),
→ UNIX_TIMESTAMP(MAX
→ (date_completed)) FROM tasks';

$r = mysqli_query($dbc, $q);

list($max_a, $max_c) =
→ mysqli_fetch_array
→ ($r, MYSQLI_NUM);

$max = ($max_a > $max_c) ?
→ $max_a : $max_c;
```

The **tasks** table contains two date/time columns—**date_added** and **date_completed**. Any time the page's content is updated, these two values are set to the current date and time (there is no delete option). The query returns the largest **date_added** and **date_completed** values. Because they would be returned in a less usable format 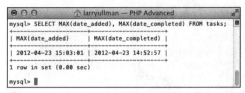, the **UNIX_TIMESTAMP()** function is applied to make them both integers . Then, the ternary operator is used to assign the largest value (and therefore the most recent date) to the **$max** variable.

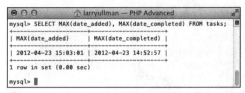

A How the timestamp fields would ordinarily be returned by the query.

B The query result used by this script.

5. Define a reasonable caching interval:

```
$interval = 60 * 60 * 6;
```

"Reasonable" depends on your page, how many visitors you get (i.e., the server load), and how often it's updated. For this value, which is in seconds, I use six hours (60 seconds times 60 minutes times 6).

6. Send the Last-Modified header:

```
header("Last-Modified: " .
→ gmdate ('r', $max));
```

This header sets the modification date of this script as the last time the database was updated. The "r" **gmdate()** (and **date()**) option will return the date formatted per the HTTP specifications.

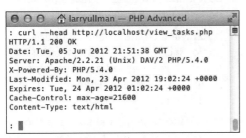

Current To-Do List

1. Another Task
    1. Subtask 3
    2. Subtask 2
        1. Subsubtask1
        2. Subsubtask 2
            1. Sub-cubed task 1
            2. Sub-cubed task 2
2. My New Task
3. This is a new task!
4. Finish Chapter 1!

C The cache-controlled Web page.

```
● ○ ○    🏠 larryullman — PHP Advanced
: curl --head http://localhost/view_tasks.php
HTTP/1.1 200 OK
Date: Tue, 05 Jun 2012 21:51:38 GMT
Server: Apache/2.2.21 (Unix) DAV/2 PHP/5.4.0
X-Powered-By: PHP/5.4.0
Last-Modified: Mon, 23 Apr 2012 19:02:24 +0000
Expires: Tue, 24 Apr 2012 01:02:24 +0000
Cache-Control: max-age=21600
Content-Type: text/html

:
```

D Using cURL to view the headers returned by the `view_tasks.php` page.

7. Set the Expires header:

```
header("Expires: " . gmdate
→ ("r", ($max + $interval)));
```

The expiration value is the current time plus the defined interval.

8. Set the Cache-Control header:

```
header("Cache-Control:
→ max-age=$interval");

?>
```

This is just the HTTP 1.1 equivalent of the Expires header. Instead of giving a date value, set **max-age** in seconds.

9. Delete the database connection that existed later on in the original script.

This has been moved to the top of the script in Step 3.

10. Save the file as **view_tasks.php**, place in your Web directory, and test in your Web browser **C**.

TIP Note that caching is, in theory, a very good thing, designed to minimize unnecessary server requests. If properly controlled, caches are great for both the server and the client.

TIP If you have cURL installed on your system, you can run this command to see a page's headers **D**:

```
curl --head http://www.example.com/
→ page.php
```

Curl is discussed in Chapter 10, "Networking with PHP."

TIP Page caching can also be affected using the META tags, placed within an HTML document's head. This may not work as reliably with some browsers as the `header()` method.

TIP This section of the chapter specifically discusses controlling browser caching. Chapter 4, "Basic Object-Oriented Programming," covers server-side caching.

Review and Pursue

If you have any problems with these sections, either in answering the questions or pursuing your own endeavors, turn to the book's supporting forum (**www.LarryUllman.com/forums/**).

Review

- What is a *bootstrap* file? (See page 57.)

- Why is it important that all user requests go through the bootstrap file (i.e., why shouldn't the individual modules be accessed directly)? (See page 61.)

- Why is the following line of code highly insecure? (See page 60.)

  ```
  include($_GET['p']);
  ```

- What two files are used to configure how the Apache Web server runs? How do the two files differ? (See page 67.)

- How can you test if **mod_rewrite** is available to use within a specific directory? (See page 71.)

- Why do *relative* references to external resources, such as images, JavaScript, and style sheets, cause problems when using **mod_rewrite**? (See page 74.)

- What is *caching*? Why is caching useful? When can caching be problematic? (See page 75.)

- What PHP function can be used to affect the caching of a page? (See page 76.)

Pursue

- Add more modules to the sample site to flesh it out.

- If you have an actual project to modularize using the techniques explained in this chapter, do so, adding in a database configuration file.

- Practice creating errors within the modularized Web site, in both live and development modes, to test the error-handling process.

- If you want, create a validation/redirection includable file that checks if a module is accessed directly and, if so, redirects the user. Then have each module include this new file.

- Modify the search page so that it shows the submitted search terms, too.

- Learn more about configuring Apache and what other features the Web server application has to offer.

- If you're using **mod_rewrite**, change the HTML so that none of the links or forms reference **index.php** anymore.

- Learn more about caching.

Advanced Database Concepts

In this book, I wanted to do a couple of things. First, I wanted to demonstrate and explain some advanced concepts and approaches. Second, I wanted to present solutions to common problems. This chapter addresses both of those goals equally.

For the first example, you'll see how to use a database to store session data. Doing so offers many advantages, with improved security at the forefront. Next, you'll find a thorough discussion on working with U.S. zip codes, including how to calculate the distances between two. The third example introduces *stored functions*, a useful database concept. The chapter ends by answering a common question: how do you lay out query results horizontally as opposed to the standard vertical layout?

Storing Sessions in a Database

By default, PHP stores all session data in text files in the server. Normally, these files are stored in a temporary folder (like **/tmp** on Unix and Mac OS X) with filenames matching the session IDs (e.g., *ei26b4i2nup742ucho9glmbh84*). However, PHP provides a mechanism for you to manage sessions in other ways, such as storing the session data in a database.

The main reason I recommend making this change is improved security. On shared hosting servers, without extra steps being taken every Web site uses the same temporary directory for its sessions. This means that dozens upon dozens of applications are all reading and writing in the same place. Knowing this, you'd find it easy to create a script that reads all the data from all the files in the sessions folder, thereby accessing the stored user data from other sites.

A second benefit to moving session data to a database is that it allows you to easily retrieve more information about your Web site's sessions in general. Queries could be run indicating the number of active sessions and session data can even be backed up.

A third reason to store session data in a database is if you have a site running on multiple servers. When this is the case, the same user may be fed pages from different servers over the course of the same session. The session data stored in a file on one server would be unavailable to the pages on other servers. This isn't a situation that the majority of developers face, but if you do, there's really no other option but to go the database route.

With an understanding of why you might want to store session data in a database, let's go through the steps you'd need to take to implement that approach.

> **TIP** Another fix for the security concern on a shared host is to change the session directory for your site. To do so, call the `session_save_path()` function prior to every `session_start()` call. You'll also need to make sure that the new directory exists, of course, and that it has the proper permissions.

Creating the session table

To store session data in a database, you must first create a special database table for that express purpose. This table can be part of an already existing database (like the rest of your application) or in its own database. At a bare minimum, the table needs three columns (**Table 3.1**).

The **session** table can have more than those three columns, but it must have those three. Keep in mind, though, that many things you might be inclined to represent in another column—a user's ID, for example—would likely be stored in the session data column.

TABLE 3.1 Session Table Columns

Column Type	Stores
CHAR(32)	The session ID
TEXT	The session data
TIMESTAMP	The last time the session data was accessed

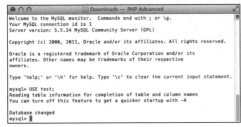

```
Welcome to the MySQL monitor.  Commands end with ; or \g.
Your MySQL connection id is 1
Server version: 5.5.24 MySQL Community Server (GPL)

Copyright (c) 2000, 2011, Oracle and/or its affiliates. All rights reserved.

Oracle is a registered trademark of Oracle Corporation and/or its
affiliates. Other names may be trademarks of their respective
owners.

Type 'help;' or '\h' for help. Type '\c' to clear the current input statement.

mysql> USE test;
Reading table information for completion of table and column names
You can turn off this feature to get a quicker startup with -A

Database changed
mysql>
```

A I'll put the **sessions** table within the **test** database for this example.

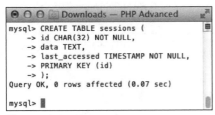

```
mysql> CREATE TABLE sessions (
    -> id CHAR(32) NOT NULL,
    -> data TEXT,
    -> last_accessed TIMESTAMP NOT NULL,
    -> PRIMARY KEY (id)
    -> );
Query OK, 0 rows affected (0.07 sec)

mysql>
```

B This one table will handle all the session data.

```
mysql> DESCRIBE sessions;
+---------------+-----------+------+-----+-------------------+-----------------------------+
| Field         | Type      | Null | Key | Default           | Extra                       |
+---------------+-----------+------+-----+-------------------+-----------------------------+
| id            | char(32)  | NO   | PRI | NULL              |                             |
| data          | text      | YES  |     | NULL              |                             |
| last_accessed | timestamp | NO   |     | CURRENT_TIMESTAMP | on update CURRENT_TIMESTAMP |
+---------------+-----------+------+-----+-------------------+-----------------------------+
3 rows in set (0.00 sec)

mysql>
```

C Confirming the table's structure.

To create the sessions table:

1. Access your MySQL database using the **mysql** client.

   You can also use phpMyAdmin or whatever other interface you prefer.

2. Select the **test** database **A**.

   USE test;

   Since this is just an example, I'll create the table within the **test** database.

3. Create the **sessions** table **B**:

   CREATE TABLE sessions (

   id CHAR(32) NOT NULL,

   data TEXT,

   last_accessed TIMESTAMP NOT NULL,

   PRIMARY KEY (id)

   );

   The table contains the basic three fields. The **id** is the primary key. It will always contain a string 32 characters long and can never be **NULL**. The **data** column is a **TEXT** type and it can be **NULL** (when the session is first started, there is no data). The **last_accessed** column is a **TIMESTAMP**. It will therefore always be updated when the session is created (on **INSERT**) or modified (on **UPDATE**).

4. Confirm the **sessions** table structure **C**:

   DESCRIBE sessions;

   TIP If your application stores a lot of data in sessions, you'd want to change the size of the session data column to **MEDIUMTEXT** or **LONGTEXT**.

Defining the session functions

After creating the database table, storing session data in a database is a two-part process (from a PHP perspective):

1. Define the functions for interacting with the database.

2. Tell PHP to use these functions.

For this second step, the **session_set_save_handler()** function is used. This function should be called with six arguments, each a function name (**Table 3.2**).

I'll briefly discuss what each function should receive (as arguments) and do while creating them in the next script. I'll say up front that all of the functions must return a Boolean value, except for the "read" function. That function must always return a string, even if that means an empty string.

Before getting into the script, it helps to understand when the different functions will be called ❶. Every time a session is started, the "open" and "read" functions are called automatically and immediately. When the "read" function is called, garbage collection *may* take place (depending on various factors).

When a script terminates, the write function is called, and then the "close" function is called. If the session is destroyed, then the "write" function won't be invoked, but the "destroy" function will be, followed by the "close" function.

TABLE 3.2 session_set_save_handler() Arguments

Order	Function to Be Called When...
1	A session is started
2	A session is closed
3	Session data is read
4	Session data is written
5	Session data is destroyed
6	Old session data should be deleted (aka garbage collection performed)

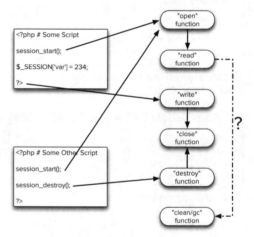

❶ The logical flow of using sessions and the various session-handling functions.

To create new session handlers:

1. Begin a new PHP script in your text editor or IDE, to be named **db_sessions. inc.php** (Script 3.1):

   ```
   <?php # Script 3.1 -
   → db_sessions.inc.php
   ```

   ```
   $sdbc = NULL;
   ```

   The **$sdbc** variable will store the database connection. I initialize it here and then make it global in each function. Note that I'm specifically giving this variable a different name than a standard database connection variable (e.g., **$dbc**), so as to minimize bugs. Normally, you'd want to use only a single database connection, in which case you'd change some of this code accordingly.

   continues on page 88

Script 3.1 This script defines all the functionality required to store session data in a database. It can be included by any page that wants that feature.

```
1    <?php # Script 3.1 - db_sessions.inc.php
2
3    /*
4     *  This page creates the functional interface for
5     *  storing session data in a database.
6     *  This page also starts the session.
7     */
8
9    // Global variable used for the database
10   // connections in all session functions:
11   $sdbc = NULL;
12
13   // Define the open_session() function:
14   // This function takes no arguments.
15   // This function should open the database connection.
16   // This function should return true.
17   function open_session() {
18       global $sdbc;
19
20       // Connect to the database:
21       $sdbc = mysqli_connect ('localhost', 'username', 'password', 'test');
22
```

script continues on next page

```
23      return true;
24   } // End of open_session() function.
25
26   // Define the close_session() function:
27   // This function takes no arguments.
28   // This function closes the database connection.
29   // This function returns the closed status.
30   function close_session() {
31      global $sdbc;
32
33      return mysqli_close($sdbc);
34   } // End of close_session() function.
35
36   // Define the read_session() function:
37   // This function takes one argument: the session ID.
38   // This function retrieves the session data.
39   // This function returns the session data as a string.
40   function read_session($sid) {
41      global $sdbc;
42
43      // Query the database:
44      $q = sprintf('SELECT data FROM sessions WHERE id="%s"', mysqli_real_escape_string($sdbc, $sid));
45      $r = mysqli_query($sdbc, $q);
46
47      // Retrieve the results:
48      if (mysqli_num_rows($r) == 1) {
49         list($data) = mysqli_fetch_array($r, MYSQLI_NUM);
50
51         // Return the data:
52         return $data;
53
54      } else { // Return an empty string.
55         return '';
56      }
57   } // End of read_session() function.
58
59   // Define the write_session() function:
60   // This function takes two arguments:
61   // the session ID and the session data.
62   function write_session($sid, $data) {
63      global $sdbc;
64
65      // Store in the database:
66      $q = sprintf('REPLACE INTO sessions (id, data) VALUES ("%s", "%s")',
         → mysqli_real_escape_string($sdbc, $sid), mysqli_real_escape_string($sdbc, $data));
```

script continues on next page

```
67        $r = mysqli_query($sdbc, $q);
68
69        return true;
70    } // End of write_session() function.
71
72    // Define the destroy_session() function:
73    // This function takes one argument: the session ID.
74    function destroy_session($sid) {
75        global $sdbc;
76
77        // Delete from the database:
78        $q = sprintf('DELETE FROM sessions WHERE id="%s"', mysqli_real_escape_string($sdbc, $sid));
79        $r = mysqli_query($sdbc, $q);
80
81        // Clear the $_SESSION array:
82        $_SESSION = array();
83
84        return true;
85    } // End of destroy_session() function.
86
87    // Define the clean_session() function:
88    // This function takes one argument: a value in seconds.
89    function clean_session($expire) {
90        global $sdbc;
91
92        // Delete old sessions:
93        $q = sprintf('DELETE FROM sessions WHERE DATE_ADD(last_accessed, INTERVAL %d SECOND) < NOW()',
          → (int) $expire);
94        $r = mysqli_query($sdbc, $q);
95
96        return true;
97    } // End of clean_session() function.
98
99    # *************************** #
100   # ***** END OF FUNCTIONS ***** #
101   # *************************** #
102
103   // Declare the functions to use:
104   session_set_save_handler('open_session', 'close_session', 'read_session', 'write_session',
          → 'destroy_session', 'clean_session');
105
106   // Make whatever other changes to the session settings, if you want.
107
108   // Start the session:
109   session_start();
```

2. Define the function for opening a session:

```php
function open_session() {
    global $sdbc;
    $sdbc = mysqli_connect
    ('localhost', 'username',
    'password', 'test');
    return true;
}
```

This function takes no arguments (which is to say that when PHP does something to open a session, it will call this function without sending any values to it). The intent of this function is merely to establish a database connection.

In a real application, without the constraints of a book's limited pages, I would update the function so that it would return a Boolean indicating the success of the given operation instead of always returning true.

3. Define the function for closing a session:

```php
function close_session() {
    global $sdbc;
    return mysqli_close($sdbc);
}
```

This function also takes no arguments. It will close the database connection, returning the success of that operation.

4. Define the function for reading the session data:

```php
function read_session($sid) {
    global $sdbc;
    $q = sprintf('SELECT data FROM
    sessions WHERE id="%s"',
    mysqli_real_escape_string
    ($sdbc, $sid));
    $r = mysqli_query($sdbc, $q);
    if (mysqli_num_rows($r) == 1) {
        list($data) = mysqli_fetch_
        array($r, MYSQLI_NUM);
        return $data;
    } else {
        return '';
    }
}
```

This function will receive one argument: the session ID (e.g., *ei26b4i2nup742u-cho9glmbh84*). The function needs to retrieve the data for that session ID from the database and return it. If the function can't do that, it should return an empty string instead. Although the session ID should be safe to use in a URL, you shouldn't make assumptions when it comes to security, so the `mysqli_real_escape_string()` function is used to make it safe (alternatively, you could use prepared statements).

If you're not familiar with the `sprintf()` function, which I use to compile the query, see Chapter 1, "Advanced PHP Techniques."

5. Define the function for writing data to the database:

```
function write_session($sid,
→ $data) {

  global $sdbc;

  $q = sprintf('REPLACE INTO
→ sessions (id, data) VALUES
→ ("%s", "%s")', mysqli_real_
→ escape_string($sdbc, $sid),
→ mysqli_real_escape_string
→ ($sdbc, $data));

  $r = mysqli_query($sdbc, $q);

  return true;

}
```

This function receives two arguments: the session ID and the session data. The session data is a serialized version of the **$_SESSION** array **E**. For the query, an **INSERT** must be run the first time the session record is created in the database and an **UPDATE** query every time thereafter. The lesser-known **REPLACE** query will achieve the same result. If a record exists whose primary key is the same as that given a value in this query (i.e., the session ID), an update will occur. Otherwise, a new record will be made.

6. Create the function for destroying the session data:

```
function destroy_session($sid) {

  global $sdbc;

  $q = sprintf('DELETE FROM
→ sessions WHERE id="%s"',
→ mysqli_real_escape_string
→ ($sdbc, $sid));

  $r = mysqli_query($sdbc, $q);

  $_SESSION = array();

  return true;

}
```

This function, which will be called when the PHP **session_destroy()** function is invoked, receives one argument, the session ID. This function then runs a **DELETE** query in the database and clears the **$_SESSION** array.

As an example of changing the returned value, you could have this function return the number of affected rows: 1 would effectively be true and 0 would be false.

continues on next page

```
● ○ ○                    Downloads — PHP Advanced                        ⤢
mysql> SELECT * FROM sessions\G
*************************** 1. row ***************************
          id: eafocan0rr7484etbslcb7lnk1
        data: blah|s:6:"umlaut";this|d:3615684.4500000002;that|s:4:"blue";
last_accessed: 2012-06-08 10:50:46
1 row in set (0.00 sec)

mysql> █
```

E Session data is stored in the database (or in a file) as a serialized array. This serialized value says that indexed at **blah** is a string six characters long with a value of *umlaut*. Indexed at **this** is a decimal with a value of *3615684.4500* (and so on). Indexed at **that** is a string four characters long with a value of *blue*.

7. Define the garbage collection function:

```php
function clean_session($expire) {
    global $sdbc;
    $q = sprintf('DELETE FROM
    → sessions WHERE DATE_ADD
    → (last_accessed, INTERVAL %d
    → SECOND) < NOW()', (int)
    → $expire);
    $r = mysqli_query($sdbc, $q);
    return true;
}
```

Garbage collection is something most PHP programmers do not think about. Garbage collection is a language or application's tool for cleaning up resources that are no longer needed. With sessions, PHP's garbage collection can wipe out old sessions that weren't formally destroyed.

There are two relevant settings in PHP: what is considered to be "old" and how likely it is that garbage collection is performed. For all session activity in a site, there is an *X* percent chance that PHP will go into garbage collection mode (the exact percent is a PHP setting; the default value is 1%). If it does, then all "old" session data will be destroyed. So garbage collection is *triggered by any session* but attempts to *clean up every session*.

As for the garbage collection function, it will receive a time, in seconds, as to what is considered to be old. This can be used in a **DELETE** query to get rid of any session that hasn't been accessed in more than the set time.

8. Tell PHP to use the session-handling functions:

```php
session_set_save_handler
→ ('open_session', 'close_session',
→ 'read_session', 'write_session',
→ 'destroy_session',
→ 'clean_session');
```

9. Start the session:

```php
session_start();
```

Two important things to note here: First, the **session_set_save_handler()** function does not start a session. You still have to invoke **session_start()**. Second, you must use these two lines in this order. Calling **session_start()** prior to **session_set_save_handler()** will result in your handlers being ignored.

The reason I'm choosing to start the session within this file is that this file will be included by any script that needs sessions. My concern is that were you to start the sessions separately in each script, it would allow for the possibility that a script could start a session without including this file first, thereby using the file system for that page's session and creating bugs.

10. Save the file as **db_sessions.inc.php** and place it in your Web directory.

As is my rule for all PHP scripts being included by other scripts, this one does not have a terminating PHP tag.

TIP Note that the "write" session function is never called until all of the output has been sent to the Web browser **D**. Then the "close" function is called.

TIP If `session.auto_start` is turned on in your PHP configuration (meaning that sessions are automatically started for each page), then you cannot use the `session_set_save_handler()` function.

TIP As of PHP 5.4, you can provide the `session_set_save_handler()` function with a single argument: an object of any class type that implements `SessionHandlerInterface`. For example, you can use the `SessionHandler` class. This will mean more after the chapters on object-oriented programming.

Using the new session handlers

Using the newly created session handlers is only a matter of invoking the `session_set_save_handler()` function, as discussed in the preceding section. Almost everything else you would do with sessions is unchanged, from storing data in them to accessing stored data to destroying a session.

To demonstrate this, the next script will create some session data if it doesn't exist, show all the session data, and even destroy the session data if a link back to this same page is clicked. As is often the case, there is one little tricky issue...

All of the session activity requires the database and, therefore, the database connection. The connection is opened when the session is started and closed when the session is closed. No problem there except that the "write" and "close" functions will be called after a script has finished running **D**.

As you may already know, PHP does you the favor of automatically closing any database connections when a script stops running. For this next script, this means that after the script runs, the database connection is automatically closed, *and then* the session functions attempt to write the data to the database and close the connection. The result will be some confusing errors (and a—trust me on this— long "Where in the World Is My Database Connection?" search).

To avoid this sequential problem, the `session_write_close()` function should be called before the script terminates. This function will invoke the "write" and "close" functions, while there's still a good database connection.

To use the new session handlers:

1. Begin a new PHP script in your text editor or IDE, to be named **sessions.php** (Script 3.2):

   `<?php # Script 3.2 - sessions.php`

continues on page 93

Script 3.2 This script includes the **db_sessions.inc.php** page (Script 3.1) so that session data is stored in a database.

```
1   <?php # Script 3.2 - sessions.php
2
3   /*  This page does some silly things with sessions.
4    *  It includes the db_sessions.inc.php script
5    *  so that the session data will be stored in a database.
6    */
```

script continues on next page

```
7
8    // Include the sessions file:
9    // The file already starts the session.
10   require('db_sessions.inc.php');
11   ?><!doctype html>
12   <html lang="en">
13   <head>
14       <meta charset="utf-8">
15       <title>DB Session Test</title>
16       <link rel="stylesheet" href="style.css">
17   </head>
18   <body>
19   <?php
20   // Store some dummy data in the session, if no data is present:
21   if (empty($_SESSION)) {
22
23       $_SESSION['blah'] = 'umlaut';
24       $_SESSION['this'] = 3615684.45;
25       $_SESSION['that'] = 'blue';
26
27       // Print a message indicating what's going on:
28       echo '<p>Session data stored.</p>';
29
30   } else { // Print the already-stored data:
31       echo '<p>Session Data Exists:<pre>' . print_r($_SESSION, 1) . '</pre></p>';
32   }
33
34   // Log the user out, if applicable:
35   if (isset($_GET['logout'])) {
36
37       session_destroy();
38       echo '<p>Session destroyed.</p>';
39
40   } else { // Otherwise, print the "Log Out" link:
41       echo '<a href="sessions.php?logout=true">Log Out</a>';
42   }
43
44   // Reprint the session data:
45   echo '<p>Session Data:<pre>' . print_r($_SESSION, 1) . '</pre></p>';
46
47   // Complete the page:
48   echo '</body>
49   </html>';
50
51   // Write and close the session:
52   session_write_close();
53   ?>
```

2. Include the **db_sessions.inc.php** file:

```
require('db_sessions.inc.php');
?>
```

The **session_start()** function, which is in **db_sessions.inc.php**, must be called before anything is sent to the Web browser, so this file must be included prior to any HTML.

3. Create the initial HTML:

```
<!doctype html>
<html lang="en">
<head>
  <meta charset="utf-8">
  <title>DB Session Test</title>
    <link rel="stylesheet"
href="style.css">
</head>
<body>
```

The style sheet can be downloaded along with all of the other code from **www.LarryUllman.com**.

4. Store some dummy data in a session if it is currently empty:

```
<?php
if (empty($_SESSION)) {
  $_SESSION['blah'] = 'umlaut';
  $_SESSION['this'] = 3615684.45;
  $_SESSION['that'] = 'blue';
  echo '<p>Session data stored.</p>';
```

Storing data in a database-managed session is no different than the regular method. This conditional is being used to replicate sessions on multiple pages. The first time the page is loaded, new data will be stored in the session.

5. Otherwise, print the currently stored data:

```
} else {
  echo '<p>Session Data Exists:
→ <pre>' . print_r($_SESSION, 1) .
→ '</pre></p>';
}
```

The second time the page is loaded, the existing data will be available. As a quick way to print the session data, the **print_r()** function will be used.

6. Create the logout functionality:

```
if (isset($_GET['logout'])) {
  session_destroy();
  echo '<p>Session destroyed.</p>';
} else {
  echo '<a href="sessions.php?
→ logout=true">Log Out</a>';
}
```

Again, this conditional is used to fake a multipage site. When the page is accessed, a "Log Out" link is displayed. If the user clicks that link, **?logout=true** is passed in the URL, telling this page to destroy the session.

7. Print the session data:

```
echo '<p>Session Data:<pre>' .
→ print_r($_SESSION, 1) .
→ '</pre></p>';
```

This is mostly a repeat of the code in Step 5. Unlike that line, this one will apply the first time the page is loaded. It will also be used to reveal the effect of destroying the session.

continues on next page

8. Complete the HTML:

```
echo '</body>
</html>';
```

9. Call the **session_write_close()** function and complete the page:

```
session_write_close();
?>
```

It really doesn't matter where in the script this function is called, as long as all the modifications to the session data are over. If you don't use this function, you might see some ugly results 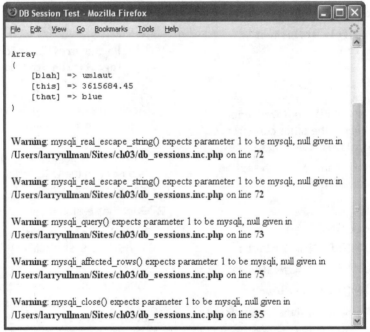.

Array
(
    [blah] => umlaut
    [this] => 3615684.45
    [that] => blue
)

Warning: mysqli_real_escape_string() expects parameter 1 to be mysqli, null given in /Users/larryullman/Sites/ch03/db_sessions.inc.php on line 72

Warning: mysqli_real_escape_string() expects parameter 1 to be mysqli, null given in /Users/larryullman/Sites/ch03/db_sessions.inc.php on line 72

Warning: mysqli_query() expects parameter 1 to be mysqli, null given in /Users/larryullman/Sites/ch03/db_sessions.inc.php on line 73

Warning: mysqli_affected_rows() expects parameter 1 to be mysqli, null given in /Users/larryullman/Sites/ch03/db_sessions.inc.php on line 75

Warning: mysqli_close() expects parameter 1 to be mysqli, null given in /Users/larryullman/Sites/ch03/db_sessions.inc.php on line 35

F Because PHP is nice enough to close open database connections after a script runs, the **write_session()** and **close_session()** functions—called after that point—would be without a database connection.

G The result the first time the page is loaded.

10. Save the file as **sessions.php**, place it in your Web directory (in the same folder as **db_sessions.inc.php**), and test in your Web browser **G**, **H**, and **I**.

> **TIP** You should also call **session_write_close()** before redirecting the browser with a **header()** call. This only applies when you're using your own session handlers.

H Reloading the page allows it to access the already-stored session data.

I Clicking the "Log Out" link ends up destroying the session.

Working with U.S. Zip Codes

A common need on many Web sites is to be able to perform distance calculations between addresses. Although you can always go the full MapQuest or Google Maps route, simple distance estimates can be managed using just zip codes (in the United States, that is).

For every zip code, there is an associated longitude and latitude (technically, zip codes represent multiple longitudes and latitudes, but one pair can be considered centrally located). Take two of these points on the earth, throw in some complicated math, and you have an approximate distance. In this section, I'll discuss how to obtain the necessary zip code data, create a "store locator" table that will provide one of the two points, and then go over the formula used to calculate distances.

Creating the zip code table

This whole example is predicated on having a database with the latitude and longitude points for every zip code in the United States. You'll find three types of sources for this information:

- Commercial zip code databases
- Free zip code databases
- Free zip code tabulation area (ZCTA) databases

The first option will provide you with the most accurate, up-to-date information, but you'll have to pay for it (not a terrible amount, normally). The second option is free (free!) but harder to find and less likely to be current. You can search the Web for "free zip code database" to find free options.

The last option, ZCTA, is a database created by the U.S. Census Bureau for its own purposes. This database ignores around 10,000 zip codes that are used internally by the U.S. Post Office or by specific corporations. It also groups some zip codes together and uses characters to represent others. But for some uses, this information will do just fine. One source of a ZCTA database is **http://zips.sourceforge.net**, found by searching SourceForge.net for "zip code."

Although having a zip code database will be necessary for subsequent examples in this chapter, what these next series of steps also convey is how to turn a comma-separated value (CSV) list of data into a usable database table.

To create the zip code database:

1. Find your data source.

Which source (of the types and specific ones outlined) you use depends on your situation. How important is accuracy? How much are you willing to spend? As a secondary consideration, what resources exist as you're reading this (search the Web and SourceForge)?

I'll use the version from **www.federalgovernmentzipcodes.us** for my example. The only real criticism of this source is that the latitude and longitude are only precise to a bit more than a half mile, but the data is current, and free! For the following steps, I specifically downloaded the "primary location only" version.

A Creating a new database to be used in this example.

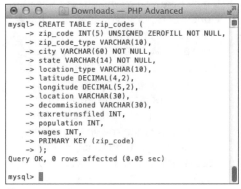

B The main table, whose structure is based on the data to be inserted **C**.

2. Create the database **A**:

```
CREATE DATABASE zips;

USE zips;
```

I'm creating a database called **zips**, in MySQL, using the **mysql** command-line client. You could do most of the following using phpMyAdmin, the MySQL Administrator, or another tool.

3. Create a table that matches the data in the data file **B**:

```
CREATE TABLE zip_codes (

zip_code INT(5) UNSIGNED ZEROFILL
→ NOT NULL,

zip_code_type VARCHAR(10),

city VARCHAR(60) NOT NULL,

state VARCHAR(14) NOT NULL,

location_type VARCHAR(10),

latitude DECIMAL(4,2),

longitude DECIMAL(5,2),

location VARCHAR(30),

decommisioned VARCHAR(30),

taxreturnsfiled INT,

population INT,

wages INT,

PRIMARY KEY (zip_code)

);
```

continues on next page

Some sources may already provide the necessary SQL commands to create the table and even insert the data, in which case you could skip Steps 3 and 4. If not, you should create a table whose structure matches the data to be inserted **C**.

The zip code column, which is the primary key, should be an unsigned, zero-filled integer five digits in length. The latitude and longitude columns should be some type of fixed-point number. My data set contains several other columns, most of which I won't actually need after the data has been imported but must be initially created in order for the import to work.

(As an aside, the word *decommissioned* is misspelled that way in the data file, hence the matching misspelling in the SQL command.)

4. Import the data **D**:

```
LOAD DATA INFILE '/tmp/zips.csv'
INTO TABLE zip_codes
FIELDS TERMINATED BY ','
ENCLOSED BY '"'
LINES TERMINATED BY '\n';
```

It may take you a while to get this step working properly (you may also have more luck using phpMyAdmin for this). The **LOAD DATA INFILE** query takes the contents of a text file and inserts them into the given table. For this step to work, the number of columns in the table must match the number of values on each row in the text file. You might also need to change the **FIELDS TERMINATED BY**, **ENCLOSED BY**, and **LINES TERMINATED BY** values to match the text file you have. See the MySQL manual for more information on this syntax.

C Part of the data file I'm working with.

D Importing the data into the table.

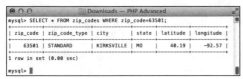

```
mysql> ALTER TABLE zip_codes DROP COLUMN location_type, DROP COLUMN location,
DROP COLUMN decommisioned, DROP COLUMN taxreturnsfiled, DROP COLUMN population
, DROP COLUMN wages;
Query OK, 42522 rows affected (0.43 sec)
Records: 42522  Duplicates: 0  Warnings: 0

mysql> UPDATE zip_codes SET latitude=NULL, longitude=NULL WHERE latitude='';
Query OK, 648 rows affected (0.06 sec)
Rows matched: 648  Changed: 648  Warnings: 0

mysql>
```

E Cleaning up the table to make the data more usable.

```
mysql> SELECT * FROM zip_codes WHERE zip_code=63501;
+----------+---------------+------------+-------+----------+-----------+
| zip_code | zip_code_type | city       | state | latitude | longitude |
+----------+---------------+------------+-------+----------+-----------+
|    63501 | STANDARD      | KIRKSVILLE | MO    |    40.19 |    -92.57 |
+----------+---------------+------------+-------+----------+-----------+
1 row in set (0.00 sec)

mysql>
```

F The information for a single zip code.

```
| Warning | 1366 | Incorrect integer value: '' for column 'population' at row 84
| Warning | 1366 | Incorrect integer value: '' for column 'wages' at row 84
| Warning | 1366 | Incorrect integer value: '' for column 'taxreturnsfiled' at row 85
| Warning | 1366 | Incorrect integer value: '' for column 'population' at row 85
| Warning | 1366 | Incorrect integer value: '' for column 'wages' at row 85
| Warning | 1366 | Incorrect integer value: '' for column 'taxreturnsfiled' at row 86
64 rows in set (0.00 sec)

mysql>
```

G Some of the warnings from the recent query (the data import).

The name of the text file should match the absolute path to the file on your computer.

Using the downloaded data that includes a header line **C**, I also had to remove that line from the CSV file prior to this point.

5. Drop any columns you will not need:

   ALTER TABLE zip_codes DROP COLUMN
   →**location_type, DROP COLUMN**
   →**location, DROP COLUMN**
   →**decommisioned, DROP COLUMN**
   →**taxreturnsfiled, DROP COLUMN**
   →**population, DROP COLUMN wages;**

   Some data sources may contain information you don't need, which you can then get rid of by running an **ALTER** query.

6. Add indexes and update the data, if necessary **E**.

   In terms of updating the data, you could, for example, turn empty latitude and longitude values into formal **NULL** values. That query is

   UPDATE zip_codes SET
   →**latitude=NULL, longitude=NULL**
   →**WHERE latitude='';**

7. Check the information for your (or any) zip code **F**:

   SELECT * FROM zip_codes

   WHERE zip_code=63501;

TIP Run the command SHOW WARNINGS within the mysql client to see reported warnings **G**.

Creating the stores table

After creating the zip code table, it's time to create the other required table. For this example, I'll want to be able to calculate the distance between a given zip code (like a user's home address) and a list of stores. Therefore, a **stores** table is necessary.

This table can contain whatever information you want. Likely, it would be something like **Table 3.3**.

Since the city and state are tied to the zip code, and that information is already in the **zip_codes** table, those columns can be removed. I'll also make the Address 2 column allow for a **NULL** option, as not all stores will use this field.

To create the stores table:

1. Access the **zips** database using the **mysql** client or another interface.

2. Create the **stores** table ⊞:

   ```
   CREATE TABLE stores (
   store_id SMALLINT(5) UNSIGNED NOT
   → NULL AUTO_INCREMENT,
   name VARCHAR(60) NOT NULL,
   address1 VARCHAR(100) NOT NULL,
   address2 VARCHAR(100) default NULL,
   zip_code INT(5) UNSIGNED ZEROFILL
   → NOT NULL,
   phone VARCHAR(15) NOT NULL,
   PRIMARY KEY (store_id),
   KEY (zip_code)
   );
   ```

TABLE 3.3 A Store's Information

Column	Example
Name	Ray's Shop
Address 1	49 Main Street
Address 2	Suite 230
City	Arlington
State	Virginia
Zip Code	22201
Phone	(123) 456-7890

```
mysql> CREATE TABLE stores (
    -> store_id SMALLINT(5) UNSIGNED NOT NULL AUTO_INCREMENT,
    -> name VARCHAR(60) NOT NULL,
    -> address1 VARCHAR(100) NOT NULL,
    -> address2 VARCHAR(100) default NULL,
    -> zip_code INT(5) UNSIGNED ZEROFILL NOT NULL,
    -> phone VARCHAR(15) NOT NULL,
    -> PRIMARY KEY (store_id),
    -> KEY (zip_code)
    -> );
Query OK, 0 rows affected (0.04 sec)

mysql>
```

⊞ Creating the second, and final, table.

The table models the data suggested in Table 3.3, except for the omission of the city and state (which are present in the **zip_codes** table). The **zip_code** column here should be defined exactly like that in the **zip_codes** table because the two fields will be used in a join (see the sidebar "Optimizing Joins").

1 Putting some sample records into the **stores** table.

3. Populate the **stores** table **1**:

   ```
   INSERT INTO stores (name,
   → address1, address2, zip_code,
   → phone) VALUES
   ('Ray''s Shop', '49 Main Street',
   → NULL, '63939', '(123) 456-7890'),
   ('Little Lulu''s', '12904 Rockville
   → Pike', '#310', '10580', '(123)
   → 654- 7890');
   ```

   You can enter whatever records you'd like. Or you can download the full SQL command from the book's corresponding Web site (**www.LarryUllman.com**).

J By performing a join on the two tables, you can fetch a store's complete address.

4. Select the complete address for a couple of stores **J**:

   ```
   SELECT stores.*, zip_codes.city,
   → zip_codes.state FROM stores LEFT
   → JOIN zip_codes USING (zip_code)
   → LIMIT 2\G
   ```

   To get a store's complete address, including the city and state, a join must be made across the two tables, using the **zip_code** column, which is common to both. If you're not familiar with it, using the **\G** closing character in the **mysql** client just returns the results in vertical groupings, not horizontal rows.

Performing distance calculations

Now that two tables exist and are populated with data, it's time to perform the distance calculations. In PHP, the formula for doing so is

$distance = sin(deg2rad($a_latitude))

* sin(deg2rad($b_latitude))

+ cos(deg2rad($a_latitude))

* cos(deg2rad($b_latitude))

* cos(deg2rad($a_longitude -
→ $b_longitude));

$distance = (rad2deg(acos($distance)))
→ * 69.09;

I could explain that formula in detail, except I don't really understand it (or, in truth, haven't tried to). All I know is that this works, and sometimes that's enough.

In MySQL, that same formula (requiring a couple of different functions) is

SELECT (DEGREES(ACOS(SIN(RADIANS(lat_a))

* SIN(RADIANS(lat_b))

+ COS(RADIANS(lat_a))

* COS(RADIANS(lat_b))

* COS(RADIANS(long_a - long_b))))) *
→ 69.09

For example, taking the latitude and longitude for two random zip codes **K**, this calculation returns a value of approximately 1,626 miles **L**.

SELECT (DEGREES(ACOS
→ (SIN(RADIANS(31.84))

* SIN(RADIANS(34.31))

+ COS(RADIANS(31.84))

* COS(RADIANS(34.31))

* COS(RADIANS(-106.43 - -78.40))))) *
→ 69.09 AS distance;

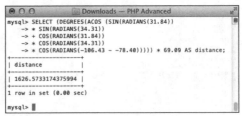

K To check the distance between two points, I select the information for two random zip codes.

L The result of the distance calculation, using the latitudes and longitudes from **K**.

Optimizing Joins

The MySQL database application does a lot of work to improve efficiency, often unbeknownst to the common user. This may involve changing the definition of a column or secretly altering how a query is run. But sometimes MySQL needs a little help.

Joins are expensive queries (in terms of database resources) because they require conditional matches to be made across two or more tables. In this example, a join will occur between the **zip_codes** and **stores** tables, using the **zip_code** column from both. To encourage MySQL to perform these joins faster, you should do two things.

First, an index should exist on both columns. Second, both columns should be defined in exactly the same way. If one column is a **TINYINT** and the other is an **INT**, MySQL will not use any indexes (which is bad).

To finally put all of this good knowledge into action, I'll create a PHP script that returns the three closest stores to a given zip code.

To calculate distances in MySQL:

1. Begin a new PHP script in your text editor or IDE, to be named **distance.php**, starting with the HTML (**Script 3.3**):

   ```
   <!doctype html>
   <html lang="en">
   <head>
     <meta charset="utf-8">
     <title>Distance Calculator</title>
     <link rel="stylesheet" href="style.css">
   </head>
   <body>
   <?php # Script 3.3 - distance.php
   ```

continues on page 105

Script 3.3 This PHP script will return the three closest stores, using a zip code calculation, to a given zip code.

```
1    <!doctype html>
2    <html lang="en">
3    <head>
4      <meta charset="utf-8">
5      <title>Distance Calculator</title>
6      <link rel="stylesheet" href="style.css">
7    </head>
8    <body>
9    <?php # Script 3.3 - distance.php
10
11   /*  This page uses the zips database to
12    *  calculate the distance between a given
13    *  point and some stores.
14    *  The three closest stores are returned.
15    */
16
17   $zip = 64154; //User's zip code.
18
```

script continues on next page

```
19   // Print a caption:
20   echo "<h1>Nearest stores to $zip:</h1>";
21
22   // Connect to the database:
23   $dbc = mysqli_connect('localhost', 'username', 'password', 'zips');
24
25   // Get the origination latitude and longitude:
26   $q = "SELECT latitude, longitude FROM zip_codes WHERE zip_code='$zip' AND latitude IS NOT NULL";
27   $r = mysqli_query($dbc, $q);
28
29   // Retrieve the results:
30   if (mysqli_num_rows($r) == 1) {
31
32      list($lat, $long) = mysqli_fetch_array($r, MYSQLI_NUM);
33
34      // Big, main, complex, wordy query:
35      $q = "SELECT name, CONCAT_WS('<br>', address1, address2), city, state, stores.zip_code, phone,
          → ROUND(DEGREES(ACOS(SIN(RADIANS($lat))
36  * SIN(RADIANS(latitude))
37  + COS(RADIANS($lat))
38  * COS(RADIANS(latitude))
39  * COS(RADIANS($long - longitude)))) * 69.09) AS distance FROM stores LEFT JOIN zip_codes USING
    → (zip_code) ORDER BY distance ASC LIMIT 3";
40      $r = mysqli_query($dbc, $q);
41
42      if (mysqli_num_rows($r) > 0) {
43
44         // Display the stores:
45         while ($row = mysqli_fetch_array($r, MYSQLI_NUM)) {
46            echo "<h2>$row[0]</h2>
47  <p>$row[1]<br />" . ucfirst(strtolower($row[2])) . ", $row[3] $row[4]<br />
48  $row[5] <br />
49  (approximately $row[6] miles)</p>\n";
50
51         } // End of WHILE loop.
52
53      } else { // No stores returned.
54
55         echo '<p class="error">No stores matched the search.</p>';
56
57      }
58
59   } else { // Invalid zip code.
60
61      echo '<p class="error">An invalid zip code was entered.</p>';
62
63   }
64
65   // Close the connection:
66   mysqli_close($dbc);
67
68   ?>
69   </body>
70   </html>
```

2. Identify the point of origin:

```
$zip = 64154;

echo "<h1>Nearest stores to
→ $zip:</h1>";
```

This value could also be taken from a form (after validating it, of course).

3. Connect to the database:

```
$dbc = mysqli_connect('localhost',
→ 'username', 'password', 'zips');
```

4. Define and execute the first query:

```
$q = "SELECT latitude, longitude
→ FROM zip_codes WHERE zip_code=
→ '$zip' AND latitude IS NOT NULL";

$r = mysqli_query($dbc, $q);
```

This first query—the script contains two—both validates the zip code (that it's an actual U.S. zip code) and retrieves that zip code's latitude and longitude. That information will be necessary for calculating distances between the given zip code and each store. Because the data I used lacks the latitude and longitude for some zip codes, I've added an **AND latitude IS NOT NULL** condition to the **WHERE** clause. This may not be necessary for all data sets.

M The result of the main, rather unwieldy, query.

5. Retrieve the results of the query:

```
if (mysqli_num_rows($r) == 1) {
  list($lat, $long) = mysqli_
  → fetch_array($r, MYSQLI_NUM);
```

If one row was returned, the zip code is valid and the returned data is assigned to these two variables.

6. Perform the main query:

```
$q = "SELECT name, CONCAT_WS
→ ('<br>', address1, address2),
→ city, state, stores.zip_code,
→ phone, ROUND(DEGREES(ACOS(SIN
→ (RADIANS($lat))
* SIN(RADIANS(latitude))
+ COS(RADIANS($lat))
* COS(RADIANS(latitude))
* COS(RADIANS($long - longitude))))
→ * 69.09) AS distance FROM stores
→ LEFT JOIN zip_codes USING
→ (zip_code) ORDER BY distance
→ ASC LIMIT 3";

$r = mysqli_query($dbc, $q);
```

Getting to this main query is really the point of the whole script. This query returns a store's name, full address, phone number, and distance from the given zip code **M**. The two addresses lines are concatenated using **CONCAT_WS()**, which will place a **
** between the lines if **address2** has a value, but return just **address1** otherwise. The store's city and state values come from the **zip_codes** table, and the **zip_code** could come from either. The phone number is also returned.

continues on next page

The big, complex calculation is also selected. For the "A" latitude and longitude, the values for the original zip code are used (already retrieved by the earlier query). For the "B" latitude and longitude, values from this query will be used. Only three stores are going to be returned, and they are ordered by the distance value, from smallest to largest. Whew!

7. Print the results:

```
if (mysqli_num_rows($r) > 0) {

  while ($row = mysqli_fetch_
  →array($r, MYSQLI_NUM)) {

    echo "<h2>$row[0]</h2>

<p>$row[1]<br />" . ucfirst
→(strtolower($row[2])) . ",
→$row[3] $row[4]<br />

$row[5] <br />

(approximately $row[6] miles)
→</p>\n";

  } // End of WHILE loop.

} else {

  echo '<p class="error">No stores
  →matched the search.</p>';

}
```

The results are going to be printed with just a modicum of formatting. If no store was returned for some reason (which shouldn't happen), that message is displayed.

8. Complete the conditional begun in Step 5:

```
} else {

  echo '<p class="error">An
  →invalid zip code was entered.
  →</p>';

}
```

This message applies if an invalid zip code is provided .

Nearest stores to 77777:

An invalid zip code was entered.

 The result should an invalid zip code (like 77777 here) be used.

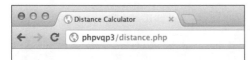

Nearest stores to 64154:

Kiosk

St. Charles Towncenter
3890 Crain Highway
Wellsville, MO 63384
(123) 888-4444
(approximately 162 miles)

Ray's Shop

49 Main Street
Fairdealing, MO 63939
(123) 456-7890
(approximately 272 miles)

O The closest stores to the 64154 zip code.

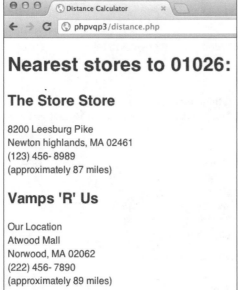

Nearest stores to 01026:

The Store Store

8200 Leesburg Pike
Newton highlands, MA 02461
(123) 456- 8989
(approximately 87 miles)

Vamps 'R' Us

Our Location
Atwood Mall
Norwood, MA 02062
(222) 456- 7890
(approximately 89 miles)

P The closest stores to the 01026 zip code.

9. Complete the page:

   ```
   mysqli_close($dbc);
   ?>
   </body>
   </html>
   ```

10. Save the file as **distance.php**, place it in your Web directory, and test in your Web browser **O**.

11. Change the zip code and test again **P**.

   To use a zip code that begins with a 0, put it in quotes:

   ```
   $zip = '01026';
   ```

   If you don't, PHP will think you're using another number format and translate it.

TIP You could easily limit the stores returned to a certain area by adding WHERE distance<=X to the main query.

Creating Stored Functions

Stored functions are half of a larger concept called *stored routines* (the other half are *stored procedures*). Present in many database applications but new to MySQL as of version 5, stored routines allow you to save a set sequence of code in the MySQL server, and then call that sequence as needed. Think of it like being able to write your own PHP functions but in SQL.

The topic of stored routines can be expansive, but I want to give you a little taste here. For more information, see the MySQL manual or my *MySQL: Visual QuickStart Guide* (Peachpit Press, 2006), where I dedicate many more pages to the subject.

Declaring Local Variables

Stored routines are like small programs, and they can even have their own variables. To do so, use the **DECLARE** statement:

```
DECLARE var_name var_type
```

The naming rules are pretty much the same as for everything else, but you absolutely want to make sure that your variables have unique identifiers. The types correspond to the MySQL data types:

```
DECLARE var1 INT
```

```
DECLARE var2 DECIMAL(5,2)
```

```
DECLARE var3 VARCHAR(20)
```

The only restrictions to declaring variables are as follows:

- The declarations must take place within a **BEGIN...END** code block.
- The declarations must take place before any other statements (i.e., declarations must be immediately after the **BEGIN**).

Once you've declared a variable, you can assign it a value using **SET**:

```
SET name = value
```

Note as well that unlike variables in PHP, these stored routine variables do not begin with a dollar sign.

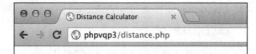

Nearest stores to 01026:

The Store Store

8200 Leesburg Pike
Newton highlands, MA 02461
(123) 456- 8989
(approximately 87 miles)

Vamps 'R' Us

Our Location
Atwood Mall
Norwood, MA 02062
(222) 456- 7890
(approximately 89 miles)

Smart Shop

9 Commercial Way
Cambridge, MA 02141
(123) 555-7890
(approximately 92 miles)

A You have to be careful when attempting to create stored routines within the **mysql** client.

The basic syntax for creating stored functions is

CREATE FUNCTION *name* **(***arguments***)**
→ **RETURNS** *type code*

For the routine's name, you should not use an existing keyword, SQL term, or function name. As with most things you name in MySQL, you should stick to alphanumeric characters and the underscore.

The arguments section is used to pass values to the routine. The listed arguments are named and given types that correspond to the available data types in MySQL:

CREATE FUNCTION myfunc (myvar1 INT,
→ **myvar2 CHAR) RETURNS** *type code*

The *code* section of this syntax is the most important. Because your routines will normally contain multiple lines, you'll want to create a block by using **BEGIN** and **END**:

CREATE FUNCTION *name* **(***arguments***)**
→ **RETURNS** *type*
BEGIN

   statement1;

   statement2;

END

Within the code block, each statement ends with a semicolon. This can cause a problem: when you go to add this stored function using the **mysql** client or php-MyAdmin, the interface will think that the semicolon indicates the end of a command to be executed immediately **A**. To prevent this, you can change the *delimiter*, which is the character used to mark the end of a query (the semicolon by default):

DELIMITER $$

You can change the delimiter to anything, as long as it's not going to appear in the subsequent commands. I normally use two dollar signs together.

Once you're done defining the function, you can change the delimiter back to the semicolon you're used to:

```
DELIMITER ;
```

Stored function definitions must contain a **RETURNS** clause, indicating the type of value returned by the function. Functions return scalar (single) values, like a number or a string. To do so, use

```
RETURN data
```

within the function's code body. The type of the data returned must match the type indicated in the function's initial definition line. You cannot return a list of values from a stored function, but because stored functions return scalar values, they can be used in queries like any of the existing MySQL functions.

All of this information, along with the blip in the accompanying sidebar "Declaring Local Variables," is the 5-minute guide to stored functions. In the next sequence of steps, I'll show you how to turn the complicated distance calculation formula (see Script 3.3) into a callable stored function.

To create a stored function:

1. Access your MySQL database using the `mysql` client.

   You can also use phpMyAdmin or any other interface you prefer.

2. Select the database where you want to define the function:

   ```
   USE zips;
   ```

3. Change the delimiter:

   ```
   DELIMITER $$
   ```

   Again, this is necessary so that the semicolons within the function definition don't trigger immediate execution of the code written to that point.

4. Start defining the function:

   ```
   CREATE FUNCTION return_distance
   → (lat_a DOUBLE, long_a DOUBLE,
   → lat_b DOUBLE, long_b DOUBLE)
   → RETURNS DOUBLE
   ```

   This code will wrap the complicated calculation within a stored function. The function is called *return_distance*. The function takes four arguments, all of type **DOUBLE**. It will return a **DOUBLE** value as well.

5. Create a local variable to store the calculated distance:

   ```
   BEGIN

   DECLARE distance DOUBLE;
   ```

   The first step in the function is to create a variable of type **DOUBLE**. Doing so will simplify the calculation to a degree (pardon the pun).

6. Assign an initial value to the **distance** variable:

   ```
   SET distance = SIN(RADIANS(lat_a))
   → * SIN(RADIANS(lat_b))

   + COS(RADIANS(lat_a))

   * COS(RADIANS(lat_b))

   * COS(RADIANS(long_a - long_b));
   ```

   The variable is assigned the value of most of the calculation.

B The stored function has been created in the database.

C The stored function is used to simplify the SQL query.

7. Return the final calculation:

RETURN((DEGREES(ACOS(distance))) * → 69.09);

The variable is then run through a couple more functions and some arithmetic, and then returned.

8. Complete the function definition **B**:

END $$

DELIMITER ;

9. Test the function by running the following query in the **mysql** client or phpMyAdmin **C**:

SELECT return_distance(31.84, → -106.43, 34.31, -78.40);

This is the same test query run earlier in the chapter, except now it calls the stored function.

10. If you want, modify **distance.php** (Script 3.3) to call the stored procedure.

To do so, just change the main query to

SELECT name, CONCAT_WS('<br>', → address1, address2), city, → state, stores.zip_code, phone, → ROUND(return_distance($lat, → $long, latitude, longitude)) → AS distance FROM stores LEFT → JOIN zip_codes USING (zip_code) → ORDER BY distance ASC LIMIT 3

TIP All stored routines are associated with a specific database. This also means that you cannot have a stored routine select a database.

TIP Because stored routines are linked with databases, if you drop the database, you'll also drop any associated stored routine.

Displaying Results Horizontally

Another of the common questions I see involves displaying query results horizontally. It's quite easy to fetch a query's results and display them vertically Ⓐ, but creating a horizontal output Ⓑ does stymie some programmers. To achieve a horizontal layout, you have to create an HTML table. The trick, truly, is knowing when to create new rows in that table.

To achieve this effect using PHP, you need a counter that tracks how many records have been placed on a row (i.e., how many columns have been created). When zero records have been placed, the new row should be started. When the maximum number of records has been placed, the old row should be concluded. That's the premise, which I'll develop in this next script. For the data, I'll use the `zip_codes` table in the `zips` database (but you could use anything).

To display results horizontally:

1. Begin a new PHP script in your text editor or IDE, to be named **display.php**, starting with the HTML (**Script 3.4**):

```
<!doctype html>
<html lang="en">
<head>
  <meta charset="utf-8">
  <title>Cities and Zip Codes
  → </title>
  <link rel="stylesheet"
  → href="style.css">
</head>
<body>
<?php # Script 3.4 - display.php
```

continues on page 115

Cities and Zip Codes found in AK
ADAK, 99546
AKIACHAK, 99551
AKIAK, 99552
AKUTAN, 99553
ALAKANUK, 99554
ALEKNAGIK, 99555
ALLAKAKET, 99720
AMBLER, 99786
ANAKTUVUK PASS, 99721
ANCHOR POINT, 99556
ANCHORAGE, 99599
ANCHORAGE, 99522

Ⓐ A traditional vertical display of some records.

Cities and Zip Codes found in AK

ADAK, 99546	AKIACHAK, 99551	AKIAK, 99552	AKUTAN, 99553	ALAKANUK, 99554
ALEKNAGIK, 99555	ALLAKAKET, 99720	AMBLER, 99786	ANAKTUVUK PASS, 99721	ANCHOR POINT, 99556
ANCHORAGE, 99599	ANCHORAGE, 99522	ANCHORAGE, 99530	ANCHORAGE, 99529	ANCHORAGE, 99524

Ⓑ The same data as in Ⓐ, laid out in table form.

Script 3.4 All of the cities and zip codes for a given state are retrieved by this PHP script. Instead of appearing as a vertical list, they'll be displayed in a table with five cells per row.

```
1    <!doctype html>
2    <html lang="en">
3    <head>
4       <meta charset="utf-8">
5       <title>Cities and Zip Codes</title>
6       <link rel="stylesheet" href="style.css">
7    </head>
8    <body>
9    <?php # Script 3.4 - display.php
10
11   /*  This page retrieves and displays all of the
12    *  cities and zip codes for a particular state.
13    *  The results will be shown in a table.
14    */
15
16   // Abbreviation of state to show:
17   $state = 'AK';
18
19   // Items to display per row:
20   $items = 5;
21
22   // Print a caption:
23   echo "<h1>Cities and Zip Codes found in $state</h1>";
24
25   // Connect to the database:
26   $dbc = mysqli_connect ('localhost', 'username', 'password', 'zips');
27
28   // Get the cities and zip codes, ordered by city:
29   $q = "SELECT city, zip_code FROM zip_codes WHERE state='$state' ORDER BY city";
30   $r = mysqli_query($dbc, $q);
31
32   // Retrieve the results:
33   if (mysqli_num_rows($r) > 0) {
34
35      // Start a table:
36      echo '<table border="2" width="90%" cellspacing="3" cellpadding="3" align="center">';
37
38      // Need a counter:
39      $i = 0;
40
41      // Retrieve each record:
42      while (list($city, $zip_code) = mysqli_fetch_array($r, MYSQLI_NUM)) {
43
44         // Do we need to start a new row?
45         if ($i == 0) {
46            echo '<tr>';
47         }
48
```

script continues on next page

```
49        // Print the record:
50        echo "<td align=\"center\">$city, $zip_code</td>";
51
52        // Increment the counter:
53        $i++;
54
55        // Do we need to end the row?
56        if ($i == $items) {
57            echo '</tr>';
58            $i = 0; // Reset counter.
59        }
60
61    } // End of while loop.
62
63    if ($i > 0) { // Last row was incomplete.
64
65        // Print the necessary number of cells:
66        for (;$i < $items; $i++) {
67            echo "<td> </td>\n";
68        }
69
70        // Complete the row.
71        echo '</tr>';
72
73    } // End of ($i > 0) IF.
74
75    // Close the table:
76    echo '</table>';
77
78 } else { // Bad state abbreviation.
79
80    echo '<p class="error">An invalid state abbreviation was used.</p>';
81
82 } // End of main IF.
83
84 // Close the database connection:
85 mysqli_close($dbc);
86
87 ?>
88 </body>
89 </html>
```

2. Establish the necessary variables and print a caption:

```
$state = 'AK';
$items = 5;
echo "<h1>Cities and Zip Codes
→ found in $state</h1>";
```

The number of items to show per row is an important variable here. Just changing this one value will allow the script to output the results in fewer or more columns.

3. Connect to and query the database:

```
$dbc = mysqli_connect
→ ('localhost', 'username',
→ 'password', 'zips');
$q = "SELECT city, zip_code FROM
→ zip_codes WHERE state='$state'
→ ORDER BY city";
$r = mysqli_query($dbc, $q);
if (mysqli_num_rows($r) > 0) {
```

The query will return every city and zip code in the state in alphabetical order by city.

4. Begin a table and initialize a counter:

```
echo '<table border="2"
→ width="90%" cellspacing="3"
→ cellpadding="3" align="center">';
$i = 0;
```

The $i counter will track how many items have already been placed on a row.

5. Retrieve each record:

```
while (list($city, $zip_code) =
→ mysqli_fetch_array($r,
→ MYSQLI_NUM)) {
```

6. Start a new row, if necessary:

```
if ($i == 0) {
  echo '<tr>';
}
```

Every time, within this **while** loop, the first item on a row is to be placed, a new row should be created by printing the **<tr>**. This applies the first time the loop is entered (because $i is initially 0) and after $i is reset (upon completing a row).

7. Print the record and increment the counter:

```
echo "<td align=\"center\">$city,
→ $zip_code</td>";
$i++;
```

8. Complete the row, if necessary:

```
if ($i == $items) {
  echo '</tr>';
  $i = 0;
}
```

Once the counter equals the number of items to be placed on a row, it's time to end that row by printing **</tr>**. Then the counter needs to be reset so that the next time the loop is entered, a new row will be started.

9. Complete the **while** loop:

```
} // End of while loop.
```

continues on next page

10. Complete the last row, if necessary:

```
if ($i > 0) {
    for (;$i < $items; $i++) {
        echo "<td> </td>\n";
    }
    echo '</tr>';
}
```

This is a step that's easy to miss. Unless the number of items displayed is easily divisible by the number to be displayed per row (i.e., there's no remainder of that division), the last row will be incomplete **C**.

If **$i** has a value other than 0, some extra cells must be added (if it has a value of 0, then the last row was completed). A **for** loop can accomplish this task easily, starting with the current value of **$i** and stopping when **$i** equals **$items**. A little-known trick with the **for** loop is that each of the three parts is optional. Since no initial expression must be evaluated (like setting **$i** to some value), the loop begins with **(;**.

```
99654</td><td align="center">WASILLA, 99687</td><td align="center">WHITE
MOUNTAIN, 99784</td></tr><tr><td align="center">WHITTIER, 99693</td><td
align="center">WILLOW, 99688</td><td align="center">WRANGELL, 99929</td><td
align="center">YAKUTAT, 99689</td><td> </td>
</tr></table></body>
```

C The last row had only four items in it, so one blank table cell had to be created.

Cities and Zip Codes found in HI

AIEA, 96701	ANAHOLA, 96703	CAMP H M SMITH, 96861	CAPTAIN COOK, 96704
ELEELE, 96705	EWA BEACH, 96706	FORT SHAFTER, 96858	HAIKU, 96708
HAKALAU, 96710	HALEIWA, 96712	HANA, 96713	HANALEI, 96714

D With two quick changes, the script now displays all the cities for another state (here, Hawaii), four per row.

11. Close the table and complete the conditional started in Step 3:

```
echo '</table>';
} else {
    echo '<p class="error">An
    → invalid state abbreviation
    → was used.</p>';
} // End of main IF.
```

12. Complete the page:

```
mysqli_close($dbc);
?>
</body>
</html>
```

13. Save the file as **display.php**, place it in your Web directory, and test in your Web browser.

14. Change the value of **$items**, change the value of **$state**, and retest in your Web browser **D**.

Review and Pursue

If you have any problems with these sections, either in answering the questions or pursuing your own endeavors, turn to the book's supporting forum (**www.Larry Ullman.com/forums/**).

Review

- What are the benefits to storing session data in a database instead of the file system? (See page 82.)

- What PHP function is invoked to change how sessions are handled? (See page 84.)

- What do you have to do differently in your other session-related PHP scripts when storing session data in the database? (See pages 91 and 94.)

- How do you import CSV data into a database table? (See page 98.)

- What are stored functions? How do you create them? (See page 108.)

- How do you change the delimiter used by the **mysql** client? Why is that sometimes necessary? (See page 109.)

Pursue

- Update **db_sessions.inc.php** so that the functions return an appropriate Boolean indicating the success of each operation.

- Try using database-stored sessions on one of your own projects.

- If you have a familiarity with OOP already, check out the **SessionHandler** class in the PHP manual.

- If you need the most accurate, up-to-date zip code information, look into purchasing a commercial data set.

- Learn more about using the **LOAD DATA INFILE SQL** command.

- Create a form that submits a user-provided zip code to the **distance.php** script (instead of using a hard-coded value).

- Expand the **distance.php** script (after you've created a corresponding form) to let the user select a maximum range to search, too.

- Learn more about stored functions and procedures in MySQL.

4

Basic
Object-Oriented
Programming

Although PHP is still not as strong in its OOP feature set as other languages, object-oriented programming in PHP has a lot going for it. And while it is possible to have a good career without learning and using OOP, you *should* familiarize yourself with the concept. At the very least, being able to use both OOP and procedural programming allows you to better choose the right approach for each individual project.

In this chapter, and the next (Chapter 5, "Advanced OOP"), I will explain not only the syntax of OOP in PHP 5 and later, but the key underlying OOP theories as well. In this chapter, I will use somewhat mundane examples, but in subsequent chapters, practical, real-world code will be used. Through multiple examples and plenty of explanation, I hope in this book to fully demonstrate not just *how* you do object-oriented programming in PHP but also *when* and *why*.

In This Chapter

OOP Theory

The first thing that you must understand about OOP is that it presents not just new syntax but a new way of thinking about a problem. By far the most common mistake beginning OOP programmers make is to inappropriately apply OOP theory. PHP will tell you when you make a syntactical mistake, but you'll need to learn how to avoid theoretical mistakes as well. To explain...

All programming comes down to *taking actions with data*: a user enters data in an HTML form; the PHP code validates it, emails it, and stores it in a database; and so forth. These are simply verbs (actions) and nouns (data). With procedural programming, the focus is on the verbs: do this, then this, then this. In OOP, the focus is on the nouns: with what types of things will the application work? In both approaches, you need to identify both the nouns and the verbs required; the difference is in the focus of the application's design.

The two most important terms for OOP are *class* and *object*. A class is a generalized definition of a thing. Think of classes as blueprints. An object is a specific implementation of that thing. Think of objects as the house built using the blueprint as a guide. To program using OOP, you design your classes and then implement them as objects in your programs when needed.

One of the tenets of OOP is *modularity*: breaking applications into specific subparts. Web sites do many, many things: interact with databases, handle forms, send emails, generate HTML, etc. Each of these things can be a module, which is to say a class. By separating unrelated (albeit interacting) elements, you can develop code independently, make maintenance and updates less messy, and simplify debugging.

Related to modularity is *abstraction*: classes should be defined broadly. This is a common and understandable beginner's mistake. As an example, instead of designing a class for interacting with a MySQL database, you should make one that interacts with a nonspecific database. From there, using *inheritance* and *overriding*, you would define a more particular class for MySQL. This class would look and act like the general database class, but some of its functionality would be customized.

Another principle of OOP is *encapsulation*: separating out and hiding how something is accomplished. A properly designed class can do everything you need it to do without your ever knowing how it's being done. Coupled with encapsulation is *access control* or *visibility*, which dictates how available components of the class are.

Those are the main concepts behind OOP. You'll see how they play out in the many OOP examples in this book. But before getting into the code, I'll talk about OOP's dark side.

First of all, know that *OOP is not a better way to program*, just a *different* way. In some cases, it *may be* better and in some cases worse.

As for the technical negatives of OOP, use of objects can be less efficient than a procedural approach. The performance difference between using an object or not may be imperceptible in some cases, but you should be aware of this potential side effect.

A second issue that arises is what I have already pointed out: misuse and overuse of objects. Whereas bad procedural programming can be a hurdle to later fix, bad OOP can be a nightmare. However, the information taught over the next several chapters should prevent that from being the case for you.

Defining a Class

OOP programming begins with *classes*, a class being an abstract definition of a thing: what information must be stored and what functionality must be possible with that information? A **User** class would be able to store information such as the user's name, ID, email address, and so forth. The functionality of a **User** could be login, logout, change password, and more.

Syntactically, a class definition begins with the word **class**, followed by the name of the class. The class name cannot be a reserved word and is often written in uppercase, as a convention. After the class name, the class definition is placed within curly braces:

```
class ClassName {
}
```

Classes contain variables and functions, which are referred to as *attributes* (or *properties*) and *methods*, respectively (you'll see other terms, too). Collectively, a class's attributes and methods are called its *members*.

Functions are easy to add to classes:

```
class ClassName {
    function functionName() {
        // Function code.
    }
}
```

The methods you define within a class are defined just like functions outside of a class. They can take arguments, have default values, return values, and so on.

Attributes within classes are a little different than variables outside of classes. First, all attributes must be prefixed with a keyword indicating the variable's *visibility*. The options are **public**, **private**, and **protected**. Unfortunately, these values won't mean anything to you until you understand *inheritance* (in Chapter 5), so until then, just use **public**:

```
class ClassName {
    public $var1, $var2;
    function functionName() {
        // Function code.
    }
}
```

As shown here, a class's attributes are listed before any method definitions.

The second distinction between attributes and normal variables is that if an attribute is initialized with a set value, that value must be a literal value and not the result of an expression:

```
class GoodClass {
    public $var1 = 123;
    public $var2 = 'string';
    public $var3 = array(1, 2, 3);
}
class BadClass {
    // These won't work!
    public $today = get_date();
    public $square = $num * $num;
}
```

Note that you don't have to initialize the attributes with a value. And, aside from declaring variables, all of a class's other code goes within its methods. You cannot execute statements outside of a class method:

```
class BadClass {
    public $num = 2;
    public $square;
    $square = $num * $num; // No!
}
```

With all of this in mind, let's create an easy, almost useless class just to make sure it's all working fine and dandy. Naturally, I'll use a *Hello, world!* example (it's either that or *foo* and *bar*). To make it a little more interesting, this class will be able to say *Hello, world!* in different languages.

To define a class:

1. Create a new PHP document in your text editor or IDE, to be named **HelloWorld.php** (Script 4.1):

   ```
   <?php # Script 4.1 - HelloWorld.php
   ```

2. Begin defining the class:

   ```
   class HelloWorld {
   ```

   Using the syntax outlined earlier, start with the keyword **class**, followed by the name of the class, followed by the opening curly brace (which could go on the next line, if you prefer).

   For the class name, I use the "upper-case camel" capitalization: initial letters are capitalized, as are the first letters of new words. This is a pseudo-standardized convention in many OOP languages.

Script 4.1 This simple class will allow you to say *Hello, world!* through the magic of objects! (Okay, so it's completely unnecessary, but it's a fine introductory demonstration.)

```
1   <?php # Script 4.1 - HelloWorld.php
2   /* This page defines the HelloWorld
    → class.
3   *  The class says "Hello, world!" in
    → different languages.
4   */
5   class HelloWorld {
6
7       // This method prints a greeting.
8       // It takes one argument: the
        → language to use.
9       // Default language is English.
10      function sayHello($language =
        → 'English') {
11
12          // Put the greeting within P tags:
13          echo '<p>';
14
15          // Print a message specific to a
            → language:
16          switch ($language) {
17              case 'Dutch':
18                  echo 'Hallo, wereld!';
19                  break;
20              case 'French':
21                  echo 'Bonjour, monde!';
22                  break;
23              case 'German':
24                  echo 'Hallo, Welt!';
25                  break;
26              case 'Italian':
27                  echo 'Ciao, mondo!';
28                  break;
29              case 'Spanish':
30                  echo '¡Hola, mundo!';
31                  break;
32              case 'English':
33              default:
34                  echo 'Hello, world!';
35                  break;
36          } // End of switch.
37
38          // Close the HTML paragraph:
39          echo '</p>';
40
41      } // End of sayHello() method.
42
43  } // End of HelloWorld class.
```

3. Begin defining the first (and only) method:

```
function sayHello($language =
→'English') {
```

This class currently contains no attributes (variables), as those would have been declared before the methods. This method is called **sayHello()**. It takes one argument: the language for the greeting.

For the methods, I normally use the "lowercase camel" convention: start with lowercase letters, separating words with an uppercase letter. This is another common convention, although not one as consistently followed as that for the class name itself.

4. Start the method's code:

```
echo '<p>';
```

The method will print *Hello, world!* in one of several languages. The message will be wrapped within HTML paragraph tags, begun here.

5. Add the method's **switch**:

```
switch ($language) {
  case 'Dutch':
    echo 'Hallo, wereld!';
    break;
  case 'French':
    echo 'Bonjour, monde!';
    break;
  case 'German':
    echo 'Hallo, Welt!';
    break;
  case 'Italian':
    echo 'Ciao, mondo!';
    break;
  case 'Spanish':
    echo '¡Hola, mundo!';
```

```
    break;
  case 'English':
  default:
    echo 'Hello, world!';
    break;
} // End of switch.
```

The **switch** prints different messages based upon the chosen language. English is the default language, both in the **switch** and as the value of the **$language** argument (see Step 3). Obviously you can easily expand this **switch** to include more languages, like non-Western ones.

6. Complete the **sayHello()** method:

```
    echo '</p>';
} // End of sayHello() method.
```

You just need to close the HTML paragraph tag.

7. Complete the class and the PHP page:

```
}
```

8. Save the file as **HelloWorld.php**.

You've now created your first class. This isn't, to be clear, a *good* use of OOP, but it starts the process and you'll learn better implementations of the concept in due time.

Note that I'm not using a closing PHP tag, which is my policy for PHP scripts to be included by other files.

TIP Class methods can also have a *visibility*, by preceding the function definition with the appropriate keyword. If not stated, all methods have an assumed definition of

```
public function functionName() {...
```

TIP The class **stdClass** is already in use internally by PHP and cannot be declared in your own code.

Creating an Object

Using OOP is a two-step process. The first—defining a class—you just did when you wrote the **HelloWorld** class. The second step is to make use of that class by creating an *object* (or a class instance).

Going back to my **User** class analogy, an instance of this class may be for the user with a username of *janedoe*. The user's attributes might be that username, a user ID of 2459, and an email address of *jane@ example.com*. This is one instance of the **User** class. A second instance, *john_doe*, has that username, a user ID of 439, and an email address of *john.doe@example. edu*. These are separate objects derived from the same class. They are the same in general, but different in specificity.

Creating an object is remarkably easy in PHP once you've defined your class. It requires the keyword **new**:

`$object = new ClassName();`

Now the variable **$object** exists and is of type **ClassName** (instead of type string or array). More technically put, **$object** is an *instance* of **ClassName**.

To call the methods of the class, you use this syntax:

`$object->methodName();`

(The **->** can be called the *object operator*.)

If a method takes arguments, you provide those within parentheses, as in any function call:

`$object->methodName('value', 32, true);`

To access an object's properties, use

`$object->propertyName;`

Note that you would not use the property variable's dollar sign, which is a common cause of parse errors:

`$object->$propertyName; // Error!`

(As you'll also see in the next chapter, the ability to reference an object's method or property in this manner depends upon the member's visibility.)

Once you've finished with an object, you can delete it as you would any variable:

`unset($object);`

Simple enough! Let's go ahead and quickly make use of the **HelloWorld** class.

To create an object:

1. Create a new PHP document in your text editor or IDE, to be named **hello_object.php**, beginning with the standard HTML (**Script 4.2**):

```
<!doctype html>
<html lang="en">
<head>
    <meta charset="utf-8">
    <title>Hello, World!</title>
    <link rel="stylesheet"
href="style.css">
</head>
<body>
<?php # Script 4.2 -
 → hello_object.php
```

The class definition file itself contains no HTML, as it's not meant to be used on its own. This PHP page will include all of the code necessary to make a valid HTML page.

Script 4.2 In this page, PHP uses the defined class in order to say *Hello, world!* in several different languages.

```
1    <!doctype html>
2    <html lang="en">
3    <head>
4       <meta charset="utf-8">
5       <title>Hello, World!</title>
6       <link rel="stylesheet"
     → href="style.css">
7    </head>
8    <body>
9    <?php # Script 4.2 - hello_object.php
10   /* This page uses the HelloWorld class.
11    * This page just says "Hello, world!".
12    */
13
14   // Include the class definition:
15   require('HelloWorld.php');
16
17   // Create the object:
18   $obj = new HelloWorld();
19
20   // Call the sayHello() method:
21   $obj->sayHello();
22
23   // Say hello in different languages:
24   $obj->sayHello('Italian');
25   $obj->sayHello('Dutch');
26   $obj->sayHello('French');
27
28   // Delete the object:
29   unset($obj);
30   ?>
31   </body>
32   </html>
```

2. Include the class definition:

`require('HelloWorld.php');`

In order to create an instance of a class, the PHP script must have access to that class definition **A**. As the definition is stored in a separate file, that file must be included here. By using **require()** (as opposed to **include()**), the script will stop executing with a fatal error if the file could not be included (and there is no point in continuing without this file).

3. Create the object:

`$obj = new HelloWorld();`

This one line of code is all there is to it! You can give the object variable any valid name you'd like, of course.

4. Invoke the **sayHello()** method:

`$obj->sayHello();`

This line of code will call the **sayHello()** method, which is part of the **$obj** object. Since the method is not being given any arguments, the greeting will be in the default language of English.

5. Say hello in a few more languages:

`$obj->sayHello('Italian');`

`$obj->sayHello('Dutch');`

`$obj->sayHello('French');`

An object's methods can be called multiple times, like any other function. Different arguments are provided to vary the result.

continues on next page

Fatal error: Class 'HelloWorld' not found in
/Users/larryullman/Sites/phpvqp3/hello_object.php on line **18**

A You'll see an error like this if you go to create an object whose class definition cannot be found.

---

6. Delete the object and complete the page:

```php
unset($obj);
?>
</body>
</html>
```

You don't technically have to delete the object—it will be deleted as soon as the script ends. Still, I think it's better programming form to tidy up like this.

7. Save the file as `hello_object.php` and place it in your Web directory, along with `HelloWorld.php`.

You don't have to place both documents in the same directory, but if they are stored separately, you will need to change the `require()` line accordingly.

8. Test `hello_object.php` by viewing it in your Web browser .

Note that you should run `hello_object.php`, not `HelloWorld.php`, in your Web browser.

TIP Class names are not case-sensitive. However, object names, like any variable in PHP, are case-sensitive.

TIP Because function names in PHP are not case-sensitive, the same is true for method names in classes.

B The resulting Web page (the examples will get better, I promise).

Analyzing the HelloWorld Example

As I state in the first section of this chapter, OOP is both syntax and theory. For this first example, the **HelloWorld** class, the emphasis is on the syntax. Hopefully you can already see that this isn't great use of OOP. But why? Well, it's both too specific and too simple. Having an object print one string is a very focused idea, whereas classes should be much more abstract. It also makes absolutely no sense to use all this code—and the extra memory required—for one **echo** statement. It's nice that the object handles different languages, but still...

The **HelloWorld** class does succeed in a couple of ways, though. It does demonstrate some of the syntax. And it is reusable: if you have a project that needs to say *Hello, world!* dozens of times, this one object will do it. And if you need to change it to *Hello, World!* (with a capital "W"), edit just the one file and you're golden. To that end, however, it'd be better for the method to return the string, rather than just print it, so the string could be used in more ways.

Finally, this class kind of reflects the notion of *encapsulation*: you can use the object to say *Hello, world!* in multiple languages without any knowledge of how the class does that.

The $this Attribute

The **HelloWorld** class actually does something, which is nice, but it's a fairly minimal example. The class includes a method, but it does not contain any attributes (variables).

As I say in the section "Defining a Class," attributes:

- Are variables
- Must be declared as **public**, **private**, or **protected** (I'll use only **public** in this chapter)
- If initialized, must be given a static value (not the result of an expression)

Those are the rules for defining a class's attributes, but using those attributes requires one more piece of information. As already explained, through the object, you can access attributes via the object notation operator (->):

$object->*propertyName*;

The issue is that within the class itself (i.e., within a class's methods), you must use an alternative syntax to access the class's attributes. You cannot do just this:

```
class BadClass {
    public $var;
    function do() {
        // This won't work:
        print $var;
    }
}
```

The **do()** method cannot access **$var** in that manner. The solution is a special variable called **$this**. The **$this** variable in a class always refers to the current instance (i.e., the object involved) of that class. Within a method, you can refer to the instance of a class and its attributes by using the **$this->*attributeName*** syntax.

Rather than over-explaining this concept, I'll go right into another example that puts this new knowledge into action. This next, much more practical, example will define a class representing a rectangle.

To use the $this variable:

1. Create a new PHP document in your text editor or IDE, to be named **Rectangle.php** (Script 4.3):

   ```
   <?php # Script 4.3 - Rectangle.php
   ```

2. Begin defining the class:

   ```
   class Rectangle {
   ```

3. Declare the attributes:

   ```
   public $width = 0;

   public $height = 0;
   ```

   This class has two attributes: one for the rectangle's width and another for its height. Both are initialized to 0.

4. Create a method for setting the rectangle's dimensions:

   ```
   function setSize($w = 0, $h = 0) {

       $this->width = $w;

       $this->height = $h;

   }
   ```

   The **setSize()** method takes two arguments, corresponding to the width and height. Both have default values of 0, just to be safe.

   Within the method, the class's attributes are given values using the numbers to be provided when this method is called (assigned to **$w** and **$h**). Using **$this->width** and **$this->height** refers to this class's **$width** and **$height** attributes.

Script 4.3 This class is much more practical than the **HelloWorld** example. It contains two attributes—for storing the rectangle's width and height—and four methods.

```
1   <?php # Script 4.3 - Rectangle.php
2   /* This page defines the Rectangle
    → class.
3   * The class contains two attributes:
    → width and height.
4   * The class contains four methods:
5   * - setSize()
6   * - getArea()
7   * - getPerimeter()
8   * - isSquare()
9   */
10
11  class Rectangle {
12
13      // Declare the attributes:
14      public $width = 0;
15      public $height = 0;
16
17      // Method to set the dimensions:
18      function setSize($w = 0, $h = 0) {
19          $this->width = $w;
20          $this->height = $h;
21      }
22
23      // Method to calculate and return
        → the area.
24      function getArea() {
25          return ($this->width *
            → $this->height);
26      }
27
28      // Method to calculate and return
        → the perimeter.
29      function getPerimeter() {
30          return ( ($this->width +
            → $this->height) * 2 );
31      }
32
33      // Method to determine if the
        → rectange
34      // is also a square.
35      function isSquare() {
36          if ($this->width ==
            → $this->height) {
37              return true; // Square
```

script continues on next page

```
38          } else {
39              return false; // Not a square
40          }
41      }
42
43  } // End of Rectangle class.
```

5. Create a method that calculates and returns the rectangle's area:

```
function getArea() {
    return ($this->width *
    → $this->height);
}
```

This method doesn't need to take any arguments, because it can access the class's attributes via **$this**. Calculating the area of a rectangle is simple: multiply the width times the height. This value is then returned.

6. Create a method that calculates and returns the rectangle's perimeter:

```
function getPerimeter() {
    return ( ($this->width +
    → $this->height) * 2 );
}
```

This method is like **getArea()**, except it uses a different formula.

7. Create a method that indicates if the rectangle is also a square:

```
function isSquare() {
    if ($this->width ==
    → $this->height) {
        return true;
    } else {
        return false;
    }
}
```

This method compares the rectangle's dimensions. If they are the same, the Boolean **true** is returned, indicating the rectangle is a square. Otherwise, **false** is returned.

8. Complete the class:

```
} // End of Rectangle class.
```

9. Save the file as **Rectangle.php**.

To use the Rectangle class:

1. Create a new PHP document in your text editor or IDE, to be named **rectangle1.php**, beginning with the standard HTML (**Script 4.4**):

```
<!doctype html>
<html lang="en">
<head>
  <meta charset="utf-8">
  <title>Rectangle</title>
  <link rel="stylesheet"
href="style.css">
</head>
<body>
<?php # Script 4.4 - rectangle1.php
```

2. Include the class definition:

```
require('Rectangle.php');
```

3. Define the necessary variables and print an introduction:

```
$width = 42;
$height = 7;
echo "<h2>With a width of $width
→ and a height of $height...</h2>";
```

4. Create the object and assign the rectangle's dimensions:

```
$r = new Rectangle();
$r->setSize($width, $height);
```

The first line creates an object of type **Rectangle**. The second line assigns the values of the variables in this script—**$width** and **$height**—to the object's attributes. The values here are assigned to **$w** and **$h** in the **setSize()** method when it's called, which are then assigned to **$this->width** and **$this->height** within that method.

5. Print the rectangle's area:

```
echo '<p>The area of the rectangle
→ is ' . $r->getArea() . '</p>';
```

To print the rectangle's area, you only need to have the object tell you what that value is by calling its **getArea()** method. As this method returns the area (instead of printing it), it can be used in an **echo** statement like this.

6. Print the rectangle's perimeter:

```
echo '<p>The perimeter
→ of the rectangle is ' .
→ $r->getPerimeter() . '</p>';
```

This is a variation on the code in Step 5.

7. Indicate whether or not this rectangle is also a square:

```
echo '<p>This rectangle is ';
if ($r->isSquare()) {
   echo 'also';
} else {
   echo 'not';
}
echo ' a square.</p>';
```

Since the **isSquare()** method returns a Boolean value, I can invoke it as a condition. This code will print either *This rectangle is also a square.* or *This rectangle is not a square.*

8. Delete the object and complete the page:

```
unset($r);
?>
</body>
</html>
```

9. Save the file as **rectangle1.php** and place it in your Web directory, along with **Rectangle.php**.

continues on page 132

```
1   <!doctype html>
2   <html lang="en">
3   <head>
4       <meta charset="utf-8">
5       <title>Rectangle</title>
6       <link rel="stylesheet" href="style.css">
7   </head>
8   <body>
9   <?php # Script 4.4 - rectangle1.php
10  /*  This page uses the Rectangle class.
11   *  This page shows a bunch of information about a rectangle.
12   */
13
14  // Include the class definition:
15  require('Rectangle.php');
16
17  // Define the necessary variables:
18  $width = 42;
19  $height = 7;
20
21  // Print a little introduction:
22  echo "<h2>With a width of $width and a height of $height...</h2>";
23
24  // Create a new object:
25  $r = new Rectangle();
26
27  // Assign the rectangle dimensions:
28  $r->setSize($width, $height);
29
30  // Print the area:
31  echo '<p>The area of the rectangle is ' . $r->getArea() . '</p>';
32
33  // Print the perimeter:
34  echo '<p>The perimeter of the rectangle is ' . $r->getPerimeter() . '</p>';
35
36  // Is this a square?
37  echo '<p>This rectangle is ';
38  if ($r->isSquare()) {
39      echo 'also';
40  } else {
41      echo 'not';
42  }
43  echo ' a square.</p>';
44
45  // Delete the object:
46  unset($r);
47
48  ?>
49  </body>
50  </html>
```

10. Test `rectangle1.php` by viewing it in your Web browser **A**.

11. Change the variables' values in `rectangle1.php` and rerun it in your Web browser **B**.

> **TIP** Having *get_*and *set* methods in a class is a common convention. Methods starting with *set* are used to assign values to class attributes. Methods starting with *get* are used to return values: either attributes or the results of calculations.

> **TIP** Methods can call each other, just as they would any other function, but you'll need to use $this again. The following is unnecessary but valid:

```
function getArea() {
    if ($this->isSquare()) {
        return ($this->width *
$this->width);
    } else {
        return ($this->width *
$this->height);
    }
}
```

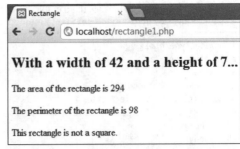

A Various attributes for a rectangle are revealed using the `Rectangle` class.

B If the width and height are the same, the rectangle is also a square.

Analyzing the Rectangle Example

The **Rectangle** class as defined isn't perfect, but it's pretty good, if I do say so myself. It encapsulates all the things you might want to do with or know about a rectangle. The methods also only handle calculations and return values; no HTML is used within the class, which is a better way to design.

One criticism may be that the class is too specific. Logically, if you've created a site that performs a lot of geometry, the **Rectangle** class might be an inherited class from a broader **Shape**. You'll learn about inheritance in the next chapter.

From the first two examples you can see the benefit of objects: the ability to create your own data type. Whereas a string is a variable type whose only power is to contain characters, the **Rectangle** is a new, powerful type with all sorts of features.

Creating Constructors

A *constructor* is a special kind of method that differs from standard ones in three ways:

- Its name is always **__construct()**.
- It is automatically and immediately called whenever an object of that class is created.
- It cannot have a **return** statement.

The syntax for defining a constructor is therefore

```
class ClassName {
    public $var;
    function __construct() {
        // Function code.
    }
}
```

A constructor could be used to connect to a database, set cookies, or establish initial values. Basically, you'll use constructors to do whatever should always be done—and done first—when an object of this class is made.

Because the constructor is still just another method, it can take arguments, and values for those arguments can be provided when the object is created:

```
class User {
    function __construct($id) {
        // Function code.
    }
}
$me = new User(2354);
```

The **Rectangle** class could benefit from having a constructor that assigns the rectangle's dimensions when the rectangle is created.

To add and use a constructor:

1. Open **Rectangle.php** (Script 4.3) in your text editor or IDE.

2. After declaring the attributes and before defining the **setSize()** method, add the constructor (**Script 4.5**):

```
function __construct($w = 0,
→ $h = 0) {
    $this->width = $w;
    $this->height = $h;
}
```

continues on next page

Script 4.5 A constructor has been added to the **Rectangle** class. This makes it possible to assign the rectangle's dimensions when the object is created.

```
1    <?php # Script 4.5 - Rectangle.php
2    /* This page defines the Rectangle class.
3     * The class contains two attributes: width and height.
4     * The class contains five methods:
5     * - __construct()
6     * - setSize()
7     * - getArea()
8     * - getPermeter()
9     * - isSquare()
10   */
```

script continues on next page

This method is exactly like the **setSize()** method, albeit with a different name. Note that constructors are normally the first method defined in a class (but still defined after the attributes).

3. Save the file as **Rectangle.php**.

4. Open **rectangle1.php** (Script 4.4) in your text editor or IDE.

5. If you want, change the values of the **$width** and **$height** variables (Script 4.6):

   $width = 160;

   $height = 75;

6. Change the way the object is created so that it reads

   $r = new Rectangle($width,
   → $height);

   The object can now be created and the rectangle assigned its dimensions in one step.

7. Delete the invocation of the **setSize()** method.

   This method is still part of the class, though, which makes sense. By keeping it in there, you ensure that a rectangle object's size can be changed after the object is created.

Script 4.5 *continued*

```
11
12   class Rectangle {
13
14     // Declare the attributes:
15     public $width = 0;
16     public $height = 0;
17
18     // Constructor:
19     function __construct($w = 0,
        → $h = 0) {
20        $this->width = $w;
21        $this->height = $h;
22     }
23
24     // Method to set the dimensions:
25     function setSize($w = 0, $h = 0) {
26        $this->width = $w;
27        $this->height = $h;
28     }
29
30     // Method to calculate and return
        → the area:
31     function getArea() {
32        return ($this->width *
           → $this->height);
33     }
34
35     // Method to calculate and return
        → the perimeter:
36     function getPerimeter() {
37        return ( ($this->width +
           → $this->height) * 2 );
38     }
39
40     // Method to determine if the
        → rectangle
41     // is also a square.
42     function isSquare() {
43        if ($this->width == $this->height)
           {
44           return true; // Square
45        } else {
46           return false; // Not a square
47        }
48
49     }
50
51   } // End of Rectangle class.
```

Script 4.6 This new version of the script assigns the rectangle's dimensions when the object is created (thanks to the constructor).

```
1    <!doctype html>
2    <html lang="en">
3    <head>
4        <meta charset="utf-8">
5        <title>Rectangle</title>
6        <link rel="stylesheet"
             → href="style.css">
7    </head>
8    <body>
9    <?php # Script 4.6 - rectangle2.php
10   /* This page uses the revised Rectangle
         → class.
11    * This page shows a bunch of
         → information
12    * about a rectangle.
13    */
14
15   // Include the class definition:
16   require('Rectangle.php');
17
18   // Define the necessary variables:
19   $width = 160;
20   $height = 75;
21
22   // Print a little introduction:
23   echo "<h2>With a width of $width and a
         → height of $height...</h2>";
24
25   // Create a new object:
26   $r = new Rectangle($width, $height);
27
28   // Print the area.
29   echo '<p>The area of the rectangle
         → is ' . $r->getArea() . '</p>';
30
31   // Print the perimeter.
32   echo '<p>The perimeter of the rectangle
         → is ' . $r->getPerimeter() . '</p>';
33
34   // Is this a square?
35   echo '<p>This rectangle is ';
36   if ($r->isSquare()) {
37       echo 'also';
38   } else {
39       echo 'not';
40   }
41   echo ' a square.</p>';
42
43   // Delete the object:
44   unset($r);
45
46   ?>
47   </body>
48   </html>
```

8. Save the file as **rectangle2.php**, place it in your Web directory along with the new **Rectangle.php** (Script 4.5), and test in your Web browser 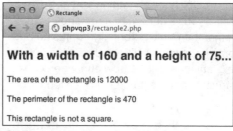.

TIP A constructor like the one just added to the Rectangle class is called a *default constructor*, as it provides default values for its arguments. This means that a Rectangle object can be created using either of these techniques:

$r = new Rectangle($width, $height);

$r = new Rectangle();

TIP You can directly call a constructor (although you will rarely need to):

$o = new SomeClass();

$o->__construct();

With the Rectangle example, this would let you get rid of the setSize() method without losing the ability to resize a rectangle.

TIP In PHP 4 and in other programming languages (like C++), a constructor is declared by creating a method whose name is the same as the class itself.

TIP If PHP 5 cannot find a __construct() method in a class, it will then try to find a constructor whose name is the same as the class (the PHP 4 constructor naming scheme).

A The resulting output is not affected by the incorporation of a constructor in the **Rectangle** class.

Creating Destructors

The corollary to the constructor is the *destructor*. Whereas a constructor is automatically invoked when an object is created, the destructor is called when the object is destroyed. This may occur when you overtly remove the object:

```
$obj = new ClassName();

unset($obj); // Calls  destructor, too.
```

Or this may occur when a script ends (at which point PHP releases the memory used by variables).

Being the smart reader that you are, you have probably already assumed that the destructor is created like so:

```
class ClassName {

    // Attributes and methods.

    function __destruct() {

        // Function code.

    }

}
```

Destructors do differ from constructors and other methods in that they cannot take any arguments.

The **Rectangle** class used in the last two examples doesn't lend itself to a logical destructor (there's nothing you need to do when you're done with a rectangle). And rather than do a potentially confusing but practical example, I'll run through a dummy example that shows how and when constructors and destructors are called.

Autoloading Classes

When you define a class in one script that is referenced in another script, you have to make sure that the second script includes the first, or there will be errors. To that end, PHP 5 supports a special function called *__autoload* (note that functions in PHP beginning with two underscores are special ones).

The **__autoload()** function is invoked when code attempts to instantiate an object of a class that hasn't yet been defined. The **__autoload()** function's goal is to include the corresponding file. In simplest form, this might be

```
function __autoload ($class) {

    require($class . '.php');

}
```

For each new object type created in the following code, the function will be invoked:

```
$obj = new Class();

$me = new Human();

$r = new Rectangle();
```

Thanks to the **__autoload()** function, those three lines will automatically include **Class.php**, **Human.php** and **Rectangle.php** (within the current directory).

Notice that this **__autoload()** function is defined outside of any class; instead, it is placed in a script that instantiates the objects.

The previous edition of this book demonstrated use of the **__autoload()** function, but that approach has been deprecated in favor of using the Standard PHP Library (SPL). It will be discussed in Chapter 8, "Using Existing Classes."

To create a destructor:

1. Create a new PHP document in your text editor or IDE, to be named **demo. php**, beginning with the standard HTML (Script 4.7):

```
<!doctype html>
<html lang="en">
<head>
    <meta charset="utf-8">
    <title>Constructors and
    → Destructors</title>
    <link rel="stylesheet"
    → href="style.css">
</head>
<body>
<?php # Script 4.7 - demo.php
```

2. Begin defining the class:

```
class Demo {
```

To make this example even simpler, I'll define and use the class in the same script.

3. Create the constructor:

```
function __construct() {
    echo '<p>In the constructor.</p>';
}
```

The constructor doesn't do anything but print a message indicating that it has been invoked. This will allow you to trace when the class's automatic methods are called.

4. Create the destructor:

```
function __destruct() {
    echo '<p>In the destructor.</p>';
}
```

5. Complete the class:

```
}
```

It's a very simple class!

continues on next page

Script 4.7 This script doesn't do anything except best convey when constructors and destructors are called.

```
1    <!doctype html>
2    <html lang="en">
3    <head>
4        <meta charset="utf-8">
5        <title>Constructors and Destructors</title>
6        <link rel="stylesheet" href="style.css">
7    </head>
8    <body>
9    <?php # Script 4.7 - demo.php
10   /*  This page defines a Demo class
11   *   and a demo() function.
12   *   Both are used to show when
13   *   constructors and destructors are called.
14   */
15
```

script continues on next page

6. Define a simple function that also creates an object:

```
function test() {
    echo '<p>In the function.
    → Creating a new object...</p>';
    $f = new Demo();
    echo '<p>About to leave the
    → function.</p>';
}
```

To best illuminate the life of objects, which affects when constructors and destructors are called, I'm adding this simple function. It prints messages and creates its own object, which will be a variable that's local to this function.

7. Create an object of class **Demo**:

```
echo '<p>Creating a new object...
→ </p>';
$o = new Demo();
```

When this object is created, the constructor will be called. So this script first prints this line (*Creating a new object...*) and will then print *In the constructor*.

8. Call the **test()** function:

```
echo '<p>Calling the function...
→ </p>';
test();
```

After printing the status statement, the function is called. Consequently, the function is entered, wherein *In the function. Creating a new object...* will first be printed. Then, in that function, a new object is created (called **$f**). Therefore, the constructor will be called again, and the *In the constructor.* message printed, as you'll see in the final output.

Script 4.7 *continued*

```
16   // Define the class:
17   class Demo {
18
19       // No attributes.
20
21       // Constructor:
22       function __construct() {
23           echo '<p>In the constructor.</p>';
24       }
25
26       // Destructor:
27       function __destruct() {
28           echo '<p>In the destructor.</p>';
29       }
30
31   } // End of Demo class.
32
33   // Define a test() function:
34   function test() {
35       echo '<p>In the function. Creating a
         → new object...</p>';
36       $f = new Demo();
37       echo '<p>About to leave the
         → function.</p>';
38   }
39
40   // Create the object:
41   echo '<p>Creating a new object...</p>';
42   $o = new Demo();
43
44   // Call the test() function:
45   echo '<p>Calling the function...</p>';
46   test();
47
48   // Delete the object:
49   echo '<p>About to delete the object...
       → </p>';
50   unset($o);
51
52   echo '<p>End of the script.</p>';
53   ?>
54   </body>
55   </html>
```

A The flow of the two objects' creation and destruction over the execution of the script is revealed by this script. In particular, you can see how the **test()** function's object, **$f**, lives and dies in the middle of this script.

B If you don't forcibly delete the object **A**, it will be deleted when the script stops running. This means that the **$o** object's destructor is called after the final printed message, even after the closing HTML tags **C**.

C The **$o** object's destructor is called as the very last script event, when the script stops running. Thus, the *In the destructor.* message gets sent to the browser after the closing HTML tag.

After the object is created in the function, the *About to leave the function.* message is printed. Then the function is exited, at which point in time the object defined in the function—**$f**—goes away, thus invoking the **$f** object's destructor, printing *In the destructor.*

9. Delete the **$o** object:

```
echo '<p>About to delete the
→ object...</p>';

unset($o);
```

Once this object is deleted, its destructor is invoked.

10. Complete the page:

```
echo '<p>End of the script.</p>';

?>

</body>

</html>
```

11. Save the file as **demo.php** and place it in your Web directory. Then test by viewing it in your Web browser **A**.

12. Delete the **unset($o)** line, save the file, and rerun it in your Web browser **B**.

    Also check the HTML source code of this page **C** to really understand the flow.

    (Arguably, you could also delete the *About to delete the object...* line, although I did not for the two figures.)

TIP In C++ and C#, the destructor's name for the class `ClassName` is `~ClassName`, the corollary of the constructor, which is `ClassName`. Java does not support destructors.

Designing Classes with UML

To this point, the chapter has discussed OOP in terms of both syntax and theory, but there are two other related topics worth exploring, both new additions to this edition. First up is an introduction to *Unified Modeling Language* (UML), a way to graphically represent your OOP designs. Entire books are written on the subject, but since this chapter covers the fundamentals of OOP, I'll also introduce the fundamentals of UML.

A class at its core has three components:

- Its name
- Its attributes
- Its methods

UML graphically represents a class by creating a *class diagram*: a three-part box for each class, with the class name at the top. The next section of the box would identify the class attributes, and the third would list the methods **Ⓐ**.

For the attributes, the attribute type (e.g., string, array, etc.) is listed after the attribute's name, as in

`userId:number`

`username:string`

If the attribute had a default value, you could reflect that too:

`width:number = 0`

To define a method in a class diagram, you would start with the method name, placing its arguments and types within parentheses. This is normally followed by the type of value the method returns:

`sayHello(language:string):void`

The `sayHello()` method doesn't return anything, so its return type is **void**.

ClassName
attribute
attribute
method()
method()

Ⓐ How UML represents a class graphically.

Benefits of a Class Design

While making a formal UML class design may at first appear to be more of an exercise than anything, there are concrete benefits to creating one. First of all, if you sketch out the design before doing any coding, you improve your chances of getting the code correct from the start. In other words, if you put the effort into your visual design, and ponder whether the design fully reflects the application's needs, you minimize the number of times you'll need to update your class definitions down the road.

Second, a principle of OOP is *encapsulation*: separating out and hiding how something is accomplished. A UML, with its listing of attributes, methods, and arguments, can act as a user guide for those classes. Any code that requires classes that have been modeled should be able to use the classes, and its methods and attributes, without ever looking at the underlying code. In fact, you can distribute the UML along with your code as a service to your clients.

HelloWorld
sayHello(language: string):void

With this in mind, you can complete the class diagram for the **HelloWorld** class **B**. In the next steps, you'll design the diagram that reflects the **Rectangle** class.

To design a class using UML:

1. Using paper or software, draw a three-part box.

   If you like the feeling of designing with paper and pencil, feel free, but there are also plenty of software tools that can fulfill this role, too. Search online for an application that will run on your platform, or for a site that can serve the same purposes within the browser.

2. Add the name of the class to the top of the box:

   Rectangle

   Use the class's proper name (i.e., the same capitalization).

3. Add the attributes to the middle section:

   width:number = 0

   height:number = 0

   Here are the two attributes for the **Rectangle** class. Both are numbers with default values of 0.

4. Add the constructor definition to the third part of the box:

   __construct(width:number =
   → 0, height:number = 0):void

   This method is named **__construct**. It takes two arguments, both of type number, and both with default values of 0. The method does not return anything, so its return value is **void**.

   continues on next page

5. Add the **setSize()** method definition:

**setSize(width:number =
→ 0, height:number = 0):void**

The **setSize()** method happens to be defined exactly like **__construct()**.

6. Add the **getArea()** method definition:

getArea():number

The **getArea()** method takes no arguments and returns a number.

7. Add the **getPerimeter()** method definition:

getPerimeter():number

The **getPerimeter()** method also takes no arguments and returns a number.

8. Add the **isSquare()** method definition:

isSquare():Boolean

This method takes no arguments but returns a Boolean value.

9. Save your design for later reference **C**.

TIP Be certain to update your class design should you later change your class definition.

TIP In the next chapter, in which more complex OOP theory is unveiled, you'll learn more UML techniques.

Rectangle
width:number = 0 height:number = 0
__construct(width:number = 0, height:number = 0):void setSize(width:number = 0, height:number = 0):void getArea():number getPerimeter():number isSquare():Boolean

C A UML representation of the simple **Rectangle** class.

Better Documentation with phpDocumentor

Along with creating a UML class design, another new topic in this edition is creating better code documentation using phpDocumentor (**www.phpdoc.org**).

In my opinion, properly documenting one's code is so vitally important that I wish PHP would generate errors when it came across a lack of comments! Having taught PHP and interacted with readers for years, I am amazed at how often programmers omit comments, occasionally under the guise of waiting until later. Proper documentation is something that should be incorporated into code for your own good, for your client's, for your co-workers' (if applicable), and for the programmer in the future who may have to alter or augment your work—even if that programmer is you.

Although you can adequately document your code using simple comments, as I do in this book, there are two obvious benefits to adopting a formal phpDocumentor approach:

- It conveys many best practices and recommended styles.

- phpDocumentor will generate documentation, in HTML and other formats, for you.

The generated HTML **Ⓐ** can also be a valuable resource for anyone using your code, particularly your classes.

Ⓐ The generated HTML documentation for the **HelloWorld** class.

phpDocumentor creates documentation by reading the PHP code and your comments. To facilitate that process, you would start writing your comments in a way that php-Documentor understands. To begin, you'll use the *docblock* syntax:

```
/**
 *
 * Short description
 *
 * Long description
 * Tags
 */
```

The short description should be a single line description. The long description can go over multiple lines and even use some HTML. Both are optional.

After the description, write one or more lines of tags. Each tag is prefaced by @, and phpDocumentor supports several kinds; which you use will depend on the thing you're documenting.

A docblock can be placed before any of the following:

- Class definition
- Function or method definition
- Variable declaration
- Constant definition
- File inclusion

A docblock should be written at the top of a script, in order to document the entire file (**Script 4.8**).

Script 4.8 A more formally documented version of the **HelloWorld** class.

```
1    <?php # Script 4.8 - HelloWorld.php #2
2    /**
3     * This page defines the HelloWorld class.
4     *
5     * Written for Chapter 4, "Basic Object-Oriented Programming"
6     * of the book "PHP Advanced and Object-Oriented Programming"
7     * @author Larry Ullman <Larry@LarryUllman.com>
8     * @copyright 2012
9     */
10
11   /**
12    * The HelloWorld class says "Hello, world!" in different languages.
13    *
14    * The HelloWorld class is mostly for
15    * demonstration purposes.
16    * It's not really a good use of OOP.
17    */
18   class HelloWorld {
19
20       /**
21        * Function that says "Hello, world!" in different languages.
22        * @param string $language Default is "English"
23        * @returns void
24        */
```

script continues on next page

```
25      function sayHello($language =
        → 'English') {
26
27          // Put the greeting within P tags:
28          echo '<p>';
29
30          // Print a message specific to a
            → language:
31          switch ($language) {
32              case 'Dutch':
33                  echo 'Hallo, wereld!';
34                  break;
35              case 'French':
36                  echo 'Bonjour, monde!';
37                  break;
38              case 'German':
39                  echo 'Hallo, Welt!';
40                  break;
41              case 'Italian':
42                  echo 'Ciao, mondo!';
43                  break;
44              case 'Spanish':
45                  echo '¡Hola, mundo!';
46                  break;
47              case 'English':
48              default:
49                  echo 'Hello, world!';
50                  break;
51          } // End of switch.
52
53          // Close the HTML paragraph:
54          echo '</p>';
55
56      } // End of sayHello() method.
57
58  } // End of HelloWorld class.
```

To document a variable declaration, you use the **@var** tag, followed by the variable's type (and optional description):

```
/**
 * @var string
 */
$name = 'Larry Ullman';
```

Notice that the docblock doesn't need to reference the variable name, as php-Documentor will be able to read that from the following line of code. The point of the docblock is to indicate the variable's intended type.

To document methods and functions, use **@param** to detail the function's parameters and **@return** to indicate the type of value the function returns (Script 4.8).

The details as to the possible types, and the full usage of all of phpDocumentor, can be found in the documentation (**www.phpdoc.org/docs/**).

Once you've written comments in the proper format, you can use the phpDocumentor tool to generate your documentation. To do that, you must first install phpDocumentor. The best way to install it is using PEAR (**http://pear.php.net**), so you must have that installed, too. PEAR already comes installed with many all-in-one WAMP, MAMP, or LAMP stacks; check your associated documentation if you're using one of these. If not, see the sidebar for some tips on installing PEAR.

To use phpDocumentor:

1. Complete the phpDocumentor-type comments for a file (Script 4.8) or application.

   For simplicity's sake, Script 4.8 shows a fully documented **HelloWorld.php**.

2. Access your computer via the command-line interface.

   My assumption is that you already know how to do this for your platform. If not, search the Web or use my support forums for answers.

3. Add the phpDocumentor PEAR channel **B**:

   ```
   pear channel-discover
   → pear.phpdoc.org
   ```

   This will allow you to download the latest version of the phpDocumentor directory from that site.

4. Install phpDocumentor **C**:

   ```
   pear install phpdoc/
   phpDocumentor-alpha
   ```

   This instruction comes straight from the phpDocumentor Web site. It may change in time; check the site for the best, current instructions.

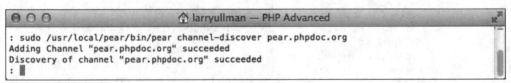

```
🏠 larryullman — PHP Advanced
: sudo /usr/local/pear/bin/pear channel-discover pear.phpdoc.org
Adding Channel "pear.phpdoc.org" succeeded
Discovery of channel "pear.phpdoc.org" succeeded
:
```

B Adding the phpDocumentor channel to my PEAR installation.

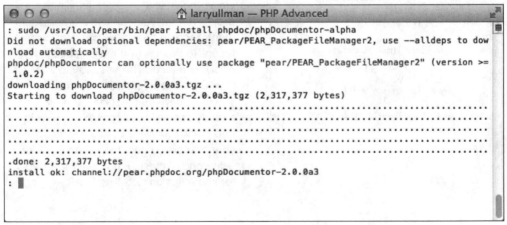

```
🏠 larryullman — PHP Advanced
: sudo /usr/local/pear/bin/pear install phpdoc/phpDocumentor-alpha
Did not download optional dependencies: pear/PEAR_PackageFileManager2, use --alldeps to dow
nload automatically
phpdoc/phpDocumentor can optionally use package "pear/PEAR_PackageFileManager2" (version >=
 1.0.2)
downloading phpDocumentor-2.0.0a3.tgz ...
Starting to download phpDocumentor-2.0.0a3.tgz (2,317,377 bytes)
.........................................................................................
.........................................................................................
.........................................................................................
.........................................................................................
......
.done: 2,317,377 bytes
install ok: channel://pear.phpdoc.org/phpDocumentor-2.0.0a3
:
```

C Installing phpDocumentor in PEAR.

Installing PEAR Packages

One PEAR-related thing I do not discuss in this book is the installation process, for two good reasons. First, with the variations of available operating systems, it's too tough to nail down comprehensive instructions for all potential readers. Second, experience tells me that many users are on hosted servers, where they cannot directly install anything.

Still, installing PEAR is not impossibly hard, and once you master the installation of a single package, installing more is a snap. If you want to try your hand at installing PEAR packages, start by checking out the PEAR manual, which has instructions. If you're still not clear as to what you should do, search the Web for articles on the subject, particular to your operating system, and/or post a question in the book's supporting forum, where I'll be happy to assist.

Some installation tips up front:

- You may need to invoke the **pear** installer as a superuser (or using **sudo**).
- Make sure that the location of your PEAR directory is in your PHP include path.
- Run the command **pear help install** to see what options are available.

If you are on a hosted server, the hosting company should be willing to install PEAR packages for you (which benefit every user on the server). If they won't do that, you ought to consider a different hosting company (seriously). Barring that, you can install PHP and PEAR on your own computer in order to use phpDocumentor.

Note that on my system, in both Step 3 and Step 4, I had to preface these commands with **sudo**, to invoke the superuser, and include the full path to PEAR (both suggestions are made in the sidebar).

5. Move to the directory where your PHP scripts are:

cd */path/to/folder*

6. Document a single file using

phpdoc -f HelloWorld.php -t docs

That line tells phpDocumentor to parse the file **HelloWorld.php** and to write the output to the target (-t) directory **docs**, which would be a folder in that same directory. phpDocumentor will attempt to create that directory, if it does not exist.

7. Open **docs/index.html** in your browser Ⓐ.

TIP For the sake of saving precious book space, the code in this book will not be documented using the full phpDocumentor syntax.

TIP To view documentation mistakes, check out the generated errors.

TIP To have phpDocumentor document an entire project, you can have it parse the current directory using

phpdoc -d . -t docs

TIP If you want, you can edit the templates used by phpDocumentor to output HTML more to your liking.

Review and Pursue

If you have any problems with these sections, either in answering the questions or pursuing your own endeavors, turn to the book's supporting forum (www.Larry Ullman.com/forums/).

Review

- How does OOP differ from procedural programming? (See page 120.)

- What is a *class*? What is an *object*? What is an *attribute* (or property)? What is a *method*? (See page 121.)

- What syntax do you use to create a class? To create an object? (See pages 121 and 124.)

- How do you create class methods? How do you call object methods? (See pages 121 and 124.)

- How do you create class attributes? How do you reference those attributes within the class? How do you reference those attributes using an object? (See pages 121, 124, and 127.)

- What is a *constructor*? How do you create one? When is a constructor called? (See page 133.)

- What is a *destructor*? How do you create one? When is a destructor called? (See page 136.)

- What is *UML*? How do you represent a class in UML? (See page 140.)

- What is *phpDocumentor*? What are the arguments for using it? (See page 143.)

- What is a *docblock*? (See page 144.)

Pursue

- Come up with another (relatively simple) class. Define and use it in PHP. Then model and document it using UML and phpDocumentor.

- Learn more about UML, if you are so inclined.

- Find UML software that you like (for your platform or online).

- Learn more about phpDocumentor, if you are so inclined.

- Add phpDocumentor-style comments to the **Rectangle** class and then generate its documentation.

5

Advanced OOP

Chapter 4, "Basic Object-Oriented Programming," covers the fundamental concepts of OOP in PHP. A fair amount of theory is also discussed there, because that's half the OOP battle. Here, things get more advanced (hence the chapter title!), going into the more abstract aspects of OOP, with ample time again given to theory.

Most of the topics discussed in this chapter involve *inheritance*, the understanding of which is crucial to using OOP. You'll learn how to have one class inherit from another, and the various ways that a class's properties and methods can be inherited. Along the way, you'll begin creating more practical examples, and encounter more theory, particularly in the sidebars.

In This Chapter

Advanced Theories

This chapter begins with a brief discussion of a few key concepts in advanced OOP. Chapter 4 introduced most of the basic terms: *class*, *object*, *modularity*, and *abstraction*. A few more were also referenced: *inheritance*, *overriding*, *encapsulation*, and *visibility*. Of these latter four notions, all of which arise in this chapter, inheritance is far and away the most important in advanced object-oriented programming.

Object inheritance is where one class is derived from another, just as humans inherit qualities from their parents. Of course, the "qualities" in the object-oriented world are *attributes* (variables) and *methods* (functions). Through inheritance, you can define one class that is "born" with the same attributes and methods as another **A**. The inherited child class can even have its own unique qualities that the parent doesn't have **B**.

```
ParentClass
─────────────
attribute1
attribute2
─────────────
method1()
method2()
method3()
```

```
ChildClass
─────────────
attribute1
attribute2
─────────────
method1()
method2()
method3()
```

A A child class inherits (i.e., has) all of the attributes and methods of its parent class (there can be exceptions to this, but assume this to be true for now).

```
ParentClass
─────────────
attribute1
attribute2
─────────────
method1()
method2()
method3()
```

```
ChildClass
─────────────
attribute1
attribute2
attribute3
─────────────
method1()
method2()
method3()
method4()
method5()
```

B Child classes can add their own members to the ones they inherited. In this way a child can separate itself (functionally speaking) from its parent.

Indicating Inheritance in UML

In a UML class diagram, inheritance is represented using an arrow between the two classes, as in these early figures. The arrow should go *from the subclass to the base class* (i.e., the arrow points to the parent). Conventionally, the parent class is placed above the child classes.

Finally, UML would *not* have you repeat the inherited attributes and properties in the child classes, as in these early figures (that is unnecessarily redundant). I've only done so to better illustrate the point that a child class often inherits the members in its parent.

Inheritance Terminology

With class definitions, the main terms are *attributes* and *methods*, meaning variables and functions, respectively. The combination of attributes and methods make up the *members* of a class.

With inheritance you have a *parent* class and a *child* class: the latter is inherited from the former. You'll also see these described as a *base* class or *superclass* and its *derived* class or *subclass*.

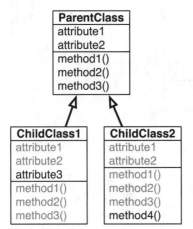

C A single parent class can have unlimited offspring, each customized in its own way.

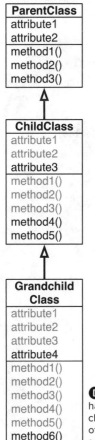

D Inheritance can theoretically have limitless depth, with each child inheriting all the members of its parent (again, not always so, but...).

But inheritance isn't necessarily a simple one-to-one relationship. There's no limit to how many times inheritance can occur: multiple classes can inherit from the same parent **C** or a class can be a child of a child **D**. This speaks to the powerful reusability of class code.

Once you've defined a class that inherits from another, it doesn't take long to start thinking how nice it'd be if it behaved just slightly differently. You can add new attributes and methods, but what if you wanted to change the behavior of the parent class's methods? It would be wrong to change the definition of the parent class (presumably it works as it should, and besides, other classes might inherit from it too **C**). Instead, you can *override* a parent class's method to customize it for the new class. This is *polymorphism*, where calling the same method can have different results, depending on the object type. This probably doesn't mean much yet, but you'll understand in time.

Acknowledging (as I just did) that it's not a good thing for one class to muck around in another, the concept of *visibility* exists. Visibility controls what members of a class can be accessed or altered by other classes (or even outside of any class).

As you can tell already, once you introduce inheritance, the OOP world expands exponentially. Just as in the previous chapter, I'll attempt to go through this sea of information slowly, to make sure that it really settles in. Some of the examples will be designed for illumination of a concept rather than real-world implementations, but you'll still see plenty of practical examples.

TIP For many of the images in this chapter, I'll use a more minimal version of UML (introduced at the end of Chapter 4). Feel free to flesh out the UML on your own, for practice.

Inheriting Classes

One of the ways in which objects make programming faster is the ability to use one class definition as the basis for another. This process is referred to as *inheritance*.

Going back to the **User** example mentioned in Chapter 4, if the **User** class has the attributes *username*, *userId*, *email*, and *password* and it has the methods *login* and *logout*, you could create another class called **Admin** that is an extension of **User**. Along with the aforementioned variables and functions, an **Admin** object might also have the attribute of *accessLevel* and the method of *editUser* 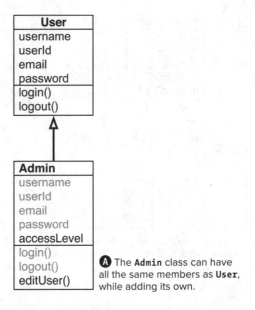.

This kind of inheritance means the two classes have an "is a" relationship, in that an **Admin** *is a* type of **User**. When you're in design situations where one thing is just a more specific type of another thing, you're probably going to want to use inheritance.

To make a child class from a parent, use the **extends** keyword. Assuming you have already defined the **ClassName** class, you can create a child like so:

```
class ChildClass extends ClassName { }
```

As written, the class **ChildClass** will possess all the members of its parent, **ClassName**. Now you can modify this class to adapt it to your specific needs without altering the original class. Ideally, once you've created a solid parent class, you will never need to modify it again and can use child classes to tailor the code to your individual requirements.

User
username
userId
email
password
login()
logout()

Admin
username
userId
email
password
accessLevel
login()
logout()
editUser()

Ⓐ The **Admin** class can have all the same members as **User**, while adding its own.

The instanceof Keyword

The **instanceof** keyword can be used to see if a particular object is of a certain class type:

```
if ($obj instanceof SomeClass) { ...
```

Notice that you don't put the class's name in quotation marks. Also—and this is important—in order for this to work, the PHP script must have access to the **SomeClass** definition.

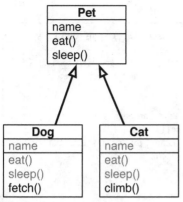

B How the pet-cat-dog relationship would be implemented as objects.

Script 5.1 This example script shows how two classes can be derived from the same parent. Each can access all the members of the parent, and each has defined its own custom method.

```
1    <!doctype html>
2    <html lang="en">
3    <head>
4       <meta charset="utf-8">
5       <title>Pets</title>
6       <link rel="stylesheet"
         → href="style.css">
7    </head>
8    <body>
9    <?php # Script 5.1 - pets1.php
10   //  This page defines and uses the Pet,
         → Cat, and Dog classes.
11
12   # ***** CLASSES ***** #
13
14   /* Class Pet.
15    *  The class contains one attribute:
         → name.
16    *  The class contains three methods:
17    *  - __construct()
18    *  - eat()
19    *  - sleep()
20    */
21   class Pet {
22
23       // Declare the attributes:
24       public $name;
25
```

script continues on next page

For an example implementation of this, I'll start with a silly (but comprehensible) pets example. Say you have two pets: a cat and a dog. Both animals have a name, and they both eat and sleep. Cats differ from dogs in that they can climb trees and dogs differ from cats in that they can fetch. Being able to describe these qualities and relationships in plain language leads to the inheritance structure you would create **B**.

To inherit from a class:

1. Begin a new PHP script in your text editor or IDE, to be named **pets1.php**, starting with the HTML (**Script 5.1**):

   ```
   <!doctype html>
   <html lang="en">
   <head>
      <meta charset="utf-8">
      <title>Pets</title>
      <link rel="stylesheet"
      → href="style.css">
   </head>
   <body>
   <?php # Script 5.1 - pets1.php
   ```

   To make things easier, I'm going to put all the class definitions and the use of these classes in this same script. In a real application, you would separate your class files from the program files that use them.

   continues on next page

2. Start declaring the **Pet** class:

```
class Pet {
   public $name;
```

Pet has one attribute: the pet's name.

3. Create the constructor:

```
function __construct($pet_name) {
   $this->name = $pet_name;
}
```

The constructor takes one argument: the name of the pet. This gets assigned to the class's **$name** attribute.

4. Define the **eat()** method:

```
function eat() {
   echo "<p>$this->name is
   → eating.</p>";
}
```

This method simply reports the name of the animal eating.

5. Define the **sleep()** method and complete the class:

```
   function sleep() {
      echo "<p>$this->name is
      → sleeping.</p>";
   }
} // End of Pet class.
```

Script 5.1 *continued*

```
26      // Constructor assigns the pet's
        → name:
27      function __construct($pet_name) {
28         $this->name = $pet_name;
29      }
30
31      // Pets can eat:
32      function eat() {
33         echo "<p>$this->name is eating.
        →</p>";
34      }
35
36      // Pets can sleep:
37      function sleep() {
38         echo "<p>$this->name is sleeping.
        →</p>";
39      }
40
41   } // End of Pet class.
42
43   /* Cat class extends Pet.
44    * Cat has additional method: climb().
45    */
46   class Cat extends Pet {
47      function climb() {
48         echo "<p>$this->name is climbing.
        →</p>";
49      }
50   } // End of Cat class.
51
52   /* Dog class extends Pet.
53    * Dog has additional method: fetch().
54    */
55   class Dog extends Pet {
56      function fetch() {
57         echo "<p>$this->name is fetching.
        → </p>";
58      }
59   } // End of Dog class.
60
61   # ***** END OF CLASSES ***** #
62
63   // Create a dog:
64   $dog = new Dog('Satchel');
65
```

script continues on next page

```
66    // Create a cat:
67    $cat = new Cat('Bucky');
68
69    // Feed them:
70    $dog->eat();
71    $cat->eat();
72
73    // Nap time:
74    $dog->sleep();
75    $cat->sleep();
76
77    // Do animal-specific thing:
78    $dog->fetch();
79    $cat->climb();
80
81    // Delete the objects:
82    unset($dog, $cat);
83
84    ?>
85    </body>
86    </html>
```

6. Declare the **Cat** class:

```
class Cat extends Pet {
   function climb() {
      echo "<p>$this->name is
      → climbing.</p>";
   }
} // End of Cat class.
```

The **Cat** class extends **Pet**, meaning that it has all the attributes and methods of **Pet**. Added to those is one new method, **climb()**. The method can refer to the **$name** attribute via **$this->name** because the attribute is also part of this class (thanks to inheritance).

7. Declare the **Dog** class:

```
class Dog extends Pet {
   function fetch() {
      echo "<p>$this->name is
      → fetching.</p>";
   }
} // End of Dog class.
```

8. Create two new pets:

```
$dog = new Dog('Satchel');
```

```
$cat = new Cat('Bucky');
```

Note that you're creating objects of the child class types, not of **Pet**.

continues on next page

9. Make the pets do the things they do:

```
$dog->eat();

$cat->eat();

$dog->sleep();

$cat->sleep();

$dog->fetch();

$cat->climb();
```

Each subclass object can invoke the methods defined in the parent class as well as its own new methods: **fetch()** and **climb()**. Note that **$dog** could not invoke the **climb()** method, nor could **$cat** call **fetch()**.

10. Complete the page:

```
unset($dog, $cat);

?>

</body>

</html>
```

You don't have to unset the objects, but it makes for tidier code.

11. Save the file as **pets1.php**, place it in your Web directory, and test in your Web browser **C**.

TIP In this example, you *could* create an object of type Pet. That object would have a name and could eat() and sleep(), but it could not fetch() or climb().

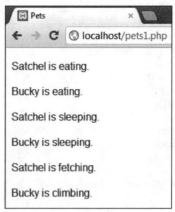

C Two objects are created from different derived classes. Then the various methods are called. Understanding this result and the code in **pets1.php** is key to the rest of the chapter's material.

Inheriting Constructors and Destructors

The pets example shows how you can create one class (i.e., **Pet**) and then derive other classes from it (**Dog** and **Cat**). These other classes can have their own methods, unique to themselves, such as **climb()** and **fetch()**.

There are two methods that are common to many classes: *constructors* and *destructors* (see Chapter 4 for a detailed description). The **Pet** class has a constructor but no need for a destructor. What would happen, then, if **Cat** or **Dog** *also* had a constructor? By definition, this method is always called **__construct()**. How does PHP determine which version of the constructor to execute?

As a rule, PHP will always call the constructor for the class just instantiated **A**. The same rule applies for destructors. Further, unlike in some other OOP languages, in PHP, when you create an object of a child class, the parent class's constructor is not automatically called.

This next, somewhat more practical, example will extend the **Rectangle** class (Script 4.5, defined in Chapter 4) to create a **Square** class (because all squares are rectangles but not all rectangles are squares).

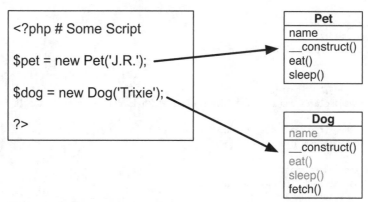

A When an object is created, PHP will always call the constructor of that object's class type.

To create subclass constructors:

1. Begin a new PHP script in your text editor or IDE, to be named **square.php**, starting with the HTML (**Script 5.2**):

```
<!doctype html>
<html lang="en">
<head>
    <meta charset="utf-8">
    <title>Square</title>
    <link rel="stylesheet"
    → href="style.css">
</head>
<body>
<?php # Script 5.2 - square.php
```

Script 5.2 The **Square** class is derived from **Rectangle** but has its own constructor. That constructor, not **Rectangle**'s, will be called when an object of type **Square** is created.

```
1    <!doctype html>
2    <html lang="en">
3    <head>
4        <meta charset="utf-8">
5        <title>Square</title>
6        <link rel="stylesheet" href="style.css">
7    </head>
8    <body>
9    <?php # Script 5.2 - square.php
10   // This page declares and uses the Square class which is derived from Rectangle (Script 4.5).
11
12   // Include the first class definition:
13   require('Rectangle.php');
14
15   // Create the Square class.
16   // The class only adds its own constructor.
17   class Square extends Rectangle {
18
19       // Constructor takes one argument.
20       // This value is assigned to the
21       // Rectangle width and height attributes.
22       function __construct($side = 0) {
23           $this->width = $side;
24           $this->height = $side;
25       }
```

script continues on next page

```
26
27   } // End of Square class.
28
29   // Rectangle dimensions:
30   $width = 21;
31   $height = 98;
32
33   // Print a little introduction:
34   echo "<h2>With a width of $width and a
     → height of $height...</h2>";
35
36   // Create a new rectangle:
37   $r = new Rectangle($width, $height);
38
39   // Print the area.
40   echo '<p>The area of the rectangle
     → is ' . $r->getArea() . '</p>';
41
42   // Print the perimeter.
43   echo '<p>The perimeter of the rectangle
     → is ' . $r->getPerimeter() . '</p>';
44
45   // Square dimensions:
46   $side = 60;
47
48   // Print a little introduction:
49   echo "<h2>With each side being $side...
     → </h2>";
50
51   // Create a new object:
52   $s = new Square($side);
53
54   // Print the area.
55   echo '<p>The area of the square
     → is ' . $s->getArea() . '</p>';
56
57   // Print the perimeter.
58   echo '<p>The perimeter of the square
     → is ' . $s->getPerimeter() . '</p>';
59
60   // Delete the objects:
61   unset($r, $s);
62
63   ?>
64   </body>
65   </html>
```

2. Include the **Rectangle** class:

   ```
   require('Rectangle.php');
   ```

   You'll need to make sure that the **Rectangle.php** file (Script 4.5) is in the same directory as this script.

3. Declare the **Square** class:

   ```
   class Square extends Rectangle {
       function __construct($side = 0) {
           $this->width = $side;
           $this->height = $side;
       }
   } // End of Square class.
   ```

   The premise is simple: there's no reason to have to pass both a height and a width value to a child of the **Rectangle** class when you know you're creating a square. So a new constructor is defined that only takes one argument. That value will be assigned, within the constructor, to the parent class's attributes.

   Note that in order for this class extension to work, it must be able to access the **Rectangle** definition (so that file must be included prior to this point).

4. Create a rectangle and report on it:

   ```
   $width = 21;
   $height = 98;
   echo "<h2>With a width of $width
   → and a height of $height...</h2>";
   $r = new Rectangle($width,
   → $height);
   echo '<p>The area of the rectangle
   → is ' . $r->getArea() . '</p>';
   echo '<p>The perimeter
   → of the rectangle is ' .
   → $r->getPerimeter() . '</p>';
   ```

continues on next page

This code is also from Chapter 4. It just creates a rectangle and prints its area and perimeter.

5. Repeat Step 4 for a square:

```
$side = 60;

echo "<h2>With each side being
→ $side...</h2>";

$s = new Square($side);

echo '<p>The area of the square
→ is ' . $s->getArea() . '</p>';

echo '<p>The perimeter
→ of the square is ' .
→ $s->getPerimeter() . '</p>';
```

This code differs from that in Step 4 in that only one value needs to be passed to the **Square** constructor. Then all the other methods can be called just the same.

6. Complete the page:

```
unset($r, $s);

?>

</body>

</html>
```

7. Save the file as **square.php**, place it in your Web directory, and test in your Web browser 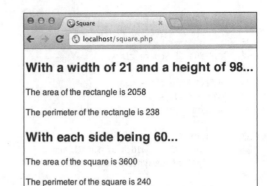.

With a width of 21 and a height of 98...

The area of the rectangle is 2058

The perimeter of the rectangle is 238

With each side being 60...

The area of the square is 3600

The perimeter of the square is 240

B Even though the **Square** constructor takes only one argument (Script 5.2), the use of the **Rectangle** methods, and the end result, works just the same.

TIP As stated in Chapter 4, by definition, constructors never return anything.

TIP A general OOP recommendation is that all classes have a constructor, inherited or otherwise.

TIP You can call the parent class's constructor, if need be, using the *scope resolution operator*, discussed later in this chapter.

Simple Inheritance Design

Any time one class inherits from another, the result should be a more specific description of a thing. Hence, I go from **Pet** to **Dog** or **Cat** and from **Rectangle** to **Square**. When deciding where to place methods, including constructors and destructors, you have to think about whether that functionality is universal or specific.

In the **Pet** example, the constructor sets the pet's name, which is universal for all pets. So the **Dog** and **Cat** classes don't need their own constructors. In the **Rectangle** example, its constructor sets the height and width. But a square doesn't have two different dimensions; having a new constructor for it is valid.

A When related classes have overridden methods, which method is called depends on the type of the object calling it. Note that for **$obj2**, the code of the overridden **scream()** method in **SomeOtherClass** is used in lieu of the original **scream()** (hence the different scream in the last three lines).

Overriding Methods

So far I've covered how one class can inherit from another class and how the child classes can have their own new methods. The previous example demonstrated that subclasses can even define their own constructors (and destructors, implicitly), which will be used in lieu of the parent class's constructors and destructors. This same thinking—creating alternative method definitions in subclasses—can be applied to the other class methods, too. This concept is called *overriding* a method.

To override a method in PHP, the subclass must define a method with the *exact same name and number of arguments* as the parent class **A**:

```php
class SomeClass {
    function scream($count = 1) {
        for ($i = 0; $i < $count; $i++) {
            echo 'Eek!<br>';
        }
    }
}
class SomeOtherClass extends
→SomeClass{
    function scream($count = 1) {
        for ($i = 0; $i < $count; $i++) {
            echo 'Whoohoo!<br>';
        }
    }
}
$obj1 = new SomeClass();
$obj1->scream();
$obj1->scream(2);
$obj2 = new SomeOtherClass();
$obj2->scream();
$obj2->scream(2);
```

Overriding methods is a common and useful feature of advanced object-oriented programming. As mentioned in the first section of this chapter, overriding methods creates *polymorphism*, where calling the same method can have different results, depending on the object type.

As a simple example of this, I'll return to the **Pet**, **Dog**, and **Cat** classes. Instead of having separate **climb()** and **fetch()** methods, you'll implement that functionality as an overridden **play()** method.

To override methods:

1. Open **pets1.php** (Script 5.1) in your text editor or IDE.

2. Add a **play()** method to the **Pet** class (Script 5.3):

   ```
   function play() {
       echo "<p>$this->name is
       → playing.</p>";
   }
   ```

   This is the method that will be overridden. It just prints the name of the pet that is playing.

Script 5.3 The **Cat** and **Dog** classes override the **Pet play()** method, giving it new functionality. Which version of **play()** gets called depends on the type of the object calling it.

```
1   <!doctype html>
2   <html lang="en">
3   <head>
4       <meta charset="utf-8">
5       <title>Pets</title>
6       <link rel="stylesheet"
        → href="style.css">
7   </head>
8   <body>
9   <?php # Script 5.3 - pets2.php
10  //  This page defines and uses the Pet,
        → Cat, and Dog classes.
11
12  # ***** CLASSES ***** #
13
14  /* Class Pet.
15   *  The class contains one attribute:
        → name.
16   *  The class contains four methods:
17   *  - __construct()
18   *  - eat()
19   *  - sleep()
20   *  - play()
21   */
22  class Pet {
23      public $name;
24      function __construct($pet_name) {
25          $this->name = $pet_name;
26      }
27      function eat() {
28          echo "<p>$this->name is eating.
            → </p>";
29      }
30      function sleep() {
31          echo "<p>$this->name is sleeping.
            → </p>";
32      }
33
34      // Pets can play:
35      function play() {
36          echo "<p>$this->name is
            → playing.</p>";
37      }
38
39  } // End of Pet class.
40
41  /* Cat class extends Pet.
```

script continues on next page

```
42      * Cat overrides play().
43      */
44     class Cat extends Pet {
45         function play() {
46             echo "<p>$this->name is climbing.
                   → </p>";
47         }
48     } // End of Cat class.
49
50     /* Dog class extends Pet.
51      * Dog overrides play().
52      */
53     class Dog extends Pet {
54         function play() {
55             echo "<p>$this->name is fetching.
                   → </p>";
56         }
57     } // End of Dog class.
58
59     # ***** END OF CLASSES ***** #
60
61     // Create a dog:
62     $dog = new Dog('Satchel');
63
64     // Create a cat:
65     $cat = new Cat('Bucky');
66
67     // Create an unknown type of pet:
68     $pet = new Pet('Rob');
69
70     // Feed them:
71     $dog->eat();
72     $cat->eat();
73     $pet->eat();
74
75     // Nap time:
76     $dog->sleep();
77     $cat->sleep();
78     $pet->sleep();
79
80     // Have them play:
81     $dog->play();
82     $cat->play();
83     $pet->play();
84
85     // Delete the objects:
86     unset($dog, $cat, $pet);
87
88     ?>
89     </body>
90     </html>
```

3. In the **Cat** class, change the name of **climb()** to **play()**.

Now the **Pet** class's **play()** method has been overridden in the **Cat** class.

4. In the **Dog** class, change the name of **fetch()** to **play()**.

5. After the class declarations, create an object of type **Pet**:

$pet = new Pet('Rob');

To see the impact of overriding a method, you'll create an object of the parent class as well.

6. Add activities for the **Pet** object:

$pet->eat();

$pet->sleep();

7. Make all three objects play:

$dog->play();

$cat->play();

$pet->play();

These three lines will reveal which class's method gets called by which object.

continues on next page

Final Methods

Most methods in classes can be overridden. The exception is if a function is defined as **final**:

final function myFunc() {...}

A final method's definition cannot be altered by any subclass.

A class can also be declared **final**, meaning that it cannot be extended.

8. Delete the calls to **$dog->fetch()** and **$cat->climb()**.

9. Also unset the **$pet** object toward the end of the script:

   ```
   unset($dog, $cat, $pet);
   ```

10. Save the file as **pets2.php**, place it in your Web directory, and test in your Web browser **B**.

TIP The combination of a function's name and its arguments (the number of arguments, specifically) is referred to as the function's *signature*. In PHP 5, except for constructors, any derived class must use the same signature when overriding a method.

TIP The Square class could logically override the Rectangle isSquare() method. It would be defined as simply

```
function isSquare() {
    return true;
}
```

TIP Overriding a method in such a way that it also takes a *different* number of arguments than the original is referred to as *overloading* a method. This can be accomplished in PHP but not as easily as overriding one.

TIP The method defined in a parent class can be called the *default* behavior, because this is what that method will do, even in instances of subclasses, unless the subclasses specifically override that behavior.

B Here, cat-specific and dog-specific **play()** methods are introduced, overriding the parent class's **play()** method. A third object, of type **Pet**, was also added.

Access Control

Access control, which is also called *visibility*, dictates how accessible a class's properties and methods are... in other words: where the class's members can be referenced and where they are inaccessible.

There are three levels of visibility: **public**, **protected**, and **private**. To establish the visibility of an attribute, prefix the variable's declaration with one of these keywords:

```
class ClassName {
    public $var1 = 'Hello';
    private $var2 = 'world';
    protected $var3 = 42;
}
```

You've already been doing this, because indicating an attribute's visibility is required in PHP. Thus far, every attribute has been declared public.

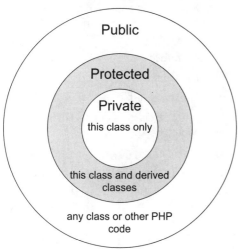

A The more restricted the visibility, the smaller the realm where the attribute or method is accessible.

To establish the visibility of a method, prefix the function's declaration with one of the keywords:

```
class ClassName {
    public function myFunction() {
        // Function code.
    }
}
```

Methods lacking the accessibility declaration are considered to be public. And because methods often are public, the visibility for them is frequently omitted.

Think of each term as prescribing a more limited circle in which the member can be accessed **A**. A public member is the most accessible: available to methods within the class itself, in inherited classes, and outside of any class. For example, because the **$name** attribute in **Pet** is public, you can do this:

```
$pet = new Pet('Charlie');
$pet->name = 'Fungo';
```

Again, because **$name** is public, it's also available within the **Dog** and **Cat** classes, as you've already seen.

Protected members can only be accessed within the class and derived subclasses. This means that should the **$name** attribute in **Pet** be made *protected*, you could still use it within methods found in the **Dog** or **Cat** classes, but not directly through an object instance of any of those classes.

Private is the most restrictive; those members are only accessible within the class that defines them. Private class members cannot be accessed by subclasses or through an object instance of that class. If the **$name** attribute in **Pet** was made *private*, you could only reference it within the **Pet** class definition (i.e., within one of its methods).

It may seem odd for a class to have attributes, or members, that are inaccessible, but this is a valuable, important OOP concept, called *encapsulation*. Simply put, encapsulation is the hiding of information (actual data or processes) that does not need to be available outside of the class. From a design perspective, a good class is a usable entity without your necessarily knowing how it works internally. Further, there are many times where some of the internal data shouldn't be accessible externally. For example, a database class needs an internal database connection, but there's no reason why that connection should be accessible outside of the class (in fact, it shouldn't be).

Looking at the **Pet** class, its **name** attribute should be made protected. It makes sense for the class and its subclasses to be able to access the name, but you shouldn't be able to change the name outside of the class. The same applies to the **$width** and **$height** attributes in **Rectangle**: they should be protected.

As with most concepts in OOP, there are two things you should learn: how visibility works and how you use it. To make clear how access control works, I'll run through a dummy example that just plays around with the accessibility of attributes. After this example, the topic of visibility will become clearer, as you'll use it in other examples.

To control member access:

1. Begin a new PHP script in your text editor or IDE, to be named **visibility. php**, starting with the HTML (**Script 5.4**):

```
<!doctype html>
<html lang="en">
<head>
    <meta charset="utf-8">
    <title>Visibility</title>
    <link rel="stylesheet"
    → href="style.css">
</head>
<body>
<?php # Script 5.4 -
→ visibility.php
```

continues on page 168

Indicating Visibility in UML

In a UML class diagram, the accessibility of a class member can be indicated by prefacing the member with:

- +, for public
- -, for private
- #, for protected

Thus, the **Pet** class as defined to this point would have:

+name:string

+__construct($pet_name:string):void

```
1    <!doctype html>
2    <html lang="en">
3    <head>
4       <meta charset="utf-8">
5       <title>Visibility</title>
6       <link rel="stylesheet" href="style.css">
7    </head>
8    <body>
9    <?php # Script 5.4 - visibility.php
10   //  This page defines and uses the Test and LittleTest classes.
11
12   # ***** CLASSES ***** #
13
14   /* Class Test.
15    *  The class contains three attributes:
16    *  - public $public
17    *  - protected $protected
18    *  - private $_private
19    *  The class defines one method: printVar().
20    */
21   class Test {
22
23      // Declare the attributes:
24      public $public = 'public';
25      protected $protected = 'protected';
26      private $_private = 'private';
27
28      // Function for printing a variable's value:
29      function printVar($var) {
30         echo "<p>In Test, \$$var: '{$this->$var}'.</p>";
31      }
32
33   } // End of Test class.
34
35   /* LittleTest class extends Test.
36    * LittleTest overrides printVar().
37    */
38   class LittleTest extends Test {
39      function printVar($var) {
40         echo "<p>In LittleTest, \$$var: '{$this->$var}'.</p>";
41      }
42   } // End of LittleTest class.
43
44   # ***** END OF CLASSES ***** #
45
46   // Create the objects:
47   $parent = new Test();
48   $child = new LittleTest();
49
```

script continues on next page

2. Begin declaring the **Test** class:

```
class Test {
    public $public = 'public';
    protected $protected =
    → 'protected';
        private $_private = 'private';
```

This class contains three attributes, one of each type. To make things even more obvious, the name and value of each attribute match its visibility.

As a convention, private variable names are often begun with an underscore. This is commonly done in many OOP languages, although it is not required.

3. Add a **printVar()** method and complete the class:

```
function printVar($var) {
    echo "<p>In Test, \$$var:
    → '{$this->$var}'.</p>";
}
} // End of Test class.
```

The **printVar()** method prints the value of a variable whose name it receives as an argument. It will print the attribute's name and value out like this:

In Test, $public: 'public'.

The **\$$var** will end up printing a dollar sign followed by the value of **$var** (the argument). The **$this->$var** code will be evaluated as **$this->public**, **$this->protected**, and **$this->private** so that it can access the class attributes.

Script 5.4 *continued*

```
50    // Print the current value of $public:
51    echo '<h1>Public</h1>';
52    echo '<h2>Initially...</h2>';
53    $parent->printVar('public');
54    $child->printVar('public');
55    // Also echo $parent->public or echo
      → $child->public.
56
57    // Modify $public and reprint:
58    echo '<h2>Modifying $parent->public...
      → </h2>';
59    $parent->public = 'modified';
60    $parent->printVar('public');
61    $child->printVar('public');
62
63    // Print the current value of
      → $protected:
64    echo '<hr><h1>Protected</h1>';
65    echo '<h2>Initially...</h2>';
66    $parent->printVar('protected');
67    $child->printVar('protected');
68
69    // Attempt to modify $protected and
      → reprint:
70    echo '<h2>Attempting to modify
      → $parent->protected...</h2>';
71    $parent->protected = 'modified';
72    $parent->printVar('protected');
73    $child->printVar('protected');
74
75    // Print the current value of $_private:
76    echo '<hr><h1>Private</h1>';
77    echo '<h2>Initially...</h2>';
78    $parent->printVar('private');
79    $child->printVar('private');
80
81    // Attempt to modify $_private and
      → reprint:
82    echo '<h2>Attempting to modify
      → $parent->_private...</h2>';
83    $parent->_private = 'modified';
84    $parent->printVar('private');
85    $child->printVar('private');
86
87    // Delete the objects:
88    unset($parent, $child);
89
90    ?>
91    </body>
92    </html>
```

4. Create a class that extends **Test**:

```
class LittleTest extends Test {
    function printVar($var) {
        echo "<p>In LittleTest,
        ↪\$$var: '{$this->$var}'.</p>";
    }
} // End of LittleTest class.
```

The **LittleTest** class, as an extension of **Test**, will inherit the **$public** and **$protected** attributes. It will not have the **$_private** attribute, as that variable's visibility is private, meaning it cannot be inherited.

This class will override the **printVar()** method, changing the printed text slightly.

B Public variables can be accessed, and modified, anywhere.

5. Create an object of each type:

```
$parent = new Test();
$child = new LittleTest();
```

6. Print the current value of the **$public** variable by calling the **printVar()** method:

```
echo '<h1>Public</h1>';
echo '<h2>Initially...</h2>';
$parent->printVar('public');
$child->printVar('public');
```

Because the **$public** variable is public, it can be accessed by either class. You could also access it outside of the class using **$parent->public** or **$child->pubic**.

7. Modify the **Test $public** attribute and reprint:

```
echo '<h2>Modifying
↪$parent->public...</h2>';
$parent->public = 'modified';
$parent->printVar('public');
$child->printVar('public');
```

Because **$public** has public visibility, it can be accessed (and therefore modified) anywhere **B**. You should note that these lines only change the value of the **$public** attribute in the **$parent** object. The **$child** object's **$public** variable still has the original value (because the **$public** attribute is represented as a separate entity in each object).

continues on next page

8. Repeat Steps 6 and 7 for the protected variable:

```
echo '<hr><h1>Protected</h1>';

echo '<h2>Initially...</h2>';

$parent->printVar('protected');

$child->printVar('protected');

echo '<h2>Attempting to modify
 →$parent->protected...</h2>';

$parent->protected = 'modified';

$parent->printVar('protected');

$child->printVar('protected');
```

As you'll see when you run this script **C**, you can access the **$protected** variable from *within* either class. But you cannot access it (which also means you cannot modify it) from outside either class, including through an object of that class type. Doing so causes a fatal error.

9. Complete the page:

```
unset($parent, $child);

?>

</body>

</html>
```

Ignore the rest of what you see in Script 5.4 for now, as I'm working you through a process!

10. Save the file as **visibility.php**, place it in your Web directory, and test in your Web browser **C**.

This is one of those rare times where I actually want you to see the error, so that you may better understand visibility. A public class member can be accessed anywhere, including outside of a class (i.e., through an object). A protected member can only be accessed in the class or in derived classes. Attempting to access the member elsewhere results in a fatal error. Thus, a protected class member is more insulated.

11. Comment out this line:

```
$parent->protected = 'modified';
```

This is the line that caused the fatal error, so let's make it inert in order to try something new.

Protected

Initially...

In Test, $protected: protected.

In LittleTest, $protected: protected.

Attempting to modify $parent->protected...

Fatal error: Cannot access protected property Test::$protected in /Users/larryullman/Sites/phpvqp3/visibility.php on line 68

C Attempting to modify the value of the protected variable using the syntax **$obj->var** results in a fatal error (which is bad).

12. Before unsetting the objects, repeat Steps 6 and 7 for the private attribute.

```
echo '<hr><h1>Private</h1>';
echo '<h2>Initially...</h2>';
$parent->printVar('private');
$child->printVar('private');
echo '<h2>Attempting to modify
 $parent->_private...</h2>';
$parent->_private = 'modified';
$parent->printVar('private');
$child->printVar('private');
```

To finish this example, let's look at where you can access *private* class members.

13. Save the file and retest **D**.

As you can see in the figure, not even the **$child** object, which is an instance of the inherited **LittleTest** class, can access **$_private**. And the script cannot refer to **$parent->_private**, which, again, causes a fatal error.

TIP Many programmers would argue that all attributes should be protected or private, so they are never directly accessible outside of the class. You would then write "get" and "set" methods as an interface for accessing them when needed.

TIP A method designed to return an attribute's value is called a *getter* or an *accessor*. A method designed to assign a value to an attribute is called a *setter* or a *mutator*.

TIP Think of access control as a firewall between your class and everything else, using visibility to prevent bugs and other inappropriate behavior (e.g., being able to change class attributes).

TIP If a class has a method that should only ever be called by the class itself, it should also be marked either protected or private.

Private

Initially...

In Test, $_private: 'private'.

Notice: Undefined property: LittleTest::$_private in **/Users/larryullman/Sites/phpvqp3/visibility.php** on line 40

In LittleTest, $_private: ''.

Attempting to modify $parent->_private...

Fatal error: Cannot access private property Test::$_private in **/Users/larryullman/Sites/phpvqp3/visibility.php** on line 83

D Attempting to refer to **$this->_private** within the **LittleTest** class—which is what happens when you call **$child->printVar('private')**—creates a notice, as the class does not contain that attribute (because it neither inherited one nor defined one itself). Attempting to refer to **$parent->_private** results in a fatal error.

Using the Scope Resolution Operator

OOP has some of its own operators, as you've already seen with ->, used by objects to access their members. Another is the *scope resolution operator*: the combination of two colons together (::). It's used to access members through classes, not objects:

ClassName::methodName();

ClassName::propertyName;

There are two places in which this construct is used:

- Within classes, to avoid confusion when inherited classes have the same attributes and methods
- Outside of classes, to access members without first creating objects

Outside of a class, you will need to specify the class name, as in the previous code. Within a class, however, are special keywords you should use. Whereas you can use **$this** within a class to refer to the current object instance, the keyword **self** is a reference to the current class:

```
class SomeClass {
   function __construct() {
      self::doThis();
   }
   protected function doThis() {
      echo 'done!';
   }
}
```

In that code, **self::doThis()** will invoke the **doThis()** method of the current class.

(As a side note on understanding visibility, the **doThis()** function defined in **SomeClass** can only be called by other methods within **SomeClass** or by methods within inherited classes, because **doThis()** is defined as **protected**.)

To refer to a member of a *parent* class, use the scope resolution operator with the keyword **parent**:

```
class SomeOtherClass extends
→ SomeClass{
   function __construct() {
      parent::doThis();
   }
}
```

For the most part, you'll use the scope resolution operator to access *overridden methods*. You'll also use it with *static* and *constant* class members, two topics yet to be discussed. In the meantime, as a simple demonstration of how you might use this new information, I'll touch up the **Pet**, **Dog**, and **Cat** classes.

To use the scope resolution operator:

1. Open **pets2.php** (Script 5.3) in your text editor or IDE.

2. Modify the **Pet** constructor so that the animals immediately sleep (**Script 5.5**):

   ```
   function __construct($pet_name) {
      $this->name = $pet_name;
      self::sleep();
   }
   ```

   It seems that many animals go to sleep as one of the first things they do. By placing this new line in the constructor, you ensure that the **sleep()** method is called as soon as the object is created.

continues on page 174

```
1   <!doctype html>
2   <html lang="en">
3   <head>
4      <meta charset="utf-8">
5      <title>Pets</title>
6      <link rel="stylesheet" href="style.css">
7   </head>
8   <body>
9   <?php # Script 5.5 - pets3.php
10  //   This page defines and uses the Pet, Cat, and Dog classes.
11
12  # ***** CLASSES ***** #
13
14  /* Class Pet.
15   *   The class contains one attribute: name.
16   *   The class contains four methods:
17   *   - __construct()
18   *   - eat()
19   *   - sleep()
20   *   - play()
21   */
22  class Pet {
23     public $name;
24     function __construct($pet_name) {
25        $this->name = $pet_name;
26        self::sleep();
27     }
28     function eat() {
29        echo "<p>$this->name is eating.</p>";
30     }
31     function sleep() {
32        echo "<p>$this->name is sleeping.</p>";
33     }
34     function play() {
35        echo "<p>$this->name is playing.</p>";
36     }
37  } // End of Pet class.
38
39  /* Cat class extends Pet.
40   * Cat overrides play().
41   */
42  class Cat extends Pet {
43     function play() {
44
45        // Call the Pet::play() method:
46        parent::play();
47
48        echo "<p>$this->name is climbing.</p>";
```

script continues on next page

3. Modify the **Cat play()** method so that it calls **Pet play()**:

```
function play() {
  parent::play();
  echo "<p>$this->name is
  → climbing.</p>";
}
```

The **play()** method in the **Pet** and **Cat** classes do slightly different things. The **Pet** method says that the object is playing. The **Cat** method says specifically what kind of play. To have the functionality of both methods, call **parent::play()** within the **Cat** method.

4. Repeat Step 3 for the **Dog** class:

```
function play() {
  parent::play();
  echo "<p>$this->name is
  → fetching.</p>";
}
```

Script 5.5 *continued*

```
49          }
50    } // End of Cat class.
51
52    /* Dog class extends Pet.
53     * Dog overrides play().
54     */
55    class Dog extends Pet {
56        function play() {
57
58            // Call the Pet::play() method:
59            parent::play();
60
61            echo "<p>$this->name is fetching.
                → </p>";
62        }
63    } // End of Dog class.
64
65    # ***** END OF CLASSES ***** #
66
67    // Create a dog:
68    $dog = new Dog('Satchel');
69
70    // Create a cat:
71    $cat = new Cat('Bucky');
72
73    // Create an unknown type of pet:
74    $pet = new Pet('Rob');
75
76    // Feed them:
77    $dog->eat();
78    $cat->eat();
79    $pet->eat();
80
81    // Nap time:
82    $dog->sleep();
83    $cat->sleep();
84    $pet->sleep();
85
86    // Have them play:
87    $dog->play();
88    $cat->play();
89    $pet->play();
90
91    // Delete the objects:
92    unset($dog, $cat, $pet);
93
94    ?>
95    </body>
96    </html>
```

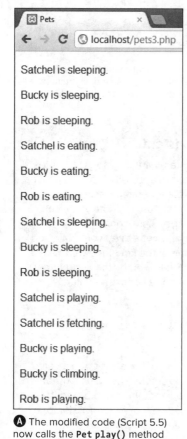

Satchel is sleeping.

Bucky is sleeping.

Rob is sleeping.

Satchel is eating.

Bucky is eating.

Rob is eating.

Satchel is sleeping.

Bucky is sleeping.

Rob is sleeping.

Satchel is playing.

Satchel is fetching.

Bucky is playing.

Bucky is climbing.

Rob is playing.

A The modified code (Script 5.5) now calls the **Pet play()** method each time a **Cat** or **Dog** plays.

5. Save the file as **pets3.php**, place it in your Web directory, and test in your Web browser **A**.

TIP In Dog and Cat, you could also use the code Pet::play(). But by using parent::play(), you minimize the chance of future problems should the class definitions change.

TIP You will often see documentation use the *ClassName*::*methodName*() syntax. When you see this, it's not suggesting that you *should* call the method this way, but rather that methodName() is part of ClassName.

Creating Static Members

Static class attributes are the class equivalent of static function variables (see Chapter 1, "Advanced PHP Techniques"). To recap, a static function variable remembers its value each time a function is called :

```php
function test() {
    static $n = 1;
    echo "$n<br>";
    $n++;
}
test();
test();
test();
```

As the figure shows, each call of the **test()** function increments the value of **$n** by 1. If **$n** was not declared as static, each call to the function would print the number 1.

With static class attributes, the concept is just the same except that a *static variable is remembered across all instances of that class* (across all objects based on the class). To declare a static attribute, use the **static** keyword after the visibility indicator:

```php
class SomeClass {
    public static $var = 'value';
}
```

A A static variable in a function retains its value over multiple calls (in the same script).

Class Constants

Class constants are like static attributes in that they are accessible to all instances of that class (or derived classes). But as with any other constant, the value can never change. Class constants are created using the **const** keyword, followed by the name of the constant (without a dollar sign), followed by the assignment operator and the constant's value:

```php
class SomeClass {
    const PI = 3.14;
}
```

Constants can only be assigned a value like in that example. The value cannot be based on another variable, and it can't be the result of an expression or a function call.

Constants, like static attributes, also cannot be accessed through the object. You cannot do this:

$obj->PI

or

$obj::PI

But you can use *ClassName*::*CONSTANT_NAME* (e.g., **SomeClass::PI**) anywhere. You can also use **self::***CONSTANT_NAME* within the class's methods.

Static variables differ from standard attributes in that you cannot access them within the class using **$this**. Instead, you must use **self**, followed by the scope resolution operator (**::**), followed by the variable name, *with its initial dollar sign*:

```
class SomeClass {
   public static $counter = 0;
   function __construct() {
     self::$counter++
   }
}
```

The preceding code creates a counter for how many objects of this class exist. Each time a new object is created:

```
$obj = new SomeClass();
```

$counter goes up by one.

Static methods are created in much the same way:

```
class SomeClass {
   public static function doThis() {
     // Code.
   }
}
```

Once you've declared a class member as static, you can access it using the class name, without creating an object. Again, the scope resolution operator is used to refer to members of a class:

```
class SomeClass {
   public static $counter = 0;
   public static function doThis() {
     // Code.
   }
}
echo SomeClass::$counter; // 0
SomeClass::doThis();
```

(In fact, not only *can* you access static members without creating an object, *static properties cannot be accessed through an object*, although static methods can be.)

To play this out, let's create a new **Pet** class that uses a static attribute and a static method. The attribute will be used to count the number of pets in existence. The static method will return the number of pets. As this is just a demonstration of this new concept, no other methods will be created.

To create static members:

1. Begin a new PHP script in your text editor or IDE, to be named **static.php**, starting with the HTML (**Script 5.6**):

```
<!doctype html>
<html lang="en">
<head>
    <meta charset="utf-8">
    <title>Static</title>
    <link rel="stylesheet"
    → href="style.css">
</head>
<body>
<?php # Script 5.6 - static.php
```

2. Begin declaring the **Pet** class:

```
class Pet {
    protected $name;
    private static $_count = 0;
```

The class still has the **$name** attribute, but it's now marked as **protected** so that only this and derived classes can access it. The **$_count** variable, which is initialized as 0, is both private and static. By making it private, only this class can access it, which is smart, because you don't want any other code to be able to change the counter. By making **$_count** static, you ensure that it retains its value for all instances of **Pet** or any derived classes.

3. Create the constructor:

```
function __construct($pet_name) {
    $this->name = $pet_name;
    self::$_count++;
}
```

Script 5.6 A static attribute and a static method are used to count the number of pets created in this script.

```
1    <!doctype html>
2    <html lang="en">
3    <head>
4        <meta charset="utf-8">
5        <title>Static</title>
6        <link rel="stylesheet"
         → href="style.css">
7    </head>
8    <body>
9    <?php # Script 5.6 - static.php
10   //  This page defines and uses the Pet,
     → Cat, and Dog classes.
11
12   # ***** CLASSES ***** #
13
14   /* Class Pet.
15    *  The class contains two attributes:
16    *  - protected name
17    *  - private static _count
18    *  The class contains three methods:
19    *  - __construct()
20    *  - __destruct()
21    *  - public static getCount()
22    */
23   class Pet {
24
25       // Declare the attributes:
26       protected $name;
27       private static $_count = 0;
28
29       // Constructor assigns the pet's name
30       // and increments the counter:
31       function __construct($pet_name) {
32
33           $this->name = $pet_name;
34
35           // Increment the counter:
36           self::$_count++;
37
38       }
39
40       // Destructor decrements the counter:
41       function __destruct() {
42           self::$_count--;
43       }
44
```

script continues on next page

```
45      // Static method for returning the
        ⤷ counter:
46      public static function getCount() {
47          return self::$_count;
48      }
49
50 } // End of Pet class.
51
52 /* Cat class extends Pet. */
53 class Cat extends Pet {
54 } // End of Cat class.
55
56 /* Dog class extends Pet. */
57 class Dog extends Pet {
58 } // End of Dog class.
59
60 /* Ferret class extends Pet. */
61 class Ferret extends Pet {
62 } // End of Ferret class.
63
64 /* PygmyMarmoset class extends Pet. */
65 class PygmyMarmoset extends Pet {
66 } // End of PygmyMarmoset class.
67
68 # ***** END OF CLASSES ***** #
69
70 // Create a dog:
71 $dog = new Dog('Old Yeller');
72
73 // Print the number of pets:
74 echo '<p>After creating a Dog, I now
        ⤷ have ' . Pet::getCount() . ' pet(s).
        ⤷ </p>';
75
76 // Create a cat:
77 $cat = new Cat('Bucky');
78 echo '<p>After creating a Cat, I now
        vhave ' . Pet::getCount() . ' pet(s).
        ⤷ </p>';
79
80 // Create another pet:
81 $ferret = new Ferret('Fungo');
82 echo '<p>After creating a Ferret, I now
        ⤷ have ' . Pet::getCount() . ' pet(s).
        ⤷ </p>';
83
84 // Tragedy strikes!
```

script continues on next page

The constructor still assigns the name to the **$name** attribute, but now it also increments the counter. Note the unique syntax for referring to a static attribute.

Every time an object of type **Pet** or of a derived type is created, this constructor gets called. So for every qualifying object, **$count** is incremented.

4. Create the destructor:

```
function __destruct() {
  self::$_count--;
}
```

Just as the constructor should increase the value of **$_count**, the destructor should decrease it. Every time an object of a qualifying type (**Pet** or a derived class) is destroyed, this destructor is called.

5. Create the static method and complete the class:

```
public static function
⤷ getCount() {
  return self::$_count;
}
} // End of Pet class.
```

The **getCount()** method is public and static. This means that it's available to be called anywhere. It returns the value of **$_count**.

6. Create a **Cat** class:

```
class Cat extends Pet {
}
```

Since the focus here is on the static members, the derived classes don't need to do anything.

continues on next page

7. Create a couple more subclasses:

```php
class Dog extends Pet {
}
class Ferret extends Pet {
}
class PygmyMarmoset extends Pet {
}
```

8. Create a new object and print the number of pets:

```php
$dog = new Dog('Old Yeller');
echo '<p>After creating a Dog,
→I now have ' . Pet::getCount() .
→' pet(s).</p>';
```

When **$dog** is created, the **Pet** constructor is called, incrementing **$_count** to 1. To return this value, invoke **Pet::getCount()**.

To avoid confusion, I'll point out that the **Pet** constructor is called when making an object of type **Dog** because **Dog** does not have its own constructor.

9. Create a couple more pets:

```php
$cat = new Cat('Bucky');
echo '<p>After creating a Cat,
→I now have ' . Pet::getCount() .
→' pet(s).</p>';
$ferret = new Ferret('Fungo');
echo '<p>After creating a Ferret,
→I now have ' . Pet::getCount() .
→' pet(s).</p>';
```

10. Have the unthinkable happen (my condolences):

```php
unset($dog);
echo '<p>After tragedy strikes,
→I now have ' . Pet::getCount() .
→' pet(s).</p>';
```

Script 5.6 *continued*

```
85   unset($dog);
86   echo '<p>After tragedy strikes, I now
     → have ' . Pet::getCount() . ' pet(s).
     → </p>';
87
88   // Pygmy Marmosets are so cute:
89   $pygmymarmoset =
     → new PygmyMarmoset('Toodles');
90   echo '<p>After creating a Pygmy
     → Marmoset, I now have ' .
     → Pet::getCount() . ' pet(s).</p>';
91
92   // Delete the objects:
93   unset($cat, $ferret, $pygmymarmoset);
94
95   ?>
96   </body>
97   </html>
```

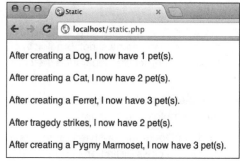

After creating a Dog, I now have 1 pet(s).

After creating a Cat, I now have 2 pet(s).

After creating a Ferret, I now have 3 pet(s).

After tragedy strikes, I now have 2 pet(s).

After creating a Pygmy Marmoset, I now have 3 pet(s).

B As the **Pet** class contains a static attribute, it can be used to count the number of objects created from derived classes.

When a **Dog** (or any other subclass) object is destroyed (here using **unset()**), the **Pet** destructor is invoked, subtracting 1 from **$_count**. (Again, the **Pet** destructor is called because no derived class has its own destructor.)

11. Recover by getting another pet:

```
$pygmymarmoset =
→ new PygmyMarmoset('Toodles');

echo '<p>After creating a
→ Pygmy Marmoset, I now have ' .
→ Pet::getCount() . ' pet(s).</p>';
```

12. Complete the page:

```
unset($cat, $ferret,
$pygmymarmoset);

?>

</body>

</html>
```

13. Save the file as **static.php**, place it in your Web directory, and test in your Web browser **B**.

TIP If you did want to have overridden constructors and destructors in the derived classes in this example (Cat, Dog, et al.), you would need them to call the Pet constructor and destructor in order to properly manage the page count. You would do so by adding parent::__construct() and parent::__destruct() to them.

TIP Static methods are almost always public because they can't be called through an object.

TIP Static attributes and methods are also sometimes called *class attributes* and *class methods* (indicating they are meant to be accessed by referencing the class itself, not through an object).

TIP The special variable $this, which always refers to the current object, is not available inside a static method, because static methods are meant to be invoked without using an object.

Review and Pursue

If you have any problems with these sections, either in answering the questions or pursuing your own endeavors, turn to the book's supporting forum (**www.Larry Ullman.com/forums/**).

Review

- What is *inheritance*? How do you implement inheritance in PHP code? (See page 152.)

- What is *polymorphism*? (See page 151.)

- What does it mean to *override* a method? How do you do that? (See page 161.)

- What is *access control* or visibility? What are the three levels of visibility and what do they mean? (See page 165.)

- What is the *scope resolution operator*? What are some of its uses? (See page 172.)

- What is a *static class attribute*? How do you reference a static class attribute within a class? What is a *static class method*? How do you invoke a static class method? (See pages 176 and 177.)

Pursue

- In situations where a class is both defined and used in the same script, break it into two (or more) scripts, separating the class definitions from their usage.

- Complete the UML diagrams for any of the examples in this chapter.

- Add phpDocumentor-style comments to any of the class definitions and scripts in this chapter.

- Once you've become comfortable with more advanced OOP, look into the subject of *overloading* a method.

6

More Advanced OOP

The previous chapter explored some advanced OOP concepts, with a particular emphasis on those related to inheritance. In this chapter, you'll learn even more advanced OOP concepts, including some introduced in more recent versions of PHP. Tip: make sure you know what version of PHP you're working with before proceeding.

The topics in this chapter get to be more esoteric, and won't always be necessary in a Web application, but these concepts should be on your radar as you become more comfortable with OOP as a programming approach. As with the past two chapters, a fair amount of OOP theory will be covered as well.

Abstract Classes and Methods

In some situations where inheritance applies, it would never be appropriate to create an instance of a parent class. For instance, in the **Pet** example, the intention would be to create a specific subclass for each pet type and never really create an object of type **Pet**. In such cases, it would be more appropriate to define an *abstract base class*, instead of a standard base class.

Abstract classes are template versions of a parent class. By defining an abstract class, you can indicate the general behavior that subclasses should have. Put another way, an abstract class defines the *interfaces*: how derived classes of this base type are to be used. The subclasses are then responsible for defining the actual *implementations* of those interfaces.

Abstract classes differ from normal classes in that attempting to create an object of an abstract class's type results in a fatal error . Instead, abstract classes are meant to be extended, and then you create an instance of that extended class.

This approach starts with the keyword **abstract**:

```
abstract class ClassName {

}
```

Abstract classes normally have abstract methods. These are defined like so:

```
abstract function methodName();
abstract function methodName
→ ($var1, $var2);
```

Fatal error: Cannot instantiate abstract class Shape in /Users/larryullman/Sites/phpvqp3/abstract.php on line **15**

Ⓐ The fatal error created by trying to make an object of an abstract class.

That's it! You do not define the functionality of the method; instead, that functionality will be determined by the class that extends the abstract class. If you want to add visibility to the definition, add the corresponding keyword after the word abstract:

```
abstract public function
→ methodName();
```

Here is how part of **Pet** might look:

```
abstract class Pet {
    protected $_name;
    abstract public function
    → getName();
}
```

Then **Cat** would contain

```
class Cat extends Pet {
    function getName() {
        return $this->_name;
    }
}
```

Note that the implementation of the abstract method in the extended class—e.g., **Cat::getName()**—must abide by the same visibility or weaker. If the abstract function is public, the extended version must also be public. If the abstract function is protected, then the extended version can only be protected or public. You would never make an abstract method private, since a private method cannot be inherited. In all cases, the implemented version of the method must also have the same number of arguments as the abstract definition (i.e., the same signature).

Note that if a class has even one abstract method, the class itself must be abstract. However, an abstract class can have non-abstract methods, as well as attributes, all of which would also be inherited by the derived class.

To put this into action, let's return to geometry examples, like **Rectangle**. That class could be an extension of a more generic **Shape** class ⑧. Let's institute the **Shape** abstract class and a child, **Triangle**.

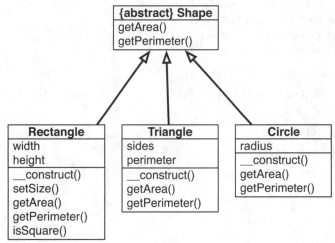

⑧ The abstract **Shape** class can be the parent to many types of (two-dimensional) shapes.

To create abstract classes and methods:

1. Begin a new PHP script in your text editor or IDE, to be named **Shape.php** (**Script 6.1**):

   `<?php # Script 6.1 - Shape.php`

2. Start defining the **Shape** class:

   `abstract class Shape {`

   Remember that when a class is abstract, it means you'll never create an object of that type. Hence, you wouldn't make an abstract **Rectangle** class because you do need to occasionally make rectangles.

3. Define the first abstract method:

   `abstract protected function`
   `→ getArea();`

   This line says that any class that extends **Shape** needs to define a **getArea()** method. Furthermore, this method should not take any arguments and have either public or protected visibility (the same visibility or weaker). Defining this as an abstract method makes sense, as every two-dimensional shape should have the ability to calculate its own area (three-dimensional shapes have volumes, not areas).

4. Define the second abstract method:

   `abstract protected function`
   `→ getPerimeter();`

5. Complete the class:

   `} // End of Shape class.`

6. Save the file as **Shape.php** and place it in your Web directory.

To create the Triangle class:

1. Begin a new PHP script in your text editor or IDE, to be named **Triangle.php** (**Script 6.2**):

   `<?php # Script 6.2 - Triangle.php`

2. Begin declaring the **Triangle** class:

   `class Triangle extends Shape {`

continues on page 188

Script 6.1 The abstract **Shape** class, with two abstract methods, will be the template for more specific shapes, like **Triangle** (Script 6.2).

```
1    <?php # Script 6.1 - Shape.php
2    /* This page defines the Shape abstract
class.
3     * The class contains no attributes.
4     * The class contains two abstract
methods:
5     * - getArea()
6     * - getPerimeter()
7     */
8
9    abstract class Shape {
10       // No attributes to declare.
11       // No constructor or destructor
defined here.
12
13       // Method to calculate and return the
area.
14       abstract protected function
getArea();
15
16       // Method to calculate and return the
perimeter.
17       abstract protected function
getPerimeter();
18
19   } // End of Shape class.
```

Script 6.2 The **Triangle** class is an extension of **Shape**. It is therefore responsible for defining how the getArea() and getPerimeter() methods work.

```php
1    <?php # Script 6.2 - Triangle.php
2    /*  This page defines the Triangle class.
3     *  The class contains two attributes:
4     *  - private $_sides (array)
5     *  - private $_perimeter (number)
6     *  The class contains three methods:
7     *  - __construct()
8     *  - getArea()
9     *  - getPerimeter()
10   */
11
12   class Triangle extends Shape {
13
14      // Declare the attributes:
15      private $_sides = array();
16      private $_perimeter = NULL;
17
18      // Constructor:
19      function __construct($s0 = 0, $s1 = 0, $s2 = 0) {
20
21         // Store the values in the array:
22         $this->_sides[] = $s0;
23         $this->_sides[] = $s1;
24         $this->_sides[] = $s2;
25
26         // Calculate the perimeter:
27         $this->_perimeter = array_sum($this->_sides);
28
29      } // End of constructor.
30
31      // Method to calculate and return the area:
32      public function getArea() {
33
34         // Calculate and return the area:
35         return (SQRT(
36         ($this->_perimeter/2) *
37         (($this->_perimeter/2) - $this->_sides[0]) *
38         (($this->_perimeter/2) - $this->_sides[1]) *
39         (($this->_perimeter/2) - $this->_sides[2])
40         ));
41
42      } // End of getArea() method.
43
44      // Method to return the perimeter:
45      public function getPerimeter() {
46         return $this->_perimeter;
47      } // End of getPerimeter() method.
48
49   } // End of Triangle class.
```

3. Declare the attributes:

```
private $_sides = array();

private $_perimeter = NULL;
```

The first attribute will store the size of the three sides (alternatively, you could make three separate variables). The second variable will store the perimeter. I'm only adding this attribute because the perimeter will be used in calculating the area (a lot), so it's nice to have it in a variable instead of retrieving it through a method call.

All the attributes are **private**, as they shouldn't be accessed outside of any class and I can't imagine how a **Triangle** class would be inherited (in which case they may need to be **protected**).

4. Define the constructor:

```
function __construct($s0 =
 0, $s1 = 0, $s2 = 0) {
  $this->_sides[] = $s0;
  $this->_sides[] = $s1;
  $this->_sides[] = $s2;
  $this->_perimeter =
   array_sum($this->_sides);
}
```

The constructor takes three arguments for the three sides of the triangle. Those values are placed in the **$_sides** array, and then the perimeter is calculated. The **array_sum()** function adds up all the values of all the elements in an array.

5. Create the **getArea()** method:

```
public function getArea() {
  return (SQRT(
  ($this->_perimeter/2) *
  (($this->_perimeter/2) -
   $this->_sides[0]) *
  (($this->_perimeter/2) -
   $this->_sides[1]) *
  (($this->_perimeter/2)
- $this->_sides[2])
  ));
}
```

If you remember your geometry, you know that the area of a triangle is equal to one-half the base times the height **C**. Of course, to make that calculation, the class would need to determine the base (the longest side, not a problem) and the height (requiring trigonometry, yikes!). So instead I'll use the formula in **D**. This code implements that formula in PHP.

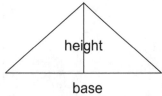

C To calculate the area of a triangle the easy way, you would need to know the height value.

$$\text{area} = \sqrt{z\,(z - a)\,(z - b)\,(z - c)}$$

D Heron's Formula says that the area of a triangle is equal to the square root of z times z minus a times z minus b times z minus c, where z is half the perimeter and a, b, and c are the three sides. (And no, I didn't know this offhand; Mr. Friendly Internet helped out.)

Script 6.3 This script makes an object of type **Triangle**, which is derived from the abstract **Shape** class.

```
1   <!doctype html>
2   <html lang="en">
3   <head>
4       <meta charset="utf-8">
5       <title>Triangle</title>
6       <link rel="stylesheet"
        → href="style.css">
7   </head>
8   <body>
9   <?php # Script 6.3 - abstract.php
10  // This page uses the Triangle class
    → (Script 6.2), which is derived from
    → Shape (Script 6.1).
11
12  // Load the class definitions:
13  require('Shape.php');
14  require('Triangle.php');
15
16  // Set the triangle's sides:
17  $side1 = 5;
18  $side2 = 10;
19  $side3 = 13;
20
21  // Print a little introduction:
22  echo "<h2>With sides of $side1, $side2,
    → and $side3...</h2>";
23
24  // Create a new triangle:
25  $t = new Triangle($side1, $side2,
    → $side3);
26
27  // Print the area.
28  echo '<p>The area of the triangle
    → is ' . $t->getArea() . '</p>';
29
30  // Print the perimeter.
31  echo '<p>The perimeter of the triangle
    → is ' . $t->getPerimeter() . '</p>';
32
33  // Delete the object:
34  unset($t);
35
36  ?>
37  </body>
38  </html>
```

6. Create the **getPerimeter()** method:

```
public function getPerimeter() {
    return $this->_perimeter;
} // End of getPerimeter() method.
```

This is the second of the abstract methods in **Shape** that must be implemented here. For this example, it simply returns the perimeter attribute. Had I not created a perimeter attribute, this method would instead return **array_sum($this->_sides)**.

7. Complete the class:

```
} // End of Triangle class.
```

8. Save the file as **Triangle.php** and place it in your Web directory.

To use the Triangle class:

1. Begin a new PHP script in your text editor or IDE, to be named **abstract.php**, starting with the HTML (**Script 6.3**):

```
<!doctype html>
<html lang="en">
<head>
    <meta charset="utf-8">
    <title>Triangle</title>
    <link rel="stylesheet"
    → href="style.css">
</head>
<body>
<?php # Script 6.3 - abstract.php
```

2. Load the class definitions:

```
require('Shape.php');
require('Triangle.php');
```

continues on next page

3. Set the sides of the triangle:

```
$side1 = 5;
$side2 = 10;
$side3 = 13;
```

Technically, a valid triangle abides by a certain rule regarding the three sides: the sum of any two sides has to be greater than the third side (I seriously brushed up on my geometry skills for this).

4. Print an introduction and create a new triangle:

```
echo "<h2>With sides of $side1,
→ $side2, and $side3...</h2>";

$t = new Triangle($side1, $side2,
→ $side3);
```

5. Print the area:

```
echo '<p>The area of the triangle
→ is ' . $t->getArea() . '</p>';
```

This code is much like the **Square** and **Rectangle** examples already demonstrated (usage redundancy is a hallmark of OOP).

6. Print the perimeter:

```
echo '<p>The perimeter of the
→ triangle is ' .
→ $t->getPerimeter() . '</p>';
```

7. Complete the page:

```
unset($t);

?>

</body>

</html>
```

8. Save the file as **abstract.php**, place it in your Web directory, and test in your Web browser **E**.

TIP In UML, a class is marked as abstract by either italicizing its name, or by placing *{abstract}* next to its name **B**.

TIP Arguably, you could have Triangle.php include Shape.php.

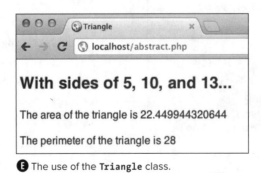

E The use of the **Triangle** class.

Interfaces

Similar to the abstract class is an *interface*. Interfaces, like abstract classes, identify the functionality (i.e., the methods) that must be defined by a specific class.

To create an interface, use the `interface` keyword. Then, within the curly brackets, define the method *signatures*, not their actual implementation:

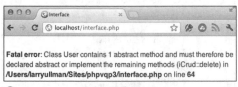

Fatal error: Class User contains 1 abstract method and must therefore be declared abstract or implement the remaining methods (iCrud::delete) in /Users/larryullman/Sites/phpvqp3/interface.php on line 64

Ⓐ The fatal error created by having a class implement an interface without implementing all of the interface's methods.

```
interface iSomething {
    public function someFunction($var);
}
```

(Conventionally, interface names often begin with a lowercase i, but this is not required.)

Note that *all methods in an interface must be public*. Also, interfaces only identify methods; they never include attributes.

To associate a class with an interface, use the `implements` operator in the class definition:

```
class Someclass implements
→ iSomething {}
```

The class must then define all of the methods listed in the interface, or a fatal error will occur **Ⓐ**.

Abstract Class vs. Interface

The difference between an interface and an abstract class may seem subtle. Remember that an abstract class is meant to be extended by a more specific class, of which you'll probably create an object instance. As you've already seen, an abstract class might define a generic object, such as a shape.

Conversely, an interface is not inherited by a class, so you should not think of an interface as a way of loosely defining an entire object. Instead, an interface establishes a *contract* for the functionality that a class must have, regardless of the class type. For example, in Chapter 8, "Using Existing Classes," you'll learn about the **Iterator** interface defined within the Standard PHP Library (SPL). The **Iterator** interface dictates the methods that must exist in a class in order for PHP to be able to loop through an instance of that class.

Another way of distinguishing between abstract classes and interfaces is that abstract classes still have an "is a" relationship with the derived class. Interfaces do not have "is a" relationships with derived classes, although you could say that the derived class has a "has the same behaviors as" relationship with an interface.

In the next example, let's create an interface for standard *CRUD* functionality. The acronym CRUD refers to the ability to *Create, Read, Update,* and *Delete* data—the four basic actions required for many different types of content used in sites and applications. Any class you use in an application that requires CRUD functionality could then implement this interface, whether it's a **User**, **Page**, or **Rectangle**.

To use interfaces:

1. Begin a new PHP script in your text editor or IDE, to be named **interface.php**, starting with the HTML (**Script 6.4**):

```
<!doctype html>
<html lang="en">
<head>
  <meta charset="utf-8">
  <title>Interface</title>
  <link rel="stylesheet"
  → href="style.css">
</head>
<body>
<?php # Script 6.4 - interface.php
```

For simplicity's sake, this one script will define and use an interface and class.

2. Declare the **iCrud** interface:

```
interface iCrud {
  public function create($data);
  public function read();
  public function update($data);
  public function delete();
}
```

The **iCrud** interface identifies four necessary methods. Two of the methods expect to take data as their lone argument. The other two methods take no arguments. You'll see in a usage of this interface how this plays out. All the methods are public, which is required.

continues on page 194

Script 6.4 The **iCrud** interface dictates the methods that must exist for a class to have full CRUD functionality.

```
1    <!doctype html>
2    <html lang="en">
3    <head>
4      <meta charset="utf-8">
5      <title>Interface</title>
6      <link rel="stylesheet"
     → href="style.css">
7    </head>
8    <body>
9    <?php # Script 6.4 - interface.php
10   // This page defines and uses the iCrud
     → interface.
11
12   /* The iCrud interface.
13    * The interface identifies four
     → methods:
14    * - create()
15    * - read()
16    * - update()
17    * - delete()
18   */
19   interface iCrud {
20     public function create($data);
21     public function read();
22     public function update($data);
23     public function delete();
24   }
25
26   /* The User class implements the iCrud
     → interface.
27    * The class contains two attributes:
28    * - private $_userId
29    * - private $_username
30    * The class contains the four interface
     → methods, plus a constructor.
31   */
32   class User implements iCrud {
33
34     private $_userId = NULL;
35     private $_username = NULL;
36
37     // Constructor takes an array of data:
38     function __construct($data) {
39       $this->_userId = uniqid();
40       $this->_username =
       → $data['username'];
41     } // End of constructor.
42
```

```
43      // This method also takes an array of data:
44      function create($data) {
45          self::__construct($data);
46      }
47
48      // Function for returning information about the current object:
49      function read() {
50          return array('userId' => $this->_userId, 'username' => $this->_username);
51      }
52
53      // Function for updating the current object:
54      function update($data) {
55          $this->_username = $data['username'];
56      }
57
58      // Function for getting rid of the current object:
59      public function delete() {
60          $this->_username = NULL;
61          $this->_userId = NULL;
62      }
63
64  } // End of User class.
65
66  // Identify the user information:
67  $user = array('username' => 'trout');
68
69  // Print a little introduction:
70  echo "<h2>Creating a New User</h2>";
71
72  // Create a new User:
73  $me = new User($user);
74
75  // Get the user's ID:
76  $info = $me->read();
77  echo "<p>The user ID is {$info['userId']}.</p>";
78
79  // Change the user's name:
80  $me->update(array('username' => 'troutster'));
81
82  // Confirm the updated name:
83  $info = $me->read();
84  echo "<p>The user name is now {$info['username']}.</p>";
85
86  // Delete the record:
87  $me->delete();
88
89  // Delete the object:
90  unset($me);
91
92  ?>
93  </body>
94  </html>
```

3. Begin defining the **User** class:

```
class User implements iCrud {
    private $_userId = NULL;
    private $_username = NULL;
```

The **User** class implements **iCrud**, which means it must define the four methods identified in the interface. To demonstrate this concept, without overwhelming you with code, I'm going to define just two attributes in the class, both of which will be private.

4. Define the constructor:

```
function __construct($data) {
    $this->_userId = uniqid();
    $this->_username =
    → $data['username'];
} // End of constructor.
```

The constructor is going to take an array of data as its lone argument. It will use this data to assign values to the internal private variables. Logically, you'd want to add some validation to the provided data here, too.

The constructor also creates a unique user ID value by invoking the PHP **uniqid()** function.

In a real-world application, the constructor might instead create a new user record in a database and assign the automatically generated primary key value to the internal attribute.

5. Define the **create()** method:

```
function create($data) {
    self::__construct($data);
}
```

By implementing the **iCrud** interface, this class is forced to have a **create()** method that takes a single argument. However, the constructor already does what's required to create a new object of this type, so this method can just call the constructor (using the keyword **self**, which refers to the current class, plus the scope resolution operator), passing along the provided data.

This method would be used in situations where a new **User** object is created (perhaps thereby creating a new record in the database) and later reused to create a new record.

6. Define the **read()** method:

```
function read() {
    return array('userId' =>
    → $this->_userId, 'username' =>
    → $this->_username);
}
```

The **read()** method takes no arguments and returns an array of information. In this hypothetical example, the information is represented by internal variables. In a real-world application, the **read()** method might fetch the associated information from the database, using the internal, private ID value to know which record to fetch.

7. Define the **update()** method:

```
function update($data) {
    $this->_username =
    →$data['username'];
}
```

Presumably, the user ID value cannot be updated, so the **update()** method as written only updates a single internal attribute. Again, you'd want to use proper validation here, instead of assuming that **$data['username']** exists.

8. Define the **delete()** method and complete the class:

```
public function delete() {
    $this->_username = NULL;
    $this->_userId = NULL;
}
} // End of User class.
```

The **delete()** method clears out the values of the attributes. In a real-world example, it might delete the corresponding record from the database instead.

9. Create a new **User** object:

```
$user = array('username' =>
→'trout');
echo "<h2>Creating a New User
→</h2>";
$me = new User($user);
```

To make the interface more useful, two of its methods expect to receive a single argument, which would be an array of data. If the **User** class also stored an email address and password, those would be represented in this one array, too.

10. Get the user's ID:

```
$info = $me->read();
echo "<p>The user ID is
→{$info['userId']}.</p>";
```

The **read()** method fetches the object's information, returned as an array.

11. Change the user's name and then confirm the change:

```
$me->update(array('username' =>
→'troutster'));
$info = $me->read();
echo "<p>The user name is now
→{$info['username']}.</p>";
```

12. Delete the record:

```
$me->delete();
```

Note that this line does not get rid of the **User** object. It only clears out the internally stored values.

continues on next page

13. Complete the page:

```php
unset($me);
?>
</body>
</html>
```

14. Save the file as **interface.php**, place it in your Web directory, and test in your Web browser **B**.

Creating a New User

The user ID is 4fe0e3883ec8f.

The user name is now troutster.

B The output from using a **User** object that implements the **iCrud** interface.

TIP *Interface* is a word with multiple meanings. Generically, interface refers to the kinds of information about classes and methods reflected by a UML diagram. In other words, an interface explains how a class or method is used. Alternatively, interface can refer to a contract that a class can be bound to, as in this section of the chapter.

TIP Another benefit that interfaces have over using abstract classes and inheritance is that classes in PHP cannot inherit from multiple parents. Classes, however, can implement multiple interfaces by separating each by a comma:

```php
class SomeClass implements iA, iB {
```

TIP The `instanceof` operator can also be used to test if a class implements an interface.

TIP In UML, an interface is indicated by prefacing its name with <<interface>> **C**.

TIP In UML, to indicate that a class implements an interface, draw a dashed arrow from the class to the interface (so that the arrow is pointing to the interface).

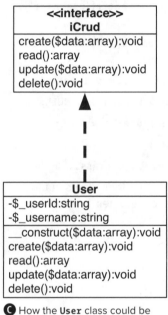

```
        <<interface>>
           iCrud
  create($data:array):void
  read():array
  update($data:array):void
  delete():void
```

```
              User
  -$_userId:string
  -$_username:string
  __construct($data:array):void
  create($data:array):void
  read():array
  update($data:array):void
  delete():void
```

C How the **User** class could be modeled.

Copying and Cloning Objects

In PHP 5, when you create a copy of an object, PHP actually creates a new reference to that object, not an entirely new object. In other words, both variables will point to the same thing, and changes made through one object will be reflected by the other:

```php
$a = new SomeClass();

$a->val = 1;

$b = $a;

$b->val = 2;

echo $a->val; // 2
```

More formally put, this means that *PHP assigns objects by reference*, not by value. PHP does this for performance reasons, as having multiple copies of entire objects, when not needed, is expensive.

If you actually want two separate, individual objects, you need to create a *clone*:

```php
$a = new SomeClass();

$a->val = 1;

$b = clone $a; // Separate objects!

$b->val = 2;

echo $a->val; // 1
```

When the clone operator is used, PHP will perform what's called a "shallow copy." If you want to change how a clone of an object is made, you can define a `__clone()` method within the class. That method would be called whenever a clone is made, and would handle the cloning as you see fit. See the PHP manual for details.

Traits

New to PHP 5.4 is support for *traits*. Traits are used to solve a problem in OOP languages such as PHP that only allow for single inheritance. For example, say you're designing a Web site that has several different classes: **User**, **Page**, **ContactForm**, etc. While you're developing the Web site, it'll help to have a debugging tool that will print out information about a given object, regardless of its type:

```php
function dumpObject() {

    // Print out the information.

}
```

You could add this definition to each class, but that'd be unnecessarily redundant (and a hurdle to overcome should you want to change the definition). Normally, when you have a method that would be needed in multiple classes, inheritance is the solution. However, in PHP each class can only inherit from a single parent class, and there is no common parent class that each of them would have. The solution, then, is traits. *Traits allow you to add functionality to a class without using inheritance*.

To create a trait, use the **trait** keyword, followed by the name and definition:

```php
trait tSomeTrait {

    // Attributes

    function someFunction() {

        // Do whatever.

    }

}
```

(Stylistically, you could begin your trait with a lowercase "t," but that is not required.)

Like an abstract class and an interface, traits cannot be instantiated (i.e., you can't make an object from a trait). Instead, you add a trait to a class via the **use** keyword *inside* the class definition:

```
class SomeClass {

    use tSomeTrait;

    // Rest of class.

}
```

Just as including an external PHP script makes that script's code usable in the current one, adding a **use TraitName** statement makes that trait's code available to the class.

Now, when you create an object of type **SomeClass**, that object has a **someFunction()** method:

```
$obj = new SomeClass();

$obj->someFunction();
```

In this next example, let's implement the debugging trait example and use it with a class. In doing so, I'm going to use three PHP functions not previously mentioned but that are virtually self-explanatory.

To use traits:

1. Begin a new PHP script in your text editor or IDE, to be named **tDebug.php** (Script 6.5):

   ```
   <?php # Script 6.5 - tDebug.php
   ```

   For this example, one script will define the trait itself. Another script will create an object that uses the trait.

2. Begin defining the trait:

   ```
   trait tDebug {
   ```

   That's all there is to it! The name of the trait is *tDebug*.

Script 6.5 The **tDebug** trait defines a useful **dumpObject()** method that can help in debugging any object type.

```
1   <?php # Script 6.5 - tDebug.php
2   // This page defines the tDebug trait.
3
4   /*  The tDebug trait.
5    *  The trait defines one method:
      → dumpObject():
6    */
7   trait tDebug {
8
9       // Method dumps out a lot of data
         → about the current object:
10      public function dumpObject() {
11
12          // Get the class name:
13          $class = get_class($this);
14
15          // Get the attributes:
16          $attributes =
             → get_object_vars($this);
17
18          // Get the methods:
19          $methods =
             → get_class_methods($this);
20
21          // Print a heading:
22          echo "<h2>Information about the
             → $class object</h2>";
23
24          // Print the attributes:
25          echo '<h3>Attributes</h3><ul>';
26          foreach ($attributes as $k => $v) {
27              echo "<li>$k: $v</li>";
28          }
29          echo '</li></ul>';
30
31          // Print the methods:
32          echo '<h3>Methods</h3><ul>';
33          foreach ($methods as $v) {
34              echo "<li>$v</li>";
35          }
36          echo '</li></ul>';
37
38      } // End of dumpObject() method.
39
40  } // End of tDebug trait.
```

3. Begin defining the **dumpObject()** method:

```
public function dumpObject() {
    $class = get_class($this);
```

The method will take no arguments but will consistently refer to **$this**, which always represents the current object.

The first thing this method does is find the class name of the current object. That's possible by invoking the **get_class()** function, providing it with the object whose class name you're trying to determine.

4. Get the object's attributes and methods:

```
$attributes =
→ get_object_vars($this);
$methods =
→ get_class_methods($this);
```

These are the other two new functions I'm using in this trait. The first gets the attributes for a given object: both the attribute names and their respective values. The second function retrieves the methods defined in the associated class. There is no **get_object_methods()** function, which is why the two have slightly different names.

5. Print a heading:

```
echo "<h2>Information about the
→ $class object</h2>";
```

This debugging method is going to be heavy on the amount of HTML it outputs, but that shouldn't be a problem as it's for debugging purposes only. And, of course, you can edit the output as needed.

6. Print the attributes:

```
echo '<h3>Attributes</h3><ul>';
foreach ($attributes as $k => $v) {
    echo "<li>$k: $v</li>";
}
echo '</li></ul>';
```

The **foreach** loop will run through the array of attributes (even if there is only one attribute, **$attributes** will still be an array). Within the loop, each attribute name and value is printed within a list.

7. Print the methods:

```
echo '<h3>Methods</h3><ul>';
foreach ($methods as $v) {
    echo "<li>$v</li>";
}
echo '</li></ul>';
```

This is a replication of the code in Step 6, although the methods don't have values to be printed.

8. Complete the method and the trait:

```
    } // End of dumpObject() method.
} // End of tDebug trait.
```

9. Save the file as **tDebug.php** and place it in your Web directory.

To use the tDebug trait:

1. Open **Rectangle.php** (Script 4.5) in your text editor or IDE.

   By design, you can use the trait with any class.

2. Within the class definition, add in the trait (**Script 6.6**):

   ```
   use tDebug;
   ```

   That's all there is to it!

3. Save the file as **Rectangle.php** and place it in your Web directory.

Interfaces vs. Traits

Traits may seem a lot like interfaces, but the two are effectively opposite approaches. An interface enforces stricter programming, ensuring that classes are designed to implement specific methods. Conversely, a trait makes methods available to a class that the class itself does not define.

As I mention in the introduction to the topic, traits can be useful in solving the occasional OOP design problem. But traits can also be mistakenly used to provide an easy solution to a problem best solved in other ways (such as rethinking your inheritance tree). Well-written traits should also avoid making assumptions about the classes that will use them.

Script 6.6 This updated version of the **Rectangle** class makes use of the **tDebug** trait.

```
1    <?php # Script 6.6 - Rectangle.php
2    /*  This page defines the Rectangle
     → class.
3     *  The class contains two attributes:
     → width and height.
4     *  The class contains five methods:
5     *  - __construct()
6     *  - setSize()
7     *  - getArea()
8     *  - getPerimeter()
9     *  - isSquare()
10   */
11
12   class Rectangle {
13
14       // Use the debug trait:
15       use tDebug;
16
17       // Declare the attributes:
18       public $width = 0;
19       public $height = 0;
20
21       // Constructor:
22       function __construct($w = 0, $h = 0) {
23           $this->width = $w;
24           $this->height = $h;
25       }
26
27       // Method to set the dimensions:
28       function setSize($w = 0, $h = 0) {
29           $this->width = $w;
30           $this->height = $h;
31       }
32
33       // Method to calculate and return
         → the area:
34       function getArea() {
35           return ($this->width *
             → $this->height);
36       }
37
38       // Method to calculate and return
         → the perimeter:
39       function getPerimeter() {
40           return ( ( $this->width +
             → $this->height) * 2 );
41       }
42
```

script continues on next page

Script 6.6 *continued*

```
43      // Method to determine if the
        → rectangle
44      // is also a square.
45      function isSquare() {
46          if ($this->width == $this->height)
        {
47              return true; // Square
48          } else {
49              return false; // Not a square
50          }
51
52      }
53
54  } // End of Rectangle class.
```

Script 6.7 This script prints out debugging information about a **Rectangle** object, made possible by the class's use of the **tDebug** trait (Script 6.6).

```
1   <!doctype html>
2   <html lang="en">
3   <head>
4       <meta charset="utf-8">
5       <title>Trait</title>
6       <link rel="stylesheet"
        → href="style.css">
7   </head>
8   <body>
9   <?php # Script 6.7 - trait.php
10  // This page uses the tDebug trait
    → through the Rectangle object.
11
12  // Include the trait definition:
13  require('tDebug.php');
14
15  // Include the class definition:
16  require('Rectangle.php');
17
18  // Create a new object:
19  $r = new Rectangle(42, 37);
20
21  // Dump the information:
22  $r->dumpObject();
23
24  // Delete the object:
25  unset($r);
26
27  ?>
28  </body>
29  </html>
```

To use the new Rectangle class:

1. Begin a new PHP script in your text editor or IDE, to be named **trait.php**, starting with the HTML (**Script 6.7**):

   <!doctype html>

   <html lang="en">

   <head>

      <meta charset="utf-8">

      <title>Trait</title>

      <link rel="stylesheet"
   → **href="style.css">**

   </head>

   <body>

   <?php # Script 6.7 - trait.php

2. Load the trait and class definitions:

   require('tDebug.php');

   require('Rectangle.php');

   Because the class references the trait, the two files must be included in this order.

   continues on next page

3. Create and debug an object:

```
$r = new Rectangle(42, 37);

$r->dumpObject();
```

The **Rectangle** class does not define the **dumpObject()** method, but it's available to the object because of the use of the trait.

4. Complete the page:

```
unset($r);

?>

</body>

</html>
```

5. Save the file as **trait.php**, place it in your Web directory, and test in your Web browser **A**.

> **TIP** If you get a parse error when you run this script, it could be because you're not using PHP 5.4 or later, and PHP does not recognize the **trait** keyword.

> **TIP** To incorporate multiple traits into a class, separate each trait by a comma:
>
> ```
> use tTrait1, tTrait2;
> ```

> **TIP** Traits can have abstract methods that must then be implemented by any class that uses the trait.

> **TIP** Again, you could arguably include the tDebug.php script within Rectangle.php instead of the main script.

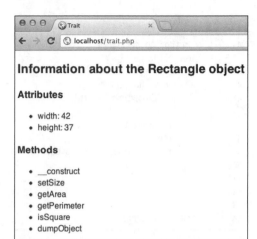

A The output generated by the **dumpObject()** method.

Trait Precedence

If a trait used by a class has a method with the same name as a method in the class, PHP has to decide which method takes precedence (i.e., which one will be executed when that method is called). If the method is defined in the class, that version will take precedence over the trait method. If the method defined in the class is actually inherited from another class, then the trait method takes precedence.

A The error message when an inappropriate type of value is sent to a function that uses type hinting.

Composition

Thus far in the book, the relationship between two classes has been one of simple inheritance: "is a" relationships (e.g., a **Dog** is a type of **Pet**). But inheritance itself is not the cornerstone of OOP; rather *code reuse* is the key concept. Inheritance is just one way you can reuse code. Another way is to implement *composition*.

Composition represents a "has a" relationship, where one class's property values are objects of another class type. For example, **Employee** is not a subtype of **Department** (i.e., a child), but rather a part of a **Department**'s composition.

In UML, composition is indicated by drawing a line with a diamond at one end from the included class (e.g., **Employee**) to the composite class (e.g., **Department**).

Type Hinting

Type hinting is the programming act of indicating what type of value is expected. For example, what type of value a function expects to receive for a parameter.

Type hinting doesn't play much of a role in procedural PHP code because you cannot hint simple types (e.g., integers or strings). But you can hint object types, which is more useful.

To perform type hinting, preface the parameter variable name with the expected class type:

```
class SomeClass {
    function doThis(OtherClass $var) {
    }
}
```

If the argument passed to the **doThis()** method is not of type **OtherClass**, or of a derived subclass, PHP will generate a fatal error **A**:

```
class OtherClass {}
$some = new SomeClass();
$other = new OtherClass();
$some->doThis($other);
$some->doThis($some);
```

For an example of type hinting, this next script will define a **Department** class with an **addEmployee()** method. That method will be used to add a new employee to the list of the department employees. The method will only accept a parameter of type **Employee**.

To use type hinting:

1. Begin a new PHP script in your text editor or IDE, to be named **hinting.php**, starting with the HTML (**Script 6.8**):

```
<!doctype html>

<html lang="en">

<head>

  <meta charset="utf-8">

  <title>Type Hinting</title>

  <link rel="stylesheet"
→ href="style.css">

</head>

<body>

<?php # Script 6.8 - hinting.php
```

2. Begin declaring the **Department** class:

```
class Department {

  private $_name;

  private $_employees;

  function __construct($name) {

    $this->_name = $name;

    $this->_employees = array();

  }
```

The **Department** class has two private attributes: one to store the department name, and the other to store an array of employees in that department. The constructor assigns the value to the private **$_name** variable and then makes **$_employees** an empty array.

Script 6.8 Type hinting is used in this script to restrict the **addEmployee()** method to only accepting arguments of type **Employee**.

```
1    <!doctype html>
2    <html lang="en">
3    <head>
4       <meta charset="utf-8">
5       <title>Type Hinting</title>
6       <link rel="stylesheet"
     → href="style.css">
7    </head>
8    <body>
9    <?php # Script 6.8 - hinting.php
10   //  This page defines and uses the
     → Department and Employee classes.
11
12   # ***** CLASSES ***** #
13
14   /* Class Department.
15    *  The class contains two attribute:
     → name and employees[].
16    *  The class contains two methods:
17    *  - __construct()
18    *  - addEmployee()
19    */
20   class Department {
21      private $_name;
22      private $_employees;
23      function __construct($name) {
24         $this->_name = $name;
25         $this->_employees = array();
26      }
27      function addEmployee(Employee $e) {
28         $this->_employees[] = $e;
29         echo "<p>{$e->getName()} has been
        → added to the {$this->_name}
        → department.</p>";
30      }
31   } // End of Department class.
32
33   /* Class Employee.
34    *  The class contains one attribute:
     → name.
35    *  The class contains two methods:
36    *  - __construct()
37    *  - getName()
38    */
39   class Employee {
40      private $_name;
41      function __construct($name) {
```

script continues on next page

```
42            $this->_name = $name;
43        }
44        function getName() {
45            return $this->_name;
46        }
47    } // End of Employee class.
48
49    # ***** END OF CLASSES ***** #
50
51    // Create a department:
52    $hr = new Department('Human Resources');
53
54    // Create employees:
55    $e1 = new Employee('Jane Doe');
56    $e2 = new Employee('John Doe');
57
58    // Add the employees to the department:
59    $hr->addEmployee($e1);
60    $hr->addEmployee($e2);
61
62    // Delete the objects:
63    unset($hr, $e1, $e2);
64
65    ?>
66    </body>
67    </html>
```

3. Define the **addEmployee()** method and complete the class:

```
function addEmployee(Employee $e) {
    $this->_employees[] = $e;
    echo "<p>{$e->getName()} has
    → been added to the {$this->_
    → name} department.</p>";
}
} // End of Department class.
```

This method will be called to add an employee to the current department object. It takes one argument, which, thanks to type hinting, must be of type **Employee**. If an appropriately typed argument is received, it will be added to the internal, private **$employees** array. For confirmation purposes (and to have the final script output something), verification of the added employee is printed.

Note that because **$e** will be an object of type **Employee**, it can invoke any of the **Employee** methods, such as **getName()**.

4. Define the **Employee** class:

```
class Employee {
    private $_name;
    function __construct($name) {
        $this->_name = $name;
    }
    function getName() {
        return $this->_name;
    }
} // End of Employee class.
```

continues on next page

I'm defining the **Employee** class in a fairly minimal way. Its constructor takes an employee's name as an argument, which will be assigned to its internal private attribute. The **getName()** method is public, and it is the proper way to fetch the name of the employee.

5. Create a **Department**:

   ```
   $hr = new Department('Human
   → Resources');
   ```

6. Create two **Employee** objects:

   ```
   $e1 = new Employee('Jane Doe');
   $e2 = new Employee('John Doe');
   ```

7. Add the employees to the department:

   ```
   $hr->addEmployee($e1);
   $hr->addEmployee($e2);
   ```

   Because these two objects are of type **Employee**, they can be passed to the **addEmployee()** method.

8. Complete the page:

   ```
   unset($hr, $e1, $e2);
   ?>
   </body>
   </html>
   ```

9. Save the file as **hinting.php**, place it in your Web directory, and test in your Web browser 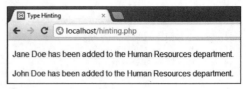.

Ⓑ The script result when the **addEmployee()** method is properly invoked.

TIP The errors triggered when the proper argument type is not submitted Ⓐ are *exceptions*, which means they can be "caught", a more graceful way of handling this problem. This will mean more in Chapter 8.

TIP Type hinting can be used in functions, too (i.e., in non-methods: functions defined outside of any class).

TIP You can also hint for interfaces, arrays (as of PHP 5.1), and functions (i.e., *callables*, as of PHP 5.4).

Namespaces

Added in version 5.3 of PHP is support for *namespaces*. Namespaces provide a solution to a common OOP problem: as you begin utilizing more and more classes, including those defined by other developers and in third-party libraries, conflicts can occur if multiple classes have the same name. Namespaces prevent these conflicts by letting you organize your code into groups. This has the effect of allowing you to safely use descriptive names without concern for conflicts.

An apt analogy (which the PHP manual also uses) is to compare namespaces to creating a directory structure on your computer. You cannot place two files named **functions.php** within the same folder. However, you can place one in the **MyUtilities** folder and another in the **YourUtilities** folder, thereby making both versions of **functions.php** available.

There are limits as to what you can place in a namespace, specifically:

- Classes
- Interfaces
- Functions
- Constants

You couldn't, for example, create a namespace just to hold some variables.

To define a namespace, you'll want to create a new file that will only store the namespaced code. This is both a virtual requirement of PHP and a best design practice. Within that file, you create a namespace by using the **namespace** keyword, followed by the identifier:

```
namespace SomeNamespace;
```

Note that this should be the first line of PHP code in a file, and that the file cannot even have any HTML before that PHP code (although, from a design perspective, you wouldn't want to mix HTML and a namespace anyway). You can have PHP comments before that line, however.

Any code that follows that line will automatically be placed within that namespace:

```
namespace SomeNamespace;

class SomeClass {}
```

Namespaces can have subnamespaces, just as you'd have levels of directories on your computer. To do that, indicate a subnamespace using the backslash:

```
namespace MyUtilities\UserManagement;

class Login {}
```

Once you've defined a namespace, you can reference it by using the backslashes again. First, though, you'd need to include the file that defines the namespace:

```
require('SomeNameSpace.php');
```

then use backslashes to indicate a namespace is being used:

```
$obj = new \SomeNameSpace\SomeClass();
```

Or:

```
require('MyUtilities\User\User.php');
$obj = new \MyUtilities\User\Login();
```

As a stylistic choice, one suggestion is to use your name or organization as the top-level namespace:

```
namespace MyName\Util\User;
```

Another suggestion is that you organize the files themselves using the same structure **A**. This isn't required, but doing so makes a lot of sense, in my mind.

As a practical example of this, let's place the **Directory** and **Employee** classes within a **MyNamespace\Company** namespace.

To use namespaces:

1. Begin a new PHP script in your text editor or IDE, to be named **Company.php** (Script 6.9):

```
<?php # Script 6.9 - Company.php
```

This script will only define a namespace, and it will not contain any HTML.

Script 6.9 The two company-related classes are now defined within their own namespace, which in turn is a subnamespace of **MyNamespace**.

```
1    <?php # Script 6.9 - Company.php
2    // This script defines the Company
     → namespace, with two classes.
3
4    // Declare the namespace:
5    namespace MyNamespace\Company;
6
7    # ***** CLASSES ***** #
8    class Department {
9        private $_name;
10       private $_employees;
11       function __construct($name) {
12           $this->_name = $name;
13           $this->_employees = array();
14       }
15       function addEmployee(Employee $e) {
16           $this->_employees[] = $e;
17           echo "<p>{$e->getName()} has been
             → added to the {$this->_name}
             → department.</p>";
18       }
19   } // End of Department class.
20
21   class Employee {
22       private $_name;
23       function __construct($name) {
24           $this->_name = $name;
25       }
26       function getName() {
27           return $this->_name;
28       }
29   } // End of Employee class.
30
31   # ***** END OF CLASSES ***** #
```

MyName — Geometry

Util — User.php

A A suggested file structure for organizing a library of code.

2. Declare the **MyNamespace\Company** namespace:

```
namespace MyNamespace\Company;
```

The premise here is that all of your reusable code would go into the **MyNamespace** namespace, whose name you would make more unique. Within that entire library, all of the classes and code related to creating company-based projects would go in the **Company** namespace, declared here.

3. Define the **Department** class:

```
class Department {
    private $_name;
    private $_employees;
```

```
    function __construct($name) {
        $this->_name = $name;
        $this->_employees = array();
    }
    function addEmployee(Employee
    → $e) {
        $this->_employees[] = $e;
        echo "<p>{$e->getName()} has
        → been added to the {$this->_
        → name} department.</p>";
    }
} // End of Department class.
```

This is the same code already explained in the type-hinting section.

continues on next page

Design Approaches

Through three chapters, this book has introduced the fundamental, and even the more advanced, concepts and theories when it comes to object-oriented programming in PHP. As with all application development, the key is the underlying design, and that is a skill only really learned through practice. Chapter 8 and Chapter 9, "Example—CMS with OOP," will provide more practice, but here are a few tips in the meantime.

First, by this point in time you probably have a good amount of experience in designing normalized databases. And while the comparison isn't perfect, some aspects of that design process apply to designing classes. In particular, you want to avoid redundancies among your classes, and try to design classes to be as small and specific as possible. Use *inheritance* and *composition* so that multiple classes together fulfill all of the application needs. And, also as with database design, understand that you won't necessarily get it right from the get-go; changes sometimes have to be made after the fact.

Toward that end, however, remember the difference between the *interface*—how a method or class is used—and the *implementation*: what the class or method does internally. A well-designed class or method can have its implementation changed without affecting any code that uses the class, as the interface should remain unchanged.

Similarly, classes, even in a complex application, should be *loosely coupled*. This means that classes should be written so they are not too strongly dependent on the design or functionality of another class.

Finally, be in the habit of using constructors that guarantee the generated object is in a safe state to be used. This means initializing internal attributes and performing any necessary setup.

4. Define the **Employee** class:

```
class Employee {
  private $_name;
  function __construct($name) {
    $this->_name = $name;
  }
  function getName() {
    return $this->_name;
  }
} // End of Employee class.
```

Again, no changes here.

5. Save the file as **Company.php**, and then place it in your Web directory within a **MyNamespace/Company** directory.

To use the namespace class:

1. Begin a new PHP script in your text editor or IDE, to be named **namespace.php**, starting with the HTML (**Script 6.10**):

```
<!doctype html>
<html lang="en">
<head>
  <meta charset="utf-8">
  <title>Namespace</title>
  <link rel="stylesheet"
  → href="style.css">
</head>
<body>
<?php # Script 6.10 - namespace.php
```

2. Include the namespace file:

```
require('MyNamespace/Company/
→ Company.php');
```

If you did not use the directory structure recommended in Step 5 of the previous sequence, change the path accordingly.

Script 6.10 This variation on Script 6.8 references two classes defined within a namespace.

```
1   <!doctype html>
2   <html lang="en">
3   <head>
4     <meta charset="utf-8">
5     <title>Namespace</title>
6     <link rel="stylesheet"
      → href="style.css">
7   </head>
8   <body>
9   <?php # Script 6.10 - namespace.php
10  //  This page defines and uses the
    → Department and Employee classes.
11
12  // Include the PHP script:
13  require('MyNamespace/Company/
    → Company.php');
14
15  // Create a department:
16  $hr = new \MyNamespace\Company\
    → Department('Accounting');
17
18  // Create employees:
19  $e1 = new \MyNamespace\Company\
    → Employee('Holden Caulfield');
20  $e2 = new \MyNamespace\Company\
    → Employee('Jane Gallagher');
21
22  // Add the employees to the department:
23  $hr->addEmployee($e1);
24  $hr->addEmployee($e2);
25
26  // Delete the objects:
27  unset($hr, $e1, $e2);
28
29  ?>
30  </body>
31  </html>
```

3. Create a **Department** object:

```
$hr = new \MyNamespace\Company\
→ Department('Accounting');
```

This is the same code used in the type hinting example, although now a full namespace reference to the **Department** class is used.

4. Create two employees:

```
$e1 = new \MyNamespace\Company\
→ Employee('Holden Caulfield');
```

```
$e2 = new \MyNamespace\Company\
→ Employee('Jane Gallagher');
```

Again, the references to the **Employee** class just need to include the full namespace, starting with a backslash.

5. Add the employees to the department:

```
$hr->addEmployee($e1);
```

```
$hr->addEmployee($e2);
```

6. Complete the page:

```
unset($hr, $e1, $e2);
```

```
?>
```

```
</body>
```

```
</html>
```

7. Save the file as **namespace.php**, place it in your Web directory, and test in your Web browser **B**.

TIP You can use the same namespace in multiple files, which will allow you to put multiple classes, each defined in separate scripts, within the same namespace.

TIP Technically, the namespace keyword can come after one particular line of PHP code: a `declare()` statement.

TIP You can define multiple namespaces within a single file, but I recommend against doing so.

TIP The `__NAMESPACE__` constant represents the current namespace.

TIP PHP allows you to more quickly reference a namespace by bringing it into current scope via the `use` keyword:

```
use MyNamespace\Company;
```

Having done that, you can now create an object by just referencing classes within the Company namespace:

```
$obj = new Department();
```

I tend to avoid these kinds of heavy-handed approaches, though, as the purpose of namespaces is to be specific.

TIP The PHP manual goes into a lot of detail about how namespaces are resolved considering various *scopes*. If you begin using namespaces on a regular basis, read through that section of the PHP manual.

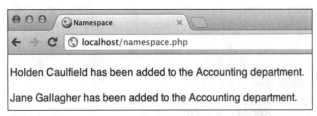

B The output is more or less the same as in the previous script, although the underlying code is now better organized thanks to namespaces.

Review and Pursue

If you have any problems with these sections, either in answering the questions or pursuing your own endeavors, turn to the book's supporting forum (**www.Larry Ullman.com/forums/**).

Review

- What is an *abstract class*? How do you create and use one? (See page 184.)

- What is an *abstract method*? How do you create and use one? (See pages 184 and 185.)

- When a class inherits an abstract method, what visibility can the subclass assign to that method? (See page 185.)

- What is an *interface*? How do you create one? How do you use one? (See page 191.)

- What visibility must interface methods have? (See page 191.)

- What is a *trait*? How do you create one? How do you use one? (See page 197.)

- What is *type hinting*? How do you perform type hinting? (See page 203.)

- What are *namespaces*? Why are they useful? How do you crate a namespace? How do you reference namespaced code? (See page 207.)

Pursue

- In situations where a class, interface, or trait is both defined and used in the same script, break it into two (or more) scripts, separating the definitions from their usage.

- Complete the UML diagrams for any of the examples in this chapter.

- Add phpDocumentor-style comments to any of the definitions and scripts in this chapter.

- Implement **Pet** as an abstract class.

- Create other classes such as **Circle** and **Rectangle** that extend **Shape**.

- If you want more practice, create abstract **Shape2D** and **Shape3D** classes. Then extend these in logical directions, including new classes like **Sphere**.

- Flesh out the **User** class used in the interface example, adding other attributes (such as email address and password) and methods (such as login and logout).

- Rewrite the **User** class so that it interacts with a database instead of using internal attributes. Hint: Keep only the **$_userId** attribute and have it store the associated primary key value.

- Test out the **tDebug** trait on other object types.

- Flesh out the **Department** and **Employee** classes.

- Check out the PHP manual's documentation for more on namespaces.

- Look up cloning in the PHP manual.

7

Design Patterns

Once you begin regularly programming using objects, it's not too long before you encounter the subject of *design patterns*. A design pattern is, simply put, a recommended best practice for solving a particular problem. In other words, if you're trying to figure out how to implement such-and-such functionality, then use this design pattern as your approach.

This chapter introduces the concept of design patterns and walks you through four commonly used ones. Be forewarned that design patterns can be rather abstract, especially if the entire subject of OOP is still new to you.

In This Chapter

Understanding Design Patterns

In the introduction, I state that a design pattern is a best practice for solving a particular problem. Before getting into some actual patterns, let's look at what this definition means in more detail.

You may be surprised to learn that the first important book on design patterns was not a programming book at all, but one on architecture and city planning: *A Pattern Language: Towns, Buildings, Construction* by Christopher Alexander, Sara Ishikawa, and Murray Silverstein (Oxford University Press, 1977). This fact goes toward the first design pattern quality to grasp: *design patterns are not specific bits of code* that you can copy and paste as needed. No, design patterns are programming approaches, where the specific code—the implementation of that approach—may change from one situation to the next.

Second, a design pattern doesn't just define a solution, but also the problem the solution is trying to address. One of the hardest things about learning design patterns is understanding which design pattern applies to a given situation.

But a design pattern is not made up of just a problem and a solution, but rather four key pieces:

- Its *name*
- A *discussion of the problem*: under what circumstances you would use the particular pattern
- The *solution*, which is not concrete in terms of code, but provides enough information for you to be able to reliably write the code
- The *consequences*: the pros and cons of the particular pattern

This last piece represents an important aspect of good software design. Identifying the consequences of an approach reflects the fact that while there may be best practices, there is no perfect solution for all possible situations. Understanding not just the problem and solution, but also the consequences will help you know when and if you should use a particular design pattern.

The rest of the chapter will introduce and demonstrate four design patterns. All of these were first defined in the "Gang of Four" book (see the sidebar). Before moving on, however, I want to add that design patterns, like OOP in general, are prone to being overly praised. Design patterns, like OOP, are a great tool to have in your developer toolbox. But neither design patterns nor OOP provides a magic bullet for all possible situations. As with any type of programming, the goal is to select the right tool for the job.

The Gang of Four

The seminal programming book on the subject of design patterns is *Design Patterns: Elements of Reusable Object-Oriented Software*, by Erich Gamma, Richard Helm, Ralph Johnson, and John Vlissides (Addison-Wesley Professional, 1994). You'll see this group of authors referred to as the "Gang of Four," abbreviated as GoF.

The *Design Patterns* book identified 23 patterns, organized into three broad categories: *creational*, *structural*, and *behavioral*. The book primarily uses C++ for its examples, along with Smalltalk, but the whole point of design patterns is that they define *approaches*, regardless of the language in use.

Creational patterns create objects, saving you from having to do so manually in your code. The *Builder*, *Factory*, *Prototype*, and *Singleton* patterns are all creational; Factory and Singleton are covered in this chapter.

Structural patterns assist in the creation and use of complex structures. Examples of structural patterns include *Adapter*, *Bridge*, *Composite* (covered in this chapter), *Decorator*, *Façade*, and *Proxy*.

Behavioral patterns address how objects within a system communicate and how a program's logic flows. The *Command*, *Iterator*, *Observer*, *State*, *Strategy* (covered in this chapter), and *Template Method* patterns are all behavioral.

As a second caveat, entire books have been written on design patterns. This one chapter is meant to be an introduction to the concept—providing what you need to get going. I've selected a range of patterns that will best demonstrate the variety of possible design patterns while sticking to those patterns that are easiest to grasp. I've also forgone the formality of covering each pattern's consequences, as I feel doing so would have just added more words and things for you to think about, thereby making the learning that much harder.

The goal in this chapter is for you to get a handle on what design patterns are, how they are used, and what types of design patterns exist. Once you are comfortable with all that, try learning one new pattern at a time, using the Gang of Four book and online articles as resources. Take copious notes, and try not to move on to another pattern until you fully comprehend the one you are studying.

TIP Some of these examples use additions to PHP's OOP model as recent as PHP 5.3 and PHP 5.4. If you see any weird errors while running an example, it's likely because you're not using a current enough version of PHP.

TIP As is the case with the Normal Forms in database design, you'll see specific design patterns described in slightly different ways, often accenting one aspect of the problem or solution over another. Along with time and practice, it may take reading several different sources before you best comprehend the true heart of a particular pattern: problem and solution.

TIP Being comfortable with design patterns makes project collaboration easier, as design patterns provide a vocabulary for common approaches.

The Singleton Pattern

The Singleton pattern is a creational pattern that will restrict an application to creating only a single instance of a particular class type. For example, a Web site will need a database connectivity object, but should have only one (you'd almost always want all database interactions going through a single connection), so you could use Singleton to enforce that restriction.

In terms of design, it's relatively easy to implement the Singleton pattern **Ⓐ**. For starters, you can use a static attribute to guarantee that only one instance of a particular class exists.

```
class SomeClass {
    static private $_instance = NULL;
}
```

As explained in Chapter 5, "Advanced OOP," because the attribute is static, it's shared by all instances of the class. Taking that idea just one step further, if you store the actual instance in that attribute (i.e., assign an object to it), then all references to this class can use that attribute.

The next step is to create a method that will create an instance of the class if one does not exist and return the instance regardless (assuming the name of the class is **SomeClass**):

```
class SomeClass {
    static private $_instance = NULL;
    static function getInstance() {
        if (self::$_instance == NULL) {
            self::$_instance =
            → new SomeClass();
        }
        return self::$_instance;
    }
}
```

It's common for a Singleton to name this method **getInstance()**. In the method, the conditional checks if the **$_instance** attribute still has a **NULL** value. If so, a new instance is created and assigned to the attribute. Finally, the instance is returned.

Now the class can be used in this manner:

```
$obj1 = SomeClass::getInstance();
```

If this is the first object in the application of that type, the instance will be created, assigned to the internal private attribute, and then returned.

Singleton
-_instance:Singleton
+getInstance():Singleton

Ⓐ The simple UML representation of the Singleton pattern. (See the previous three chapters for more on UML symbols.)

Script 7.1 The `Config` class implements the Singleton pattern so that an entire Web application can make use of the same configuration object.

```php
1    <?php # Script 7.1 - Config.php
2    // This page defines a Config class
   → which uses the Singleton pattern.
3
4    /* The Config class.
5     * The class contains two attributes:
   → $_instance and $settings.
6     * The class contains four methods:
7     * - __construct()
8     * - getInstance()
9     * - set()
10    * - get()
11    */
12   class Config {
13
14       // Store a single instance of
   → this class:
15       static private $_instance = NULL;
16
17       // Store settings:
18       private $_settings = array();
19
20       // Private methods cannot be called:
21       private function __construct() {}
22       private function __clone() {}
23
24       // Method for returning the instance:
25       static function getInstance() {
26           if (self::$_instance == NULL) {
27               self::$_instance = new Config();
28           }
29           return self::$_instance;
30       }
31
32       // Method for defining a setting
   → settings:
33       function set($index, $value) {
34           $this->_settings[$index] = $value;
35       }
36
37       // Method for retrieving a setting:
38       function get($index) {
39           return $this->_settings[$index];
40       }
41
42   } // End of Config class definition.
```

When a second object also calls that code, the *same instance* will be returned:

$obj2 = SomeClass::getInstance();

Now both **$obj1** and **$obj2** refer to the same instance of **ClassName**.

There is one catch, however. If a user tries to create a new object of that class type using **new** or **clone**, you would end up with multiple instances, defeating the purpose of a Singleton. The trick to preventing that from happening is to make a private constructor that does nothing:

private function __construct() {}

Now the following code will trigger an error **B**:

$obj = new ClassName();

Another good use for a Singleton is to create one global object, such as a configuration object used by an entire site. Let's do that in the next series of steps.

To create a Singleton class:

1. Begin a new PHP script in your text editor or IDE, to be named **Config.php** (**Script 7.1**):

   <?php # Script 7.1 - Config.php

2. Start defining the **Config** class:

   class Config {

   Note that this is not an abstract class, as an instance of this class will be created.

   continues on next page

Fatal error: Call to private Config::__construct() from invalid context in
/Users/larryullman/Sites/phpvqp3/singleton.php on line **16**

B Because the class's constructor is private, you cannot use **new** to create an object of this type.

3. Declare the two private attributes:

```
static private $_instance = NULL;
private $_settings = array();
```

The first attribute, **$_instance**, will represent a single instance of the class. The second attribute, **$_settings**, will store all the configuration settings. Both are initialized here.

4. Define a private constructor and a private __clone() method:

```
private function __construct() {}
private function __clone() {}
```

This code prevents the class from being instantiated using **new** or **clone**.

5. Define the **getInstance()** method:

```
static function getInstance() {
    if (self::$_instance == NULL) {
        self::$_instance =
        → new Config();
    }
    return self::$_instance;
}
```

This method is defined using the code already explained.

6. Define the **set()** method:

```
function set($index, $value) {
    $this->_settings[$index] =
    → $value;
}
```

This method takes two arguments: a setting name, or index, and its value. The two arguments are used to manipulate the **$_settings** array.

7. Define the **get()** method:

```
function get($index) {
    return $this->_settings[$index];
}
```

The **get()** method is used to return a current setting. After reading Chapter 8, "Using Existing Classes," you'd likely want to have this method *throw an exception* should the function not be provided with an index that matches a previously stored value.

8. Complete the class:

```
} // End of Config class
→ definition.
```

9. Save the file as **Config.php** and place it in your Web directory.

To use the Config class:

1. Begin a new PHP script in your text editor or IDE, to be named **singleton.php**, starting with the HTML (**Script 7.2**):

```
<!doctype html>
<html lang="en">
<head>
    <meta charset="utf-8">
    <title>Singleton</title>
    <link rel="stylesheet"
    → href="style.css">
</head>
<body>
<h2>Using a Singleton Config
→ Object</h2>
<?php # Script 7.2 - singleton.php
```

2. Load the class definition:

```
require('Config.php');
```

C Both variables refer to the same, lone class instance, thanks to the Singleton pattern.

Script 7.2 Thanks to the Singleton pattern, multiple variables will always reference the same object.

```
1    <!doctype html>
2    <html lang="en">
3    <head>
4       <meta charset="utf-8">
5       <title>Singleton</title>
6       <link rel="stylesheet"
        → href="style.css">
7    </head>
8    <body>
9    <h2>Using a Singleton Config Object</h2>
10   <?php # Script 7.2 - singleton.php
11   // This page uses the Config class
       → (Script 7.1).
12
13   // Load the class definition:
14   require('Config.php');
15
16   // Create the object:
17   $CONFIG = Config::getInstance();
18
19   // Set some value:
20   $CONFIG->set('live', 'true');
21
22   // Confirm the current value:
23   echo '<p>$CONFIG["live"]: ' .
       → $CONFIG->get('live') . '</p>';
24
25   // Create a second object to confirm:
26   $TEST = Config::getInstance();
27   echo '<p>$TEST["live"]: ' .
       → $TEST->get('live') . '</p>';
28
29   // Delete the objects:
30   unset($CONFIG, $TEST);
31
32   ?>
33   </body>
34   </html>
```

3. Create a **Config** instance:

`$CONFIG = Config::getInstance();`

Remember that an instance is obtained through the static **getInstance()** method.

Frequently, an object which is a Singleton instance uses all capital letters (like a constant) for its name, although this is not required.

4. Establish a setting:

`$CONFIG->set('live', 'true');`

At this point, **$CONFIG** is an object of **Config** type, usable like any other object.

5. Print the setting's value:

`echo '<p>$CONFIG["live"]: ' .`
`→ $CONFIG->get('live') . '</p>';`

6. Create another configuration object and confirm the set value:

`$TEST = Config::getInstance();`

`echo '<p>$TEST["live"]: ' .`
`→ $TEST->get('live') . '</p>';`

7. Complete the page:

`unset($CONFIG, $TEST);`

`?>`

`</body>`

`</html>`

8. Save the file as **singleton.php**, place it in your Web directory, and test in your Web browser **C**.

TIP In theory, code outside of any class could regulate the number of class instances. However, since you're using OOP, and a single instance is a requirement of a class, it'd be best to design that functionality in the class.

The Factory Pattern

The Factory pattern is another creation pattern, like Singleton. But unlike Singleton, which creates and manages a single object of a single class type, the Factory pattern is used to manufacture potentially multiple objects of many different class types.

Of course, you already know how to create objects of a specific type:

`$obj = SomeClass();`

So why would you need a Factory to do that for you?

The Factory pattern becomes useful in situations where the type of object that needs to be generated isn't known when the program is written but only once the program is running. In very dynamic applications, this can often be the case.

Another clue for when the Factory pattern might be appropriate is when there's an abstract base class, and different derived subclasses will need to be created on the fly. This particular design structure is important with the Factory pattern, as once you've created the object, regardless of its specific type, the use of that object will be consistent.

The Factory pattern works via a static method, conventionally named **Create()**,

`factory()`, `factoryMethod()`, or `createInstance()`. The method takes at least one argument, which indicates the type of object to create. The method then returns an object of that type **A**:

```
static function Create($type) {
    // Validate $type.
    return new SomeClassType();
}
```

That's the basic idea. Let's see how this will be implemented in the following example, which will create a different type of **Shape** based on input provided to the page through the URL. This example will use the **Shape**, **Rectangle**, and **Triangle** classes from Chapter 6, "More Advanced OOP." You will need to copy those to the same directory as the following files. Also, you can either also copy over the **tDebug.php** file, or remove that trait reference from the **Rectangle** class (see Chapter 6).

To create a Factory:

1. Begin a new PHP script in your text editor or IDE, to be named **ShapeFactory.php** (Script 7.3):

   ```
   <?php # Script 7.3 -
   → ShapeFactory.php
   ```

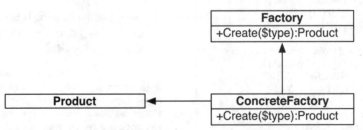

A In the Factory pattern, the abstract Factory base class is extended by concrete Factory classes that will output objects of that class type (aka, products).

2. Start defining the **ShapeFactory** class:

```
abstract class ShapeFactory {
```

The Factory class will be abstract, just as **Shape** itself is. You'll never create an instance of the **ShapeFactory** class.

The class has no attributes.

3. Start defining the static method:

```
static function Create($type,
 array $sizes) {
```

This static method will take two arguments: the type of shape to create and an array of sizes. For a rectangle, that array would contain two values; for a triangle, three; and for a circle, only one (the radius).

Type hinting is used to enforce the requirement that **$sizes** be an array.

4. Create a different object based on the type value:

```
switch ($type) {
  case 'rectangle':
    return new Rectangle
     ($sizes[0], $sizes[1]);
    break;
  case 'triangle':
    return new Triangle($sizes[0],
     $sizes[1], $sizes[2]);
    break;
} // End of switch.
```

The switch checks the value of **$type** against the expected values. For now, just these two **Shape** types are recognized.

continues on next page

Script 7.3 The **ShapeFactory** class generates different **Shape**-derived objects on the fly.

```
1   <?php # Script 7.3 - ShapeFactory.php
2   // This page defines a ShapeFactory class which uses the Factory pattern.
3
4   /* The ShapeFactory class.
5    * The class contains no attributes.
6    * The class contains one method: Create().
7    */
8   abstract class ShapeFactory {
9
10     // Static method that creates objects:
11     static function Create($type, array $sizes) {
12
13        // Determine the object type based upon the parameters received.
14        switch ($type) {
15           case 'rectangle':
16              return new Rectangle($sizes[0], $sizes[1]);
17              break;
18           case 'triangle':
19              return new Triangle($sizes[0], $sizes[1], $sizes[2]);
20              break;
21        } // End of switch.
22
23     } // End of Create() method.
24
25  } // End of ShapeFactory class.
```

Again, a more complete version of this class would throw an exception if improper values were provided.

5. Complete the method and the class:

```
    } // End of Create() method.
} // End of ShapeFactory class.
```

6. Save the file as **ShapeFactory.php** and place it in your Web directory.

To use the ShapeFactory class:

1. Begin a new PHP script in your text editor or IDE, to be named **factory.php**, starting with the HTML (**Script 7.4**):

```
<!doctype html>
<html lang="en">
<head>
    <meta charset="utf-8">
    <title>Factory</title>
    <link rel="stylesheet"
    → href="style.css">
</head>
<body>
<?php # Script 7.4 - factory.php
```

2. Load the class definitions:

```
require('ShapeFactory.php');
require('Shape.php');
require('Triangle.php');
require('Rectangle.php');
```

This script needs access to any possible **Shape**-derived class that might be used, as well as the **Shape** class definition itself, and **ShapeFactory**.

In the next chapter, you'll learn how to establish an autoloader, so that the required class files can be included only when needed.

3. Perform some minimal validation:

```
if (isset($_GET['shape'],
→ $_GET['dimensions'])) {
```

To make this example shorter, I've forgone the HTML form that the user might fill out to create different shapes and will just take values straight from the URL. The URL needs to include both a *shape* value and a *dimensions* value.

4. Create the object:

```
$obj = ShapeFactory::Create
→ ($_GET['shape'],
→ $_GET['dimensions']);
```

To create the object, the static method of the **ShapeFactory** class is invoked, passing it the values that came from the URL.

In a more realized version of this script, I'd add error handling here to confirm that the shape object was created before attempting to use it in the following steps.

5. Print an introduction:

```
echo "<h2>Creating a
→ {$_GET['shape']}...</h2>";
```

6. Print the area:

```
echo '<p>The area is ' .
→ $obj->getArea() . '</p>';
```

As **$obj** is now some sort of **Shape**-based object, you know it has a **getArea()** method that can be called.

7. Print the perimeter:

```
echo '<p>The perimeter is ' .
→ $obj->getPerimeter() . '</p>';
```

continues on page 224

```php
1    <!doctype html>
2    <html lang="en">
3    <head>
4       <meta charset="utf-8">
5       <title>Factory</title>
6       <link rel="stylesheet" href="style.css">
7    </head>
8    <body>
9    <?php # Script 7.4 - factory.php
10   // This page uses the ShapeFactory class (Script 7.2).
11
12   // Load the class definitions:
13   require('ShapeFactory.php');
14   require('Shape.php');
15   require('Triangle.php');
16   require('Rectangle.php');
17
18   // Minimal validation:
19   if (isset($_GET['shape'], $_GET['dimensions'])) {
20
21      // Create the new object:
22      $obj = ShapeFactory::Create($_GET['shape'], $_GET['dimensions']);
23
24      // Print a little introduction:
25      echo "<h2>Creating a {$_GET['shape']}...</h2>";
26
27      // Print the area:
28      echo '<p>The area is ' . $obj->getArea() . '</p>';
29
30      // Print the perimeter:
31      echo '<p>The perimeter is ' . $obj->getPerimeter() . '</p>';
32
33   } else {
34      echo '<p class="error">Please provide a shape type and size.</p>';
35   }
36
37   // Delete the object:
38   unset($obj);
39
40   ?>
41   </body>
42   </html>
```

8. Complete the minimal validation:

```
} else {
    echo '<p class="error">
    →Please provide a shape type
    →and size.</p>';
}
```

9. Complete the page:

```
unset($obj);

?>

</body>

</html>
```

10. Save the file as **factory.php**, place it in your Web directory, along with the other class files, and test in your Web browser **B**.

You'll need to use a URL like **factory.php?shape=rectangle& dimensions[]=10&dimensions[]=14**.

11. Provide new parameters in the URL and retest in your Web browser **C**.

TIP The Factory pattern is also meant to be easily extendible (i.e., supporting new classes as they are defined).

TIP One of the consequences of using the Factory pattern is that the Factory class is very tightly coupled with the rest of the application, due to its internal validation. You can see this in the `ShapeFactory Create()` method, which makes assumptions about the incoming `$sizes` array.

TIP A variation on the Factory pattern is Abstract Factory. Whereas the Factory pattern outputs different objects, all derived from the same parent, the Abstract Factory outputs *other factories*.

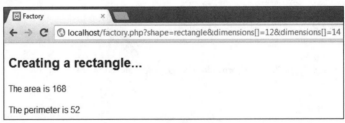

B Based on values passed in the URL, this script reports the area and perimeter of a rectangle.

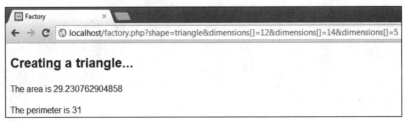

C Just changing the URL parameters, without touching the underlying code, now reports on a triangle.

The Composite Pattern

The Singleton and Factory patterns are *creational*: used to generate one or more objects. Another category of patterns is *structural*. These patterns apply in situations where a nontraditional class structure, or a modification of an existing class structure, is required. For an example of a structural pattern, I want to introduce Composite.

The focus in Chapter 5 is on inheritance as a way of basing one class definition on another. In Chapter 6, I talk about *composition*, which is another design approach. The composition explained there involves one class type (e.g., **Department**) being composed of other class types (e.g., **Employee**s), which will commonly happen. Similarly, the Composite pattern applies in situations where you have an object that might represent a single entity or a composite entity, but still needs to be usable in the same manner.

For example, an HTML form contains one or more form elements. From a programming perspective, certain behaviors will apply to both the entire form and its individual components:

- Display
- Validate
- Show errors

Addressing these needs without using patterns would require that you replicate a lot of code in two different classes (i.e., **Form** and **FormElement**). And, as you should know by now, replication makes for bad programming. The solution to this problem is to apply Composite so that the entire form or just an individual component can be treated the same. For example, you could show errors on the form or on a single element; you could validate the entire form at once or just a single element (e.g., validate the availability of a username via Ajax).

Another sign that the Composite pattern may apply is when you're working with a tree-like structure. For example, the whole form is the root of the tree, and the different form elements would be the branches (often called "leaves" in Composite jargon).

To implement the Composite pattern, you'll normally start with an abstract base class that will be extended by the different subclasses. The base class needs to identify the methods for adding and removing "leaves" (or composite items). The base class also needs to identify any functionality that the composite, or its subelements, needs to do:

```
abstract class FormComponent {
    abstract function add
    → (FormComponent $obj);
    abstract function remove
    → (FormComponent $obj);
    abstract function display();
    abstract function validate();
    abstract function showError();
}
```

As you can see, the abstract class here is also using type hinting (see Chapter 6). The first two methods are key to Composite. The other three represent the specific functionality needed by this particular example.

Each subclass now inherits from this derived class. By definition, each must also define the implementation of the abstract methods. Here's a partial example:

```php
class Form extends FormComponent {
   private $_elements = array();
   function add(FormComponent $obj) {
      $this->_elements[] = $obj;
   }
   function display() {
      // Display the entire form.
   }
}
class FormElement extends
→ FormComponent {
   function add(FormComponent $obj) {
      return $obj; // Or false.
   }
   function display() {
      // Display the element.
   }
}
```

As you can see in that code, the **Form** class implements a true **add()** method, which allows you to add elements to a form:

```php
$form = new Form();
$email = new FormElement();
$form->add($email);
```

Note that the **FormElement** class still has to define the **add()** method, but the method shouldn't do anything, because you don't add subelements to that class type. Instead, such add methods will conventionally return the object that's being added, or false, or throw an exception.

With these class definitions, you can now treat entire forms or individual form elements in the same manner.

To demonstrate another implementation of the Composite pattern, let's create a variation on the **Department-Employee** example. Here, there will be two types of work units: employees and teams, with the latter being made up of employees. Jobs to be done can be assigned to, and completed by, either.

To create a Composite design:

1. Begin a new PHP script in your text editor or IDE, to be named **WorkUnit.php** (**Script 7.5**):

   ```php
   <?php # Script 7.5 - WorkUnit.php
   ```

2. Start defining the **WorkUnit** class:

   ```php
   abstract class WorkUnit {
   ```

   Again, this is an abstract class, because you won't create objects of this class type.

3. Declare two protected attributes:

   ```php
   protected $tasks = array();
   protected $name = NULL;
   ```

   These two attributes will be used by any class that extends this one. The first attribute stores the jobs to be done. The second stores the name of the current object, be it a team or an employee.

4. Define the constructor:

   ```php
   function __construct($name) {
      $this->name = $name;
   }
   ```

   The constructor is not abstract; it's fully implemented and assigns the name of the team or employee to the protected attribute.

continues on page 229

Script 7.5 The **WorkUnit** abstract class is extended by two concrete classes to implement the Composite pattern.

```php
1    <?php # Script 7.5 - WorkUnit.php
2    // This page defines a WorkUnit class which uses the Composite pattern.
3    // This page also defines Team and Employee classes, which extend WorkUnit.
4
5    /* The WorkUnit class.
6     * The class contains two attributes: $tasks and $name.
7     * The class contains five methods: __construct(), getName(), add(), remove(), assignTask(),
     → and completeTask().
8     */
9    abstract class WorkUnit {
10
11       // For storing work to be done:
12       protected $tasks = array();
13
14       // For storing the employee or team name:
15       protected $name = NULL;
16
17       // Constructor assigns the name:
18       function __construct($name) {
19          $this->name = $name;
20       }
21
22       // Method that returns the name:
23       function getName() {
24          return $this->name;
25       }
26
27       // Abstract functions to be implemented:
28       abstract function add(Employee $e);
29       abstract function remove(Employee $e);
30       abstract function assignTask($task);
31       abstract function completeTask($task);
32
33    } // End of WorkUnit class.
34
35    /* The Team class extends WorkUnit.
36     * The class has one new attribute: $_employees.
37     * The class has one new method: getCount().
38     */
39    class Team extends WorkUnit {
40
41       // For storing team members:
42       private $_employees = array();
43
44       // Implement the abstract methods...
45       function add(Employee $e) {
46          $this->_employees[] = $e;
47          echo "<p>{$e->getName()} has been added to team {$this->getName()}.</p>";
48       }
```

script continues on next page

```
49        function remove(Employee $e) {
50            $index = array_search($e, $this->_employees);
51            unset($this->_employees[$index]);
52            echo "<p>{$e->getName()} has been removed from team {$this->getName()}.</p>";
53        }
54        function assignTask($task) {
55            $this->tasks[] = $task;
56            echo "<p>A new task has been assigned to team {$this->getName()}. It should be easy to
    → do with {$this->getCount()} team member(s).</p>";
57        }
58         function completeTask($task) {
59             $index = array_search($task, $this->tasks);
60             unset($this->tasks[$index]);
61             echo "<p>The '$task' task has been completed by team {$this->getName()}.</p>";
62         }
63
64        // Method for returning the number of team members:
65        function getCount() {
66            return count($this->_employees);
67        }
68
69    } // End of Team class.
70
71    /* The Employee class extends WorkUnit.
72     * The class has no new attributes or methods.
73     */
74    class Employee extends WorkUnit {
75
76        // Empty functions:
77        function add(Employee $e) {
78            return false;
79        }
80        function remove(Employee $e) {
81            return false;
82        }
83
84        // Implement the abstract methods...
85        function assignTask($task) {
86            $this->tasks[] = $task;
87            echo "<p>A new task has been assigned to {$this->getName()}. It will be done by
    → {$this->getName()} alone.</p>";
88        }
89        function completeTask($task) {
90            $index = array_search($task, $this->tasks);
91            unset($this->tasks[$index]);
92            echo "<p>The '$task' task has been completed by employee {$this->getName()}.</p>";
93        }
94
95    } // End of Employee class.
```

5. Define the **getName()** method:

```
function getName() {
    return $this->name;
}
```

This method is just a "getter" for the **$name** attribute. I created this method only for better output in the final script (i.e., to be able to see which employee or team is doing what), but it is not inherent to the Composite pattern approach.

6. Identify the abstract methods:

```
abstract function add
→ (Employee $e);

abstract function remove
→ (Employee $e);

abstract function assignTask
→ ($task);

abstract function completeTask
→ ($task);
```

For this example, I'm defining four abstract methods. Two are required by Composite: one for adding composite pieces (i.e., employees) and one for removing them. The other two methods are unique to this example and demonstrate the functionality that both specific classes can do.

7. Complete the class:

```
} // End of WorkUnit class.
```

8. Start defining the **Team** class:

```
class Team extends WorkUnit {
    private $_employees = array();
```

The **Team** class extends **WorkUnit**, meaning that it inherits the constructor and **getName()** methods, as well as the two protected attributes. It adds a new attribute, which will store the "leaves."

9. Implement the **add()** method:

```
function add(Employee $e) {
    $this->_employees[] = $e;
    echo "<p>{$e->getName()}
→ has been added to team
→ {$this->getName()}.</p>";
}
```

This method will be used to add composite members to the class. It uses type hinting to expect an **Employee** object, which is then added to the internal array. So that the script has something to show, a message reports the name of the employee added to the team.

10. Implement the **remove()** method:

```
function remove(Employee $e) {
    $index = array_search($e,
    → $this->_employees);
    unset($this->_employees[$index]);
    echo "<p>{$e->getName()}
→ has been removed from team
→ {$this->getName()}.</p>";
}
```

This method is for removing team members from the composite object. To do so, the index must first be found for the employee being removed. Then this element is unset from the array. In a more fleshed-out class, I'd check that **$index** has a positive value first.

Again, a message indicates what's happening.

continues on next page

11. Define the **assignTask()** method:

```
function assignTask($task) {
    $this->tasks[] = $task;
    echo "<p>A new task has
    → been assigned to team
    → {$this->getName()}. It should
    → be easy to do with
    → {$this->getCount()} team
    → member(s).</p>";
}
```

Here, a new job is added to the ongoing list of responsibilities for the team. A message indicates that the task has been added, and shows how many employees (i.e., members of this team) will be available to work on the task.

12. Define the **completeTask()** method:

```
function completeTask($task) {
    $index = array_search($task,
    → $this->tasks);
    unset($this->tasks[$index]);
    echo "<p>The '$task' task
    → has been completed by team
    → {$this->getName()}.</p>";
}
```

This method is similar to **remove()**, this time removing completed tasks.

13. Define the **getCount()** method and complete the class:

```
function getCount() {
    return count
    → ($this->_employees);
}
} // End of Team class.
```

This method simply returns the number of employees in the team.

14. Begin defining the **Employee** class:

```
class Employee extends WorkUnit {
    function add(Employee $e) {
        return false;
    }
    function remove(Employee $e) {
        return false;
    }
```

The **Employee** class also extends **WorkUnit**, so it must define the **add()** and **remove()** methods, even if both just return false.

15. Implement the two remaining abstract methods:

```
function assignTask($task) {
    $this->tasks[] = $task;
    echo "<p>A new task has been
    → assigned to {$this->getName()}.
    → It will be done by
    → {$this->getName()} alone.</p>";
}
function completeTask($task) {
    $index = array_search($task,
    → $this->tasks);
    unset($this->tasks[$index]);
    echo "<p>The '$task' task has
    → been completed by employee
    → {$this->getName()}.</p>";
}
```

These two methods work similarly to those in **Team**, with a couple of employee-specific changes.

16. Complete the class:

```
} // End of Employee class.
```

17. Save the file as **WorkUnit.php** and place it in your Web directory.

```
1    <!doctype html>
2    <html lang="en">
3    <head>
4       <meta charset="utf-8">
5       <title>Composite</title>
6       <link rel="stylesheet"
       → href="style.css">
7    </head>
8    <body>
9    <h2>Using Composite</h2>
10   <?php # Script 7.6 - composite.php
11   // This page uses the WorkUnit, Team,
       → and Employee classes (Script 7.5).
12
13   // Load the class definition:
14   require('WorkUnit.php');
15
16   // Create the objects:
17   $alpha = new Team('Alpha');
18   $john = new Employee('John');
19   $cynthia = new Employee('Cynthia');
20   $rashid = new Employee('Rashid');
21
22   // Assign employees to the team:
23   $alpha->add($john);
24   $alpha->add($rashid);
25
26   // Assign tasks:
27   $alpha->assignTask('Do something great.');
28   $cynthia->assignTask('Do something
       → grand.');
29
30   // Complete a task:
31   $alpha->completeTask('Do something
       → great.');
32
33   // Remove a team member:
34   $alpha->remove($john);
35
36   // Delete the objects:
37   unset($alpha, $john, $cynthia, $rashid);
38   ?>
39   </body>
40   </html>
```

To use the Composite classes:

1. Begin a new PHP script in your text editor or IDE, to be named **composite.php**, starting with the HTML (**Script 7.6**):

   ```
   <!doctype html>

   <html lang="en">

   <head>

      <meta charset="utf-8">

      <title>Composite</title>

      <link rel="stylesheet"
    → href="style.css">

   </head>

   <body>

   <h2>Using Composite</h2>

   <?php # Script 7.6 - composite.php
   ```

2. Load the class definition:

   ```
   require('WorkUnit.php');
   ```

3. Create the objects:

   ```
   $alpha = new Team('Alpha');

   $john = new Employee('John');

   $cynthia = new Employee
    → ('Cynthia');

   $rashid = new Employee('Rashid');
   ```

   Here are four different objects: one **Team** and three **Employee**s.

4. Assign employees to the team:

   ```
   $alpha->add($john);

   $alpha->add($rashid);
   ```

continues on next page

5. Assign tasks:

```
$alpha->assignTask('Do something
→ great.');
```

```
$cynthia->assignTask('Do something
→ grand.');
```

Because **WorkUnit** uses the **Composite** pattern, all four objects can be treated the same from this point forward.

6. Complete a task and remove a team member:

```
$alpha->completeTask('Do something
→ great.');
```

```
$alpha->remove($john);
```

This is just a test of the functionality of the class.

7. Complete the page:

```
unset($alpha, $john, $cynthia,
→ $rashid);
```

```
?>
```

```
</body>
```

```
</html>
```

8. Save the file as **composite.php**, place it in your Web directory, and test in your Web browser **A**.

TIP The Visitor pattern, which allows for operations across structures, is often used in conjunction with Composite.

TIP This example could be extended so that teams could be made up of employees or other teams.

TIP Another way of implementing this example using the Composite pattern would be to focus on the tasks. New tasks could be treated individually, or created as steps in other tasks. Then an individual task or a group of tasks could be assigned to work units.

Antipatterns

In learning about design patterns, you'll often come across the term *antipattern*. A design pattern is a best practice; an antipattern is, therefore, an example of what we know did not work. As any developer comes to know, you learn as much, if not more, from your failures as from your successes.

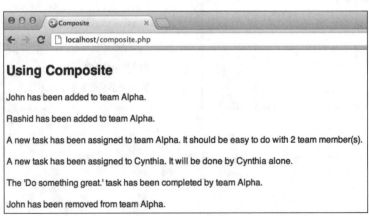

A The Composite pattern allows one class type to be used like another, even if one is composed of the other class type.

The Strategy Pattern

The final pattern example to be explained in this chapter, Strategy, is a type of *behavioral* pattern. Behavioral patterns are used to address how an application runs. As a comparison, the Factory pattern can change the *object type* on the fly, but the Strategy pattern can change an *algorithm* on the fly (an algorithm just being a process or set of code used to perform a calculation or solve a problem). Strategy is most useful in situations where you have classes that may be similar, but not related, and differ only in their specific behavior.

For example, say you need a filtering system for strings. Different filters might include:

- Stripping out HTML
- Crossing out swear words
- Catching character combinations that can be used to send spam through contact forms and the like

The only quality that these three approaches have in common is that they're all applied to strings. Other than that, there are no commonalities that might suggest they'd make sense as derived subclasses from a common base class.

Furthermore, these filters might be applied differently on the fly. For example, an application switch might indicate whether or not HTML or swear words are allowed in text. This, then, is a good candidate for the Strategy pattern.

First, start by defining an interface that dictates the needed functionality:

```
interface Filter {
    function filter($str);
}
```

(For a refresher on interfaces, see Chapter 6.)

Specific filter types then implement their specific versions of the interface's method:

```
class HtmlFilter implements Filter {
    function filter($str) {
        // Strip out the HTML.
        return $str;
    }
}
class SwearFilter implements Filter {
    function filter($str) {
        // Cross out swear words.
        return $str;
    }
}
```

Finally, another class would be written that could use any filter 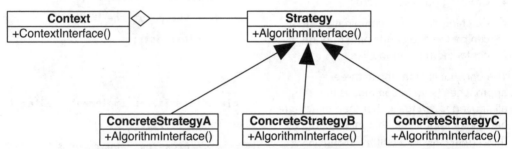:

```
class FormData {
    private $_data = NULL;
    function __construct($input) {
        $this->_data = $input;
    }
    function process(Filter $type) {
        $this->_data =
        → $type->filter($this->_data);
    }
}
```

In that code, the **process()** method expects to receive an object of type **Filter** through which the data would then be run.

And here's how you would use this:

```
$form = new FormData($someUserInput);
if (/* No HTML allowed. */) {
    $form->process(new HtmlFilter());
}
if (/* No swear words allowed. */) {
    $form->process(new SwearFilter());
}
```

As an alternative use of Strategy, let's take the multidimensional sort example from Chapter 1, "Advanced PHP Techniques," and implement it using objects. To make the algorithms as reusable as possible, each algorithm will take constructor arguments to more finely tune its behavior.

A In the Strategy pattern, an interface is extended by more concrete classes, which in turn are used by a specific object (the Context).

Script 7.7 The **iSort** interface is implemented by
two classes in order to create different sorting
algorithms.

```
1    <?php # Script 7.7 - iSort.php
2    // This page defines an iSort interface
     → and two classes.
3    // This page implements the Strategy
     → pattern.
4
5    // The Sort interface defines the sort()
     → method:
6    interface iSort {
7        function sort(array $list);
8    }
9
10   // The MultiAlphaSort sorts a
     → multidimensional array alphabetically.
11   class MultiAlphaSort implements iSort {
12
13       // How to sort:
14       private $_order;
15
16       // Sort index:
17       private $_index;
18
19       // Constructor sets the sort index
         → and order:
20       function __construct($index, $order =
         → 'ascending') {
21           $this->_index = $index;
22           $this->_order = $order;
23       }
24
25       // Function does the actual sorting:
26       function sort(array $list) {
27
28           // Change the algorithm to match
             → the sort preference:
29           if ($this->_order == 'ascending') {
30               uasort($list, array($this,
                 → 'ascSort'));
31           } else {
32               uasort($list, array($this,
                 → 'descSort'));
33           }
34
35           // Return the sorted list:
36           return $list;
37
```

script continues on next page

To create a Strategy design:

1. Begin a new PHP script in your text
   editor or IDE, to be named **iSort.php**
   (Script 7.7):

   `<?php # Script 7.7 - iSort.php`

2. Define the **iSort** interface:

   ```
   interface iSort {
       function sort(array $list);
   }
   ```

   This interface is very simple, requiring only a single method: **sort()**. That
   method takes an array as its lone argument and will return the sorted version
   of the array (although the return value is
   not indicated in the interface).

3. Begin defining the **MultiAlphaSort** class:

   ```
   class MultiAlphaSort implements
   → iSort {
       private $_order;
       private $_index;
   ```

   The **MultiAlphaSort** class implements
   iSort, per the Strategy design. The
   class has two private attributes, both of
   which will customize how the sort works.

   I've chosen to name this *MultiAlphaSort*
   to indicate that it's used to perform alphabetical sorts of multidimensional arrays.
   Another sort class might perform alphabetical sorts of one-dimensional arrays.

   continues on page 237

```
38      }// End of sort() method.
39
40      // Functions that compares two values:
41      function ascSort($x, $y) {
42          return strcasecmp($x[$this->_index], $y[$this->_index]);
43      }
44      function descSort($x, $y) {
45          return strcasecmp($y[$this->_index], $x[$this->_index]);
46      }
47
48  } // End of MultiAlphaSort class.
49
50  // The MultiNumberSort sorts a multidimensional array numerically.
51  class MultiNumberSort implements iSort {
52
53      // How to sort:
54      private $_order;
55
56      // Sort index:
57      private $_index;
58
59      // Constructor sets the sort index and order:
60      function __construct($index, $order = 'ascending') {
61          $this->_index = $index;
62          $this->_order = $order;
63      }
64
65      // Function does the actual sorting:
66      function sort(array $list) {
67
68          // Change the algorithm to match the sort preference:
69          if ($this->_order == 'ascending') {
70              uasort($list, array($this, 'ascSort'));
71          } else {
72              uasort($list, array($this, 'descSort'));
73          }
74
75          // Return the sorted list:
76          return $list;
77
78      }// End of sort() method.
79
80      // Functions that compares two values:
81      function ascSort($x, $y) {
82          return ($x[$this->_index] > $y[$this->_index]);
83      }
84      function descSort($x, $y) {
85          return ($x[$this->_index] < $y[$this->_index]);
86      }
87
88  } // End of MultiNumberSort class.
```

4. Define the constructor:

```
function __construct($index,
→ $order = 'ascending') {

  $this->_index = $index;

  $this->_order = $order;

}
```

When a new object of this type is created, the sort order and index—the element in the array to be used as the basis of the sort—are assigned to the private attributes. As you'll see in the code, this class can be used like so:

```
$obj = new MultiAlphaSort
→ ('indexName', 'descending');
```

5. Begin defining the **sort()** method:

```
function sort(array $list) {
```

This method must have the same signature as that in the **iSort** interface. That just means a name of *sort* and a single argument.

6. Change the sorting algorithm based on the desired sort order:

```
if ($this->_order == 'ascending') {

  uasort($list, array($this,
  → 'ascSort'));

} else {

  uasort($list, array($this,
  → 'descSort'));

}
```

Within the method, the **uasort()** function is used to sort a multidimensional array (see Chapter 1). How that array is sorted will depend upon the chosen order, already stored in a private attribute.

The second argument to the **uasort()** function should be the name of the function to use for the comparison. Because that function—**ascSort()** or **descSort()**—is defined as a method in this current object, you can use this construct to reference it: **array($this, 'methodName')**.

7. Complete the **sort()** method:

```
  return $list;

}// End of sort() method.
```

The last step in the **sort()** method is to return the newly sorted array.

8. Define the comparison functions and complete the class:

```
function ascSort($x, $y) {

  return strcasecmp
  → ($x[$this->_index],
  → $y[$this->_index]);

}

function descSort($x, $y) {

  return strcasecmp
  → ($y[$this->_index],
  → $x[$this->_index]);

}

} // End of MultiAlphaSort class.
```

These functions, as explained in Chapter 1, take two arguments and return a value based upon the comparison of them. In this case, both **$x** and **$y** will be an array, and **$this->_index** represents what indexed value to sort upon.

continues on next page

9. Start defining the **MultiNumberSort** class:

```php
class MultiNumberSort implements
→ iSort {

  private $_order;

  private $_index;

  function __construct($index,
  → $order = 'ascending') {

    $this->_index = $index;

    $this->_order = $order;

  }
```

This class is largely defined exactly like **MultiAlphaSort**.

10. Implement the **sort()** method:

```php
function sort(array $list) {

  if ($this->_order ==
  → 'ascending') {

    uasort($list, array($this,
    → 'ascSort'));

  } else {

    uasort($list, array($this,
    → 'descSort'));

  }

  return $list;

}// End of sort() method.
```

This code is virtually the same as that in the other class.

11. Implement the comparison functions and complete the class:

```php
function ascSort($x, $y) {

  return ($x[$this->_index] >
  → $y[$this->_index]);

}

function descSort($x, $y) {

  return ($x[$this->_index] <
  → $y[$this->_index]);

}

} // End of MultiNumberSort class.
```

12. Save the file as **iSort.php** and place it in your Web directory.

To use the iSort classes:

1. Begin a new PHP script in your text editor or IDE, to be named **strategy.php**, starting with the HTML (**Script 7.8**):

```html
<!doctype html>

<html lang="en">

<head>

  <meta charset="utf-8">

  <title>Strategy</title>

  <link rel="stylesheet"
  → href="style.css">

</head>

<body>

<?php # Script 7.8 - strategy.php
```

Script 7.8 This script applies the **iSort** Strategy pattern to a multidimensional array.

```
1   <!doctype html>
2   <html lang="en">
3   <head>
4       <meta charset="utf-8">
5       <title>Strategy</title>
6       <link rel="stylesheet"
        → href="style.css">
7   </head>
8   <body>
9   <?php # Script 7.8 - strategy.php
10  // This page uses the iSort interface,
    → plus the MultiAlphaSort and
    → MultiNumberSort classes (Script 7.7).
11
12  // Load the class definition:
13  require('iSort.php');
14
15  /* The StudentsList class.
16   * The class contains one attribute:
     → $_students.
17   * The class contains three methods:
18   * - __construct()
19   * - sort()
20   * - display()
21   */
22  class StudentsList {
23
24      // Stores the list of students:
25      private $_students = array();
26
27      // Constructors stores the list
        → internally:
28      function __construct($list) {
29          $this->_students = $list;
30      }
31
32      // Perform a sort using an iSort
        → implementation:
33      function sort(iSort $type) {
34          $this->_students =
            → $type->sort($this->_students);
35      }
36
37      // Display the students as an
        → HTML list:
38      function display() {
39          echo '<ol>';
40          foreach ($this->_students as
            → $student) {
```

script continues on next page

2. Load the class definition:

```
require('iSort.php');
```

3. Begin defining the **StudentsList** class:

```
class StudentsList {
    private $_students = array();
    function __construct($list) {
        $this->_students = $list;
    }
```

An object of the **StudentsList** type will actually use the sorting algorithms (this object plays the role of *Context* in Ⓐ). This class's constructor stores the multidimensional array internally.

4. Define the **sort()** method:

```
function sort(iSort $type) {
    $this->_students =
    → $type->sort($this->_students);
}
```

This **sort()** method will use the various algorithms (it doesn't have to be named *sort*; it just makes sense to use that name here, too). This simple method is the heart of the Strategy pattern. On the fly, this method will receive an object of **iSort** type (you can do type hinting on interfaces, too). Within the method, that **iSort** object's **sort()** method will be called, passing it the list of students. Because the implementations of **sort()** return the sorted list, the results of the method call have to be assigned to the **StudentsList** private attribute.

continues on next page

5. Create a **display()** method:

```
function display() {
  echo '<ol>';
  foreach ($this->_students as
  → $student) {
    echo "<li>{$student['name']}
    → {$student['grade']}</li>";
  }
  echo '</ol>';
}
```

This method is just used to display the list of students as an ordered HTML list.

6. Complete the **StudentsList** class:

```
} // End of StudentsList class.
```

7. Create a multidimensional array:

```
$students = array(
  256 => array('name' => 'Jon',
  → 'grade' => 98.5),
  2 => array('name' => 'Vance',
  → 'grade' => 85.1),
  9 => array('name' => 'Stephen',
  → 'grade' => 94.0),
  364 => array('name' => 'Steve',
  → 'grade' => 85.1),
  68 => array('name' => 'Rob',
  → 'grade' => 74.6)
);
```

This code comes from Chapter 1.

8. Create the **StudentsList** object and display the original list:

```
$list = new StudentsList
→ ($students);
echo '<h2>Original Array</h2>';
$list->display();
```

Script 7.8 *continued*

```
41           echo "<li>{$student['name']}
             → {$student['grade']}</li>";
42         }
43       echo '</ol>';
44     }
45
46   } // End of StudentsList class.
47
48   // Create the array...
49   // Array structure:
50   // studentID => array('name' =>
     → 'Name', 'grade' => XX.X)
51   $students = array(
52       256 => array('name' => 'Jon',
         → 'grade' => 98.5),
53       2 => array('name' => 'Vance',
         → 'grade' => 85.1),
54       9 => array('name' => 'Stephen',
         → 'grade' => 94.0),
55       364 => array('name' => 'Steve',
         → 'grade' => 85.1),
56       68 => array('name' => 'Rob',
         → 'grade' => 74.6)
57   );
58
59   // Create the main object:
60   $list = new StudentsList($students);
61
62   // Show the original array:
63   echo '<h2>Original Array</h2>';
64   $list->display();
65
66   // Sort by name:
67   $list->sort(new MultiAlphaSort('name'));
68   echo '<h2>Sorted by Name</h2>';
69   $list->display();
70
71   // Sort by grade:
72   $list->sort(new MultiNumberSort('grade',
     → 'descending'));
73   echo '<h2>Sorted by Grade</h2>';
74   $list->display();
75
76   // Delete the object:
77   unset($list);
78   ?>
79   </body>
80   </html>
```

Original Array

1. Jon 98.5
2. Vance 85.1
3. Stephen 94
4. Steve 85.1
5. Rob 74.6

Sorted by Name

1. Jon 98.5
2. Rob 74.6
3. Stephen 94
4. Steve 85.1
5. Vance 85.1

Sorted by Grade

1. Jon 98.5
2. Stephen 94
3. Vance 85.1
4. Steve 85.1
5. Rob 74.6

B The list of students is sorted two different ways using algorithms implemented via Strategy.

9. Sort the array alphabetically and redisplay:

```
$list->sort(new MultiAlphaSort
→ ('name'));
```

```
echo '<h2>Sorted by Name</h2>';
```

```
$list->display();
```

To sort the list alphabetically by name, in ascending order, you need to pass the **StudentList** object's **sort()** method an **iSort** class instance. That specific instance should also know that the index to be used in the sort is *name*. You could create the **iSort** instance using

```
$isort = new MultiAlphaSort
→ ('name');
```

To save space, the creation of the object is done within the method call instead.

10. Sort the array numerically in descending order and redisplay:

```
$list->sort(new MultiNumberSort
→ ('grade', 'descending'));
```

```
echo '<h2>Sorted by Grade</h2>';
```

```
$list->display();
```

Only the first line of code here is significantly different.

11. Complete the page:

```
unset($list);
```

```
?>
```

```
</body>
```

```
</html>
```

12. Save the file as **strategy.php**, place it in your Web directory, and test in your Web browser **B**.

Review and Pursue

If you have any problems with these sections, either in answering the questions or pursuing your own endeavors, turn to the book's supporting forum (**www.Larry Ullman.com/forums/**).

Review

- What is a *design pattern*? What are the four components of a design pattern definition? (See page 214.)

- What is the *GoF*? (See page 215.)

- What is the Singleton pattern? Under what circumstances is it useful? How does the Singleton pattern ensure a single instance of a class type? (See pages 216 and 217.)

- What is the Factory pattern? Under what circumstances is it useful? How does the Factory pattern generate new objects? (See page 220.)

- What is the Composite pattern? Under what circumstances is it useful? How do you design a Composite pattern? (See page 225.)

- What is the Strategy pattern? Under what circumstances is it useful? How do you design a Strategy pattern? (See page 233.)

Pursue

- Modify **singleton.php** so that the second **Config** object changes a setting. Then confirm the setting's value via the first **Config** object.

- Create an HTML form that passes values to **factory.php** to create new shapes on the fly.

- Create a **Circle** class that extends **Shape**. Then update **ShapeFactory** to generate **Circle** objects, too.

- Update the Composite example to create a **Department** class. The **Department** class can be made up of teams and employees, and can also be assigned and complete tasks.

- Update the Composite example to create a **Task** class. Then modify the other classes to use type hinting for this object type.

- Create an implementation of **iSort** that sorts a single-dimensional array.

- Change the **MultiNumberSort** and **MultiAlphaSort** classes so that they inherit from a base class that defines the attributes and the constructor. Hint: The base class would implement the interface.

- After reading Chapter 8, add exception handling to this chapter's examples.

- Learn more about design patterns using as many different sources as you can!

8

Using Existing Classes

The preceding four chapters discuss object-oriented programming, discussing both syntax and theory. The majority of the examples in those chapters tend to be as much demonstrative as practical (e.g., the **Rectangle**, **Square**, **Shape**, and **Triangle** classes are useful, but only if you're doing geometric work). Philosophical examples are best for teaching OOP, I believe, but real-world object-oriented programming hammers the points home. And nothing best demonstrates real-world OOP than using some of the many existing classes created by other developers.

All of the examples in this chapter are based on classes that are already defined in PHP. This includes the **Exception** class, PHP Data Objects (PDO), and the Standard PHP Library (SPL). In using these classes, not only will you learn about some valuable resources, but you'll also see variations on many of the design ideas already explained.

In This Chapter

Catching Exceptions

While introducing the concept of OOP in Chapter 4, "Basic Object-Oriented Programming," I explained that programming is entirely about *nouns* and *verbs*. Procedural programming focuses on the verbs and OOP focuses on the nouns. Another difference is that procedural code creates *errors*, while OOP has *exceptions*.

The difference between errors and exceptions is structural, but both represent problems with your code. (As you'll see, an exception is really just an error in an object form.) Instead of using conditionals in procedural code to watch for errors, OOP has the **try** and **catch** statements for handling exceptions.

The premise is that you *try* to do certain things in your PHP code, specifically the kinds of things that might fail (like connecting to a database or including a file). If an error occurs, an exception is *thrown*. Your code will then *catch* the exception and respond accordingly.

The basic syntax is

```
try {
    // Do something.
    // An exception is thrown on error.
} catch (exception) {
    // Do whatever now.
}
```

This is a more sophisticated version of

```
if (/* Do something. */) {
} else {
    /* Do whatever because a problem
    → occurred. */
}
```

One benefit that exception handling has over the conditional is that it further separates the functionality and logic from the error handling. Furthermore, multiple errors can be handled without having to use lots of nested conditionals.

Exceptions are thrown using the syntax

```
throw new Exception('error message');
```

This code throws an object of type **Exception**, a class defined in PHP. To catch this exception, you would have

```
catch (Exception $e)
```

where **$e** is an object of the **Exception** type.

The **Exception** class contains the methods indicated in **Table 8.1**, which you can use to access information about the error. A **try...catch** example might therefore look like this:

```
try {
    // Do something.
} catch (Exception $e) {
    echo $e->getMessage();
}
```

You should note that any code within a **try** block after an exception is thrown will never run. Conversely, if no exception ever occurs, the code in the **catch** block will never be executed.

For an example of this, let's create a class used to write some data to a file. If a problem occurs, an exception will be thrown.

TABLE 8.1 Exception Class Methods

Name	Returns
getCode()	The numeric exception code received, if any
getMessage()	The string exception message received, if any
getFile()	The name of the file where the exception occurred
getLine()	The line number from which the exception was thrown
getTrace()	An array of information, like the file name, line number, and so on
getTraceAsString()	The same information as getTrace() but as a string
__toString()	All of the preceding information as a string

Script 8.1 If any of three different steps in this class cannot be completed, exceptions are thrown.

```
1    <?php # Script 8.1 - WriteToFile.php
2    // This page defines a WriteToFile class.
3
4    /* The WriteToFile class.
5     * The class contains one attribute:
         → $_fp.
6     * The class contains three methods:
         → __construct(), write(), close(),
         → and __destruct().
7     */
8    class WriteToFile {
9
10       // For storing the file pointer:
11       private $_fp = NULL;
12
13       // Constructor opens the file for
           → writing:
14       function __construct($file) {
15
16           // Check that the file exists and
               → is a file:
```

script continues on next page

To define the WriteToFile class:

1. Begin a new PHP script in your text editor or IDE, to be named **WriteToFile.php** (Script 8.1):

   ```
   <?php # Script 8.1 -
   → WriteToFile.php
   ```

2. Start defining the **WriteToFile** class:

   ```
   class WriteToFile {
       private $_fp = NULL;
   ```

   This class will define all the functionality for writing data to a file. The attribute will act as the file pointer and is made private as it need not (in fact, shouldn't) be available outside of this class.

3. Begin defining the constructor:

   ```
   function __construct($file) {
       if (!file_exists($file) ||
       → !is_file($file)) {
           throw new Exception('The file
           → does not exist.');
       }
   ```

   The constructor is called when a new **WriteToFile** object is created. It takes one argument: the file to be used. The purpose of the constructor is to confirm that the file exists and is writable, and then to open that file for writing.

   As you can see, the first conditional within the constructor checks if the file does not exist or if it is not a file (**file_exists()** will return true for directories, too). If either of these conditions is true, an exception is thrown.

   continues on next page

4. Complete the constructor:

```
if (!$this->_fp =
→ @fopen($file, 'w')) {

    throw new Exception('Could
    → not open the file.');

}

} // End of constructor.
```

The next conditional throws an exception if the file could not be opened for writing. The mode is assumed to be "w," but you'll make this class more flexible in just a couple of pages.

If you're not familiar with how to write data to a file in PHP, see the PHP manual.

Note that the **fopen()** call is prefaced with the error suppression operator so that PHP itself does not generate any errors should a problem occur (because the class should throw an exception instead).

5. Define the **write()** method:

```
function write($data) {

    if (@!fwrite($this->_fp,
    → $data . "\n")) {

        throw new Exception('Could
        → not write to the file.');

    }

} // End of write() method.
```

This method will be called to write data to the opened file. It takes the data to be written as its lone argument. If the data cannot be written, another exception is thrown.

Again, the error suppression operator prefaces the function call.

Script 8.1 *continued*

```
17      if (!file_exists($file) ||
        → !is_file($file)) {
18          throw new Exception('The file
            → does not exist.');
19      }
20
21      // Open the file:
22      if (!$this->_fp =
        → @fopen($file, 'w')) {
23          throw new Exception('Could not
            → open the file.');
24      }
25
26  } // End of constructor.
27
28  // This method writes data to the
    → file:
29  function write($data) {
30
31      // Confirm the write:
32      if (@!fwrite($this->_fp,
        → $data . "\n")) {
33          throw new Exception('Could not
            → write to the file.');
34      }
35
36  } // End of write() method.
37
38  // This method closes the file:
39  function close() {
40
41      // Make sure it's open:
42      if ($this->_fp) {
43          fclose($this->_fp);
44          $this->_fp = NULL;
45      }
46
47  } // End of close() method.
48
49  // The destructor calls close(),
    → just in case:
50  function __destruct() {
51      $this->close();
52  } // End of destructor.
53
54  } // End of WriteToFile class.
```

6. Define the **close()** method:

```
function close() {
  if ($this->_fp) {
    fclose($this->_fp);
    $this->_fp = NULL;
  }
} // End of close() method.
```

This method closes the open file.

7. Define the destructor and complete the class:

```
  function __destruct() {
    $this->close();
  } // End of destructor.
} // End of WriteToFile class.
```

In case the code that uses this class never formally closes the file, this code will call the **close()** method when the object is deleted.

8. Save the file as **WriteToFile.php** and place it in your Web directory.

To use the WriteToFile class:

1. Begin a new PHP script in your text editor or IDE, to be named **write_to_file. php**, starting with the HTML (**Script 8.2**):

```
<!doctype html>
<html lang="en">
<head>
  <meta charset="utf-8">
  <title>Handling
→ Exceptions</title>
  <link rel="stylesheet"
→ href="style.css">
</head>
<body>
<?php # Script 8.2 -
→ write_to_file.php
```

2. Load the class definition:

```
require('WriteToFile.php');
```

continues on next page

Script 8.2 Exceptions thrown by the code in the **try** block will be caught and displayed by the **catch**.

```
1   <!doctype html>
2   <html lang="en">
3   <head>
4       <meta charset="utf-8">
5       <title>Handling Exceptions</title>
6       <link rel="stylesheet" href="style.css">
7   </head>
8   <body>
9   <?php # Script 8.2 - write_to_file.php
10  // This page uses the WriteToFile class (Script 8.1).
11
12  // Load the class definition:
13  require('WriteToFile.php');
14
15  // Start the try...catch block:
16  try {
17
```

script continues on next page

3. Begin a **try** block:

```
try {
```

The bulk of the functionality of the script will go within this block.

4. Create the object:

```
$fp = new WriteToFile('data.txt');
```

This code will not only create the object but also attempt to open the file for writing. Opening a file for writing is a common cause of problems, most likely because the file doesn't exist, the file's name and path are incorrect, or the file does not have the proper permissions. If the file could not be opened in writing mode, an exception is thrown with the message *could not open the file* (see the class's constructor).

Note that the provided file value should represent the full path (relative or absolute) to the text file.

5. Attempt to write data to the file:

```
$fp->write('This is a line
→ of data.');
```

This piece of code will only be executed if no exception was thrown by the code in Step 4. Logically, if the file could be opened for writing, the object should be able to use **fwrite()** without complaint.

6. Close the file and delete the object:

```
$fp->close();

unset($fp);
```

7. Print a message indicating success of the operation:

```
echo '<p>The data has been
→ written.</p>';
```

This line of code will be executed only if no exceptions were thrown prior to this point.

Script 8.2 *continued*

```
18      // Create the object:
19      $fp = new WriteToFile('data.txt');
20
21      // Write the data:
22      $fp->write('This is a line of data.');
23
24      // Close the file:
25      $fp->close();
26
27      // Delete the object:
28      unset($fp);
29
30      // If we got this far, everything
        → worked!
31      echo '<p>The data has been written.
        → </p>';
32
33   } catch (Exception $e) {
34      echo '<p>The process could not
        → be completed because the script:
        → ' . $e->getMessage() . '</p>';
35   }
36
37   echo '<p>This is the end of the script.
        → </p>';
38
39   ?>
40   </body>
41   </html>
```

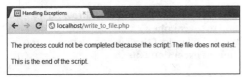

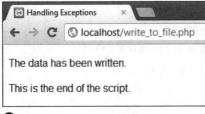

A Although it may not be apparent in the end result, this script uses a **try...catch** block to throw, and then catch, an object of **Exception** type.

B If no problems occurred, this is the end result.

8. Catch, and handle, the exception:

```
} catch (Exception $e) {
    echo '<p>The process could not
    ↪ be completed because the
    ↪ script: ' . $e->getMessage() .
    ↪ '</p>';
}
```

The variable **$e** will be an object of **Exception** type, matching the kinds of exceptions thrown by the **WriteToFile** object. Within this block, the received message is printed (by calling the **getMessage()** method) within context.

9. Print another message:

```
echo '<p>This is the end of the
↪ script.</p>';
```

This code, outside of the **try...catch** block, will always be executed, even if exceptions occur. I've included this statement just to demonstrate that.

10. Complete the page:

```
?>
</body>
</html>
```

11. Save the file as **write_to_file.php**, place it in your Web directory, and test in your Web browser **A**.

Without first creating a text file called **data.txt**, with the proper permissions, you'll see something like **A**.

12. Create a file called **data.txt** in the same directory as **write_to_file.php**, and adjust its permissions if necessary. Then rerun the PHP page in your Web browser **B**.

TIP To see the other exception error messages, you'll need to introduce errors into the code. For example, changing the fopen() mode to *r* will create an exception in the write() method.

TIP Failure to catch a thrown exception results in a fatal error 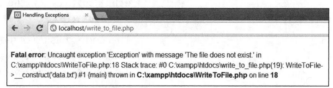.

TIP The Exception class's constructor can take anywhere from zero to two arguments. The first argument is an error message, and the second is an error code.

TIP As constructors, by definition, cannot return anything (such as an error or error code), it's appropriate to have constructors throw errors upon improper use.

TIP A catch block can also throw an exception to be caught by a subsequent catch block. The object thrown can be new or the current exception object:

```
try {
    // Code.
} catch (Exception $e) {
    // Do whatever.
    throw $e;
} catch (Exception $e) {
    // Now do this.
}
```

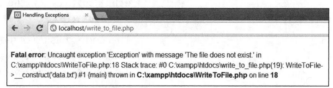

C When using **try**, you must ensure that all exceptions are caught, lest you're left with ugly fatal errors like this one.

Extending the Exception Class

The preceding example demonstrates basic usage of a **try...catch** block by using a class that throws standard exceptions. The basic PHP **Exception** class is very simple **A**, designed to be extended so that you can add, or change, functionality as needed.

Extending the **Exception** class is accomplished just like extending any class (see Chapter 5, "Advanced OOP"):

class MyException extends Exception {

Note that only the **Exception** constructor and **__toString()** methods can be overridden, because the others are all defined as **final**.

To use your extended class, you would write

```
throw new MyException('error
→ message');
```

Thanks to type hinting, introduced in Chapter 6, "More Advanced OOP," you can catch different kinds of exceptions from the same **try** block:

```
try {
    // Some code.
    throw new MyException1('error
    → message');
    // Some more code.
    throw new MyException2('error
    → message');
} catch (MyException1 $e) {
} catch (MyException2 $e) {
}
```

Using this new information, the next script will update the preceding example, but now the **WriteToFile** class will throw exceptions of a specific type.

Exception
#$message:string
#$code:int
#$file:string
#$line:int
__construct($message, $code, $previous)
getMessage():string
getPrevious():Exception
getCode:mixed
getFile():string
getLine():int
getTrace():array
getTraceAsString():string
__toString():string
-__clone():void

A A UML representation of PHP's built-in **Exception** class.

To extend the Exception class:

1. Open **WriteToFile.php** (Script 8.1) in your text editor or IDE, if it is not already.

2. Before the **WriteToFile** definition, begin defining an extension to the **Exception** class (**Script 8.3**):

   ```
   class FileException extends
   → Exception {
   ```

   This class, called **FileException**, will specifically handle file opening, writing, and closing errors. It will add one method to the inherited **Exception** methods.

3. Begin defining the **getDetails()** method:

   ```
   function getDetails() {
     switch ($this->code) {
       case 0:
           return 'No filename was
           → provided';
           break;
   ```

   Any time an exception occurs, up to two arguments can be passed to the **Exception** class: the message and the error code. The **WriteToFile** class, to be updated shortly, will generate its own error codes. This class, **FileException**, will associate those error codes with more specific error messages. This **getDetails()** method returns the message that goes with each code, using a **switch**.

4. Complete the **switch**:

   ```
   case 1:
       return 'The file does not
       → exist.';
       break;
   case 2:
       return 'The file is not a
       → file.';
       break;
   case 3:
       return 'The file is not
       → writable.';
       break;
   case 4:
       return 'An invalid mode was
       → provided.';
       break;
   case 5:
       return 'The data could not
       → be written.';
       break;
   case 6:
       return 'The file could not
       → be closed.';
       break;
   default:
       return 'No further
       → information is available.';
       break;
   } // End of SWITCH.
   ```

   Each of these messages will mean more once you see the updated **WriteToFile** class.

continues on page 255

Script 8.3 This script extends the **Exception** class to create a more specific type of exception handler. Exceptions of this new type are thrown by the **WriteToFile** class.

```php
1   <?php # Script 8.3 - WriteToFile.php
2   // This page defines a WriteToFile and a FileException class.
3
4   /* The FileException class.
5    * The class creates one new method: getDetails().
6    */
7   class FileException extends Exception {
8
9       // For returning more detailed error messages:
10      function getDetails() {
11
12          // Return a different message based upon the code:
13          switch ($this->code) {
14              case 0:
15                  return 'No filename was provided';
16                  break;
17              case 1:
18                  return 'The file does not exist.';
19                  break;
20              case 2:
21                  return 'The file is not a file.';
22                  break;
23              case 3:
24                  return 'The file is not writable.';
25                  break;
26              case 4:
27                  return 'An invalid mode was provided.';
28                  break;
29              case 5:
30                  return 'The data could not be written.';
31                  break;
32              case 6:
33                  return 'The file could not be closed.';
34                  break;
35              default:
36                  return 'No further information is available.';
37                  break;
38          } // End of SWITCH.
39
40      } // End of getDetails() method.
41
42  } // End of FileException class.
43
44  /* The WriteToFile class.
45   * The class contains one attribute: $_fp.
46   * The class contains three methods: __construct(), write(), close(), and __destruct().
47   */
48  class WriteToFile {
49
50      // For storing the file pointer:
51      private $_fp = NULL;
52
53      // For storing an error message:
```

script continues on next page

```php
54        private $_message = '';
55
56        // Constructor opens the file:
57        function __construct($file = null, $mode = 'w') {
58
59            // Assign the file name and mode
60            // to the message attribute:
61            $this->_message = "File: $file Mode: $mode";
62
63            // Make sure a file name was provided:
64            if (empty($file)) throw new FileException($this->_message, 0);
65
66            // Make sure the file exists:
67            if (!file_exists($file)) throw new FileException($this->_message, 1);
68
69            // Make sure the file is a file:
70            if (!is_file($file)) throw new FileException($this->_message, 2);
71
72            // Make sure the file is writable, when necessary
73            if (!is_writable($file)) throw new FileException($this->_message, 3);
74
75            // Validate the mode:
76            if (!in_array($mode, array('a', 'a+', 'w', 'w+'))) throw new FileException($this->_message,
4);
77
78            // Open the file:
79            $this->_fp = fopen($file, $mode);
80
81        } // End of constructor.
82
83        // This method writes data to the file:
84        function write($data) {
85
86            // Confirm the write:
87            if (@!fwrite($this->_fp, $data . "\n")) throw new FileException($this->_message .
          → " Data: $data", 5);
88
89        } // End of write() method.
90
91        // This method closes the file:
92        function close() {
93
94            // Make sure it's open:
95            if ($this->_fp) {
96                if (@!fclose($this->_fp)) throw new FileException($this->_message, 6);
97                $this->_fp = NULL;
98            }
99
100       } // End of close() method.
101
102       // The destructor calls close(), just in case:
103       function __destruct() {
104           $this->close();
105       } // End of destructor.
106
107   } // End of WriteToFile class.
```

5. Complete the **getDetails()** method and the **FileException** class:

```
} // End of getDetails()
→ method.

} // End of FileException class.
```

6. Within the **WriteToFile** class, add a new private attribute:

```
private $_message = '';
```

This new attribute will be assigned an error message, built up over the course of several methods.

7. Begin replacing the existing constructor with this new definition:

```
function __construct($file =
→ null, $mode = 'w') {

  $this->message = "File: $file
  → Mode: $mode";
```

The constructor now takes two arguments: the file and the mode. The mode's default value is *w*. The constructor will also start building an error message, which, for debugging purposes, will contain the filename and the mode.

8. Make sure that a filename was provided:

```
if (empty($file)) throw new
→ FileException($this->message, 0);
```

The first validation routine checks that some filename was passed to the class. If not, an exception of type **FileException** is thrown, using the default message and an error code of 0. This error code matches the more specific message in the **FileException getDetails()** method.

Note that I rarely use conditionals without the curly braces, but this is a reasonable exception (pun!).

9. Make sure that the file exists and that it is a file:

```
if (!file_exists($file)) throw new
→ FileException ($this->message, 1);

if (!is_file($file)) throw new
→ FileException($this->message, 2);
```

For more specific exceptions, the class now checks each possible problem separately. If either of these checks fails, an exception is thrown, providing different error codes accordingly.

10. Confirm that the file is writable:

```
if (!is_writable($file)) throw new
→ FileException($this->message, 3);
```

11. Confirm that a valid mode was used:

```
if (!in_array($mode, array('a',
→ 'a+', 'w', 'w+'))) throw new
→ FileException($this->message, 4);
```

Because I don't want to try to open the file in an invalid mode, this check is necessary. I've omitted some valid modes (like *ab*) and all reading modes (because I'm creating a write-specific class) to keep it simple.

12. Open the file and complete the constructor:

```
  $this->_fp = fopen($file,
  → $mode);

} // End of constructor.
```

If all of the validation tests were passed, the file is opened in the given mode, assigning the result to the attribute.

continues on next page

13. Update the **write()** method:

```
function write ($data) {

    if (@!fwrite($this->_fp,
    → $data . "\n")) throw new
    → FileException($this->
    → message . " Data: $data", 5);

} // End of writeData() method.
```

This method now throws its own exception code.

14. Update the **close()** method:

```
function close() {

    if ($this->_fp) {

        if (@!fclose($this->_fp)) throw
        → new FileException
        → ($this->message, 6);

        $this->_fp = NULL;

    }

} // End of close() method.
```

15. Save the file.

16. Open **write_to_file.php** in your text editor or IDE, if it is not already.

17. Change the **catch** statement to read (**Script 8.4**) as follows:

```
} catch (FileException $e) {

    echo '<p>The process could
    → not be completed. Debugging
    → information:<br>' .
    → $e->getMessage() . '<br>' .
    → $e->getDetails() . '</p>';

}
```

Script 8.4 Now the script is written to catch a specific type of exception.

```
1    <!doctype html>
2    <html lang="en">
3    <head>
4        <meta charset="utf-8">
5        <title>Extending Exceptions</title>
6        <link rel="stylesheet"
         href="style.css">
7    </head>
8    <body>
9    <?php # Script 8.4 - write_to_file.php #2
10   // This page uses the WriteToFile class
     → (Script 8.3).
11
12   // Load the class definition:
13   require('WriteToFile.php');
14
15   // Start the try...catch block:
16   try {
17
18       // Create the object:
19       $fp = new WriteToFile('data.txt', 'w');
20
21       // Write the data:
22       $fp->write('This is a line of data.');
23
24       // Close the file:
25       $fp->close();
26
27       // Delete the object:
28       unset($fp);
29
30       // If we got this far, everything
         → worked!
31       echo '<p>The data has been written.
         → </p>';
32
33   } catch (FileException $e) {
34       echo '<p>The process could not be
         → completed. Debugging information:
         → <br>' . $e->getMessage() . '<br>' .
         → $e->getDetails() . '</p>';
35   }
36
37   echo '<p>This is the end of the script.
     </p>';
38
39   ?>
40   </body>
41   </html>
```

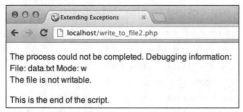

B The result if the file exists but is not writable. The first line of debugging information comes from the **Exception getMessage()** class. The rest comes from **FileException getDetails()**.

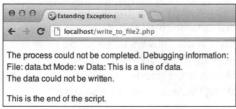

C If the data cannot be written to the file, the debugging information also shows what data was received.

This **catch** expects exceptions of type **FileException**, which will be thrown by the **WriteToFile** object. Within the **catch**, debugging information is printed using both the **Exception getMessage()** method (which should print the file, mode, and possibly data) and the **FileException get_details()** method.

18. Save the file, place it in your Web directory, and test in your Web browser **B**.

19. Introduce some errors and retest **C**.

TIP Because PHP generates an ugly error should an uncaught exception occur, you can create your own exception handler to handle this situation more gracefully:

```
function my_ex_handler(Exception $e) {

    // Do whatever.

}

set_exception_handler('my_ex_handler');
```

TIP Every **try** statement requires at least one **catch**. You can have multiple **catch** statements, each catching a different exception type:

```
try {
} catch (SomeType $e) {
} catch (Exception $e) {
}
```

Note that you should always catch **Exception** types last, as it's the most generic type.

TIP If your extended **Exception** class has its own constructor, it should also call the **Exception** constructor using **parent::__construct()**.

Using PDO

New in this edition of this book is a discussion of PHP Data Objects (PDO), an alternative way to interact with a database. Built into PHP as of version 5.1, PDO provide a consistent way to execute queries regardless of the database application in use.

At the time of this writing, PDO works with MySQL (of course), PostgreSQL, SQLite, Oracle, Microsoft SQL Server, and more. Once you've embraced PDO on a project, changing literally one line of code will allow you to seamlessly switch to another database application, should the need arise.

To confirm what applications are supported with your PHP installation, invoke the **getAvailableDrivers()** method of the PDO class **A**:

```
print_r(PDO::getAvailableDrivers());
```

Over the next several pages, I'll cover how to perform several fundamental tasks using PDO, rewriting one of the book's existing examples in the process.

TIP To use PDO, your PHP installation must have the PDO extension enabled, and you must have the proper PDO driver for the database application you intend to use **A**.

Connecting to the database

All of the customization of the PDO experience comes when making a connection to the database. The connection is made by creating a new object of type **PDO**. As you would expect, this is done via the **new** keyword. You should provide to the **PDO** constructor three values:

```
$pdo = new PDO('dsn', 'username',
→ 'password');
```

Technically, the username and password are optional, but most database applications should always be requiring them anyway. The *DSN*, short for *Data Source Name*, is the important part. The DSN is a string that indicates several things:

- The database driver to use
- The database name
- In the case of SQLite, the location of the database file
- Optionally, the hostname
- Optionally, the port

You can also put the username and password in the DSN, if you'd prefer, as opposed to providing them to the **PDO** constructor.

A Test for PDO support on your installation, prior to running any code.

To create the DSN, first you indicate the database driver. Then, after a colon, use *name=value* pairs, each separated by a semicolon:

driver:name1=value1;name2=value2

For example, with MySQL, accessing the **test** database on localhost, the proper DSN is *mysql:dbname=test;host=localhost*.

Thus, this is how you use PDO to connect to MySQL:

```
$pdo = new PDO('mysql:dbname=test;
→ host=localhost', 'username',
→ 'password');
```

If you're using, for example, SQLite, that connection could be

```
$pdo = new PDO('sqlite:/path/to/
→ somedb.sq3');
```

Note that SQLite connections are made to specific files on the server and do not require usernames and passwords.

To close the database connection, simply unset the PDO object:

```
unset($pdo);
```

Or set it to null:

```
$pdo = null;
```

TIP See the PHP manual for the correct DSN value to use with other database applications, should you have that need.

Catching exceptions

Before getting into how you'd use PDO to execute queries, let's first look at how you handle any database-related errors that might occur when using PDO. This includes a range of possible problems, from an inability to connect to the database to an error in a query's syntax.

Being a class, PDO does not generate errors but rather throws exceptions. Specifically, PDO throws exceptions of type **PDOException**.

With this in mind, to interact with the database, you'll want to use a **try...catch** block like **B**:

```
try {
    $pdo = new PDO('mysql:dbname=
    → test;host=localhost', 'username',
    → 'password');
    // Execute queries.
    // Do whatever else.
} catch (PDOException $e) {
    // Use $e and $e->getMessage().
}
```

Let's put all this together and start creating a PHP script that connects to the database. For this example, I'll rewrite the **add_task2. php** file (Script 1.7) from Chapter 1.

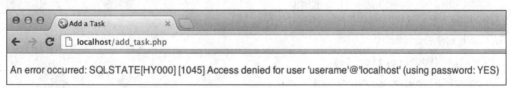

An error occurred: SQLSTATE[HY000] [1045] Access denied for user 'userame'@'localhost' (using password: YES)

B An exception thrown by PDO's inability to connect to the database.

To use PDO:

1. Begin a new PHP script in your text editor or IDE, to be named **add_task.php**, starting with the HTML (**Script 8.5**):

```
<!doctype html>
<html lang="en">
<head>
    <meta charset="utf-8">
    <title>Add a Task</title>
    <link rel="stylesheet"
    → href="style.css">
</head>
<body>
<?php # Script 8.5 - add_task.php
```

2. Begin a **try** block:

```
try {
```

All of the database interactions will go within this **try** block of the script.

3. Create the **PDO** object:

```
$pdo = new PDO('mysql:dbname=
→ test;host=localhost', 'username',
→ 'password');
```

Naturally, you'll need to change these particulars to match your environment.

4. Close the connection:

```
unset($pdo);
```

This isn't formally required—PHP will close the connection when the script terminates—but it makes for good form.

5. Catch any exceptions:

```
} catch (PDOException $e) {
```

Again, PDO throws exceptions of type **PDOException**, so that's what this block tries to catch.

Script 8.5 To start writing the **add_task.php** script, first a database connection is made within a **try... catch** block.

```
1   <!doctype html>
2   <html lang="en">
3   <head>
4       <meta charset="utf-8">
5       <title>Add a Task</title>
6       <link rel="stylesheet"
    → href="style.css">
7   </head>
8   <body>
9   <?php # Script 8.5 - add_task.php
10  //  This page adds tasks to the tasks
    → table using PDO.
11
12  // Try to connect to the database:
13  try {
14
15      // Create the object:
16      $pdo = new PDO('mysql:dbname=test;
    → host=localhost', 'username',
    → 'password');
17
18      // Unset the object:
19      unset($pdo);
20
21  } catch (PDOException $e) { // Report
    → the error!
22      echo '<p class="error">An error
    → occurred: ' . $e->getMessage() .
    → '</p>';
23  }
24
25  ?>
26  </body>
27  </html>
```

6. Report the error and complete the **catch**:

```
echo '<p class="error">
→ An error occurred: ' .
→ $e->getMessage() . '</p>';
}
```

Showing the exceptions message is good for debugging, but it's not something you'd want to do on a live site. On a live site, you'd probably show a generic message to the user and log the specific error message.

7. Complete the page:

```
?>

</body>

</html>
```

8. Save the file as **add_task.php**, place it in your Web directory, and test in your Web browser 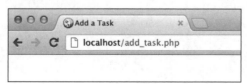.

If you see a blank page, then no problems occurred. You may need to introduce an error to see a message as in **B**.

TIP You can change the level of database error reporting using the PDO **setAttribute()** method and the proper constants. See the PHP manual for details.

Executing simple queries

Once you've established a database connection (and a **PDO** object), you can run queries on the database. Doing so requires one of two methods, depending on the type of query being executed.

For simple queries that do not return results—**INSERT**, **UPDATE**, and **DELETE**, for example, use the **exec()** method. It takes the query to be run as its argument (which I'll represent as **$q**):

```
$q = 'DELETE FROM tablename';
$pdo->exec($q);
```

For these simple queries, **exec()** will return the number of rows affected by the query:

```
$num = $pdo->exec($q);
// Use $num.
```

If you just ran an **INSERT** query and need to know the dynamically generated primary key value, call the **lastInsertId()** method:

```
$id = $pdo->lastInsertId();
```

This is equivalent to calling **mysqli_insert_id()** when using the MySQL Improved extension.

The last thing to be aware of when running simple queries is how to prevent *SQL injection attacks*. When you use the MySQL Improved extension, data can be made safe to use in a query by running it through **mysqli_real_escape_string()** first:

```
$data = mysqli_real_escape_string
→ ($dbc, $unsafe_data);
```

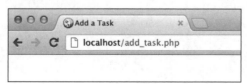

C At this point, a blank page is good (i.e., nothing bad happened).

For PDO, call the **quote()** method:

```
$data = $pdo->quote($unsafe_data);
```

This method not only prevents SQL injection attacks, but it also wraps the strings in quotes so you don't have to in your query:

```
$data = $pdo->quote($unsafe_data);

$pdo->exec("INSERT INTO tablename
→ (column1) VALUES ($data)");
```

Given all that, you should instead use prepared statements, as explained in just a couple of pages.

TIP If the query ran through the **exec()** method affects no records, the number 0 is returned. If the query generates an error, false is returned.

TIP The quote() method relies on the database's default character set being established.

Executing select queries

Simple queries—those that don't return records—are run through the **exec()** method. Queries that *do* return results (such as **SELECT**) should be run using the **query()** method, assigning the results to a new variable:

```
$results = $pdo->query($q);
```

To see how many records were returned by the query, invoke the new variable's **rowCount()** method:

```
$results->rowCount();
```

This is equivalent to calling **mysqli_num_rows()**.

Interestingly, the **$results** variable will be an object of type **PDOStatement**, which is one of the three most important PDO classes, along with **PDO** and **PDOException**.

Once you have executed a query that returned some results, you can fetch those results using the **fetch()** method of the **PDOStatement** object (e.g., **$results**). First, though, you should tell PHP *how* you want to fetch the records. This is accomplished by providing the **setFetchMode()** method with a constant. The most commonly used ones are:

- **PDO::FETCH_ASSOC**, for an associative array
- **PDO::FETCH_NUM**, for a numerically indexed array
- **PDO::FETCH_OBJ**, for a generic object
- **PDO::FETCH_CLASS**, for a specific type of object

Fetching Results Directly

The **query()** method allows you to fetch results directly in a loop without using **fetch()**. That syntax is

```
foreach ($pdo->query($q) as $row) {

    // Use $row.

}
```

Although it might seem like the query would be executed with each iteration of the loop, that's not actually the case. Still, I prefer the more overt strategy of using the **fetch()** method.

For example:

```
$results = $pdo->query('SELECT id,
→ username FROM users');

$results->setFetchMode(PDO::FETCH_NUM);

while ($row = $results->fetch()) {

    // Use $row[0] for the id.

    // Use $row[1] for the username.

}
```

A more interesting option is to have the returned records be turned into specific types of objects, logically, objects you're already using in your application. For example, say you've defined a **User** class:

```
class User {

    private $id;

    private $username;

    public getUsername() {

        return $this->username;

    }

}
```

Now you can fetch database records into new **User** objects:

```
$results = $pdo->query('SELECT id,
→ username FROM users');

$results->setFetchMode
→ (PDO::FETCH_CLASS, 'User');

while ($row = $results->fetch()) {

    echo $row->getUsername();

}
```

As you can see in that code, **$row** will be a **User** object, and it can invoke the **User** methods.

This approach can be beneficial in an object-based site. The thing to watch out for is that PHP directly maps the returned column names to matching class attributes. If no comparable class attribute exists, PHP will create the column name as a new public attribute. For this reason, I had to use **$id** as the private class attribute instead of **$_id**.

Let's use this information to update **add_task.php** so that it now shows a form for adding new tasks. Per the example in Chapter 1, the form will display the current tasks in a menu so that a new task can be created as a subtask **D**.

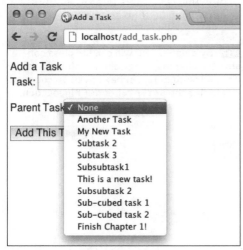

D A SELECT query is used to fetch all the currently incomplete tasks shown in the form.

To run a SELECT query:

1. Open **add_task.php** (Script 8.5) in your text editor or IDE, if it is not already.

2. Within the **try** block, after the **PDO** object has been created, start the form (Script 8.6):

   ```
   echo '<form action="add_task.php"
   → method="post">
   <fieldset>
       <legend>Add a Task</legend>
       <p>Task: <input name="task"
   → type="text" size="60"
   → maxlength="100"></p>
       <p>Parent Task: <select
   → name="parent_id"><option
   → value="0">None</option>';
   ```

   This code comes verbatim from Chapter 1. See that chapter if you need any explanations.

   Note that this code is being added *within* the **try** block, because that's where the database connection is made, and all database interactions will occur.

3. Run the query:

   ```
   $q = 'SELECT task_id, task
   → FROM tasks WHERE date_completed=
   → "0000-00-00 00:00:00" ORDER BY
   → date_added ASC';
   $r = $pdo->query($q);
   ```

   The SQL query is the same as in Chapter 1, but now it is run through a **PDO** instance.

4. Set the fetch mode:

   ```
   $r->setFetchMode(PDO::FETCH_NUM);
   ```

   The rows will be fetched as numerically indexed arrays.

5. Show the results:

   ```
   while ($row = $r->fetch()) {
       echo "<option
   value=\"$row[0]\">$row[1]
   → </option>\n";
   }
   ```

   Again, aside from the new PDO code, this is the same idea as in Chapter 1.

6. Complete the form:

   ```
   echo '</select></p>
   <input name="submit" type="submit"
   → value="Add This Task">
   </fieldset>
   </form>';
   ```

7. Save the file, place it in your Web directory, and test in your Web browser **D**.

   There's no point in submitting the form, though, as no code has yet been written to handle form submissions.

TIP By default, PHP will call the class constructor *after* mapping column values to the class attributes. This behavior can be changed by altering the setFetchMode() invocation. See the PHP manual for details.

Script 8.6 The next step in developing this script is to use a **SELECT** query to populate a menu in the form.

```
1    <!doctype html>
2    <html lang="en">
3    <head>
4       <meta charset="utf-8">
5       <title>Add a Task</title>
6       <link rel="stylesheet" href="style.css">
7    </head>
8    <body>
9    <?php # Script 8.6 - add_task.php #2 (in this chapter)
10   //   This page adds tasks to the tasks table using PDO.
11
12   // Try to connect to the database:
13   try {
14
15       // Create the object:
16       $pdo = new PDO('mysql:dbname=test;host=localhost', 'username', 'password');
17
18       // Start the form:
19       echo '<form action="add_task.php" method="post">
20       <fieldset>
21          <legend>Add a Task</legend>
22          <p>Task: <input name="task" type="text" size="60" maxlength="100"></p>
23          <p>Parent Task: <select name="parent_id"><option value="0">None</option>';
24
25       // Run the query:
26       $q = 'SELECT task_id,  task FROM tasks WHERE date_completed="0000-00-00 00:00:00"
         → ORDER BY date_added ASC';
27       $r = $pdo->query($q);
28
29       // Set the fetch mode:
30       $r->setFetchMode(PDO::FETCH_NUM);
31
32       // Show the results:
33       while ($row = $r->fetch()) {
34          echo "<option value=\"$row[0]\">$row[1]</option>\n";
35       }
36
37       // Complete the form:
38       echo '</select></p>
39       <input name="submit" type="submit" value="Add This Task">
40       </fieldset>
41       </form>';
42
43       // Unset the object:
44       unset($pdo);
45
46   } catch (PDOException $e) { // Report the error!
47       echo '<p class="error">An error occurred: ' . $e->getMessage() . '</p>';
48   }
49
50   ?>
51   </body>
52   </html>
```

Prepared statements

The final concept I want to introduce is how to use *prepared statements* through PDO. Using prepared statements, in case you're not familiar with them, is a different way of running queries. Most queries aren't static but rather contain a combination of SQL keywords, specific table and column references, and some data that changes on the fly, such as that provided by users. Traditionally, the whole query is assembled and sent to the database as one step:

```
$results = $pdo->query("SELECT *
→ FROM users WHERE email='$email'
→ AND pass=SHA1('$pass')");
```

With prepared statements, the query is sent as one step and the specific data is sent separately. The end result can be much better performance and easier security management: because the data is sent separately from the query, it does not need to be protected against SQL injection attacks.

To use prepared statements with PDO, start with the **prepare()** method. Provide to this method the query, with the dynamic data represented by *placeholders* (question marks):

```
$stmt = $pdo->prepare('SELECT *
→ FROM users WHERE email=?
→ AND pass=SHA1(?)');
```

Note that even though the two pieces of data in this query are strings, the placeholders do not need to be within quotation marks (as in the original query).

This method returns a **PDOStatement** object, which will be used in subsequent steps.

Next, invoke the **execute()** method of the **PDOStatement** object, providing to it an array of actual values:

```
$stmt->execute(array('me@example.com',
→ 'mypass'));
```

The values should be supplied in the same order as they'll be used in the query.

Using the question marks as placeholders is one option. A more overt alternative is to use *named placeholders*. Named placeholders start with a colon, followed by a label:

```
$stmt = $pdo->prepare('SELECT *
→ FROM users WHERE email=:email
→ AND pass=SHA1(:pass)');
```

Then, use the named placeholders as keys in the array passed to the **execute()** method:

```
$stmt->execute(array(':email' =>
→ 'me@example.com', ':pass' =>
→ 'mypass'));
```

The net effect is the same, but using named placeholders is more obvious and less likely to mix up the placeholders and values.

Let's use prepared statements to complete the **add_task.php** script, adding form validation and an **INSERT** query.

To use prepared statements:

1. Open **add_task.php** (Script 8.6) in your text editor or IDE, if it is not already.

2. Within the **try** block, after the **PDO** object has been created, start validating the form data (**Script 8.7**):

```
if (($_SERVER['REQUEST_METHOD'] ==
→ 'POST') && !empty($_POST['task'])) {
    if (isset($_POST['parent_id']) &&
    filter_var($_POST['parent_id'],
    → FILTER_VALIDATE_INT,
    → array('min_range' => 1)) ) {
        $parent_id =
        → $_POST['parent_id'];
    } else {
        $parent_id = 0;
    }
```

Again, this code comes verbatim from Chapter 1. See that chapter if you need any explanations.

3. Prepare the query:

```
$q = 'INSERT INTO tasks
→ (parent_id, task) VALUES
→ (:parent_id, :task)';

$stmt = $pdo->prepare($q);
```

The SQL query is the same as from Chapter 1, but it now uses named place-holders for the two dynamic values.

4. Execute the query and report on the results:

```
if ($stmt->execute(array
→ (':parent_id' => $parent_id,
→ ':task' => $_POST['task']))) {

    echo '<p>The task has been
→ added!</p>';

} else {

    echo '<p>The task could not be
→ added!</p>';

}
```

The **execute()** method returns a Boolean indicating its success, so it can be used in a conditional as in this code.

continues on page 269

Script 8.7 Finally, the script performs a minimal amount of validation, and then adds the new task to the database, using prepared statements.

```
1    <!doctype html>
2    <html lang="en">
3    <head>
4        <meta charset="utf-8">
5        <title>Add a Task</title>
6        <link rel="stylesheet" href="style.css">
7    </head>
8    <body>
9    <?php # Script 8.7 - add_task.php #3 (in this chapter)
10   //  This page adds tasks to the tasks table using PDO.
11
12   // Try to connect to the database:
13   try {
14
15       // Create the object:
16       $pdo = new PDO('mysql:dbname=test;host=localhost', 'username', 'password');
17
18       // Check for a form submission:
19       if (($_SERVER['REQUEST_METHOD'] == 'POST') && !empty($_POST['task'])) {
20
21           // Minimal validation:
22           if (isset($_POST['parent_id']) &&
23           filter_var($_POST['parent_id'], FILTER_VALIDATE_INT, array('min_range' => 1)) ) {
24               $parent_id = $_POST['parent_id'];
25           } else {
26               $parent_id = 0;
```

script continues on next page

```
27          }
28
29          // Add the task to the database:
30          $q = 'INSERT INTO tasks (parent_id, task) VALUES (:parent_id, :task)';
31          $stmt = $pdo->prepare($q);
32
33          // Confirm the results:
34          if ($stmt->execute(array(':parent_id' => $parent_id, ':task' => $_POST['task']))) {
35              echo '<p>The task has been added!</p>';
36          } else {
37              echo '<p>The task could not be added!</p>';
38          }
39
40      } // End of submission IF.
41
42      // Start the form:
43      echo '<form action="add_task.php" method="post">
44      <fieldset>
45          <legend>Add a Task</legend>
46          <p>Task: <input name="task" type="text" size="60" maxlength="100"></p>
47          <p>Parent Task: <select name="parent_id"><option value="0">None</option>';
48
49      // Run the query:
50      $q = 'SELECT task_id, task FROM tasks WHERE date_completed="0000-00-00 00:00:00" ORDER BY
        �e date_added ASC';
51      $r = $pdo->query($q);
52
53      // Set the fetch mode:
54      $r->setFetchMode(PDO::FETCH_NUM);
55
56      // Show the results:
57      while ($row = $r->fetch()) {
58          echo "<option value=\"$row[0]\">$row[1]</option>\n";
59      }
60
61      // Complete the form:
62      echo '</select></p>
63      <input name="submit" type="submit" value="Add This Task">
64      </fieldset>
65      </form>';
66
67      // Unset the object:
68      unset($pdo);
69
70  } catch (PDOException $e) { // Report the error!
71      echo '<p class="error">An error occurred: ' . $e->getMessage() . '</p>';
72  }
73
74  ?>
75  </body>
76  </html>
```

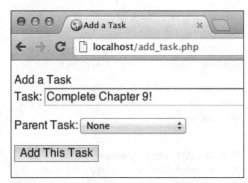

E Filling out the form...

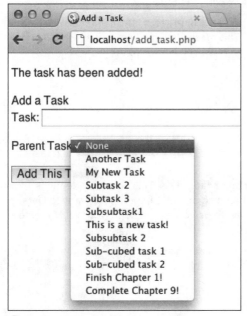

F ...and the new task has been added (as also shown in the select menu).

5. Complete the conditional begun in Step 2:

```
} // End of submission IF.
```

6. Save the file, place it in your Web directory, and test in your Web browser **E** and **F**.

TIP Prepared statements will have the largest performance benefits in scripts that execute the same query multiple times with only the data changing on each execution.

TIP PDO also supports *transactions*, assuming that the database application does.

Using the Standard PHP Library

A key component to the success of the C programming language over the years has been its C Standard Library: a collection of commonly needed tools that can easily be used in your own programs. Because PHP is written in C, it's only logical that it would eventually have its own counterpart: the Standard PHP Library (SPL), built into PHP as of version 5.0.

The initial focus of the SPL was on *iterators* (to be explained shortly) and exceptions. Version 5.3 of the language added even more classes, in particular a host of new data structures (think of them like new variable types). There are also classes for working with files and directories, as well as some useful OOP-related functions.

Through the rest of the chapter, I'll demonstrate some of the range of things that the SPL has to offer.

> **TIP** The SPL also implements many Gang of Four design patterns, such as Iterator and Observer. For this reason, I purposefully did not cover those in Chapter 7, "Design Patterns."

> **TIP** As of PHP 5.3, SPL cannot be disabled. This means that if you're using PHP 5.3 or greater, you have support for SPL.

The SessionHandlerInterface Class

Added in version 5.4 of PHP is the **SessionHandlerInterface** class. This interface identifies what functionality is required to create your own session-handling object. Chapter 3, "Advanced Database Concepts," explained how to do this procedurally. To use objects instead, you would create a class that implements **SessionHandlerInterface**:

```
class SessionHandler implements SessionHandlerInterface {
```

The class would need to define these methods:

- open()
- read()
- write()
- close()
- destroy()
- gc()

Those methods would do the same things that the procedural functions covered in Chapter 3 do. Then you'd use this class like so:

```
$sh = new SessionHandler();
session_set_save_handler($sh, true);
```

And that's it!

File handling

To start with some easy examples, the SPL has defined a few classes for working with files and directories. First, there's the **SplFileInfo** class, which creates an object from a file reference:

```
$file = new SplFileInfo
→ ('filename.ext');
```

Once you have created that object, you can invoke various methods to get information about the file:

- **getBasename()**
- **getExtension()**
- **getMTime()**
- **getPathname()**
- **getSize()**
- **getType()**
- **isDir()**
- **isFile()**
- **isWritable()**

This is just a sampling of the available methods; see the PHP manual for the full list. For example **A**:

```
$file = new SplFileInfo('test.php');
echo "<p>Extension:
→ {$file->getExtension()}</p>";
echo "<p>Size (bytes):
→ {$file->getSize()}</p>";
echo "<p>Real path:
→ {$file->getRealPath()}</p>";
```

If you also want file manipulation functionality, such as the ability to write to or read from a file, you can use **SplFileObject**. This class inherits from **SplFileInfo**. Hence, you have all of the previous methods, plus some new ones like **fgets()** and **fwrite()**, which correspond to the procedural equivalents.

To create a new object of type **SplFileObject**, provide the filename (and path, if needed) as the first argument and the mode as the second:

```
$file = new SplFileObject
→ ('somefile.txt', 'r');
```

Now, for example, you can read the file's data:

```
while (!$file->eof()) {
    echo $file->fgets();
}
```

With this in mind, let's create a new version of the **write_to_file.php** example that uses SPL.

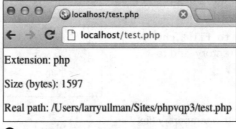

A A sampling of the available information for a specific file.

To use SplFileObject:

1. Open **write_to_file.php** (Script 8.2), in your text editor or IDE.

   Note that I'm going to be editing the first version of the **write_to_file.php** script. This is because that script handles generic exceptions, which is what **SplFileObject** will throw in case of problems.

2. Remove the inclusion of the **WriteToFile** class (**Script 8.8**).

3. Change the creation of the **$fp** object to

   $fp = new SplFileObject
   → ('data.txt', 'w');

   Instead of creating an object of type **WriteToFile**, now the script will create one of type **SplFileObject**.

4. Change the data writing line to

   $fp->fwrite("This is a line of
   → data.\n");

   There are two changes here. First, the method to invoke is now **fwrite()**, not **write()**. Second, the newline character, which the original class added automatically, must now be part of the data to be written.

5. Remove the call to the **close()** method.

   The **SplFileObject** does not have a **close()** or **fclose()** method. The file will be closed when the object is deleted.

6. Save the file as **write_to_file3.php**, place it in your Web directory, and test in your Web browser **Ⓑ**.

TIP The **SplTempFileObject** class provides a way to create and work with a temporary file.

Script 8.8 This updated version of **write_to_file.php** now uses the SPL **SplFileObject** class.

```
1   <!doctype html>
2   <html lang="en">
3   <head>
4       <meta charset="utf-8">
5       <title>Using SplFileObject</title>
6       <link rel="stylesheet"
        → href="style.css">
7   </head>
8   <body>
9   <?php # Script 8.8 - write_to_file3.php
10  // This page uses the SplFileObject
    → class.
11
12  // Start the try...catch block:
13  try {
14
15      // Create the object:
16      $fp = new SplFileObject
        → ('data.txt', 'w');
17
18      // Write the data:
19      $fp->fwrite("This is a line of
        → data.\n");
20
21      // Delete the object:
22      unset($fp);
23
24      // If we got this far, everything
        → worked!
25      echo '<p>The data has been written.
        → </p>';
26
27  } catch (Exception $e) {
28      echo '<p>The process could not
        → be completed because the script:
        → ' . $e->getMessage() . '</p>';
29  }
30
31  echo '<p>This is the end of the script.
    → </p>';
32
33  ?>
34  </body>
35  </html>
```

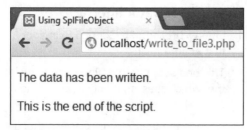

B Unbeknownst to the end user, the script now uses an object of type `SplFileObject`.

Iterators

Iterator is a design pattern that makes it possible to access the components of any kind of complex data structure using a loop. That probably sounds more complicated than it really is.

For example, as you know, the **foreach** loop can iterate through an array, a **while** loop is used to fetch query results, and PHP has functions for iterating through directory and file contents. Although the underlying data structure is different in each of these cases, the premise for looping through them is the same.

An iterator, then, is just a "one ring to rule them all" solution: regardless of the data being iterated, you can use the same code (normally, **foreach**).

There are more than a dozen types of iterators defined in the SPL, including these:

- **ArrayIterator**
- **RecursiveArrayIterator**
- **LimitIterator**
- **DirectoryIterator**

For example, to loop through a directory of files, you can use the **DirectoryIterator** class:

```
// Reference to current directory:
$dir = new DirectoryIterator('.');
foreach ($dir as $item) {
    // Use $item.
}
```

A nice thing about this example is that **DirectoryIterator** returns each item in the loop as an **SplFileObject**. This means that within the loop, you can use the methods just explained.

Of course, since they are classes, you can extend any of these iterators to create your own variations on them. If you look online, you'll find examples that extend **DirectoryIterator**.

As an easy example, let's start with the basic **Iterator** interface. As an interface (see Chapter 6), **Iterator** identifies the methods needed by a class in order for PHP to be able to loop through instances of that class. Those methods are as follows:

- **current()**, which returns the current item
- **key()**, which returns the current key, or position in the list
- **next()**, which increments the key or position
- **rewind()**, which resets the key or position
- **valid()**, which returns a Boolean indicating if a value exists at the current key or position

Once you've defined these methods (assuming you've defined them correctly), PHP will have the knowledge it needs to iterate through objects of that class type.

For an example of this, let's take the **Department** and **Employee** classes from Chapter 6 and make **Department** implement **Iterator**, so that a loop can be used to access the employees in a department.

To use the Iterator interface:

1. Open **hinting.php** (Script 6.8) in your text editor or IDE.

   This one script both defined and used the two classes, so it only needs to be edited here.

2. Change the **Department** class so that it implements **Iterator** (Script 8.9):

   ```
   class Department implements
   →Iterator {
   ```

   Now that this class implements that interface, it must define the five methods already identified, or an error will occur (again, see Chapter 6 for details).

3. Within the class, add a new private attribute:

   ```
   private $_position = 0;
   ```

   This private attribute will be used to track iterations through the **$_employees** array.

4. Within the constructor, set **$_position** to 0:

   ```
   $this->_position = 0;
   ```

   This isn't absolutely necessary—the code in Step 3 also does this—but it makes for good programming form.

5. Define the **current()** method:

   ```
   function current() {
       return $this->_employees
       →[$this->_position];
   }
   ```

   The **current()** method should return the current item. The "items" for a **Department** are stored in the **$_employees** array, so this method just needs to return the element in that array indexed at the current position.

   continues on page 277

Script 8.9 By implementing **Iterator**, a **Department** object can now be used in a loop, to fetch every employee in that department.

```
1    <!doctype html>
2    <html lang="en">
3    <head>
4        <meta charset="utf-8">
5        <title>Iterators</title>
6        <link rel="stylesheet" href="style.css">
7    </head>
8    <body>
9    <?php # Script 8.9 - iterator.php
10   //   This page defines and uses the Department and Employee classes.
11
12   # ***** CLASSES ***** #
13
14   /* Class Department.
15    *   The class contains two attribute: name and employees[].
16    *   The class contains seven methods now!
17    */
18   class Department implements Iterator {
19       private $_name;
20       private $_employees;
21
22       // For tracking iterations:
23       private $_position = 0;
24
25       function __construct($name) {
26           $this->_name = $name;
27           $this->_employees = array();
28           $this->_position = 0;
29       }
30       function addEmployee(Employee $e) {
31           $this->_employees[] = $e;
32           echo "<p>{$e->getName()} has been added to the {$this->_name} department.</p>";
33       }
34
35       // Required by Iterator; returns the current value:
36       function current() {
37           return $this->_employees[$this->_position];
38       }
39
40       // Required by Iterator; returns the current key:
41       function key() {
42           return $this->_position;
43       }
44
45       // Required by Iterator; increments the position:
46       function next() {
47           $this->_position++;
48       }
```

script continues on next page

```
49
50      // Required by Iterator; returns the position to the first spot:
51      function rewind() {
52          $this->_position = 0;
53      }
54
55      // Required by Iterator; returns a Boolean indiating if a value is indexed at this position:
56      function valid() {
57          return (isset($this->_employees[$this->_position]));
58      }
59
60  } // End of Department class.
61
62  class Employee {
63      private $_name;
64      function __construct($name) {
65          $this->_name = $name;
66      }
67      function getName() {
68          return $this->_name;
69      }
70  } // End of Employee class.
71
72  # ***** END OF CLASSES ***** #
73
74  // Create a department:
75  $hr = new Department('Human Resources');
76
77  // Create employees:
78  $e1 = new Employee('Jane Doe');
79  $e2 = new Employee('John Doe');
80
81  // Add the employees to the department:
82  $hr->addEmployee($e1);
83  $hr->addEmployee($e2);
84
85  // Loop through the department:
86  echo "<h2>Department Employees</h2>";
87  foreach ($hr as $e) {
88      echo "<p>{$e->getName()}</p>";
89  }
90
91  // Delete the objects:
92  unset($hr, $e1, $e2);
93
94  ?>
95  </body>
96  </html>
```

6. Define the **key()** method:

```
function key() {
    return $this->_position;
}
```

The **key()** method returns the current position.

7. Define the **next()** method:

```
function next() {
    $this->_position++;
}
```

The **next()** method should increment the position indicator so that it will point to the next item.

8. Define the **rewind()** method:

```
function rewind() {
    $this->_position = 0;
}
```

The **rewind()** method resets the position indicator back to its original value.

C The employees are easily listed at the bottom of the page because **Department** now implements the **Iterator** pattern.

9. Define the **valid()** method:

```
function valid() {
    return (isset($this->_employees
    [$this->_position]));
}
```

This method needs to return a Boolean indicating if a value exists at the current position. If this method returns false, then the iterating structure (i.e., the **foreach** loop) will know to stop looping through the data.

10. Outside of the class, after creating all the objects, loop through the department:

```
echo "<h2>Department Employees
</h2>";
foreach ($hr as $e) {
    echo "<p>{$e->getName()}</p>";
}
```

Since **Department** implements **Iterator**, a **Department** object can be passed to a **foreach** loop. Since each item within the **foreach** loop is an **Employee** object—because that's what the **Department::current()** method returns—you can call **getName()** on the **$e** object within the loop.

11. Save the file as **iterator.php**, place it in your Web directory, and test in your Web browser **C**.

TIP The **FilterIterator** can be used with a **DirectoryIterator** to limit what kinds of files are iterated.

TIP The **LimitIterator** allows you to page through a list, similar to using a **LIMIT** clause in a SQL command.

TIP The SPL defines a couple of recursive iterators that make it easier to navigate nested lists (such as directories or multidimensional arrays).

Data structures

In more recent versions of PHP, the SPL also has classes that define new data structures. Most of these use objects to create more specific, limited variations on arrays. You might think that would be bad, but the flexibility and openness of PHP arrays can have adverse performance effects and allow for sloppier coding.

As an example, take **SplFixedArray**. This array type has the following characteristics:

- Has a fixed number of elements
- Only uses integers greater than or equal to 0 for its keys
- Cannot use any of the existing array functions

That may all sound like a bad deal, but what the **SplFixedArray** provides is better performance than a traditional array. In situations where you know the number of array elements in advance and are using numeric indexes, this is a reasonable trade-off. And, wisely, **SplFixedArray** implements **Iterator**, so you can access the entire array using a loop, as you would a standard array. (Technically, you can change the number of elements in an **SplFixedArray** after you've created it, but doing so eradicates any performance benefits of using the format in the first place.)

As another example, the *stack* is a commonly used structure in programming. A stack is a list of items that has a last-in, first-out (LIFO) order. In other words, the only item in the stack that is available is the one added most recently:

```
$names = new SplStack();
// Add items:
$names->push('Lucian');
$names->push('Priscilla');
$names->push('Travis');
$names->push('Greta');
$names->pop(); // Greta
```

Again, this is just a more restricted type of array, but restrictions are sometimes for the best. For example, if you have an array that stores a sequence of steps, you might only let the user go back a step, not to any random step. That kind of restriction can be enforced with a stack, but not a standard array.

Similar to the stack is the *queue*, implemented in SPL as **SplQueue**. This list type uses the first-in, first-out (FIFO) structure.

Autoloading classes

With OOP, a logical way to modularize the files in an application is to place each class definition in its own file. You've done this multiple times over by now. In such examples, the class file has to be required by the script that needs to create an object of that type:

```
require('Rectangle.php');
$r = new Rectangle(43, 902);
```

When including just one class file, this isn't much of a hardship, but as your programs use more and more objects, including all the requisite files can become tedious. Thankfully, the developers behind PHP created a workaround to the tiresome process of always including class definition files.

To start, define a function that will know how to include class files for you:

```php
function class_loader($class) {
    require('classes/' . $class .
    →'.php');
}
```

That code assumes that all class files are in the **classes** subdirectory. Now you can load a class file using

```php
class_loader('Rectangle');
```

However, the point of creating a class loading function isn't to call it directly but rather to have PHP call it for you when a class definition is required. This is known as *autoloading*.

To enable autoloading, register your loading function with PHP:

```php
spl_autoload_register
→('class_loader');
```

For each new object type created in the following code, the function will be invoked:

```php
$obj = new Class();
$me = new Human();
$r = new Rectangle();
```

Other Interfaces

There are a couple of SPL interfaces that do not fit neatly into any of the chapter's categories of SPL topics. For example, the **Countable** interface dictates the method signature that a class must have in order to use the PHP **count()** method on objects of that class type. Specifically, **Countable** needs you to create a method called **count()** that takes no arguments, and returns an integer:

```php
class Department implements Iterator, Countable {
    // Attributes.
    // Other methods.
    function count() {
        return count($this->_employees);
    }
} // End of Department class.
echo count($hr);
```

Another interface, **ArrayAccess**, allows you to make an object treatable like it was an array. To implement it, you define four methods that then let you add, reference, and remove object components using array notation.

Thanks to the autoloader function, those three lines will automatically include **Class.php**, **Human.php**, and **Rectangle.php** (within the **classes** directory). Note that this does assume that the classes and class files use the same exact names (minus the extensions).

Notice that the **class_loader()** function and the **spl_autoload_register()** call are defined outside of any class. Instead, you would place those lines of code in a script that instantiates objects.

As an example of this, let's rewrite **factory.php** (Script 7.4) to autoload the class definitions. The factory example is particularly good for autoloading because the specific **Shape** type—e.g., **Rectangle** or **Triangle**—will only be known at runtime. By using the autoloader, instead of automatically loading all the classes that could be used, no memory will be wasted by loading unused classes.

To autoload class definition files:

1. Open **factory.php** (Script 7.4) in your text editor or IDE.

2. Remove the four **require()** lines (**Script 8.10**).

3. Add the definition of the **class_loader()** function:

```
function class_loader($class) {
    require($class . '.php');
}
```

This assumes that all class files will be in the same directory as this script, which has been how I've been doing things in this book, for simplicity's sake.

4. Tell PHP to use the function:

```
spl_autoload_register
→ ('class_loader');
```

5. Save the file as **autoload.php**, place it in your Web directory along all the necessary class files, and test in your Web browser **D**.

Remember that you have to pass certain values along in the URL in order for the script to work. See Chapter 7 for details.

TIP In earlier versions of PHP, before the `spl_autoload_register()` function was added, the `__autoload()` function was used for this same purpose.

TIP Although class names in PHP are case-insensitive, some operating systems use case-sensitive file structures. If your class is called `MyClass`, you'll be better off naming the file exactly `MyClass.php` and creating objects using

```
$obj = new MyClass();
```

D The script seems to work exactly the same as before, but now class definition files are loaded on an as-needed basis.

Script 8.10 Using the SPL autoloading capability, this script no longer has to manually include each class file that it may need.

```
1    <!doctype html>
2    <html lang="en">
3    <head>
4        <meta charset="utf-8">
5        <title>Autoloading</title>
6        <link rel="stylesheet" href="style.css">
7    </head>
8    <body>
9    <?php # Script 8.10 - autoload.php
10   // This page uses the ShapeFactory class (Script 7.2).
11
12   // Create the autoloader:
13   function class_loader($class) {
14       require($class . '.php');
15   }
16   spl_autoload_register('class_loader');
17
18   // Minimal validation:
19   if (isset($_GET['shape'], $_GET['dimensions'])) {
20
21       // Create the new object:
22       $obj = ShapeFactory::Create($_GET['shape'], $_GET['dimensions']);
23
24       // Print a little introduction:
25       echo "<h2>Creating a {$_GET['shape']}...</h2>";
26
27       // Print the area:
28       echo '<p>The area is ' . $obj->getArea() . '</p>';
29
30       // Print the perimeter:
31       echo '<p>The perimeter is ' . $obj->getPerimeter() . '</p>';
32
33   } else {
34       echo '<p class="error">Please provide a shape type and size.</p>';
35   }
36
37   // Delete the object:
38   unset($obj);
39
40   ?>
41   </body>
42   </html>
```

Review and Pursue

If you have any problems with these sections, either in answering the questions or pursuing your own endeavors, turn to the book's supporting forum (www.Larry Ullman.com/forums/).

Review

- What is an *exception*? How do exceptions differ from errors? (See page 244.)
- What exception methods will you commonly use? (See page 245.)
- What is the **try...catch** syntax? (See page 244.)
- How do you create different exception types? (See page 251.)
- What is *PDO*? What are the benefits of using PDO? (See page 258.)
- How do you connect to a database using PDO? (See pages 258 and 259.)
- How do you execute a simple query using PDO? (See page 261.)
- How do you execute a query that returns results, and fetch those results, using PDO? (See page 262.)
- What are *prepared statements*? How do you execute them using PDO? (See page 266.)
- What is the *SPL*? (See page 270.)
- What SPL classes exist for working with files? (See page 271.)
- What is an *iterator*? (See page 273.)
- What are some of the new data structures added in the SPL? What advantages are there in using them? (See page 278.)
- What are the benefits of having PHP autoload class files for you? How do you set that up? (See page 279.)

Pursue

- If you're not familiar with how to write data to a file in PHP, see the PHP manual.
- Introduce errors into the **WriteTo-File** class in order to see some other exceptions.
- Check out the PHP manual's pages on PDO. Specifically investigate how to
  - Change the level of error reporting.
  - Perform transactions.
- If you're unfamiliar with what *SQL injection attacks* are, look them up online.
- If you've never used prepared statements, do more research on what they are and why they're beneficial.
- Update the **add_task.php** example to create a **Task** class. Then fetch existing tasks from the database into **Task** objects.
- If you're using PHP 5.4 or later, rewrite the **db_sessions.inc.php** script from Chapter 3, this time using an extension of the **SessionHandlerInterface** class.
- Try implementing the **Directory Iterator** example, using the **SplFileObject** within the loop to print out information about each file.
- Try having the **Department** class also implement **Countable**, so that you can apply the **count()** function to **Department** objects.
- Check out the PHP manual examples for the **ArrayAccess** interface.
- Spend an afternoon (or two) reading up on the Standard PHP Library, both in the PHP manual and in various tutorials and articles online.

Example— CMS with OOP

New in this edition of the book is this example chapter. A popular feature of my other PHP books, an example chapter walks through the entire implementation of a real-world site...well, as "entire" as is possible within the confines of a single chapter, that is.

For the example, I'll create a content management system (CMS), with users who can create and view pages of content. In keeping with the material taught over the previous five chapters, the example will use OOP. Still, the most relevant information will come from Chapter 4, "Basic Object-Oriented Programming," and Chapter 8, "Using Existing Classes." While using those ideas to create this site, you will still learn a few new things and get plenty of suggestions for how you could extend this example.

In This Chapter

Identifying the Goals

The goal for this chapter is to implement an example site using OOP. The specific example I came up with is a content management system, both because I haven't used that example in previous books and because CMS represents a large percentage of existing Web sites, often created using WordPress, Drupal, or the like.

That being said, there's a limit to how much of the site can be implemented and explained in a single chapter of a book (I could write a short book on the subject alone). This chapter focuses on the two most important aspects of a CMS:

- Pages (i.e., the content)
- Users (the people both creating and reading the content)

Just implementing the most critical features for these two aspects requires 16 PHP scripts and HTML files (and, consequently, about 50 book pages). But I've managed to define all the requisite functionality:

- Pages can be added.
- The most recent pages are previewed on the home page.
- An individual page can be seen in its entirety.
- A user can log in.
- A user can log out.
- Only administrative users, or the author of the currently viewed page of content, will be provided access to edit the page.
- Only administrative users or author users can create new pages.

Because it's an object-based system, you can easily extend this initial functionality to fit your needs. I'll provide many such recommendations along the way.

As an added bonus, the example will use a light, makeshift *Model-View-Controller* (MVC) approach. MVC is a common software architectural pattern (it's not technically a design pattern), first introduced in the Smalltalk programming language. MVC is very popular, and for good reason. Using MVC, you separate the data (i.e., the Model), from the output (i.e., the View), using the Controller as the agent.

MVC can be used for application design just as it can Web design. In a Web environment, the Models are normally represented by database tables, although some Models can also represent form data that doesn't get stored in the database (such as that used in a contact form). Naturally, on a Web page, the Views are the HTML pages—the final, dynamically generated output—that the user actually sees. The Controllers react to user actions, such as the request of a single page or the submission of a form. Controllers implement the logic: validate some data, insert it into a database, show the results, and so forth.

By using MVC, you'll find that your project will be both easier to expand and easier to maintain. You can add and change any of the three components without necessarily touching the others. For example, you can change how a certain bit of logic is executed in a Controller without adjusting the associated Model or View. And since each component is its own file, edits are quicker, since you don't have to scan through oodles of integrated PHP, SQL, and HTML.

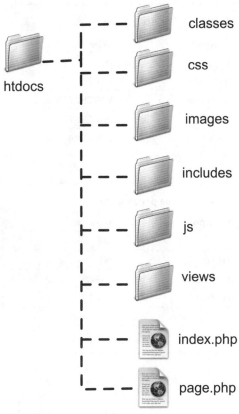

classes

css

images

includes

js

views

index.php

page.php

htdocs

A The organization of the site.

In more formal MVC structures, you would use objects as Controllers. Here, individual PHP scripts will act as the Controllers. However, just as in formal MVC, the Controllers will not contain or generate any HTML, pushing that onto the Views, which are individual HTML files. As you'll see, the View files are primarily HTML, with very little logic, which is to say only the bare minimum of PHP code. The Models will always be classes.

The Controllers are represented by top-level PHP scripts. All of the classes go into a separate directory, as do the View files **A**. Three other PHP scripts, which don't fit neatly into one of these three categories, go in the **includes** directory.

Through the rest of the chapter, you'll walk through the implementation of this example in much the same order as I developed the site itself.

Making Improvements with Apache

In Chapter 2, "Developing Web Applications," I discuss how to configure the Apache Web server to change how a site operates. Two primary concepts were introduced:

- Using **mod_rewrite** to create prettier, more SEO-friendly URLs
- Using **.htaccess** to limit access to a directory

Although I don't do so in this chapter, both ideas could be applied to this site.

For example, with **mod_rewrite**, the URL for a page of content could be changed from **page.php?id=X** to **page/X/The+Content+Title**. The X values would still be used to pull the content from the database (on **page.php**), the URL would be much prettier, informative, and SEO-friendly.

As for using **.htaccess** to protect a directory, that would be most appropriate for the **includes** directory. Also, adding that same restriction to the **views** directory would prevent someone from trying to load a page from that folder directly (assuming the malicious user knows it exists, of course).

Creating the Database

For me, when it comes to Web development, I almost always begin with the underlying database. In the MVC approach, the database tables tend to represent most of the Models, too. For this example, as I've implemented it in this chapter, there are two tables: **users** (Table 9.1) and **pages** (Table 9.2). The **id** column from the **users** table is a foreign key in the **pages** table, indicating who created the page.

Some CMS systems distinguish between "pages," which are intended as longstanding, time-insensitive, types of content, versus "posts," which are time-sensitive. For example, an "about" page would be a *page* but news would be put into a post. This site does not do that, but you'd just need to create a **posts** table if you wanted that ability. It would be designed just like **pages**.

If you want the ability to associate categories or tags with pages or posts, you would need to create a **categories** or **tags** table. Then you would need to create a **pages_categories** (or **pages_tags** or **posts_categories** or **posts_tags**) table that would act as the intermediary for the many-to-many relationship between pages/posts and categories/tags.

If you want users to be able to add comments to a page (or post), create a **comments** table. It would need to store the page ID, the comment content, the date submitted, and some reference to the user. What that reference would be would depend on whether or not only registered users could comment.

TABLE 9.1 The users Table

Column	Type
id	INT
userType	ENUM
username	VARCHAR(30)
email	VARCHAR(40)
pass	CHAR(40)

TABLE 9.2 The pages Table

Column	Type
id	INT
creatorId	INT
title	VARCHAR(100)
content	TEXT
dateUpdated	TIMESTAMP
dateAdded	TIMESTAMP

To create the database:

1. Access MySQL (or other database application) via whatever interface you prefer.

   I'll be using the command-line mysql client, but you can use phpMyAdmin or whatever.

   Also, because this site will use PDO (see Chapter 8) for all database interactions, changing database applications will only require that you edit a single line of code.

2. Create and use a new database:

   ```
   CREATE DATABASE cms;
   ```

   ```
   USE cms;
   ```

   I'm creating a new database for this example. If that's not possible for you (e.g., you're using a hosted site), just select your existing database.

3. Create the **users** table 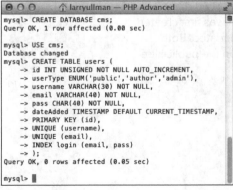:

   ```
   CREATE TABLE users (
   id INT UNSIGNED NOT NULL
   → AUTO_INCREMENT,
   userType ENUM('public','author',
   → 'admin'),
   username VARCHAR(30) NOT NULL,
   email VARCHAR(40) NOT NULL,
   pass CHAR(40) NOT NULL,
   dateAdded TIMESTAMP DEFAULT
   → CURRENT_TIMESTAMP,
   PRIMARY KEY (id),
   UNIQUE (username),
   UNIQUE (email),
   INDEX login (email, pass)
   );
   ```

   The **users** table uses the **id** column as its primary key. The **userType** column represents three possible types of users. Users can have usernames, which must be unique, as must the email address. The password will be encrypted using **SHA1()**, which outputs a string 40 characters long.

continues on next page

```
⊖ ○ ○          ⬆ larryullman — PHP Advanced
mysql> CREATE DATABASE cms;
Query OK, 1 row affected (0.00 sec)

mysql> USE cms;
Database changed
mysql> CREATE TABLE users (
    -> id INT UNSIGNED NOT NULL AUTO_INCREMENT,
    -> userType ENUM('public','author','admin'),
    -> username VARCHAR(30) NOT NULL,
    -> email VARCHAR(40) NOT NULL,
    -> pass CHAR(40) NOT NULL,
    -> dateAdded TIMESTAMP DEFAULT CURRENT_TIMESTAMP,
    -> PRIMARY KEY (id),
    -> UNIQUE (username),
    -> UNIQUE (email),
    -> INDEX login (email, pass)
    -> );
Query OK, 0 rows affected (0.05 sec)

mysql> ▋
```

Ⓐ Creating the first table.

Note that because I'm using OOP on the programming side of things, I'm naming my database columns using conventional OOP lower camel-case syntax. For example, it's **userType**, not **user_type**. This allows my class code to be **$this->userType**, which is more standard than **$this->user_type**.

4. Create the **pages** table 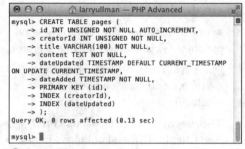:

```
CREATE TABLE pages (
id INT UNSIGNED NOT NULL
→ AUTO_INCREMENT,
creatorId INT UNSIGNED NOT NULL,
title VARCHAR(100) NOT NULL,
content TEXT NOT NULL,
dateUpdated TIMESTAMP DEFAULT
→ CURRENT_TIMESTAMP ON UPDATE
→ CURRENT_TIMESTAMP,
dateAdded TIMESTAMP NOT NULL,
PRIMARY KEY (id),
INDEX (creatorId),
INDEX (dateUpdated)
);
```

The **pages** table is also pretty simple. It uses the **id** column as the primary key, and identifies the creator of the page via **creatorId**. A page itself is made up of a title and its content. Two dates are stored: when the page was first created and when it was last updated. Both could be meaningful on the public side of things.

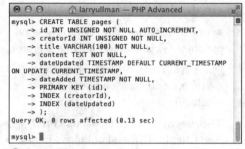
B Creating the second table.

5. Create a couple of users **C**:

```
INSERT INTO users VALUES
(NULL, 'public', 'publicUser',
→'public@example.com',
→SHA1('publicPass'), NULL),
(NULL, 'author', 'authorUser',
→'author@example.com',
→SHA1('authorPass'), NULL),
(NULL, 'admin', 'adminUser',
→'admin@example.com',
→SHA1('adminPass'), NULL);
```

Given the limitations of a book, I haven't implemented a registration process, so create a couple of usable users via this **INSERT** command. Later in the book you'll see how easy it will be to create a registration process, using the site's classes.

6. Create a couple of pages:

```
INSERT INTO pages VALUES
(NULL, 2, 'This is a post',
→'<p>Lorem ipsum dolor sit amet,
→consectetur adipisicing elit,
→sed do eiusmod tempor
→incididunt ut labore et dolore
→magna aliqua.</p>', NULL, NOW());
```

The script for adding new pages of content won't be written until the end of the chapter. In the interim, use an **INSERT** command to create at least three pages of content.

Use whatever combination of text and HTML you want for the content.

TIP You can download a couple of sample SQL commands along with the site's code from www.LarryUllman.com.

TIP If you wanted to allow for a more flexible user type structure, create a userTypes table. Then relate that back into the users table.

```
mysql> INSERT INTO users VALUES
    -> (NULL, 'public', 'publicUser', 'public@example.com', SHA1('publicPass'), NULL),
    -> (NULL, 'author', 'authorUser', 'author@example.com', SHA1('authorPass'), NULL),
    -> (NULL, 'admin', 'adminUser', 'admin@example.com', SHA1('adminPass'), NULL);
Query OK, 3 rows affected (0.01 sec)
Records: 3  Duplicates: 0  Warnings: 0

mysql>
```

C Prepopulating the **users** table.

Making the Template

Next in the process, I often turn from the most hidden component—the database—to the most obvious: the HTML template. Having no design skills myself, I was fortunate that Tjobbe Andrews (**http://tawd.co.uk**) volunteered to create an HTML5 template for me to use with this chapter of the book. Tjobbe had let me freely use one of his existing templates in the previous edition of this book, and it was so kind of him to take the time to create a new one for this chapter's example.

With that template developed, the entire site can use a three-include approach **A**:

```
include('includes/header.inc.php');

include('views/specific_content.html');

include('includes/footer.inc.php');
```

The header file has a little bit of PHP logic to set the page title based on the presence of a variable. Second, both it and the footer will toggle the login/logout link, based on whether or not the user is currently logged in.

The footer file also creates an "add page" link if the current user is either an author or an administrator.

All of the code can be downloaded from the corresponding Web site at **www.LarryUllman.com**. In fact, that's clearly a better way of creating the two template files, in particular. In the following sequence, I'll only highlight the dynamic PHP code found in both files. Also see the first image in the chapter for the site's overall directory structure.

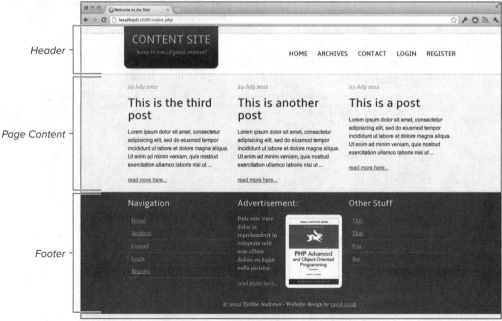

A How a page of content is broken into three distinct files.

To create the header and footer:

1. In **header.inc.php**, print the page title based on the existence of a variable (Script 9.1):

```
<title><?php echo
→ (isset($pageTitle)) ?
→ $pageTitle : 'Some Content
→ Site'; ?></title>
```

This code checks if the **$pageTitle** variable is set (has a non-empty value). If so, its value is printed. Otherwise, a default page title is printed. This is simplified to a single line thanks to the ternary operator.

Normally, in procedural code, I would name the variable **$page_title**, but because I'm using OOP conventions here, I've chosen to use **$pageTitle**, despite the fact that it won't be an object.

continues on next page

Script 9.1 The header file begins the HTML page, dynamically sets the title value, and toggles the login/logout link.

```
1    <!DOCTYPE HTML>
2    <html>
3    <head>
4        <meta http-equiv="Content-Type" content="text/html; charset=utf-8">
5        <meta name="viewport" content="width=device-width, initial-scale=1.0">
6        <title><?php echo (isset($pageTitle)) ? $pageTitle : 'Some Content Site'; ?></title>
7        <!--[if IE]>
8        <script src="http://html5shiv.googlecode.com/svn/trunk/html5.js"></script>
9        <![endif]-->
10       <script src="https://ajax.googleapis.com/ajax/libs/jquery/1.7.2/jquery.min.js"></script>
11       <script src="js/custom-jquery.js"></script>
12       <link rel="stylesheet" href="css/reset.css">
13       <link rel="stylesheet" href="css/fonts/fonts.css">
14       <link rel="stylesheet" href="css/main.css">
15       <!--[if lt IE 8]>
16       <link rel="stylesheet" href="css/ie6-7.css">
17       <![endif]-->
18   </head>
19   <!-- # header.inc.php - Script 9.1 -->
20   <body>
21       <header>
22           <h1>Content Site<span>Home to lots of great content!</span></h1>
23           <nav>
24               <ul>
25                   <li><a href="index.php">Home</a></li><li><a href="#">Archives</a></li><li><a
                     → href="contact.php">Contact</a></li><li><?php if ($user) { echo '<a
                     → href="logout.php">Logout</a>'; } else { echo '<a href="login.php">
                     → Login</a>'; } ?></li><li><a href="#">Register</a></li>
26               </ul>
27           </nav>
28       </header>
```

2. Within the header navigation links, toggle the login/logout link:

```
<li><?php if ($user) { echo '<a
→ href="logout.php">Logout</a>';
→ } else { echo '<a href=
→ "login.php">Login</a>'; } ?></li>
```

The **$user** variable will represent the currently logged-in user, or have a **NULL** value if the user is not logged in. Thus, **if ($user)** is enough of a conditional to determine whether the login or the logout link should be shown.

3. Save the file as **header.inc.php** in the **includes** directory.

I'm using **.inc** to indicate that this file is meant to be included by others.

4. Within **footer.inc.php**, again toggle the login/logout links (**Script 9.2**):

```
<li><?php if ($user) { echo '<a
→ href="logout.php">Logout</a>';
→ } else { echo '<a href=
→ "login.php">Login</a>'; } ?></li>
```

This is the same code as in the header, since all the links are just repeated.

Script 9.2 The footer file also toggles the login/logout link, and creates a new link for certain users.

```
1    <!-- # footer.inc.php - Script 9.2 -->
2      <div class="footerBox">
3        <footer class="threeColumns">
4          <article>
5            <h1>Navigation</h1>
6            <nav>
7              <ul>
8                <li><a href="index.php">Home</a></li><li><a href="#">Archives</a></li><li>
                 → <a href="#">Contact</a></li><li><?php if ($user) { echo '<a href=
                 → "logout.php">Logout</a>'; } else { echo '<a href="login.php">
                 → Login</a>'; } ?></li><li><a href="#">Register</a></li>
9              </ul>
10           </nav>
11         </article>
12         <article>
13           <h1>Advertisement:</h1>
14           <img src="images/book.png" class="alignright">
15           <p>Duis aute irure dolor in reprehenderit in voluptate velit esse cillum dolore eu
                 → fugiat nulla pariatur.</p>
16           <p><a href="#">read more here..</a></p>
17         </article>
18         <article>
19           <h1>Other Stuff</h1>
20           <ul>
21             <?php if ($user && $user->canCreatePage()) echo '<li><a
                 → href="add_page.php">Add a New Page</a></li>'; ?>
22             <li><a href="#">This</a></li>
23             <li><a href="#">That</a></li>
24             <li><a href="#">Foo</a></li>
25             <li><a href="#">Bar</a></li>
26           </ul>
```

script continues on next page

```
27              </article>
28              <small>&copy; <?php echo
       → date('Y'); ?> Tjobbe
       → Andrews - Website design by
       → <a href="http://www.tawd.
       → co.uk">tawd.co.uk</a></small>
29          </footer>
30      </div>
31  </body>
32  </html>
```

5. Create a link to the **add_page.php** script, should the user be logged in and have the power to add pages:

```
<?php if ($user && $user->can
→ CreatePage()) echo '<li><a href=
→ "add_page.php">Add a New Page
→ </a></li>'; ?>
```

Two types of users, authors and administrators, can create new pages of content. You *could* write a conditional here that checks for either of those types:

```
if (($user->getUserType() ==
→ 'admin') || ($user->getUserType()
→ == 'author')) {
```

But that ends up being a lot of logic and specificity (i.e., the particular values being watched for) buried among this other PHP code and HTML. Therefore, it makes more sense to write an object method that can return a Boolean value indicating the user's ability to perform this task. That's all the **canCreatePage()** method does. You'll see it in a few pages.

6. Save the file as **footer.inc.php**, also in your **includes** directory.

Writing a Utilities File

The next step I took in developing this site was to create a utilities file. This file will be included by every primary PHP script (i.e., every Controller). On other sites, I might call this a *configuration* file, but this one does a bit more than just that.

As written for the relatively straightforward site, the utilities file fulfills three needs:

- It defines the class loading function (see Chapter 8).
- It starts the session and checks for the presence of a **User** object previously stored in the session.
- It opens the database connection, creating a PDO object in the process.

The only truly new idea here involves the *serializing* of objects, which I'll explain.

It's very easy to store simple data types, such as strings and numbers, in a session, file, or database, as you already know. But complex data types, such as arrays and objects, are not easily stored in their original state. Those flat storage mediums cannot directly support multifaceted formats like arrays and objects. The solution is to convert the complex data type into a simple data type. This is done in PHP using the **serialize()** function:

```
$data = array('Karen' => 'Toronto',
→'Stephanie' => 'Boston',
→'Jessica' => 'State College');
$sData = serialize($data);
```

The **serialize()** function outputs a string that represents the complex data. Now, **$sData** would have a value of

```
a:3:{s:5:"Karen";s:7:"Toronto";s:9:
→"Stephanie";s:6:"Boston";s:7:
→"Jessica";s:13:"State College";}
```

(That says that the data is an array, consisting of three elements. The first element uses a string for its key, containing five characters, with a value of *Karen*. That element has a string for its value, containing seven characters, with a value of *Toronto*. And so on.)

From that string, the data can be reconstituted into its complex format via the **unserialize()** function:

```
$data = unserialize($sData);
```

The process is the same with objects, with two exceptions. First, the serialized version of the object will only store the values of the object's attributes, along with the name of the object's class. The object's methods will not be stored (this is fine; they'll come back to the object when the object is unserialized).

The second difference is that PHP needs access to the object's class definition in order to re-create the object. As long as PHP can do that, the original object will be properly reconstituted, retaining its attribute values and able to invoke its methods once again.

Now, given that long explanation, if you go to store an object in the session, PHP will automatically serialize and unserialize the data on the fly. This process will work as long as PHP can access the corresponding class definitions when the session is started again.

```
1   <?php # utilities.inc.php - Script 9.3
2   // This page needs to do the setup and
    → configuration required by every
    → other page.
3
4   // Autoload classes from "classes"
    → directory:
5   function class_loader($class) {
6       require('classes/' . $class . '.php');
7   }
8   spl_autoload_register('class_loader');
9
10  // Start the session:
11  session_start();
12
13  // Check for a user in the session:
14  $user = (isset($_SESSION['user'])) ?
    → $_SESSION['user'] : null;
15
16  // Create the database connection as
    → a PDO object:
17  try {
18
19      // Create the object:
20      $pdo = new PDO('mysql:dbname=cms;
        → host=localhost', 'username',
        → 'password');
21
22  } catch (PDOException $e) { // Report
    → the error!
23
24      $pageTitle = 'Error!';
25      include('includes/header.inc.php');
26      include('views/error.html');
27      include('includes/footer.inc.php');
28      exit();
29
30  }
```

To create the utilities file:

1. Begin a new PHP script in your text editor or IDE, to be named **utilities.inc. php** (Script 9.3):

   ```
   <?php # utilities.inc.php -
   → Script 9.3
   ```

2. Define a function that will autoload the classes:

   ```
   function class_loader($class) {
       require('classes/' . $class .
       → '.php');
   }
   spl_autoload_register
   → ('class_loader');
   ```

   This code comes from Chapter 8. The only difference here is that the class definition files will be placed in the **classes** subdirectory.

3. Start the session:

   ```
   session_start();
   ```

   Again, the session is being started at this point so that it can access all the class definitions (thanks to the autoloader). This order is required should there be a stored, serialized object in the session.

4. Check for a user in the session:

   ```
   $user = (isset($_SESSION['user']))
   → ? $_SESSION['user'] : null;
   ```

   The **$user** variable, as already explained in the discussion of the header and footer files, will be a reference to the currently logged-in user. The user object will be stored in the session upon successfully logging in. On subsequent pages, the **$user** variable will be reconstituted from the session.

continues on next page

If the user is not logged in, then the **$user** variable is set to **null**. This will make uses of the variable, as in

```
if ($user) {
```

be false and not create an error (for referencing an undefined variable.

5. Create the database connection as a PDO object:

```
try {

    $pdo = new PDO('mysql:dbname=
    → cms;host=localhost',
    → 'username', 'password');
```

This code also comes from Chapter 8. Change the particulars of the DSN to match your setup.

6. Catch any PDO exception:

```
} catch (PDOException $e) {

    $pageTitle = 'Error!';

    include('includes/
    → header.inc.php');

    include('views/error.html');

    include('includes/
    → footer.inc.php');

    exit();

}
```

The site will make frequent use of exception handling, starting with this **try...catch** block. If the database connection could not be made, then the page title is set to *Error!*, the header is included, as is the **error.html** view file, and the footer. As this script will be included by other scripts, the **exit()** function must then be called to stop the including script from continuing to execute, as almost every page does require a database connection.

As you'll see in the next section, the **$e** exception will be used in the error view file **Ⓐ**.

7. Save the file as **utilities.inc.php**, in the **includes** directory.

> **TIP** To be clear, if you were storing an object in a database or a file, you would need to formally serialize the object prior to storage. Upon retrieval, you would unserialize the object.

Ⓐ How a database connection error is treated during development of the site.

Creating the Error View File

The **utilities.inc.php** (Script 9.3) page makes reference to **views/error.html**, so let's go ahead and write that script now.

To create the error view file:

1. Begin a new HTML document in your text editor or IDE, to be named **error.html** (Script 9.4):

   ```
   <!-- # error.html - Script 9.4 -->
   ```

2. Begin the page-specific content:

   ```
   <section class="fullWidth">
       <article>
           <h1>An Error Occurred!</h1>
   ```

   As you'll see in time, the site has been designed so that all page-specific content goes within its own **section**. The **section** element's **class** attribute dictates how much of the page is taken up by that **section**. This **section** will use the full width.

continues on next page

Script 9.4 All significant problems will be handled by this single view file.

```
1   <!-- # error.html - Script 9.4 -->
2   <section class="fullWidth">
3       <article>
4           <h1>An Error Occurred!</h1>
5           <p>The content is not viewable because an error occurred. We apologize for any
              → inconvenience. The system administrator has been notified and will correct the
              → problem as soon as possible.</p>
6           <p>Details (not for public consumption): <span class="error"><?php echo
              → $e->getMessage(); ?></span></p>
7       </article>
8   </section>
```

3. Add a generic message:

```
<p>The content is not viewable
→ because an error occurred.
→ We apologize for any
→ inconvenience. The system
→ administrator has been notified
→ and will correct the problem as
→ soon as possible.</p>
```

This is essentially what the public user would see, or a variation on this. Of course, you'd want to add code to make sure the system administrator is actually notified!

4. Add a detailed debugging message:

```
<p>Details (not for public
→ consumption): <span class=
→ "error"><?php echo $e->
→ getMessage(); ?></span></p>
```

Here the exception is being used to report what the problem was (as in Ⓐ in the previous section). You would never want to show this to the public, because it's both unprofessional and not secure.

When the site goes live, you could just remove this section and replace it with the code that emails the administrator with the details of the problem.

5. Complete the HTML:

```
    </article>

</section>
```

6. Save the file as **error.html** in the **views** directory.

Defining the Classes

Surprisingly, I was able to pull off this entire site defining only two classes. That's a misleading count, of course, since the site uses PDO (and the corresponding **PDOStatement** and **PDOException** classes), as you've already seen. And, as you'll see soon enough, another series of existing classes are used to create and validate the forms. So, in full disclosure, aside from all the excellent existing classes used by the site, there are two new, user-defined classes:

- **Page**
- **User**

Let's look at both in detail.

The Page class

The **Page** class will be used to represent a page of content. This will come up in several places:

- On the home page, which shows the three most recent additions
- On an individual page, which displays an entire page of content
- When new pages of content are added

The definition of the **Page** class starts with one attribute for each corresponding database column. This makes sense, because PDO will be used to fetch records from the **pages** table into new objects of type **Page**, assigning column values to class attributes (see Chapter 8).

From there, I created six methods to return the values of each protected attribute (i.e., "getters"). Finally, the **Page** class has a method that returns the first X number of characters of the page's content. This method will initially be used on the home page.

To create the Page class:

1. Begin a new PHP script in your text editor or IDE, to be named **Page.php** (Script 9.5):

   `<?php # Page.php - Script 9.5`

   continues on next page

Script 9.5 This class represents a page of content.

```
1    <?php # Page.php - Script 9.5
2    // This script defines the Page class.
3
4    /*  Class Page.
5     *  The class contains six attributes: id, creatorId, title, content, dateAdded, and dateUpdated.
6     *  The attributes match the corresponding database columns.
7     *  The class contains seven methods:
8     *  - getId()
9     *  - getCreatorId()
10    *  - getTitle()
11    *  - getContent()
12    *  - getDateAdded()
13    *  - getDateUpdated()
```

script continues on next page

2. Begin defining the class:

```
class Page {
    protected $id = null;
    protected $creatorId = null;
    protected $title = null;
    protected $content = null;
    protected $dateAdded = null;
    protected $dateUpdated = null;
```

Here are the six attributes that correspond to the database columns. Each is initialized to **null**, just in case that column isn't selected from the database when the time comes.

3. Define the six "getter" methods:

```
function getId() {
    return $this->id;
}
function getCreatorId() {
    return $this->creatorId;
}
function getTitle() {
    return $this->title;
}
function getContent() {
    return $this->content;
}
function getDateAdded() {
    return $this->dateAdded;
}
function getDateUpdated() {
    return $this->dateUpdated;
}
```

There's nothing particularly notable about these methods.

Script 9.5 *continued*

```
14    *  - getIntro()
15    */
16   class Page {
17
18       // All attributes correspond to
         → database columns.
19       // All attributes are protected.
20       protected $id = null;
21       protected $creatorId = null;
22       protected $title = null;
23       protected $content = null;
24       protected $dateAdded = null;
25       protected $dateUpdated = null;
26
27       // No need for a constructor!
28
29       // Six methods for returning
         → attribute values:
30       function getId() {
31           return $this->id;
32       }
33       function getCreatorId() {
34           return $this->creatorId;
35       }
36       function getTitle() {
37           return $this->title;
38       }
39       function getContent() {
40           return $this->content;
41       }
42       function getDateAdded() {
43           return $this->dateAdded;
44       }
45       function getDateUpdated() {
46           return $this->dateUpdated;
47       }
48
49       // Method returns the first X
         → characters from the content:
50       function getIntro($count = 200) {
51           return substr(strip_tags
             → ($this->content), 0, $count) .
             → '...';
52       }
53
54   } // End of Page class.
```

4. Define the **getIntro()** method:

```
function getIntro($count = 200) {
    return substr(strip_tags
    ↪($this->content), 0, $count) .
    ↪'...';
}
```

The purpose of this method is to return an abbreviated, initial part of the page's content as a way of previewing the page. In theory, this is just a matter of returning the first X number of characters. To make the method more flexible, it takes an argument to indicate how many characters are desired (e.g., the home page may want 200 but a sidebar only 100).

However, if the content begins with HTML, that will throw off the count. For example, an early image in the content could require 50 characters—not to mention the fact that the HTML could throw off the layout of the page requesting the snippet. For that reason, **strip_tags()** is first applied to the content, *and then* the first X number of characters will be returned.

5. Complete the class:

```
} // End of Page class.
```

6. Save the file as **Page.php** in the **classes** directory.

TIP A fancier version of the **getIntro()** method would break the returned text on a space, comma, period, semicolon, question mark, or exclamation point.

The User class

The other new class being defined is **User**, which represents registered and logged-in users only (i.e., users not logged in are not represented by this class). Like the **Page** class, **User** begins with attributes for the database columns already defined.

From there, to address the needs of the site as written for this chapter, there are four methods. One method returns the user's ID, which will be necessary when a user adds a new page of content: the user's ID will need to be added to the page record as the **creatorId** value.

The remaining three methods return Boolean values indicating qualities and capabilities of the user:

- Is the user an administrator?
- Can the user edit the current page?
- Can the user create new pages?

To create the User class:

1. Begin a new PHP script in your text editor or IDE, to be named **User.php** (Script 9.6):

```
<?php # User.php - Script 9.6
```

2. Begin defining the class:

```
class User {
    protected $id = null;
    protected $userType = null;
    protected $username = null;
    protected $email = null;
    protected $pass = null;
    protected $dateAdded = null;
```

continues on page 303

Script 9.6 This class represents the currently logged-in user.

```php
1    <?php # User.php - Script 9.6
2    // This script defines the User class.
3
4    /*  Class User.
5     *  The class contains six attributes: id, userType, username, email, pass, and dateAdded.
6     *  The attributes match the corresponding database columns.
7     *  The class contains four methods:
8     *  - getId()
9     *  - isAdmin()
10    *  - canEditPage()
11    *  - canCreatePage()
12    */
13   class User {
14
15       // All attributes correspond to database columns.
16       // All attributes are protected.
17       protected $id = null;
18       protected $userType = null;
19       protected $username = null;
20       protected $email = null;
21       protected $pass = null;
22       protected $dateAdded = null;
23
24       // Method returns the user ID:
25       function getId() {
26           return $this->id;
27       }
28
29       // Method returns a Boolean if the user is an administrator:
30       function isAdmin() {
31           return ($this->userType == 'admin');
32       }
33
34       // Method returns a Boolean indicating if the user is an administrator
35       // or if the user is the original author of the provided page:
36       function canEditPage(Page $p) {
37           return ($this->isAdmin() || ($this->id == $page->getCreatorId()));
38       }
39
40       // Method returns a Boolean indicating if the user is an administrator or an author:
41       function canCreatePage() {
42           return ($this->isAdmin() || ($this->userType == 'author'));
43       }
44
45   } // End of User class.
```

3. Define the **getId()** method:

```
function getId() {
    return $this->id;
}
```

This method merely returns the attribute value.

4. Define the **isAdmin()** method:

```
function isAdmin() {
    return ($this->userType ==
    → 'admin');
}
```

Administrators in the site can create new pages or edit any page. Presumably, administrators would be able to do other things, such as edit user records. Therefore, it's useful to have a method that can be determined if the user is an administrator.

One option would be to just return the **userType** value. However, then the underlying logic—**$userType == 'admin'**—would need to be written into multiple scripts. If for whatever reason you later change the type to *administrator*, or create other types that would be treated like an administrator, all of that embedded code would need to be found and edited.

By placing the logic in the class, only one line of code would ever need to be tweaked to enact changes like those.

5. Define the **canEditPage()** method:

```
function canEditPage(Page $p) {
    return ($this->isAdmin() ||
    → ($this->id == $page->
    → getCreatorId()));
}
```

This method returns true if the user is an administrator—determined by invoking the **isAdmin()** method—or if the current user's ID equals the page's **creatorID** value.

This method uses class type hinting, as explained in Chapter 6, "More Advanced OOP."

6. Define the **canCreatePage()** method:

```
function canCreatePage() {
    return ($this->isAdmin() ||
    → ($this->userType == 'author'));
}
```

This method returns true if the user is an administrator or an author.

7. Complete the class:

```
} // End of User class.
```

8. Save the file as **User.php** in the **classes** directory.

Creating the Home Page

With all of the core functionality—the database, the template, the utilities file, the main classes—in place, it's time to start creating the PHP scripts that do the actual work. (Again, in the MVC-lite approach being implemented, I'm talking about the Controllers here.) To start, let's create the home page, **index.php**. It will retrieve the three most recent pages of content, display previews of them, and link to the script where the viewer can see the entire content.

Along with this PHP script, you'll need to create the View file that's included by this page.

To create the home page:

1. Begin a new PHP script in your text editor or IDE, to be named **index.php** (**Script 9.7**):

   ```
   <?php # index.php - Script 9.7
   ```

2. Include the utilities file:

   ```
   require('includes/utilities.inc.
   → php');
   ```

   Because the utilities file is so important, I've chosen to use **require()** for it, not **include()**.

Script 9.7 The home page uses a **try...catch** block to pull three records from the table, and then includes the proper View file.

```
1    <?php # index.php - Script 9.7
2
3    // Need the utilities file:
4    require('includes/utilities.inc.php');
5
6    // Include the header:
7    $pageTitle = 'Welcome to the Site!';
8    include('includes/header.inc.php');
9
10   // Fetch the three most recent pages:
11   try {
12
13       $q = 'SELECT id, title, content,
         → DATE_FORMAT(dateAdded, "%e %M %Y")
         → AS dateAdded FROM pages ORDER BY
         → dateAdded DESC LIMIT 3';
14       $r = $pdo->query($q);
15
16       // Check that rows were returned:
17       if ($r && $r->rowCount() > 0) {
18
19           // Set the fetch mode:
20           $r->setFetchMode(PDO::FETCH_CLASS,
             → 'Page');
21
22           // Records will be fetched in
             → the view:
23           include('views/index.html');
24
25       } else { // Problem!
26           throw new Exception('No content is
             → available to be viewed at this
             → time.');
27       }
28
29   } catch (Exception $e) { // Catch generic
     → Exceptions.
30       include('views/error.html');
31   }
32
33   // Include the footer:
34   include('includes/footer.inc.php');
35   ?>
```

3. Define the page title and include the header:

$pageTitle = 'Welcome to the Site!';

include('includes/header.inc.php');

The **$pageTitle** variable will be used within the header, as already explained. The header file is then included. Because it's not the worst thing in the world if the header and the footer aren't included (quite ugly, yes, but still...), I will use **include()** for them. This way, the script will not be terminated if the file cannot be included.

4. Fetch the three most recent pages:

```
try {
    $q = 'SELECT id, title, content,
→ DATE_FORMAT(dateAdded, "%e
→ %M %Y") AS dateAdded FROM
→ pages ORDER BY dateAdded DESC
→ LIMIT 3';
    $r = $pdo->query($q);
```

The query fetches four columns from the **pages** table, formatting the date in the process **A**. Note that you want to create an alias of the formatted date—back to the original column name—or else the resulting records won't have a **dateAdded** value **B** (and, therefore, the generated class won't have that attribute).

continues on next page

A The results returned by the home page's query.

B Without using an alias, the last value selected—the formatted date—will not have the name expected by the class.

5. Check that some rows were returned:

```
if ($r && $r->rowCount() > 0) {
```

This is just a nice precaution to take.

6. Set the fetch mode:

```
$r->setFetchMode(PDO::FETCH_CLASS,
→ 'Page');
```

This line, as explained in Chapter 8, will fetch each record as a new **Page** object.

7. Include the View:

```
include('views/index.html');
```

As you saw in **error.html**, the View will do all the handling and displaying of the data.

8. Throw an exception if no rows were returned:

```
} else {
  throw new Exception('No content
  → is available to be viewed at
  → this time.');
}
```

If no rows were returned, then there was probably a problem with the query (or, less likely, you haven't created any pages of content yet). In either case, the problem needs to be addressed, so a generic **Exception** is thrown, indicating the problem.

9. Catch any exceptions:

```
} catch (Exception $e) {
  include('views/error.html');
}
```

Exceptions could have been thrown by any of the PDO functionality within the **try** block, or simply because the query did not return any records. Any thrown exception will be caught here and then handled in the error view file ⓒ.

Note that you must catch generic **Exceptions** here, which will cover both **PDOExceptions** (as that class extends **Exception**) and the possible exception thrown in Step 8. If you only caught **PDOExceptions** here, then the exception thrown in Step 8 would not be caught.

10. Complete the page:

```
include('includes/footer.inc.php');
?>
```

11. Save the file as **index.php** in the main web directory.

To create the home page view:

1. Begin a new HTML script in your text editor or IDE, to be named **index.html** (**Script 9.8**):

```
<!-- # index.html - Script 9.8 -->
```

2. Begin a new **section**:

```
<section class="threeColumns">
```

Again, this comes from the wonderful template created by Tjobbe Andrews.

An Error Occurred!

The content is not viewable because an error occurred. We apologize for any inconvenience. and will correct the problem as soon as possible.

Details (not for public consumption): No content is available to be viewed at this time.

ⓒ If the query had an error in it, or there is no content, an exception is thrown.

Script 9.8 The View file for the home page fetches and displays the preview of three items.

```
1    <!-- # index.html - Script 9.8 -->
2    <section class="threeColumns">
3    <?php // Fetch the results and display
     →  them:
4    while ($page = $r->fetch()) {
5        echo "<article>
6        <h1><span>{$page->getDateAdded()}
         →  </span>{$page->getTitle()}</h1>
7        <p>{$page->getIntro()}</p>
8        <p><a href=\"page.php?id={$page->
         →  getId()}\">read more here...</a></p>
9        </article>
10       ";
11   }
12   ?>
13   </section>
```

3. Fetch the results and display them:

```
<?php
while ($page = $r->fetch()) {
    echo "<article>
    <h1><span>{$page->getDateAdded
    →  ()}</span>{$page->getTitle()}
    v</h1>
    <p>{$page->getIntro()}</p>
    <p><a href=\"page.php?id=
    →  {$page->getId()}\">read more
    →  here...</a></p>
    </article>
    ";
}
?>
```

The loop fetches each record from the database and creates a new **Page** object in the process. That object can then invoke any of the **Page** class methods in order to create the proper output.

4. Complete the HTML:

```
</section>
```

5. Save the file as **index.html** in the **views** directory, and test by going to **index.php** in your Web browser **D**.

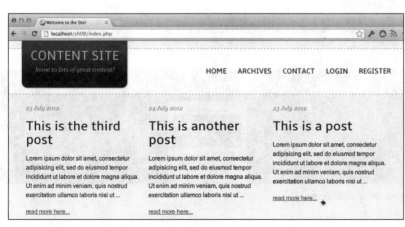

D The final home page.

Viewing a Page

Moving onward into the site, the home page shows previews of the three most recently added pages of content. Each is linked to **page.php**, passing along the page's ID value in the URL. The purpose of **page.php** is to display the full content . This is a simple process:

- Validate the page ID
- Retrieve the corresponding database record
- Include the View file

Again, let's first create the PHP script and then the simple View file.

To create the page-viewing page:

1. Begin a new PHP script in your text editor or IDE, to be named **page.php** (**Script 9.9**):

   ```php
   <?php # page.php - Script 9.9
   require('includes/utilities.inc.
   ⇥ php');
   ```

continues on page 310

Ⓐ A single page of content, in its entirety.

Script 9.9 This is the "Controller" file for displaying a single, full page of content.

```php
1    <?php # page.php - Script 9.9
2    // This page displays a single page of content.
3
4    // Need the utilities file:
5    require('includes/utilities.inc.php');
6
7    try {
8
9        // Validate the page ID:
10       if (!isset($_GET['id']) || !filter_var($_GET['id'], FILTER_VALIDATE_INT, array
     → ('min_range' => 1))) {
11           throw new Exception('An invalid page ID was provided to this page.');
12       }
13
14       // Fetch the page from the database:
15       $q = 'SELECT id, title, content, DATE_FORMAT(dateAdded, "%e %M %Y") AS dateAdded
     → FROM pages WHERE id=:id';
16       $stmt = $pdo->prepare($q);
17       $r = $stmt->execute(array(':id' => $_GET['id']));
18
19       // If the query ran okay, fetch the record into an object:
20       if ($r) {
21           $stmt->setFetchMode(PDO::FETCH_CLASS, 'Page');
22           $page = $stmt->fetch();
23
24           // Confirm that it exists:
25           if ($page) {
26
27               // Set the browser title to the page title:
28               $pageTitle = $page->getTitle();
29
30               // Create the page:
31               include('includes/header.inc.php');
32               include('views/page.html');
33
34           } else {
35               throw new Exception('An invalid page ID was provided to this page.');
36           }
37
38       } else {
39           throw new Exception('An invalid page ID was provided to this page.');
40       }
41
42    } catch (Exception $e) { // Catch generic Exceptions.
43
44        $pageTitle = 'Error!';
45        include('includes/header.inc.php');
46        include('views/error.html');
47
48    }
49
50    // Include the footer:
51    include('includes/footer.inc.php');
52    ?>
```

2. Validate the page ID:

```
try {
    if (!isset($_GET['id']) ||
→ !filter_var($_GET['id'],
→ FILTER_VALIDATE_INT,
→ array('min_range' => 1))) {
        throw new Exception('An
        → invalid page ID was
        → provided to this page.');
    }
```

The page ID should have been received in the URL. The conditional first verifies that a page ID was received, and then uses PHP's Filter extension to validate that it's an integer greater than or equal to 1.

If this conditional is false, an exception is thrown.

3. Query the database:

```
$q = 'SELECT id, title, content,
→ DATE_FORMAT(dateAdded, "%e %M
→ %Y") AS dateAdded FROM pages
→ WHERE id=:id';
$stmt = $pdo->prepare($q);
$r = $stmt->execute(array(':id' =>
→ $_GET['id']));
```

The query itself is much like that on the index page.

4. Fetch the record into an object:

```
if ($r) {
    $stmt->setFetchMode
    → (PDO::FETCH_CLASS, 'Page');
    $page = $stmt->fetch();
```

5. If an object was made, create the page:

```
if ($page) {
    $pageTitle = $page->getTitle();
        include('includes/header.inc.
        → php');
    include('views/page.html');
```

The order of this page is a bit different than the others, because I want the content title to also be the browser window title.

6. Throw exceptions for the conditionals begun in Step 4 and Step 5:

```
    } else {
        throw new Exception('An
        → invalid page ID was
        → provided to this page.');
    }
} else {
    throw new Exception('An invalid
    → page ID was provided to this
    → page.');
}
```

7. Catch any exceptions:

```
} catch (Exception $e) {
    $pageTitle = 'Error!';
        include('includes/header.inc.
        → php');
    include('views/error.html');
}
```

Again, generic **Exception** objects must be caught, not just **PDOException** objects.

8. Complete the page:

```
include('includes/footer.inc.php');
?>
```

9. Save the file as **page.php**.

To create the page-viewing View:

1. Begin a new HTML script in your text editor or IDE, to be named **page.html** (Script 9.10):

   ```
   <!-- # page.html - Script 9.10 -->
   ```

2. Begin a new **section**:

   ```
   <section class="fullWidth">
       <article>
   ```

   In the template, the **fullWidth** class sections use the entire browser window width, which is preferred here.

3. Display the page content:

   ```
   <h1><span><?php echo $page->
   → getDateAdded(); ?></span><?php
   → echo $page->getTitle(); ?></h1>

   <?php echo $page->getContent(); ?>

   <?php if ($user && $user->
   → canEditPage($page)) {

   echo '<p><a href="edit_page.
   → php?id=' . $page->getId() .
   → '">EDIT</a></p>';

   } ?>
   ```

This View will have access to the **$page** variable, which will be an object of type **Page**. From there, it's just a matter of invoking the right methods to generate the desired output.

Along with the actual content, a link to an edit page is created if the user has the authority to edit this particular page. The conditional first checks that **$user** has a non-false value (users not logged in will have a **$user** value of **null**). Then the conditional invokes the **canEditPage()** method of the **User** object. That method takes the current page as its argument. The method will return true if the user is an administrator or the original author of this page.

4. Complete the HTML:

   ```
       </article>
   </section>
   ```

5. Save the file as **page.html** in the **views** directory, and test by clicking one of the page links on the home page Ⓐ.

Script 9.10 This View file outputs the page content within a few HTML tags.

```
1    <!-- # page.html - Script 9.10 -->
2    <section class="fullWidth">
3       <article>
4          <h1><span><?php echo $page->getDateAdded(); ?></span><?php echo $page->getTitle(); ?></h1>
5          <?php echo $page->getContent(); ?>
6          <?php if ($user && $user->canEditPage($page)) {
7          echo '<p><a href="edit_page.php?id=' . $page->getId() . '">EDIT</a></p>';
8          } ?>
9       </article>
10   </section>
```

Using HTML_QuickForm2

In creating the requisite classes for this example, I began designing a class for creating and validating the different forms. Such classes are very useful but a bit tricky: they must be designed to handle:

- Different types of form elements
- Different ways to validate data (numbers vs. emails address vs. anything else you can think of)
- Displaying of errors
- And more

Fortunately, before I got too far along, I remembered my old friend **HTML_QuickForm**. **HTML_QuickForm** is a PEAR (**http://pear.php.net**) class that does all of the above. I wrote about it in the previous edition of the book. Now, there's **HTML_QuickForm2**, rewritten to take advantage of the object features available in PHP5.

The site as written has two forms, one for logging in **Ⓐ**, and another for creating new pages of content **Ⓑ**. Both are created and validated using **HTML_QuickForm2**. I'll briefly explain how to use the class, and then walk through the specific forms.

Note that to use **HTML_QuickForm2**, you must install it. This is normally a matter of executing this line from a command-line interface:

```
pear install HTML_QuickForm2
```

Note that, on some operating systems, you might have to preface that with **sudo**, or provide a full path to PEAR. If you have any trouble installing PEAR, see the PEAR manual, search online, or ask in my support forums.

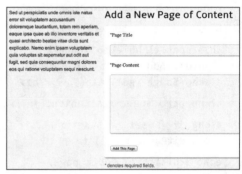

Sed ut perspiciatis unde omnis iste natus error sit voluptatem accusantium doloremque laudantium, totam rem aperiam, eaque ipsa quae ab illo inventore veritatis et quasi architecto beatae vitae dicta sunt explicabo. Nemo enim ipsam voluptatem quia voluptas sit aspernatur aut odit aut fugit, sed quia consequuntur magni dolores eos qui ratione voluptatem sequi nesciunt.

Login

*Email Address

*Password

Login

* denotes required fields.

Ⓐ The login form.

Sed ut perspiciatis unde omnis iste natus error sit voluptatem accusantium doloremque laudantium, totam rem aperiam, eaque ipsa quae ab illo inventore veritatis et quasi architecto beatae vitae dicta sunt explicabo. Nemo enim ipsam voluptatem quia voluptas sit aspernatur aut odit aut fugit, sed quia consequuntur magni dolores eos qui ratione voluptatem sequi nesciunt.

Add a New Page of Content

*Page Title

*Page Content

Add This Page

* denotes required fields.

Ⓑ The form for adding new pages of content.

TABLE 9.3 Standard HTML Element Types

Name	Creates
button	Button
checkbox	Single check box
fieldset	Fieldset
file	File upload prompt
hidden	Hidden input
image	Image input
password	Password input
radio	Radio button
reset	Reset button
select	Select menu
submit	Submit button
text	Text input
textarea	Textarea field

TABLE 9.4 Custom QuickForm2 Element Types

Name	Creates
date	Series of select menus for the month, day, and year
group	Group of related elements
hierselect	Two chained select inputs, the second controlled by the first
script	Inline JavaScript
static	Block of text or HTML

Creating a form

After you've installed the PEAR class, you must first include it in scripts that will use it:

```
require('HTML/QuickForm2.php');
```

Then create an object of type **HTML_QuickForm2**, providing the constructor with a unique ID value for the form:

```
$form = new HTML_QuickForm2
→('someForm');
```

When creating this object, you can pass other parameters to the constructor to change the form method (the default is POST) or add other attributes to the opening **form** tag.

From there you want to add elements to the form. There are many element types, from the standard HTML ones with which you are accustomed (**Table 9.3**) to useful ones defined by QuickForm2 (**Table 9.4**). The syntax for adding a form element is

```
$form->addElement('type', 'name',
→'attributes', 'data');
```

You may want to create a reference to the element being created for future manipulations. If so, just assign the **addElement()** call to another variable:

```
$elem = $form->addElement(/* ... */);
```

To set the label for a form element, invoke the **setLabel()** method on the element:

```
$element->setLabel('Prompt: ');
```

Once you've added all the elements, you show the form by simply printing it:

```
echo $form;
```

The class will take care of the rest.

Filtering and validating form data

Commonly, you'll want to apply some sort of *filter* to your form data: send it through a process that changes the data in some way. The **addFilter()** method does this, taking the name of the PHP function to apply as its arguments:

```
$elem->addFilter('function_name');
```

For example, this line will apply the **trim()** function to whatever value a user entered in the name field:

```
$name->addFilter('trim');
```

Or you might want to apply **nl2br()** to a text area field:

```
$comments->addFilter('nl2br');
```

Along with filters, you can add *rules* to form elements. Rules can apply validation techniques to the form data. The **addRule()** method is used here:

```
$elem->addRule('rule_type',
→'error message');
```

Table 9.5 lists some of the available validation rules. For example, to make a field required, use

```
$elem->addRule('required',
→'Enter this value.');
```

If a rule, like *length*, takes another argument, that would come after the rule type:

```
$age->addRule('length', 'Please enter
→your age.', array('min' => 1,
→'max' => 120));
```

The **HTML_QuickForm2** class will automatically add error messages when rules aren't passed .

 **HTML_QuickForm2** will add appropriate errors next to the form elements.

TABLE 9.5 **QuickForm2 Validation Rules**

Name	Meaning
compare	Compare two or more elements
email	Must be a syntactically valid email address
eq	Must be identical to a value
gt	Must be greater than a value
gte	Must be greater than or equal to a value
length	Must be within the given limits
lt	Must be less than a value
lte	Must be less than or equal to a value
maxlength	Cannot have more characters than
minlength	Must be at least this many characters
nonempty	A non-empty value must be provided
required	Some value required

TIP Better yet, you can have QuickForm2 perform not only server-side validation (using PHP) but also client-side (by generating the necessary JavaScript). See the QuickForm2 documentation for details.

TIP You can create your own validation rules and then declare them for use by invoking `registerRule()`. This could be done, for example, to make sure that a username or email address has not already been registered. The function involved would check your database for that name or address's presence. Again, see the QuickForm2 documentation for the specifics.

Script 9.11 The login process is made much easier thanks to the **HTML_QuickForm2** PEAR class.

```
1    <?php # login.php - 9.11
2    // This page both displays and handles
     → the login form.
3
4    // Need the utilities file:
5    require('includes/utilities.inc.php');
6
7    // Create a new form:
8    set_include_path(get_include_path() .
     → PATH_SEPARATOR . '/usr/local/pear/
     → share/pear/');
9    require('HTML/QuickForm2.php');
10   $form = new HTML_QuickForm2('loginForm');
11
12   // Add the email address:
13   $email = $form->addElement('text',
     → 'email');
14   $email->setLabel('Email Address');
15   $email->addFilter('trim');
16   $email->addRule('required', 'Please enter
     → your email address.');
17   $email->addRule('email', 'Please enter
     → your email address.');
18
19   // Add the password field:
20   $password = $form->addElement
     → ('password', 'pass');
21   $password->setLabel('Password');
22   $password->addFilter('trim');
23   $password->addRule('required',
     → 'Please enter your password.');
```

script continues on next page

Processing form data

The final step in the whole form dance is to do something with the form data. Quick-Form2 provides a method that returns a Boolean value indicating if the form passes the server-side validation. This method can be used in a conditional:

```
if ($form->validate()) {
    // Good to go!
}
```

The form data will pass the **validate()** test if every form element passes all of the applicable rules you've established.

To then access the form values, refer to **$elem->getValue()**. This method returns the processed version of the submitted data after running the data through the filters.

With this quick introduction to **HTML_QuickForm2** in place, let's implement the login process.

To create the login.php script:

1. Begin a new PHP script in your text editor or IDE, to be named **login.php** (Script 9.11):

   ```
   <?php # login.php - 9.11
   require('includes/utilities.inc.
   → php');
   ```

   continues on page 317

```
24
25    // Add the submit button:
26    $form->addElement('submit', 'submit', array('value'=>'Login'));
27
28    // Check for a form submission:
29    if ($_SERVER['REQUEST_METHOD'] == 'POST') { // Handle the form submission
30
31        // Validate the form data:
32        if ($form->validate()) {
33
34            // Check against the database:
35            $q = 'SELECT id, userType, username, email FROM users WHERE email=:email AND
              ⇢ pass=SHA1(:pass)';
36            $stmt = $pdo->prepare($q);
37            $r = $stmt->execute(array(':email' => $email->getValue(), ':pass' => $password->getValue()));
38
39            // Try to fetch the results:
40            if ($r) {
41                $stmt->setFetchMode(PDO::FETCH_CLASS, 'User');
42                $user = $stmt->fetch();
43            }
44
45            // Store the user in the session and redirect:
46            if ($user) {
47
48                // Store in a session:
49                $_SESSION['user'] = $user;
50
51                // Redirect:
52                header("Location:index.php");
53                exit;
54
55            }
56
57        } // End of form validation IF.
58
59    } // End of form submission IF.
60
61    // Show the login page:
62    $pageTitle = 'Login';
63    include('includes/header.inc.php');
64    include('views/login.html');
65    include('includes/footer.inc.php');
66    ?>
```

2. Create a new form:

```
require('HTML/QuickForm2.php');
$form = new HTML_QuickForm2
→('loginForm');
```

As a reminder, you must have already installed the PEAR class for this to work. If you know you installed it and the PHP script cannot find the class, you can add the include path using this code, prior to the **require()** line:

```
set_include_path(get_include_
→path() . PATH_SEPARATOR .
→'/usr/local/pear/share/pear/');
```

The **set_include_path()** function changes where PHP can find files to include. It takes as its argument the new include path. So as not to overwrite the existing include path, you can set this value as the current include path, plus the path separator for the operating system, plus the location of where the PEAR files are, as in this line of code.

Again, if you have any problems with this, search online or ask in my support forums (**www.LarryUllman.com/forums/**).

3. Add the email address:

```
$email = $form->addElement('text',
→'email');
$email->setLabel('Email Address');
$email->addFilter('trim');
$email->addRule('required', 'Please
→enter your email address.');
$email->addRule('email', 'Please
→enter your email address.');
```

First the email address element is added as a text input. Then its label is set. The trim filter is added next. Finally, two rules are applied. The first says that the field is required and the second says that it must be a syntactically valid email address.

4. Add the password field:

```
$password = $form->addElement
→('password', 'pass');
$password->setLabel('Password');
$password->addFilter('trim');
$password->addRule('required',
→'Please enter your password.');
```

5. Add the submit button:

```
$form->addElement('submit',
→'submit', array('value'=>'Login'));
```

6. Check for a form submission:

```
if ($_SERVER['REQUEST_METHOD'] ==
→'POST') {
```

Next, the script will check for a form submission in order to process that login attempt.

7. Validate the form data:

```
if ($form->validate()) {
```

That's all that's required to validate the form data, given the rules already established!

8. Check the submitted values against the database:

```
$q = 'SELECT id, userType,
→username, email FROM users
→WHERE email=:email AND
→pass=SHA1(:pass)';
$stmt = $pdo->prepare($q);
$r = $stmt->execute(array(':email'
→=> $email->getValue(), ':pass' =>
→$password->getValue()));
```

The query uses prepared statements to select four columns from the **users** table. For the values, call the **getValue()** method of the corresponding element object to retrieve the filtered data.

continues on next page

9. Fetch the results:

```
if ($r) {
    $stmt->setFetchMode(PDO::FETCH_
    → CLASS, 'User');
    $user = $stmt->fetch();
}
```

If the query was executed, the next step is to fetch the query results, assuming there were any.

10. If there was one record returned, store it in a session and redirect the user:

```
if ($user) {
    $_SESSION['user'] = $user;
    header("Location:index.php");
    exit;
}
```

There's no great way to see how many records were returned by a **SELECT** prepared statement. The solution then is to fetch the record (or all of them, if necessary), and count how many were fetched. Or, in this case, just confirm that **$user** has a non-false value.

11. Complete the conditionals begun in Step 6 and Step 7:

```
    } // End of form validation IF.
} // End of form submission IF.
```

12. Create the login page:

```
$pageTitle = 'Login';
include('includes/header.inc.php');
include('views/login.html');
include('includes/footer.inc.php');
```

13. Complete the script:

```
?>
```

14. Save the file as **login.php**.

To create the login View:

1. Begin a new HTML script in your text editor or IDE, to be named **login.html** (Script 9.12):

```
<!-- # login.html - Script 9.12 -->
```

2. Begin a new **section**:

```
<section class="threeColumns">
    <article>
        <p>Sed ut perspiciatis unde
        → omnis iste natus error sit
        → voluptatem accusantium
        → doloremque laudantium,
        → totam rem aperiam, eaque
        → ipsa quae ab illo inventore
        → veritatis et quasi
        → architecto beatae vitae
        → dicta sunt explicabo. Nemo
        → enim ipsam voluptatem quia
        → voluptas sit aspernatur
        → aut odit aut fugit, sed
        → quia consequuntur magni
        → dolores eos qui ratione
        → voluptatem sequi
        → nesciunt.</p>
    </article>
```

Presumably, some instructions might go in this area.

3. Add the form:

```
<article class="twoThirds">
    <h1>Login</h1>
    <?php if ($form->isSubmitted()
    → && $form->validate()) {
        echo '<p class="error">The
        → values submitted do not
        → match those on file!</p>';
    }?>
    <?php echo $form; ?>
</article>
```

D The result if the form was completed but the values were incorrect.

Showing the form is just a matter of printing the form object. Prior to this, a conditional checks if the form was submitted and passed validation. If so, the only reason the form is being shown again is because the provided values didn't match those in the database **D**.

4. Complete the HTML:

   `</section>`

5. Save the file as **login.html** in the **views** directory, and test by attempting to log in.

   Use the values from the earlier **INSERT** commands.

Script 9.12 The login View file only needs to print the form and possibly an error message.

```
1    <!-- # login.html - Script 9.12 -->
2    <section class="threeColumns">
3      <article>
4        <p>Sed ut perspiciatis unde omnis iste natus error sit voluptatem accusantium doloremque
         → laudantium, totam rem aperiam, eaque ipsa quae ab illo inventore veritatis et
         → quasi architecto beatae vitae dicta sunt explicabo. Nemo enim ipsam voluptatem quia
         → voluptas sit aspernatur aut odit aut fugit, sed quia consequuntur magni dolores eos
         → qui ratione voluptatem sequi nesciunt.</p>
5      </article>
6      <article class="twoThirds">
7        <h1>Login</h1>
8        <?php if ($form->isSubmitted() && $form->validate()) {
9          echo '<p class="error">The values submitted do not match those on file!</p>';
10       }?>
11       <?php echo $form; ?>
12     </article>
13   </section>
```

Logging Out

Logging out is really simple. All the script has to do is:

- Clear the session data in the array
- Clear the session cookie
- Destroy the session data on the server (i.e., the session file)

This is fairly standard stuff and not impacted by the use of objects at all.

The View file is quite simple (**Script 9.13**) and doesn't require any further instructions. It should be named **logout.html**, and stored in the **views** directory.

To create the logout script:

1. Begin a new PHP script in your text editor or IDE, to be named **logout.php** (**Script 9.14**):

   ```
   <?php # logout.php - Script 9.14
   require('includes/utilities.inc.
   ⇢ php');
   ```

2. Check that the user is logged in:

   ```
   if ($user) {
   ```

   Just in case this page is somehow accessed accidentally (such as the user clicking the back button to return to it after already logging out), the actual logging out will only take place if the user is, in fact, logged in.

Script 9.13 The logout View file only contains literal HTML.

```
1   <!-- # logout.html - Script 9.13 -->
2   <section class="fullWidth">
3       <article>
4           <h1>You are now logged out.</h1>
5           <p>Thank you for visiting!</p>
6       </article>
7   </section>
```

Script 9.14 The logout page clears out all the session data.

```
1   <?php # logout.php - Script 9.14
2   // This page logs the user out.
3
4   // Need the utilities file:
5   require('includes/utilities.inc.php');
6
7   // Check for a user before attempting to
    ⇢ actually log them out:
8   if ($user) {
9
10      // Clear the variable:
11      $user = null;
12
13      // Clear the session data:
14      $_SESSION = array();
15
16      // Clear the cookie:
17      setcookie(session_name(), false,
        ⇢ time()-3600);
18
19      // Destroy the session data:
20      session_destroy();
21
22  } // End of $user IF.
23
24  // Set the page title and include the
    ⇢ header:
25  $pageTitle = 'Logout';
26  include('includes/header.inc.php');
27
28  // Need the view:
29  include('views/logout.html');
30
31  // Include the footer:
32  include('includes/footer.inc.php');
33  ?>
```

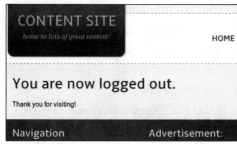

A The user can now be logged out.

3. Clear the variable:

```
$user = null;
```

The variable should be set to **null**, not entirely unset, because other code (such as in the footer) expects this variable to exist.

4. Clear the session data:

```
$_SESSION = array();
```

5. Clear the cookie:

```
setcookie(session_name(), false,
→ time()-3600);
```

6. Destroy the session data:

```
session_destroy();
```

7. Complete the conditional begun in Step 2:

```
} // End of $user IF.
```

8. Create the page:

```
$pageTitle = 'Logout';
include('includes/header.inc.php');
include('views/logout.html');
include('includes/footer.inc.php');
```

9. Complete the page:

```
?>
```

10. Save the file as **logout.php** and test by logging in and then clicking the logout link **A**.

Adding Pages

Finally, there's the most important feature of a content management system: the ability to dynamically add content. Thanks to **HTML_QuickForm2**, this isn't that much harder than the login form. In fact, aside from checking to ensure that the current user has permission to create new pages, the process is very similar.

I have made one assumption here: that the content is just simple HTML that the user would hand-edit. Naturally, full-fledged CMS systems use plug-ins to aid in the creation of HTML, the adding of media, and so forth. That is something that could be added here, too, using TinyMCE (**www.tinymce.com**) or the like.

To create the add_page.php script:

1. Begin a new PHP script in your text editor or IDE, to be named **add_page.php** (Script 9.15):

   ```
   <?php # add_page.php - Script 9.15
   require('includes/utilities.inc.
   → php');
   ```

2. Create a new form:

   ```
   require('HTML/QuickForm2.php');
   $form = new HTML_QuickForm2
   → ('addPageForm');
   ```

3. Add the title field:

   ```
   $title = $form->addElement('text',
   → 'title');
   $title->setLabel('Page Title');
   $title->addFilter('strip_tags');
   $title->addRule('required', 'Please
   → enter a page title.');
   ```

   The title field is a text input. The **strip_tags()** function will be applied to it, just in case.

4. Add the content field:

   ```
   $content = $form->addElement
   → ('textarea', 'content');
   $content->setLabel('Page Content');
   $content->addFilter('trim');
   $content->addRule('required',
   → 'Please enter the page
   → content.');
   ```

continues on page 324

Script 9.15 HTML_QuickForm2 is also used here to easily create and validate a form.

```
1   <?php # add_page.php - Script 9.15
2   // This page both displays and handles the "add a page" form.
3
4   // Need the utilities file:
5   require('includes/utilities.inc.php');
6
7   // Redirect if the user doesn't have permission:
8   if (!$user->canCreatePage()) {
9       header("Location:index.php");
10      exit;
11  }
12
13  // Create a new form:
14  set_include_path(get_include_path() . PATH_SEPARATOR . '/usr/local/pear/share/pear/');
```

script continues on next page

Script 9.15 *continued*

```
15   require('HTML/QuickForm2.php');
16   $form = new HTML_QuickForm2('addPageForm');
17
18   // Add the title field:
19   $title = $form->addElement('text', 'title');
20   $title->setLabel('Page Title');
21   $title->addFilter('strip_tags');
22   $title->addRule('required', 'Please enter a page title.');
23
24   // Add the content field:
25   $content = $form->addElement('textarea', 'content');
26   $content->setLabel('Page Content');
27   $content->addFilter('trim');
28   $content->addRule('required', 'Please enter the page content.');
29
30   // Add the submit button:
31   $submit = $form->addElement('submit', 'submit', array('value'=>'Add This Page'));
32
33   // Check for a form submission:
34   if ($_SERVER['REQUEST_METHOD'] == 'POST') { // Handle the form submission
35
36      // Validate the form data:
37      if ($form->validate()) {
38
39         // Insert into the database:
40         $q = 'INSERT INTO pages (creatorId, title, content, dateAdded) VALUES (:creatorId, :title,
      → :content, NOW())';
41         $stmt = $pdo->prepare($q);
42         $r = $stmt->execute(array(':creatorId' => $user->getId(), ':title' => $title->getValue(),
      → ':content' => $content->getValue()));
43
44         // Freeze the form upon success:
45         if ($r) {
46            $form->toggleFrozen(true);
47            $form->removeChild($submit);
48         }
49
50      } // End of form validation IF.
51
52   } // End of form submission IF.
53
54   // Show the page:
55   $pageTitle = 'Add a Page';
56   include('includes/header.inc.php');
57   include('views/add_page.html');
58   include('includes/footer.inc.php');
59   ?>
```

5. Add the submit button:

```
$submit = $form->addElement
→('submit', 'submit', array
→('value'=>'Add This Page'));
```

For a reason to be explained shortly, the script will later make reference to the submit button, so that element must be created as a variable, too.

6. Check for a form submission and validate:

```
if ($_SERVER['REQUEST_METHOD'] ==
→'POST') {
  if ($form->validate()) {
```

7. Insert the record into the database:

```
$q = 'INSERT INTO pages
→(creatorId, title, content,
→dateAdded) VALUES (:creatorId,
→:title, :content, NOW())';
$stmt = $pdo->prepare($q);
$r = $stmt->execute(array
→(':creatorId' => $user->getId(),
→':title' => $title->getValue(),
→':content' => $content->
→getValue()));
```

Two of the values come from the processed form data, and the **creatorId** value comes from the **$user** object.

8. If the insert query worked, freeze the form to show the results:

```
if ($r) {
  $form->toggleFrozen(true);
  $form->removeChild($submit);
}
```

Here is a bit of new information about **HTML_QuickForm2**: the **toggleFrozen()** method, when passed a value of **true**, will "freeze" the form, which makes the form elements no longer editable. This is one way of showing the user what they just accomplished. In addition, the submit button will be removed so that the frozen form cannot be submitted again.

9. Complete the conditionals begun in Step 6:

```
  } // End of form validation IF.
} // End of form submission IF.
```

10. Create the page:

```
$pageTitle = 'Add a Page';
include('includes/header.inc.php');
include('views/add_page.html');
include('includes/footer.inc.php');
```

11. Complete the script:

```
?>
```

12. Save the file as **add_page.php**.

To create the "add a page" view file:

1. Begin a new HTML script in your text editor or IDE, to be named **add_page.html** (Script 9.16):

```
<!-- # add_page.html - Script 9.16
-->
```

2. Begin a new **section**:

```
<section class="threeColumns">
  <article>
    <p>Sed ut perspiciatis unde
→omnis iste natus error sit
→voluptatem accusantium
→doloremque laudantium,
→totam rem aperiam, eaque
→ipsa quae ab illo
→inventore veritatis et
→quasi architecto beatae
→vitae dicta sunt explicabo.
→Nemo enim ipsam voluptatem
→quia voluptas sit
→aspernatur aut odit aut
→fugit, sed quia
→consequuntur magni dolores
→eos qui ratione voluptatem
→sequi nesciunt.</p>
  </article>
```

Presumably, this first section would provide instructions.

3. Add the **section** for the form:

```
<article class="twoThirds">
<h1>Add a New Page of Content</h1>
```

Add a New Page of Content

The page has been added!

*Page Title

This is a Test.
*Page Content

<p>Sed ut perspiciatis unde omnis iste natus error sit voluptatem accusantium doloremque laudantium, totam rem aperiam, eaque ipsa quae ab illo inventore veritatis et quasi architecto beatae vitae dicta sunt explicabo. Nemo enim ipsam voluptatem quia voluptas sit aspernatur aut odit aut fugit, sed quia consequuntur magni dolores eos qui ratione voluptatem sequi nesciunt.</p>

<p>Sed ut perspiciatis unde omnis iste natus error sit voluptatem accusantium doloremque laudantium, totam rem aperiam, eaque ipsa quae ab illo inventore veritatis et quasi architecto beatae vitae dicta sunt explicabo. Nemo enim ipsam voluptatem quia voluptas sit aspernatur aut odit aut fugit, sed quia consequuntur magni dolores eos qui ratione voluptatem sequi nesciunt.</p>

Ⓐ This page of content has successfully been added.

4. Print a message if the previous submission worked:

```
<?php if ($form->isSubmitted() &&
 $form->validate()) {
echo '<p>The page has been added!
 </p>';
}?>
```

The page should display something to the user to indicate success (errors will automatically be indicated by **HTML_ QuickForm2**). One way of testing for success is confirming that the form has been submitted and that it did validate.

5. Display the form:

```
<?php echo $form; ?>
```

6. Complete the HTML:

```
    </article>

</section>
```

7. Save the file as **add_page.html** in the **views** directory, and test by logging in as the proper user type and clicking the link in the footer Ⓐ.

Script 9.16 Like the logout page View, the "add a page" View simply displays the form. This file does present a message upon success, though.

```
1    <!-- # add_page.html - Script 9.16 -->
2    <section class="threeColumns">
3       <article>
4          <p>Sed ut perspiciatis unde omnis iste natus error sit voluptatem accusantium doloremque
laudantium, totam rem aperiam, eaque ipsa quae ab illo inventore veritatis et quasi architecto
beatae vitae dicta sunt explicabo. Nemo enim ipsam voluptatem quia voluptas sit aspernatur aut odit
aut fugit, sed quia consequuntur magni dolores eos qui ratione voluptatem sequi nesciunt.</p>
5       </article>
6       <article class="twoThirds">
7          <h1>Add a New Page of Content</h1>
8          <?php if ($form->isSubmitted() && $form->validate()) {
9          echo '<p>The page has been added!</p>';
10         }?>
11         <?php echo $form; ?>
12      </article>
13   </section>
```

Review and Pursue

If you have any problems with these sections, either in answering the questions or pursuing your own endeavors, turn to the book's supporting forum (**www.Larry Ullman.com/forums/**).

Review

- What is *MVC*? How is MVC implemented in this chapter? What are the benefits to using MVC? (See pages 284 and 285.)

- What does an *autoloading* function do? Why must it be defined before the session is started? (See pages 279 and 294.)

- What does it mean to *serialize* and *unserialize* data? (See page 294.)

- Why must some of the **catch** blocks catch generic **Exception** objects, not **PDOException** objects? (See page 251.)

Pursue

- Use the information about Apache covered in Chapter 2 to make improvements to how this project runs.

- If you want a site that supports both pages and posts, create a **posts** table and then all the requisite code. For example, the home page would select the most recent posts and link to **post. php**, passing along the post ID in the URL. The "about" page would be linked to **page.php**, passing along the page ID in the URL.

- If you want to support the ability to add categories or tags, do so using the suggestions on page 286.

- If you want the ability to support comments, do so using the suggestions on page 286.

- Create a user-registration process using **HTML_QuickForm2**.

- Change **error.html** so that it works as it should on a live site. Have the script email you when a problem occurs, rather than showing the error to the end user.

- Implement the fancier version of **Page::getIntro()**, as suggested in the tip on page 301.

- If you like **HTML_QuickForm2**, read more about what it can do and how to make the most of its capabilities.

- Implement the ability to edit an existing page.

- Create an "archives" page that lists the pages in reverse chronological order, linking to the full version of each.

- Create a "contact" page that uses **HTML_QuickForm2** to create and validate the form.

10

Networking with PHP

The vast bulk of what PHP is used to do is based on taking information from the server (like a database or a text file) and sending it to the client (the end-user's Web browser), or vice versa. But PHP also supports a slew of features for the purpose of interacting with other Web sites, communicating with other servers, and even FTP'ing files. In this chapter, I'll discuss and demonstrate some of PHP's network-related functions and capabilities.

In the first example, you'll see how to read data from another Web site as if it were any old text file. In the second, a Web site verifier will be created (a tool for checking whether a link is good). In the third section of the chapter, you'll learn how to identify from what country a user is connecting to your server. The fourth example introduces cURL, a powerful networking utility. And finally, you'll learn how to start creating your own *Web services* using PHP.

In This Chapter

Accessing Other Web Sites

Even though PHP itself is normally used to create Web sites, it can also access and interact with Web pages on its own. This can be useful for retrieving information, writing spiders (applications that scour the Internet for particular data), and more. Surprisingly, you can access other Web sites in much the same way you would access a text file on your hard drive: by using **fopen()**:

```
fopen ('http://www.example.com/', 'r');
```

The same **fopen()** function used for opening files can also open Web pages because they are, after all, just files on a server. The parameters for using **fopen()** are the same (**r**, **w**, and **a**), although you will be limited to opening a file only for reading.

One caveat, though, is that you must use a trailing slash after a directory because **fopen()** will not support redirects. The preceding example and this one are fine:

```
fopen ('http://www.example.com/
→ index.php', 'r');
```

But this will fail:

```
fopen ('http://www.example.com/
→ dir', 'r');
```

(Many people are unaware that the URL **www.example.com/dir** is redirected to **www.example.com/dir/**.)

Another caveat is that PHP must be configured to allow for **fopen()** calls over a network, which not all PHP installations are **A**.

Once you have opened a file, you can treat it as you otherwise would, using **file()**, **fgets()**, etc., to retrieve the data.

I'll demonstrate this concept by making use of Yahoo!'s financial pages that return New York Stock Exchange quotes for different stocks. Before proceeding, I should state that the legality of retrieving information from another Web site is an issue you would want to investigate before permanently implementing something like this. Most sites contain copyrighted information, and using it without permission would be a violation. This demonstration with Yahoo! is just a demonstration, not a suggestion that you make a habit of this!

Warning: fopen(): http:// wrapper is disabled in the server configuration by allow_url_fopen=0 in **/Users/larryullman/Sites/phpvqp3/get_quote.php** on line **18**

Warning: fopen(http://quote.yahoo.com/d/quotes.csv?s=aapl&f=nl1): failed to open stream: no suitable wrapper could be found in **/Users/larryullman/Sites/phpvqp3/get_quote.php** on line **18**

A If your PHP installation does not allow **fopen()** to be used over a network, you'll see errors like these.

To read a Web site with PHP:

1. Create a new PHP document in your text editor or IDE, to be named **get_quote.php**, beginning with the HTML (**Script 10.1**):

```
<!doctype html>
<html lang="en">
<head>
   <meta charset="utf-8">
   <title>Get Stock Quotes</title>
   <link rel="stylesheet"
→ href="style.css">
</head>
<body>
<?php # Script 10.1 -
→ get_quote.php
```

The CSS script, available in the downloads at the book's corresponding Web site (**www.LarryUllman.com**), defines two classes that will be used to format the results.

2. Check if the form has been submitted:

```
if (isset($_GET['symbol']) &&
→ !empty($_GET['symbol'])) {
```

This page will both display and handle a form. The form itself takes just one input: the symbol for a stock. As the form uses the GET method, the handling PHP code checks for the presence of a **$_GET['symbol']**.

continues on next page

Script 10.1 The code in this example will retrieve stock quotes by opening up Yahoo!'s quote page and parsing the data therein.

```
1    <!doctype html>
2    <html lang="en">
3    <head>
4       <meta charset="utf-8">
5       <title>Get Stock Quotes</title>
6       <link rel="stylesheet" href="style.css">
7    </head>
8    <body>
9    <?php # Script 11.1 - get_quote.php
10   //   This page retrieves a stock price from Yahoo!.
11
12   if (isset($_GET['symbol']) && !empty($_GET['symbol'])) { // Handle the form.
13
14       // Identify the URL:
15       $url = sprintf('http://quote.yahoo.com/d/quotes.csv?s=%s&f=nl1', $_GET['symbol']);
16
17       // Open the "file".
18       $fp = fopen($url, 'r');
19
20       // Get the data:
21       $read = fgetcsv($fp);
22
23       // Close the "file":
```

script continues on next page

3. Define the URL to be opened:

```
$url = sprintf('http://quote.
→ yahoo.com/d/quotes.csv?s=
→ %s&f=nl1', $_GET['symbol']);
```

The most important consideration when accessing and reading other Web pages is to know exactly what data will be there and in what form. In other words, unless you are merely copying the entire contents of a file, you'll need to develop some system for gleaning the parts of the page you want according to how the data is structured.

In this example, a URL such as **http://quote.yahoo.com/d/quotes.csv** takes two arguments: the stock (or stocks) to check and the formatting parameters.

It will then return CSV (comma-separated value) data.

For this example, I want to know the stock's name and the latest price, so the formatting would be **nl1** (see **www.gummy-stuff.org/Yahoo-data.htm** for the options and what they mean). That gets added to the URL, along with the ticker symbol.

If you were to run this URL directly in a Web browser—a good debugging step—you'd see that the result will be in the format (where *XX.XX* is the price):

"STOCK NAME",XX.XX

Script 10.1 *continued*

```
24      fclose($fp);
25
26      // Check the results for improper symbols:
27      if (strcasecmp($read[0], $_GET['symbol']) !== 0) {
28
29          // Print the results:
30          echo '<div>The latest value for <span class="quote">' . $read[0] . '</span> (<span
            → class="quote">' . $_GET['symbol'] . '</span>) is $<span class="quote">' . $read[1] .
            → '</span>.</div>';
31
32      } else {
33          echo '<div class="error">Invalid symbol!</div>';
34      }
35
36  } // End of form submission IF.
37
38  // Show the form:
39  ?><form action="get_quote.php" method="get">
40      <fieldset>
41          <legend>Enter a NYSE stock symbol to get the latest price:</legend>
42          <p><label for="symbol">Symbol</label>: <input type="text" name="symbol" size="5"
            → maxlength="5"></p>
43          <p><input type="submit" name="submit" value="Fetch the Quote!" /></p>
44      </fieldset>
45  </form>
46  </body>
47  </html>
```

4. Open the Web page and read in the data:

```
$fp = fopen($url, 'r');
$read = fgetcsv($fp);
fclose($fp);
```

Now that the URL is defined, I can open the "file" for reading. Since I know that the returned data is in CSV form, I can use `fgetcsv()` to read it. This function will automatically turn the line it reads into an array, using commas as the delimiter. Then I close the file pointer. Note that if the URL were a proper HTML document (this one is not), the first line read would be something like `<!doctype html...`

5. Validate that a legitimate stock symbol was used:

```
if (strcasecmp($read[0],
→ $_GET['symbol']) !== 0) {
```

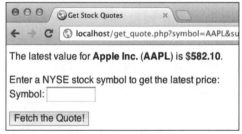

B The script has determined, by accessing the Yahoo! page, that Apple Computer is currently at $582.10.

If an invalid stock symbol is used, then the Yahoo! page will return that symbol as the stock name and $0.00 as the price. To weed out these instances, check if the returned name is the same as the symbol. I use the `strcasecmp()` function to perform a case-insensitive equality check between them. If they are the same, the function will return 0. If they are not the same, a nonzero value is returned, meaning it's safe to print the result.

6. Print the stock's value:

```
echo '<div>The latest value
→ for <span class="quote">' .
→ $read[0] . '</span> (<span
→ class="quote">' .
→ $_GET['symbol'] . '</span>) is
→ $<span class="quote">' .
→ $read[1] . '</span>.</div>';
```

The code in Step 4 takes the information retrieved (e.g., *"STOCK NAME",24.34*) and turns it into an array. The first element in the array is the stock's name, and the second is the current stock value. Both are printed, along with the stock's symbol, within some CSS formatting **B**. Note that the `fgetcsv()` function will strip the quotes from around the stock's name.

7. Complete the `strcasecmp()` conditional:

```
} else {
  echo '<div class="error">Invalid
→ symbol!</div>';
}
```

8. Complete the `$_GET['symbol']` conditional and the PHP section.

```
} // End of form submission IF.
?>
```

continues on next page

9. Create the HTML form:

```
<form action="get_quote.php"
→method="get">
    <fieldset>
        <legend>Enter a NYSE stock
        →symbol to get the latest
        →price:</legend>
        <p><label for="symbol">
        →Symbol</label>: <input
        →type="text" name="symbol"
        →size="5" maxlength="5"></p>
        <p><input type="submit"
        →name="submit" value="Fetch
        →the Quote!" /></p>
    </fieldset>
</form>
```

The form takes just one input: a text box for the stock's symbol **C**.

10. Complete the page:

```
</body>
</html>
```

11. Save the file as **get_quote.php**, place it in your Web directory, and test in your Web browser **D**.

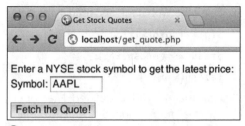

C The form takes just a stock symbol from the user.

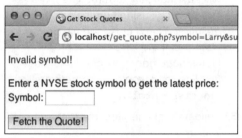

D The result if an invalid ticker symbol is entered.

TIP PEAR (PHP Extension and Application Repository) contains dozens of networking-related classes. See http://pear.php.net for more.

TIP The Zend Framework (http://framework.zend.com) has some network-related classes as well. As of this writing, classes are available specifically for connecting to Amazon, Flickr, and Yahoo!.

TIP More complex Web pages might require use of regular expressions to retrieve the particular pieces you want from the returned data.

Working with Sockets

The **fopen()** function is one way to access Web pages, but a more sophisticated method for interacting with another server is to use *sockets*. A socket, in case you are not familiar, is a channel through which two computers can communicate with each other. To open a socket in PHP, use **fsockopen()**:

```
$fp = fsockopen ($url, $port,
→ $error_number, $error_string,
→ $timeout);
```

You use **fsockopen()** to establish a file pointer, just as you would use **fopen()**. The parameters the function takes are the URL, the port, an error number variable, an error string variable, and the timeout (only the first argument is required).

In layman's terms, a *port* is the door through which different protocols (methods of communication) go. For Web pages, the port is normally 80 (see **Table 10.1**, which lists the most commonly used of the more than 60,000 ports in existence). The error number and string variables are interesting in that they are not really sent to the function (as they have no value initially) so much as they are a way for the function to return error information should one occur. Finally, the timeout simply states for how many seconds the function should try to connect.

Once the file has been successfully opened, you can again use **fwrite()**, **fgets()**, and so forth to manipulate the data.

Another function I'll explain before writing the **fsockopen()** example is **parse_url()**. This function takes a URL and turns it into an associative array by breaking the structure into its parts:

```
$url_pieces = parse_url($url);
```

The primary pieces of the URL will be *scheme*, *host*, *port*, *path*, and *query*. **Table 10.2** shows how the URL

http://www.example.com/view.php?week=
→ **1#demo**

would be broken down by **parse_url()**. The *user* and *pass* indexes would have values if the URL were of the format **http://username:password@www.example.com**.

TABLE 10.1 Some Common Ports

Number	Primary Purpose
21	FTP
22	SSH
23	Telnet
25	SMTP
80	Web
81	Web (alternate)
110	POP
143	IMAP
389	LDAP
443	SSL

TABLE 10.2 parse_url() Example

Index	Value
scheme	http
host	www.example.com
port	80
user	
pass	
path	view.php
query	week=1
fragment	#demo

The **parse_url()** function can be handy in all sorts of instances. I'll demonstrate one example in the following script. The code developed there will run through a list of URLs and check each to make sure they are still active. To do so, a user-defined function will take a provided URL, parse it, and then use **fsockopen()** to connect to it. The server's HTTP response code will indicate the validity of that link. (**Table 10.3** lists some common HTTP status codes, which you can also find by searching the Web.)

To use fsockopen():

1. Create a new PHP document in your text editor or IDE, to be named **check_urls.php**, beginning with the HTML (**Script 10.2**):

```
<!doctype html>
<html lang="en">
<head>
    <meta charset="utf-8">
    <title>Validate URLs</title>
    <link rel="stylesheet"
    → href="style.css">
</head>
<body>
<?php # Script 10.1 -
→ check_urls.php
```

Again, download the CSS script from **www.LarryUllman.com** to properly format the results.

2. Begin defining the **check_url()** function:

```
function check_url($url) {
```

The function takes one argument: the URL to be validated.

continues on page 336

TABLE 10.3 Common HTTP Status Codes

Code	Meaning
200	OK
204	No content
400	Bad request
401	Unauthorized
403	Forbidden
404	Not found
408	Timeout
500	Internal server error

Script 10.2 By making a socket connection, this script can quickly check if a given URL is still valid.

```
1    <!doctype html>
2    <html lang="en">
3    <head>
4        <meta charset="utf-8">
5        <title>Validate URLs</title>
6        <link rel="stylesheet"
         → href="style.css">
7    </head>
8    <body>
9    <?php # Script 11.2 - check_urls.php
10   // This page validates a list of URLs.
     → It uses fsockopen() and parse_url()
     → to do so.
11
12   // This function will try to connect
     → to a URL:
13   function check_url($url) {
14
15       // Break the URL down into its parts:
16       $url_pieces = parse_url($url);
17
18       // Set the $path and $port:
19       $path = (isset($url_pieces['path'])) ?
         → $url_pieces['path'] :  '/';
20       $port = (isset($url_pieces['port'])) ?
         → $url_pieces['port'] : 80;
21
22       // Connect using fsockopen():
23       if ($fp = fsockopen
         → ($url_pieces['host'], $port,
         → $errno, $errstr, 30)) {
```

script continues on next page

```
24
25        // Send some data:
26        $send = "HEAD $path HTTP/1.1\r\n";
27        $send .= "HOST: {$url_pieces['host']}\r\n";
28        $send .= "CONNECTION: Close\r\n\r\n";
29        fwrite($fp, $send);
30
31        // Read the response:
32        $data = fgets($fp, 128);
33
34        // Close the connection:
35        fclose($fp);
36
37        // Return the response code:
38        list($response, $code) = explode(' ', $data);
39        if ($code == 200) {
40            return array($code, 'good');
41        } else {
42            return array($code, 'bad');
43        }
44
45    } else { // No connection, return the error message:
46        return array($errstr, 'bad');
47    }
48
49 } // End of check_url() function.
50
51 // Create the list of URLs:
52 $urls = array(
53 'http://www.larryullman.com/',
54 'http://www.larryullman.com/wp-admin/',
55 'http://www.yiiframework.com/tutorials/',
56 'http://video.google.com/videoplay?docid=-5137581991288263801&q=loose+change'
57 );
58
59 // Print a header:
60 echo '<h2>Validating URLs</h2>';
61
62 // Kill the PHP time limit:
63 set_time_limit(0);
64
65 // Validate each URL:
66 foreach ($urls as $url) {
67    list($code, $class) = check_url($url);
68    echo "<p><a href=\"$url\" target=\"hew\">$url</a> (<span class=\"$class\">$code</span>)</p>\n";
69 }
70 ?>
71 </body>
72 </html>
```

3. Parse the URL:

```
$url_pieces = parse_url($url);
```

4. Set the proper path and port values:

```
$path =
→ (isset($url_pieces['path'])) ?
→ $url_pieces['path'] :  '/';

$port =
→ (isset($url_pieces['port'])) ?
→ $url_pieces['port'] : 80;
```

I want to make sure that I've got the right path and port when testing the connection later on, so I set the **$path** variable to be either the existing path, if any, or a slash, as the default. For the URL **www.example.com/dir**, the path would be **/dir**. For **www.example.com**, the path would be **/**.

The same treatment is given to the **$port**, with the default as 80.

5. Attempt to connect using **fsockopen()**:

```
if ($fp =
→ fsockopen($url_pieces['host'],
→ $port, $errno, $errstr, 30)) {
```

6. If a connection is established, write some data to the server:

```
$send = "HEAD $path HTTP/1.1\r\n";

$send .=
→ "HOST: {$url_pieces['host']}\r\n";

$send .=
→ "CONNECTION: Close\r\n\r\n";

fwrite($fp, $send);
```

These lines may seem confusing, but what they are essentially doing is sending a series of HTTP headers to the server to initiate communication. The type of request being made is HEAD Ⓐ. Such a request is like GET, except that the server will only return a response and not the entire page Ⓑ. The **fsockopen()** line connects to the server; the **HEAD $path** line here requests a specific page. This could be just **/** or **/somefolder/somepage.php**.

The **\r\n** code is required for properly formatting the request.

```
: curl --head http://www.larryullman.com
HTTP/1.1 200 OK
Date: Sat, 23 Jun 2012 15:08:19 GMT
Server: Apache/2.0.63 (CentOS)
Last-Modified: Sat, 23 Jun 2012 14:01:24 GMT
ETag: "ab0d-2f247500"
Accept-Ranges: bytes
Content-Length: 43789
Cache-Control: public, must-revalidate, proxy-revalidate
Expires: Sat, 23 Jun 2012 15:01:24 GMT
Vary: Accept-Encoding,Cookie
X-Pingback: http://www.larryullman.com/xmlrpc.php
X-Powered-By: W3 Total Cache/0.9.2.4
Pragma: public
Content-Type: text/html; charset=UTF-8
:
```

Ⓐ A HEAD request returns only the basic headers for a page.

```
: curl http://www.larryullman.com
<!DOCTYPE html PUBLIC "-//W3C//DTD XHTML 1.0 Transitional/
/EN" "http://www.w3.org/TR/xhtml1/DTD/xhtml1-transitional.
dtd"><html
xmlns="http://www.w3.org/1999/xhtml" dir="ltr" lang="en-US
"><head
profile="http://gmpg.org/xfn/11"><script type="text/javasc
ript" src="http://cloudfront.larryullman.com/wp-content/w3
tc/min/da7ca/default.include.216c0a.js.gzip"></script><met
a
http-equiv="content-type" content="text/html; charset=UTF-
8" /><title>Larry Ullman - Translating Geek Into English</
title><link
rel="alternate" type="application/rss+xml" href="http://ww
w.larryullman.com/feed/" title="Larry Ullman latest posts"
 /><link
rel="alternate" type="application/rss+xml" href="http://ww
```

Ⓑ A normal (GET) request returns the entire page (this figure just shows the first few lines of the HTML source code returned).

7. Retrieve the response code:

```
$data = fgets($fp, 128);
fclose($fp);
list($response, $code) =
→ explode(' ', $data);
```

Once the URL has been hit with a header, it will respond with its own HTTP headers Ⓐ. This code will read in the first 128 characters of the response and then break that string down into an array. The second element returned will be the HTTP code. Table 10.3 lists some of the possible response codes.

8. Return the code and a class message:

```
if ($code == 200) {
  return array($code, 'good');
} else {
  return array($code, 'bad');
}
```

This function should indicate, via its return values, what code was received and whether that code is good or bad (these strings match up to the CSS classes). An HTTP status code of 200 is considered normal (OK, technically); anything else indicates some sort of problem.

Reasonably, other status codes are considered to be acceptable, including other numbers in the 200s and 300s.

9. Finish the conditional begun in Step 5 and the function:

```
  } else {
    return array($errstr, 'bad');
  }
} // End of check_url() function.
```

If a socket connection was not made, the returned error message will be sent back from the **check_urls()** function.

10. Create a list of URLs:

```
$urls = array(
'http://www.larryullman.com/',
'http://www.larryullman.com/
→ wp-admin/',
'http://www.yiiframework.com/
→ tutorials/',
'http://video.google.com/
→ videoplay?docid=
→ -5137581991288263801&q=
→ loose+change'
);
```

For sake of simplicity, I'm creating an array of hard-coded URLs. You might retrieve your own URLs from a database or from a file instead.

11. Print a header and adjust the PHP scripts' time limit:

```
echo '<h2>Validating URLs</h2>';
set_time_limit(0);
```

Making these socket connections can take some time, especially if you have a lot of URLs to validate. By calling the **set_time_limit()** function with a value of 0, the PHP script is given limitless time to do its thing.

continues on next page

12. Validate each URL:

```
foreach ($urls as $url) {
    list($code, $class) =
    → check_url($url);

    echo "<p><a href=\"$url\"
    → target=\"new\">$url</a> (<span
    class=\"$class\">$code</span>)
    → </p>\n";

}
```

The **foreach** loop goes through each URL in the array. Then the **check_url()** function is called. It returns two values: the code (or an error message) and the CSS class name to use (either good or bad). Then the URL is printed, as a link, followed by the code or error message.

13. Finish the PHP and the HTML:

```
?>
</body>
</html>
```

14. Save the file as **check_urls.php**, place it in your Web directory, and test in your Web browser **C**.

TIP Another benefit that **fsockopen()** has over the **fopen()** method used in the first section of the chapter is that the **fopen()** technique will fail unless PHP's **allow_url_fopen** setting is **true**.

TIP This is just one example of using sockets in PHP. You can create your own socket server using PHP and the socket functions. If you don't already know why you might want to do this, you'll likely never need to touch these functions. But for more information, see **www.php.net/sockets**.

C How the validation panned out for the provided four URLs.

Performing IP Geolocation

One of the questions that I am commonly asked is how to identify in which country a user resides. Although the server where your PHP script is housed could be anywhere in the world and the user could be located anywhere in the world, it is still possible to make a geographic match.

The premise is this: Every computer must have an IP address to have Internet access (or to connect to any network). An Internet service provider (ISP) assigns a computer an IP address from a pool of valid addresses only they have access to. By knowing a computer's IP address, which PHP stores in `$_SERVER['REMOTE_ADDR']`, you can determine the ISP and, therefore, the country—hence, the name *IP geolocation*. New GeoIP databases can even predict the city and state (or territory or whatnot), although with less accuracy.

To perform IP geolocation, you must have access to a GeoIP database (see the sidebar). In this section, I'll use a simple online service, provided by freegeoip. net (**www.freegeoip.net**). Besides being free and not requiring any installation on your server, the service is easy to use: just perform a GET request of a specific URL. As you've now seen in the chapter, such a request can be made using either **fopen()** or **fsockopen()**.

This next example will make use of another network-related PHP function. The **gethostbyname()** function returns the IP address for a given domain name.

To find a user's location:

1. Create a new PHP script in your text editor or IDE, to be named `ip_geo.php`, beginning with the HTML (**Script 10.3**):

```
<!doctype html>
<html lang="en">
<head>
    <meta charset="utf-8">
    <title>IP Geolocation</title>
    <link rel="stylesheet"
    ➝ href="style.css">
</head>
<body>
<?php # Script 10.3 - ip_geo.php
```

2. Begin defining a function:

```
function show_ip_info($ip) {
    $url = 'http://freegeoip.net/
    ➝ csv/' . $ip;
```

This function will perform the request of the service and output the results. It takes an IP address as its lone argument. That IP address is added to the URL to be requested.

As you can see at the freegeoip.net Web site, the URL should be in the format **http://freegeoip.net/ {*data_format*}/{*IP_address*}**. The data formats returned by the service can be CSV, XML (Extensible Markup Language), or JSON (JavaScript Object Notation). Here, the request is for the data to be returned in CSV format.

Script 10.3 This script fetches geographic location information about the current user based on an IP address.

```
1   <!doctype html>
2   <html lang="en">
3   <head>
4      <meta charset="utf-8">
5      <title>IP Geolocation</title>
6      <link rel="stylesheet" href="style.css">
7   </head>
8   <body>
9   <?php # Script 11.3 - ip_geo.php
10  //  This page uses a Web service to retrieve a user's geographic location.
11
12  // This function will perform the IP Geolocation request:
13  function show_ip_info($ip) {
14
15     // Identify the URL to connect to:
16     $url = 'http://freegeoip.net/csv/' . $ip;
17
18     // Open the connection:
19     $fp = fopen($url, 'r');
20
21     // Get the data:
22     $read = fgetcsv($fp);
23
24     // Close the "file":
25     fclose($fp);
26
27     // Print whatever about the IP:
28     echo "<p>IP Address: $ip<br>
29     Country: $read[2]<br>
30     City, State: $read[5], $read[3]<br>
31     Latitude: $read[7]<br>
32     Longitude: $read[8]</p>";
33
34  } // End of show_ip_info() function.
35
36  // Get the client's IP address:
37  echo '<h2>Our spies tell us the following information about you</h2>';
38  show_ip_info($_SERVER['REMOTE_ADDR']);
39
40  // Print something about a site:
41  $url = 'www.entropy.ch';
42  echo "<h2>Our spies tell us the following information about the URL $url</h2>";
43  show_ip_info(gethostbyname($url));
44
45  ?>
46  </body>
47  </html>
```

3. Make the request and read in the result:

```
$fp = fopen($url, 'r');
$read = fgetcsv($fp);
fclose($fp);
```

Since the service returns CSV data, the same code as in **get_quote.php** can be used to read and parse it.

4. Print the results:

```
echo "<p>IP Address: $ip<br>
Country: $read[2]<br>
City, State: $read[5], $read[3]<br>
Latitude: $read[7]<br>
Longitude: $read[8]</p>";
```

The Web service returns CSV data, which the code in Step 3 turns into an array **Ⓐ**. Once you know that result, outputting the information is just a matter of referencing the correct indexes.

```
Array ( [0] => 174.49.133.225 [1] => US [2] => United States [3] => PA
[4] => Pennsylvania [5] => York [6] => 17403 [7] => 39.9171 [8] =>
-76.7256 [9] => 566 )
```

Ⓐ The array of data returned by the Web service.

5. Complete the function:

```
}
```

6. Get the user's IP address:

```
echo '<h2>Our spies tell us the
→ following information about
  → you</h2>';
show_ip_info($_SERVER
→ ['REMOTE_ADDR']);
```

Again, PHP will store the user's IP address in **$_SERVER['REMOTE_ADDR']**. This value just needs to be passed to the function that will use it for the IP geolocation call.

7. Identify a URL to report on and get its IP address:

```
$url = 'www.entropy.ch';
echo "<h2>Our spies tell us the
→ following information about
→ the URL $url</h2>";
show_ip_info(gethostbyname($url));
```

continues on next page

Choosing an IP Geolocation Option

In this chapter, I chose to use the freegioip.net Web service as the IP geolocation source for two reasons: it's free and it's easy to use. But free comes at a cost: this service is unlikely to be as accurate or fast as some other options. If you're using IP geolocation on a live site, particularly an active and/or commercial one, you'll want to consider other sources.

If you search the Internet, you'll find plenty of alternatives, but the one I most commonly use is MaxMind (**www.maxmind.com**). MaxMind provides both free and commercial versions of an IP database that can be downloaded and installed on your computer. By using a local database, you'll get better performance and not be susceptible to network issues.

MaxMind's databases are not that hard to install and use, and there are instructions on their site. The free database is perfectly fine for most people, but you can pay a modest amount to use the more accurate commercial version.

While playing around with IP geolocation, the script will also fetch the information for a Web site. This is to say that the script will try to identify the physical location of the server on which that particular site is running. In this case, I'm choosing Marc Liyanage's invaluable site, **www.entropy.ch**.

8. Complete the page:

    ```
    ?>

    </body>

    </html>
    ```

9. Save the file as **net_geo.php**, place it in your Web directory, and test in your Web browser **B**.

10. Hop into a plane, train, or automobile; travel to another country; get online; and retest the script in your Web browser **C**.

    Alternatively, you could insert another IP address in place of **$_SERVER['REMOTE_ADDR']**.

TIP The trick to using any Web service is understanding what URL to use and what the result will be. For debugging purposes, try to load the service in your Web browser to confirm the results, or have the PHP script output them.

TIP IP addresses aren't always reliable because, for example, multiple users on the same network could potentially be presented as having the same IP address. In this particular case, however, that particular problem wouldn't be a hindrance.

TIP One resource I found suggested that IP geolocation is very accurate on the country level, probably close to 95 percent. On the city and state level, that accuracy may dip down to 50–80 percent, depending on the database being used. In my case, it did not accurately pick the city but suggested one about 20 miles away. As I suggest in the sidebar, using a commercial database would garner more accurate results.

TIP If you have the need to find out the hostname associated with an IP address, use the corresponding gethostbyaddr() function.

TIP If a URL might be on multiple servers, the gethostbyname1() function returns all the possible IP addresses. You can then check one or every IP.

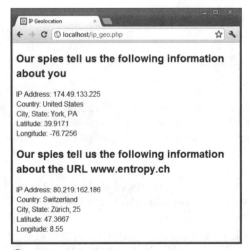

B The IP geolocation results for my IP address and the URL **www.entropy.ch**.

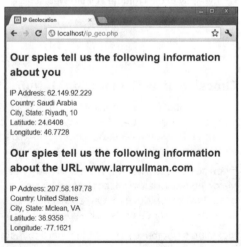

C Running the script again, after flying to Saudi Arabia. I also changed the URL to **www.LarryUllman.com** to see those results.

Using cURL

The next network-related topic to be discussed in this chapter is a technology called cURL. This utility, which stands for *client URLs* (and is also written as just *curl* or *Curl*), is a command-line tool for working with URLs. With cURL you can access Web sites and FTP files, and do much, much more. cURL provides an excellent way to interact with payment gateways for an e-commerce site. You can even use cURL to update your Facebook status or post to your blog!

PHP can invoke cURL via the **shell_exec()** and other system functions. But PHP also supports *libcurl*, a cURL library, which I'll talk about here.

The process starts by calling **curl_init()**, providing to this function the name of the URL to be accessed:

```
$curl = curl_init('www.example.com');
```

The value returned by the function should be assigned to a variable, which will act as a pointer or a handle to the transaction.

Next, the **curl_setopt()** function is used (a lot) to set any options for the request. The syntax is

```
curl_setopt($curl, CONSTANT, value);
```

Unfortunately, there are way too many options to even provide a subset here. In the following example I'll highlight a handful of them. If you like cURL, check out the PHP manual for the full list of settings.

After setting all the options (and note that you can set them in any order), use **curl_exec()** to execute the transaction:

```
$result = curl_exec($curl);
```

You should assign the result of the **curl_exec()** command to a variable, in case you need to print the result.

Finally, close the connection:

```
curl_close($curl);
```

The great thing about cURL is that it can be used to do everything that the other examples in the chapter also accomplish. But for this next example, let's use it for something that **fopen()**, **fsockopen()**, and the rest can't do: open a Web page and *post* data to it (as if the script submitted a form via the POST method).

This first script will post arbitrary data to another page. That receiving page will be written in the subsequent example.

To use cURL:

1. Create a new PHP script in your text editor or IDE, to be named **curl.php**, beginning with the HTML (**Script 10.4**):

```
<!doctype html>
<html lang="en">
<head>
    <meta charset="utf-8">
    <title>Using cURL</title>
    <link rel="stylesheet"
    → href="style.css">
</head>
<body>
<h2>cURL Results:</h2>
<?php # Script 10.4 - curl.php
```

continues on page 345

Script 10.4 The cURL library is used by PHP to post data to a page.

```
1    <!doctype html>
2    <html lang="en">
3    <head>
4        <meta charset="utf-8">
5        <title>Using cURL</title>
6        <link rel="stylesheet" href="style.css">
7    </head>
8    <body>
9    <h2>cURL Results:</h2>
10   <?php # Script 11.4 - curl.php
11   // This page uses cURL to post data to a Web service.
12
13   // Identify the URL:
14   $url = 'http://localhost/service.php';
15
16   // Start the process:
17   $curl = curl_init($url);
18
19   // Tell cURL to fail if an error occurs:
20   curl_setopt($curl, CURLOPT_FAILONERROR, 1);
21
22   // Allow for redirects:
23   curl_setopt($curl, CURLOPT_FOLLOWLOCATION, 1);
24
25   // Assign the returned data to a variable:
26   curl_setopt($curl, CURLOPT_RETURNTRANSFER, 1);
27
28   // Set the timeout:
29   curl_setopt($curl, CURLOPT_TIMEOUT, 5);
30
31   // Use POST:
32   curl_setopt($curl, CURLOPT_POST, 1);
33
34   // Set the POST data:
35   curl_setopt($curl, CURLOPT_POSTFIELDS, 'name=foo&pass=bar&format=csv');
36
37   // Execute the transaction:
38   $r = curl_exec($curl);
39
40   // Close the connection:
41   curl_close($curl);
42
43   // Print the results:
44   print_r($r);
45
46   ?>
47   </body>
48   </html>
```

2. Begin the cURL transaction:

```
$url = 'http://localhost/
→ service.php';

$curl = curl_init($url);
```

You don't have to assign the URL to a variable prior to the **curl_init()** line, of course. But this URL does need to be a valid value. The destination itself, **service.php**, will be written in the next sequence of steps. If you're not using localhost, with the default port, and the Web root directory, you'll need to change the URL accordingly.

3. Tell cURL to fail if an error occurs:

```
curl_setopt($curl,
→ CURLOPT_FAILONERROR, 1);
```

The first of the options is **CURLOPT_FAILONERROR**. By setting this to **true** (or 1), you tell cURL to stop the process if an error occurs (rather than continuing on blindly).

4. Tell cURL to allow for redirects:

```
curl_setopt($curl,
→ CURLOPT_FOLLOWLOCATION, 1);
```

This second option sets whether or not server redirections—think of a PHP **header('Location: somepage.php')** call—should stop the transaction or redirections should be followed. Here, I'm saying to follow redirections.

5. Opt to assign the returned data to a variable:

```
curl_setopt($curl,
→ CURLOPT_RETURNTRANSFER, 1);
```

If you won't use the data that would be returned by a cURL request, you don't need to enable this option. In this script, that data will be printed for verification, so this value is set to 1.

6. Set the timeout:

```
curl_setopt($curl,
→ CURLOPT_TIMEOUT, 5);
```

This is the maximum amount of time to attempt the transaction, in seconds. Five seconds may not seem like much in the real world, but in Internet time, it's an eon!

7. Tell cURL to use the POST method:

```
curl_setopt($curl,
→ CURLOPT_POST, 1);
```

In this example, data will be posted to the page (**http://localhost/service. php**) as if a form were submitted. Alternatively, some of the other examples in this chapter would perform a GET request.

8. Set the POST data:

```
curl_setopt($curl,
→ CURLOPT_POSTFIELDS,
→ 'name=foo&pass=bar&format=csv');
```

The **CURLOPT_POSTFIELDS** option is where you set the POST data. The syntax is a series of *name=value* pairs, separated by ampersands. For the **service.php** script (to be written next), you can pass almost anything and the service will report back the results.

Note that if you wanted to send more complex values through cURL, you'd want to URL-encode the data.

9. Execute the transaction:

```
$r = curl_exec($curl);
```

10. Close the connection:

```
curl_close($curl);
```

continues on next page

11. Print the results:

```
print_r($r);
```

Everything returned by the request is assigned to the $r variable. I'll just dump that out for debugging purposes.

12. Complete the page:

```
?>
</body>
</html>
```

13. Save the file as **curl.php** and place it in your Web directory.

Note that you can't run it yet, because you have to write **service.php** first.

> **TIP** If a page is protected by HTTP authentication, use this option (obviously replacing the username and password values with proper ones):
>
> ```
> curl_setopt($curl, CURLOPT_USERPWD,
> → 'username:password');
> ```

> **TIP** The curl_getinfo() function returns an array of information about the transaction **A**. If you want to use it, you must call it before closing the connection.

> **TIP** The cURL utility can also be used to send and receive cookies, handle file uploads, work over SSL connections, even FTP files.

> **TIP** Use the curl_errno() and curl_error() functions to retrieve the error number and message, should one occur.

```
Array
(
    [url] => http://localhost/service.php
    [content_type] => text/csv
    [http_code] => 200
    [header_size] => 171
    [request_size] => 157
    [filetime] => -1
    [ssl_verify_result] => 0
    [redirect_count] => 0
    [total_time] => 0.828884
    [namelookup_time] => 2.9E-5
    [connect_time] => 0.000215
    [pretransfer_time] => 0.000216
    [size_upload] => 28
    [size_download] => 30
    [speed_download] => 36
    [speed_upload] => 33
    [download_content_length] => 30
    [upload_content_length] => 28
    [starttransfer_time] => 0.828859
    [redirect_time] => 0
```

A Some of the information about the most recent cURL request.

Creating Web Services

The previous four examples in this chapter all demonstrate various ways you can use PHP to interact with another server. The IP geolocation example specifically makes use of a *Web service*. A Web service is a generic term for a server resource that provides a function that, unlike a normal Web page, is meant to be accessed directly by another computer, not a user. For example, a PHP script on server A (such as `ip_geo.php`) would make a request of a script on server B (in that case, the `freegeoip.net` server).

The principle behind a service is simple, but services can be implemented in many different ways. In fact, entire books have been written on the subject. But in this chapter, I'll present an overview of the Web services field and then show you how to implement a simple type of Web service.

Introduction to Web services

Web services can vary greatly in their complexity. In fact, that complexity is well represented by the multiple acronyms involved. Loosely speaking, you can group all Web services into two broad categories: complex and simple.

Complex services are what have been historically known as true "Web services" (as opposed to the generic term). In a complex service, the client is able to dynamically discover and use the service. For example, the server may use Web Services Description Language (WSDL) to describe the service provided. That WSDL document is then readable by clients tapping into the service.

Complex Web services often transmit data using custom, non-scalar types. This might require a protocol such as Simple Object Access Protocol (SOAP). This means that instead of just transmitting, say, plain text or XML between the client and the server, the server may send back data in an agreed-upon object format.

As you can tell, complex Web services tend to have tighter integration between the client and the server. And there may be several iterations of communication over the course of a transaction.

Conversely, simple Web services are stateless: just a basic request-response dynamic. The client makes standard requests in the hopes that the server understands that request and is able to reply. These are also known as application programming interface (API)-based services, where the developer has to find the documentation that explains how to use the service. All of the examples in this chapter have been of this type.

A popular type of simple service is called REST-ful, short for Representational State Transfer (REST). These are normally HTTP requests, with data often being passed to the service, which will in turn impact the data returned by the service. For example, an IP address and a returned data format are sent to the IP geolocation service, which then returns information in the given format.

Now that you've seen different ways of having a PHP script interact with a simple Web service (i.e., having PHP act as the client), let's create a PHP script to act as a barebones service. First, though, you need to know how to return different types of data using a PHP script.

Returning types of data

For the most part, Web developers use PHP to create HTML content. But a service does not normally create HTML; it outputs data. In both cases, PHP is still just printing the output, but when using a script as a service, the PHP script has to take the extra step of indicating its alternative usage. In other words, the PHP script has to communicate the type of content being outputted. Normally a server associates the content type of a PHP script with HTML. To change that, send a content-type header, indicating the type to be expected.

If the data being returned by the service is in plain text format, you would use

`header('Content-Type: text/plain');`

Note that, as with any time you use `header()`, this line must be called prior to anything being sent out.

If the PHP script is outputting data in CSV format, you'd use

`header('Content-Type: text/csv');`

More complex data is normally transmitted using either XML or JSON. Those content types are

`header('Content-Type: text/xml');`

and

`header('Content-Type:`
`→ application/json');`

XML, which has long been the standard for representing complex data, is discussed in great detail in Chapter 13, "XML and PHP." In that chapter, you'll see how to have a PHP script return XML data, so I won't explain how to do so any further here.

The JSON format is most commonly used in services that expect to be accessed via JavaScript, although that is not required. To have PHP output data in JSON format, you just need to invoke the `json_encode()` function:

`echo json_encode($data);`

The `json_encode()` function is part of the JSON extension, built into PHP as of version 5.2.

Creating a simple service

With a quick explanation of how you output different, standard data types from a PHP script, let's create an example. To demonstrate as much information in one fell swoop, this next script will be quite flexible, able to output data in one of four possible formats:

- Plain text
- CSV
- JSON
- XML (after some additional work)

For the data itself, the script will merely return the data provided to the service during the request. This is somewhat trivial, although it does make for a good debugging tool. Still, with a basic understanding of PHP and MySQL, however, it would be easy to have this script return information from a database or other source.

Script 10.5 This simple Web service returns data in different formats, based on how it's accessed.

```php
1    <?php # Script 11.5 - service.php
2    // This script acts as a simple Web
     → service.
3    // The script only reports back the
     → data received, along with a bit of
     → extra information.
4
5    // Check for proper usage:
6    if (isset($_POST['format'])) {
7
8        // Switch the content type based
         → upon the format:
9        switch ($_POST['format']) {
10           case 'csv':
11               $type = 'text/csv';
12               break;
13           case 'json':
14               $type = 'application/json';
15               break;
16           case 'xml':
17               $type = 'text/xml';
18               break;
19           default:
20               $type = 'text/plain';
21               break;
22       }
23
24       // Create the response:
25       $data = array();
26       $data['timestamp'] = time();
27
28       // Add back in the received data:
29       foreach ($_POST as $k => $v) {
30           $data[$k] = $v;
31       }
32
33       // Format the data accordingly:
34       if ($type == 'application/json') {
35           $output = json_encode($data);
36
37       } elseif ($type == 'text/csv') {
38
39           // Convert to a string:
40           $output = '';
41           foreach ($data as $v) {
42               $output .= '"' . $v . '",';
43           }
44
```

script continues on next page

To create a service:

1. Create a new PHP script in your text editor or IDE, to be named **service.php** (Script 10.5):

`<?php # Script 10.5 - service.php`

This script will not output any HTML!

2. Check that a format was passed to the service in POST:

`if (isset($_POST['format'])) {`

The only requirement of this script is that a desired data format is sent via POST.

3. Identify the content type based on the desired format:

```php
switch ($_POST['format']) {
  case 'csv':
      $type = 'text/csv';
      break;
  case 'json':
      $type = 'application/json';
      break;
  case 'xml':
      $type = 'text/xml';
      break;
  default:
      $type = 'text/plain';
      break;
}
```

These values match those already explained.

continues on next page

4. Start building up the response:

```
$data = array();
$data['timestamp'] = time();
```

The response will be an array of data, starting with the current timestamp.

5. Add the received data to the array:

```
foreach ($_POST as $k => $v) {
   $data[$k] = $v;
}
```

To give this service something to do, it will report back the data received.

6. Create the output in the proper format:

```
if ($type == 'application/json') {
   $output = json_encode($data);
```

The next step is to turn the data into the proper format based on what the requester submitted. For JSON data, this just means running the data through the **json_encode()** function.

7. Create the output in CSV format:

```
} elseif ($type == 'text/csv') {
   $output = '';
   foreach ($data as $v) {
      $output .= '"' . $v . '",';
   }
   $output = substr($output,
   → 0, -1);
```

The CSV data should obviously have each piece of information separated by commas. To make the data more reliable, however, each value will be wrapped in quotes (e.g., in case there are commas within the values).

Script 10.5 *continued*

```
45         // Chop off the final comma:
46         $output = substr($output, 0, -1);
47
48    } elseif ($type == 'text/plain') {
49        $output = print_r($data, 1);
50    }
51
52 } else { // Incorrectly used!
53    $type = 'text/plain';
54    $output = 'This service has been
   → incorrectly used.';
55 }
56
57 // Set the content-type header:
58 header("Content-Type: $type");
59 echo $output;
```

8. Create the output in plain text format:

```
} elseif ($type == 'text/plain') {
    $output = print_r($data, 1);
}
```

If the requested data should be in plain text format, it'll just be a variable dump.

9. Complete the conditional begun in Step 2:

```
} else {
    $type = 'text/plain';
    $output = 'This service has
    → been incorrectly used.';
}
```

If no format was provided via POST, a plain text message will indicate that the service was incorrectly used.

10. Set the content-type header:

```
header("Content-Type: $type");
```

11. Send the data:

```
echo $output;
```

Remember that "sending" is really just printing, as the output of the script is what the requesting script will receive.

12. Save the file as **service.php** and place it in your Web directory.

13. Test the service by running **curl.php** in your Web browser **A**.

14. Change the POST data in **curl.php** and rerun the script **B**.

TIP The `curl.php` and `service.php` scripts would not normally be on the same server, but it's fine for them to be together for testing purposes.

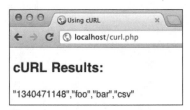

A The script displays the service results, which is in the requested CSV format.

B Different data from another service request, now in JSON format.

Review and Pursue

If you have any problems with these sections, either in answering the questions or pursuing your own endeavors, turn to the book's supporting forum (www.Larry Ullman.com/forums/).

Review

- How do you use **fopen()** to access another Web site? What restrictions exist when you do so? (See page 328.)

- What are *sockets*? What is a *port*? What PHP function do you use to communicate over sockets? (See page 333.)

- What are HTTP status codes? (See page 334.)

- What does the **parse_url()** function do? (See page 333.)

- What does the **set_time_limit()** function do? Why is it necessary in the **check_urls.php** script? (See page 337.)

- In what variable will PHP store a user's IP address? (See page 339.)

- What PHP function can be used to find the IP address associated with a domain name? (See page 339.)

- What is cURL? What kinds of things can it be used for? (See page 343.)

- What are Web services? How does a PHP script used as a Web service, as opposed to an HTML page, differ? (See page 347.)

Pursue

- If you want to practice your OOP skills, rewrite any of this chapter's examples using classes.

- Look into the Zend Framework's tools for interacting with other Web sites.

- Learn more about *sockets* and *ports*.

- Update **check_urls.php** to qualify a wider range of status codes as "good."

- If you want, update the **ip_geo.php** script to use **fsockopen()** instead of **fopen()**. Note that you'll want to perform a GET request, not a HEAD request as in **check_urls.php**.

- Learn more about using cURL.

- Rewrite any of the other chapter examples using cURL.

- Create a new, more useful service script.

PHP and the Server

A lot of the standard PHP actions, such as communicating with databases and sending emails, actually occur between applications on the server and PHP (as opposed to between the server and the client). As PHP is increasingly used for advanced purposes and not simply to generate Web content, its ability to manipulate and use the features the server has to offer becomes more important.

This chapter will show you how to better take advantage of the other services and libraries that your server may have. Starting off is a demonstration of how to compress files using PHP. The second topic shows how to automatically run your PHP scripts using `cron` on Unix (and Mac OS X). The chapter ends with instructions for implementing cryptography for better security.

Compressing Files

Most users are familiar with client-based GUI compression utilities such as WinZip or StuffIt, used to compress and decompress files. Thanks to zlib, available from **www.zlib.net**, you can have PHP compress files as well. The zlib library was written by two of the major compression/decompression developers as a patent-free, lossless data-compression tool. Zlib is available on every major platform and is frequently built into a server's configuration. I would be surprised if a Unix brand of operating system did not include zlib, and PHP on Windows has built-in support for zlib ever since version 4.3.

Once zlib is installed and PHP is made to support it **Ⓐ**, you can use it for writing to or reading from compressed files. Most of the functions work exactly like the standard file functions: **fopen()**, **fwrite()**, **fclose()**, and so forth. You start by opening a file, indicating the mode:

```
$fp = gzopen('filename.gz', 'mode');
```

The modes, shown in **Table 11.1**, are the same as those used with **fopen()**. Added to this can be a compression level on a scale of 1 (least compressed) to 9 (most). And you can add the *f*, *h*, and *b* flags to further modify the mode.

With an open file, you can then write data to it:

```
$fp = gzopen('filename.gz', 'w5');
gzwrite($fp, 'data');
```

Finally, close the file:

```
gzclose($fp);
```

Reading from files can be even easier. You can use **readgzfile()**, which reads in a compressed file, decompresses the data, and sends it to the output. There is also the **gzfile()** function, which reads in a compressed file, decompresses it, and returns it as an array (one element for each line in the file).

In this next example, I'll have PHP create a compressed file on the fly. The PHP script itself will retrieve all of the data stored in a named database and will create files listing said data in comma-delineated format. In short, this PHP script will create a compressed backup of a database's records.

zlib

ZLib Support	enabled
Stream Wrapper	compress.zlib://
Stream Filter	zlib.inflate, zlib.deflate
Compiled Version	1.2.3
Linked Version	1.2.5

Directive	Local Value	Master Value
zlib.output_compression	Off	Off
zlib.output_compression_level	-1	-1
zlib.output_handler	no value	no value

Ⓐ Before attempting to use the zlib functions, run a **phpinfo()** script to confirm PHP's support for the library.

TABLE 11.1 File Open Modes

Mode	Open for...
r	Reading only, starting at the beginning of the file.
r+	Reading and writing, starting at the beginning of the file.
w	Writing only, starting at the beginning of the file; empty the file if it exists, create it if it doesn't.
w+	Reading and writing, starting at the beginning of the file; empty the file if it exists, create it if it doesn't.
a	Writing only, starting at the end of the file; create the file if it doesn't exist.
a+	Reading and writing, starting at the end of the file; create the file if it doesn't exist.
x	Writing only, starting at the beginning of the file; create the file if it doesn't exist, indicate failure if it does.
x	Reading and writing, starting at the beginning of the file; create the file if it doesn't exist, indicate failure if it does.
f	Filtered data
h	Huffman-only compression
b	Binary mode

To compress a file:

1. Create a new PHP document in your text editor or IDE, to be named **db_backup.php**, beginning with the standard HTML (**Script 11.1**):

```
<!doctype html>
<html lang="en">
<head>
    <meta charset="utf-8">
    <title>Database Backup</title>
</head>
<body>
<?php # Script 11.1 - db_backup.php
```

2. Set the name of the database:

```
$db_name = 'test';
```

First, I set a variable with the name of the database to be backed up. I do so mostly because the database name will be referenced several times over in this script and I want to make changes easily.

continues on page 358

Script 11.1 This very useful script will back up a database, table by table, to a compressed, comma-separated text file.

```
1    <!doctype html>
2    <html lang="en">
3    <head>
4      <meta charset="utf-8">
5      <title>Database Backup</title>
6    </head>
7    <body>
8    <?php # Script 11.1 - db_backup.php
9
10   /*  This page retrieves all the data from a database
11    *  and writes that data to a text file.
12    *  The text file is then compressed using zlib.
13    */
14
15   // Establish variables and setup:
16   $db_name = 'test';
17
18   // Backup directory:
19   $dir = "backups/$db_name";
20
21   // Make the database-specific directory, if it doesn't exist:
22   if (!is_dir($dir)) {
23       if (!@mkdir($dir)) {
24           die("<p>The backup directory--$dir--could not be created.</p></body></html>");
25       }
26   }
27
28   // Get the current time for use in all filenames:
29   $time = time();
30
31   // Connect to the database:
32   $dbc = @mysqli_connect('localhost', 'username', 'password', $db_name) OR die("<p>The database--
     ↪ $db_name--could not be backed up.</p></body></html>");
33
34   // Retrieve the tables:
35   $r = mysqli_query($dbc, 'SHOW TABLES');
36
37   // Back up if at least one table exists:
38   if (mysqli_num_rows($r) > 0) {
39
40       // Indicate what is happening:
41       echo "<p>Backing up database '$db_name'.</p>";
42
43       // Fetch each table name:
44       while (list($table) = mysqli_fetch_array($r, MYSQLI_NUM)) {
45
```

script continues on next page

```
46        // Get the records for this table:
47        $q = "SELECT * FROM $table";
48        $r2 = mysqli_query($dbc, $q);
49
50        // Back up if records exist:
51        if (mysqli_num_rows($r2) > 0) {
52
53            // Attempt to open the file:
54            if ($fp = gzopen ("$dir/{$table}_{$time}.sql.gz", 'w9')) {
55
56                // Fetch all the records for this table:
57                while ($row = mysqli_fetch_array($r2, MYSQLI_NUM)) {
58
59                    // Write the data as a comma-delineated row:
60                    foreach ($row as $value) {
61                        $value = addslashes($value);
62                        gzwrite ($fp, "'$value', ");
63                    }
64
65                    // Add a new line to each row:
66                    gzwrite ($fp, "\n");
67
68                } // End of WHILE loop.
69
70                // Close the file:
71                gzclose ($fp);
72
73                // Print the success:
74                echo "<p>Table '$table' backed up.</p>";
75
76            } else { // Could not create the file!
77                echo "<p>The file--$dir/{$table}_{$time}.sql.gz--could not be opened for
   → writing.</p>";
78                break; // Leave the WHILE loop.
79            } // End of gzopen() IF.
80
81        } // End of mysqli_num_rows() IF.
82
83    } // End of WHILE loop.
84
85 } else {
86    echo "<p>The submitted database--$db_name--contains no tables.</p>";
87 }
88
89 ?>
90 </body>
91 </html>
```

3. Make sure that the backup directory exists:

```
$dir = "backups/$db_name";
if (!is_dir($dir)) {
  if (!@mkdir($dir)) {
    die("<p>The backup
    → directory--$dir--could
    → not be created.</p></body>
    → </html>");
  }
}
```

The backups will be stored in a directory called *backups*. Within this directory, each database will have its own directory. First, a variable is given the value of the final destination. Next, the script checks to see if that directory already exists. If not, the script attempts to create it. The script terminates if the directory could not be created **B**, since there'd be no point in continuing.

One assumption here is that an existing directory is already writable, something you could easily check for (using the **is_writable()** function). This section of the code, which is secondary to what's really being taught, assumes you already understand what permissions must exist for PHP to write to directories. And you'll obviously need to change the particulars to match your system.

4. Get the current time:

```
$time = time();
```

Each table backup will be its own file and this value will be used in each filename. Because every file should reflect the same backup time, I assign this to a variable once, instead of invoking the function once for each file.

5. Connect to the database:

```
$dbc = @mysqli_connect
→ ('localhost', 'username',
→ 'password', $db_name) OR die
→ ("<p>The database--$db_name--
→ could not be backed up.</p>
→ </body></html>");
```

Next, the script attempts to connect to the named database. If it can't, a message indicating a problem is displayed in the Web browser **C**, and the HTML page is concluded. Again, you'll obviously need to change the parameters to match what's appropriate for your server.

6. Retrieve the tables in this database:

```
$r = mysqli_query($dbc,
→ 'SHOW TABLES');
```

This query will return a list of every table in the current database **D**.

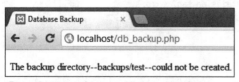

B The result if the destination directory does not exist and could not be created.

C The result if a database connection could not be made.

```
mysql> SHOW TABLES;
+---------------------------+
| Tables_in_test            |
+---------------------------+
| Department                |
| Employee                  |
| User                      |
| child                     |
| parent                    |
| phorum_banlists           |
| phorum_files              |
| phorum_forum_group_xref   |
| phorum_forums             |
| phorum_groups             |
| phorum_messages           |
| phorum_messages_edittrack |
| phorum_pm_buddies         |
| phorum_pm_folders         |
| phorum_pm_messages        |
| phorum_pm_xref            |
| phorum_search             |
```

D Running the same query that the script runs (the first of two) using the **mysql** client.

7. Confirm that at least one record was returned and print a message:

```
if (mysqli_num_rows($r) > 0) {
    echo "<p>Backing up database
→'$db_name'.</p>\n";
```

No need to back up an empty database!

8. Create a loop that fetches each table name:

```
while (list($table) = mysqli_
→fetch_array($r, MYSQLI_NUM)) {
```

9. Retrieve all the records for this table:

```
$q = "SELECT * FROM $table";
```

```
$r2 = mysqli_query($dbc, $q);
```

This query returns every record for a given table **E**. Since this query is run within a **while** loop for another query, you have to use a different result variable (**$r2** here instead of **$r**), or you'll overwrite the first query's results.

continues on next page

```
mysql> SELECT * FROM tasks;
+---------+-----------+-------------------+---------------------+---------------------+
| task_id | parent_id | task              | date_added          | date_completed      |
+---------+-----------+-------------------+---------------------+---------------------+
|       1 |         0 | Must Do This!     | 2012-04-23 14:52:57 | 2012-04-23 14:52:57 |
|       2 |         0 | Another Task      | 2012-04-22 16:06:42 | 0000-00-00 00:00:00 |
|       3 |         0 | My New Task       | 2012-04-22 16:06:42 | 0000-00-00 00:00:00 |
|       4 |         2 | Subtask 1         | 2012-04-23 14:52:57 | 2012-04-23 14:52:57 |
|       5 |         2 | Subtask 2         | 2012-04-22 16:06:42 | 0000-00-00 00:00:00 |
|       6 |         2 | Subtask 3         | 2012-04-22 16:06:42 | 0000-00-00 00:00:00 |
|       7 |         5 | Subsubtask1       | 2012-04-23 16:07:12 | 0000-00-00 00:00:00 |
|       8 |         0 | This is a new task! | 2012-04-23 13:17:51 | 0000-00-00 00:00:00 |
|       9 |         5 | Subsubtask 2      | 2012-04-23 13:59:14 | 0000-00-00 00:00:00 |
|      10 |         9 | Sub-cubed task 1  | 2012-04-23 13:59:24 | 0000-00-00 00:00:00 |
|      11 |         9 | Sub-cubed task 2  | 2012-04-23 13:59:29 | 0000-00-00 00:00:00 |
|      12 |         9 | Sub-cubed task 3  | 2012-04-23 14:52:57 | 2012-04-23 14:52:57 |
|      13 |         0 | Finish Chapter 1! | 2012-04-23 15:02:24 | 0000-00-00 00:00:00 |
|      14 |         0 | Finish Chapter 1! | 2012-04-23 15:02:48 | 0000-00-00 00:00:00 |
|      15 |         0 | F                 | 2012-04-23 15:02:57 | 0000-00-00 00:00:00 |
|      16 |         0 | Finish Chapter 1! | 2012-04-23 15:03:01 | 0000-00-00 00:00:00 |
+---------+-----------+-------------------+---------------------+---------------------+
16 rows in set (0.01 sec)

mysql>
```

E The main query, the results of which will be written to a file.

10. If the table contains some records, open the text file for writing:

```
if (mysqli_num_rows($r2) > 0) {
  if ($fp = gzopen
→ ("$dir/{$table}_{$time}.sql.gz",
→ 'w9')) {
```

Each table will be backed up to its own file, the name of which is derived from the table name (**$table**), the current timestamp (**$time**), and a **.sql.gz** extension. All of the files will be written to a database-specific folder within a backup folder. Both directories must have appropriate permissions for PHP to write to them.

The **gzopen()** function takes two parameters: the filename and the mode of opening. The modes correspond directly to **fopen()**'s modes (**w**, **r**, **a** along with **b** for writing binary data) but can also indicate a level of compression. The acceptable compression levels are on a scale from 1 (minimal compression) to 9 (maximum) with a trade-off between compression and performance. For relatively small files like these text documents, maximum compression is fine.

11. Retrieve all of the table's data, and write it to the file:

```
while ($row = mysqli_fetch_
→ array($r2, MYSQLI_NUM)) {
  foreach ($row as $value) {
    $value = addslashes($value);
    gzwrite ($fp, "'$value', ");
  }
  gzwrite ($fp, "\n");
} // End of WHILE loop.
```

This loop will take every row out of the table and write that to a text file in the format **'value',[SPACE]**. Instead of using the **fwrite()** function that you may be familiar with, there is **gzwrite()**, which works just the same (except that it writes to a compressed file).

In case the retrieved data contains an apostrophe, it's run through the **addslashes()** function prior to storage.

12. Close the file and print a message to the browser:

```
gzclose ($fp);
echo "<p>Table '$table' backed up.
→ </p>";
```

```
Backing up database 'test'.

Table 'Department' backed up.

Table 'Employee' backed up.

Table 'User' backed up.

Table 'child' backed up.

Table 'parent' backed up.

Table 'phorum_forums' backed up.

Table 'phorum_messages' backed up.

Table 'phorum_search' backed up.

Table 'phorum_settings' backed up.

Table 'phorum_users' backed up.

Table 'tasks' backed up.

Table 'test2' backed up.
```

F What the Web page shows after successfully backing up the tables found within the **test** database.

13. Complete the conditionals:

```php
                } else {
                    echo "<p>The file--$dir/
                    → {$table}_{$time}.sql.
                    → gz--could not be
                    → opened for writing.
                    → </p>\n";
                    break;
                } // End of gzopen() IF.
            } // End of mysqli_num_
            → rows() IF.
        } // End of WHILE loop.
    } else {
        echo "<p>The submitted
        → database--$db_name--contains
        → no tables.</p>\n";
    }
```

14. Complete the page:

```php
?>
```

15. Save the file as **db_backup.php** and place it in your Web directory.

16. Create a folder called **backups**, in the same directory as **db_backup.php**, and change the folder's permissions (if necessary).

    How you do this depends on your operating system, which I assume as an experienced PHP developer you've already discovered. If you don't know how to change a directory's permissions, search the Web or check out the book's corresponding support forum (**www.LarryUllman.com/forums/**).

17. Test the PHP script in your Web browser **F**.

continues on next page

18. Check the directory on your computer to see the new files **G**.

TIP The zlib functions can also work with compressed binary files. (Windows makes a distinction between binary and plain text files, but Unix and Mac OS X do not.) Binary files offer the advantage of being readable and writable in a nonlinear fashion.

TIP The zlib library can also be used to automatically compress PHP output on the fly. By sending compressed data to the browser, which the browser would automatically decompress, less data will need to be transmitted, thereby improving the page's performance.

TIP You can create ZIP archives using the zlib library and the PHP ZIP extension.

Name	Date Modified	Size	Kind
child_1337738682.sql.gz	10:04 PM	49 bytes	gzip compressed archive
Department_1337738682.sql.gz	10:04 PM	59 bytes	gzip compressed archive
Employee_1337738682.sql.gz	10:04 PM	75 bytes	gzip compressed archive
parent_1337738682.sql.gz	10:04 PM	38 bytes	gzip compressed archive
phorum_forums_1337738682.sql.gz	10:04 PM	291 bytes	gzip compressed archive
phorum_messages_1337738682.sql.gz	10:04 PM	291 bytes	gzip compressed archive
phorum_search_1337738682.sql.gz	10:04 PM	202 bytes	gzip compressed archive
phorum_settings_1337738682.sql.gz	10:04 PM	4 KB	gzip compressed archive
phorum_users_1337738682.sql.gz	10:04 PM	278 bytes	gzip compressed archive
tasks_1337738682.sql.gz	10:04 PM	284 bytes	gzip compressed archive
test2_1337738682.sql.gz	10:04 PM	61 bytes	gzip compressed archive
User_1337738682.sql.gz	10:04 PM	101 bytes	gzip compressed archive

G Viewing the directory within my computer shows the newly created compressed files, one for each table in the database.

Establishing a cron

A **cron** is a service on Unix servers that allows tasks to be scheduled and executed automatically. The **cron** application runs constantly and will carry out its orders when instructed to do so. These orders are stored in a file called **crontab**. This file is a to-do list that contains lines that might look like

```
30 22 * * * wget -q
 http://www.example.com
```

The **crontab** format dictates that each line contain six fields separated by spaces or tabs. The first five fields represent, in order: minutes, hours, days, months, and day of the week (from 0 to 6, with 0 being Sunday). You can specify the day of operation as either a day of the month (1–31) or a day of the week (Sunday through Saturday), the latter being date-indifferent.

An asterisk as one of the first five parameters means that value is not limited (i.e., it always applies). In the preceding example, the instruction is to be carried out at 10:30 p.m. (22 being 10 p.m. on the 24-hour clock) every day of the month, every month of the year.

You can also set ranges using the hyphen (1–6 for the month field would mean that the job applies to the first six months of the year) or list elements separated by comma (1, 3, 5 for Monday, Wednesday, Friday). The sixth field on each line is the task itself.

Looking at the preceding example, the actual command is to open the URL **http://www.example.com** with **wget**, a command-line URL tool built into Unix. The **-q** flag says to access the page quietly. This command would be, for example, how I might run a script whose output is not important (like **db_backups.php**).

To use **cron** to run a PHP script, you have a couple of options. The first is to use the server's own Web browser—like wget—to run a PHP script, as just explained. Another would be to use the server's installation of cURL. This program is designed to access URLs, although it's not a Web browser per se (Chapter 10, "Networking with PHP," discusses cURL in some detail). A final option is to run the PHP script using the Command-Line Interface (see Chapter 12, "PHP's Command-Line Interface").

For this example, I'll run the **db_backup.php** script (Script 11.1) created earlier in the chapter, using cURL. The syntax for using cURL is easy:

```
curl yourURLhere
```

So:

```
curl http://www.example.com/page.php
```

To add an item to the **crontab** file, you can manually edit it by typing **crontab -e** in a command prompt. This will allow you to edit the file using your default command-line text editor. Unfortunately, if you don't know how to already use said text editor—a surprisingly daunting task—this does you no good. So instead I'll show you another method.

To establish a cron for a PHP file:

1. Access your server via a command-line interface.

   If you're not clear as to how to do this, see the next chapter. If you're using a remote (i.e., hosted) server, there may just be a control panel for you to set cron jobs instead of using a command-line interface.

2. Test the command 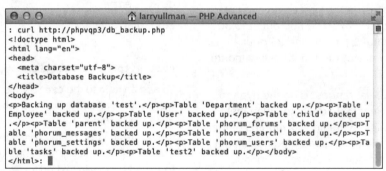:

   ```
   curl http://localhost/db_backup.php
   ```

   It's always best to test the command you'll have **cron** execute so that you know that it works. Do so just by entering the command within the command-line interface you're using. You'll obviously need to change your URL to match where you put your copy of **db_backup.php** (as in the figure). In my case, the PHP script is running on the same server as this cron job.

3. View the current contents of the **crontab** file:

   ```
   crontab -l
   ```

   This command will show you the current **crontab**, which you should be careful with, as the following steps will replace any existing instructions. If you've never worked with the **crontab** file before, it's probably blank, but better safe than sorry!

   If there are already commands entered, copy them for later.

```
: curl http://phpvqp3/db_backup.php
<!doctype html>
<html lang="en">
<head>
  <meta charset="utf-8">
  <title>Database Backup</title>
</head>
<body>
<p>Backing up database 'test'.</p><p>Table 'Department' backed up.</p><p>Table '
Employee' backed up.</p><p>Table 'User' backed up.</p><p>Table 'child' backed up
.</p><p>Table 'parent' backed up.</p><p>Table 'phorum_forums' backed up.</p><p>T
able 'phorum_messages' backed up.</p><p>Table 'phorum_search' backed up.</p><p>T
able 'phorum_settings' backed up.</p><p>Table 'phorum_users' backed up.</p><p>Ta
ble 'tasks' backed up.</p><p>Table 'test2' backed up.</p></body>
</html>:
```

Ⓐ Before entering the command into the **crontab** file, I test it once to confirm the results.

4. Create a new document in your text editor or IDE (**Script 11.2**):

```
1 0 * * 5 curl http://localhost/
→ db_backup.php
```

First, you'll write a dummy **cronjob** file, and then you'll install this into the actual **crontab**. This file should contain the entire command. Make sure you press Enter/Return once at the end of the line.

The command itself says that cURL should be invoked with that URL every Friday (5) at 12:01 a.m.

5. If Step 3 revealed anything in the current **crontab**, add it to the text document begun in Step 4.

Just copy-paste whatever was returned in Step 3 to the text document. Each task should be on its own line. It won't matter, in this case, which instruction comes first.

6. Save this file as **cronjob1** (without any extension) and upload it to the server in a convenient location (not necessarily within the Web document root).

Script 11.2 The **cronjob1** file lists the command to be added to **crontab**.

```
1    # Script 11.2 - cronjob
2    # Run a PHP script every Friday at
     → 12:01 am:
3    1 0 * * 5 curl http://localhost/
     → db_backup.php
```

7. Within your server's command prompt, enter the following code and then press Enter/Return once:

```
crontab /path/to/cronjob1
```

In my example **B**, **cronjob1** is stored on my desktop. The full path is therefore **/Users/larryullman/Desktop/cronjob1**, and the shortcut reference is **~/Desktop/cronjob1**. Replace that part of the code with the applicable location of your **cronjob1** file on the server.

8. Confirm the **cron** task list by viewing the **crontab** file **C**.

```
crontab -l
```

TIP The **crontab** file is unique for each user on the server. This also means that the instructions in the **crontab** file will run as that user, so permissions conflicts may arise. This is another reason why it's a good idea to test the command before entering it into the **crontab** file.

TIP On Windows, you can replicate **cron** using *scheduled tasks*. Search online or use my support forums (www.LarryUllman.com/forums/) if you need assistance with this.

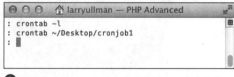

```
: crontab -l
: crontab ~/Desktop/cronjob1
:
```

B Adding the new instruction to the **crontab** file.

```
: crontab -l
# Script 11.2 – cronjob
# Run a PHP script every Friday at 12:01 am:
1 0 * * 5 curl http://localhost/db_backup.php:
```

C Confirming the contents of the **crontab** file.

Using MCrypt

Frequently, Web applications will encrypt and decrypt data stored in a database, using the database-supplied functions. This is appropriate, as you want the database to do the bulk of the work whenever possible. But what if you want to encrypt and decrypt data that's *not* being stored in a database? In that situation, MCrypt provides a good solution. To use MCrypt with PHP, you'll need to install the MCrypt library (libmcrypt, available from **http://sourceforge.net/projects/mcrypt/**) and configure PHP to support it Ⓐ. As of PHP 5, you need at least version 2.5.6 of MCrypt. It is built into PHP on Windows since PHP 5.3.

For this next example, I'll show you how to encrypt data stored in the session. As you should know, session data is normally stored as plain text in readily available files. In other words, session data normally has few security protections. Using MCrypt, you could encrypt that stored data, adding a layer of security. As the encryption process creates binary data, the **base64_encode()** function will be applied to the encrypted data, to convert it to a textual format prior to storing it. Therefore, the corresponding **base64_decode()** function needs to be used prior to decoding the data. Other than that little tidbit, the focus in the next two scripts is entirely on using MCrypt.

Do keep in mind that in the next several pages I'll be introducing and teaching security concepts to which people have dedicated entire careers. The information covered here will be secure, useful, and valid, but it's just the tip of the proverbial security iceberg.

mcrypt		
mcrypt support	enabled	
mcrypt_filter support	enabled	
Version	2.5.8	
Api No	20021217	
Supported ciphers	cast-128 gost rijndael-128 twofish arcfour cast-256 loki97 rijndael-192 saferplus wake blowfish-compat des rijndael-256 serpent xtea blowfish enigma rc2 tripledes	
Supported modes	cbc cfb ctr ecb ncfb nofb ofb stream	

Directive	Local Value	Master Value
mcrypt.algorithms_dir	no value	no value
mcrypt.modes_dir	no value	no value

Ⓐ Check your PHP installation for MCrypt support before trying this next script.

```
Array
(
    [0] => cast-128
    [1] => gost
    [2] => rijndael-128
    [3] => twofish
    [4] => arcfour
    [5] => cast-256
    [6] => loki97
    [7] => rijndael-192
    [8] => saferplus
    [9] => wake
    [10] => blowfish-compat
    [11] => des
    [12] => rijndael-256
    [13] => serpent
    [14] => xtea
    [15] => blowfish
    [16] => enigma
    [17] => rc2
    [18] => tripledes
)
```

B The list of MCrypt *algorithms* supported by this PHP installation.

```
Array
(
    [0] => cbc
    [1] => cfb
    [2] => ctr
    [3] => ecb
    [4] => ncfb
    [5] => nofb
    [6] => ofb
    [7] => stream
)
```

C The list of MCrypt *modes* supported by this PHP installation.

Encrypting data

With MCrypt libraries 2.4.x and higher, you start by identifying which *algorithm* and *mode* to use by invoking the **mcrypt_module_open()** function:

$m = mcrypt_module_open (algorithm,
→ *algorithm_dir*, mode, *mode_dir*);

MCrypt comes with dozens of different algorithms, or *ciphers*, each of which encrypts data differently. You can run the **mcrypt_list_algorithms()** function to see which ones your installation supports **B**. If you are interested in how each works, see the MCrypt home page or search the Web. In my examples, I'll be using the Rijndael algorithm, also known as the Advanced Encryption Standard (AES). It's a very popular and secure encryption algorithm, even up to United States government standards. I'll be using it with 256-bit keys, for extra security.

As for the mode, there are four main modes: ECB (electronic codebook), CBC (cipher block chaining), CFB (cipher feedback), and OFB (output feedback). CBC will suit most of your needs, especially when encrypting blocks of text as in this example. The **mcrypt_list_modes()** function shows which modes are available **C** to your installation.

With the algorithm and mode selected, to indicate that you want to use Rijndael 256 in CBC mode, you would code

$m = mcrypt_module_open
→ ('rijndael-256', '', 'cbc', '');

The second and fourth arguments fed to the **mcrypt_module_open()** function are for explicitly stating where PHP can find the algorithm and mode files. These are not required unless PHP is unable to find a cipher and you know for certain it is installed.

Once the module is open, you create an *IV* (initialization vector). This may be required, optional, or unnecessary, depending on the mode being used. I'll use it with CBC to increase the security. Here's how the PHP manual recommends an IV be created:

```
$iv = mcrypt_create_iv(mcrypt_enc_
→ get_iv_size ($m), MCRYPT_DEV_
→ RANDOM);
```

By using the `mcrypt_enc_get_iv_size()` function, a properly sized IV will be created for the cipher being used. Note that on Windows with versions of PHP before 5.3, you should use `MCRYPT_RAND` instead of `MCRYPT_DEV_RANDOM`.

The final step before you are ready to encrypt data is to create the *buffers* that MCrypt needs to perform encryption:

```
mcrypt_generic_init($m, $key, $iv);
```

The second argument is a key, which should be a hard-to-guess string. The key must be of a particular length, corresponding to the cipher you use. The Rijndael cipher I'm using takes a 256-bit key. Divide 256 by 8 (because there are 8 bits in a byte and each character in the key string takes 1 byte) and you'll see that the key needs to be exactly 32 characters long. To accomplish that, and to randomize the key even more, I'll run it through `md5()`, which always returns a 32-character string:

```
$key = md5('some string');
```

Once you have gone through these steps, you are ready to encrypt data:

```
$encrypted = mcrypt_generic($m,
→ $data);
```

You can encrypt as much, or as many individual pieces, of data as you need.

Finally, after you have finished encrypting everything, you should close all the buffers and modules:

```
mcrypt_generic_deinit($m);

mcrypt_module_close($m);
```

For this next example, I'm going to store an encrypted value in the session. The data will be decrypted in the subsequent example. The key and data to be encrypted will be hard-coded into this script, but I'll mention alternatives in the following steps. Also, because the same key and IV are needed to decrypt the data, the IV will also be stored in the session. Surprisingly, doing so doesn't hurt the security of the application, although I will again discuss alternative approaches.

To encrypt data:

1. Begin a new PHP script in your text editor or IDE, to be named **set_mcrypt. php** (Script 11.3):

   ```
   <?php # Script 11.3 -
   → set_mcrypt.php
   session_start(); ?>
   ```

   Because the script will store data in the session, the session must be begun before any HTML is created.

2. Add the HTML head:

   ```
   <!doctype html>
   <html lang="en">
   <head>
     <meta charset="utf-8">
     <title>A More Secure Session
     → </title>
   </head>
   <body>
   ```

Script 11.3 This script uses MCrypt to encrypt some data to be stored in a session.

```
1   <?php # Script 11.3 - set_mcrypt.php
2
3   /* This page uses the MCrypt library
4    * to encrypt some data.
5    * The data will then be stored in a
     → session,
6    * as will the encryption IV.
7    */
8
9   // Start the session:
10  session_start(); ?>
11  <!doctype html>
12  <html lang="en">
13  <head>
14    <meta charset="utf-8">
15    <title>A More Secure Session</title>
16  </head>
17  <body>
```

script continues on next page

3. Define the key and the data:

   ```
   <?php
   $key = md5('77 public drop-shadow
   → Java');
   $data = 'rosebud';
   ```

   For the key, some random words and numbers are run through the **md5()** function, creating a 32-character-long string. Ideally, the key should be stored in a safe place, such as a configuration file located outside of the Web document root. Or it could be retrieved from a database.

   The data being encrypted is the word *rosebud*, although in real applications this data might come from the user or another source (and be something more worth protecting).

4. Open the cipher:

   ```
   $m = mcrypt_module_open
   → ('rijndael-256', '', 'cbc', '');
   ```

   This is the same code outlined in the text before these steps.

5. Create the IV:

   ```
   $iv = mcrypt_create_iv
   → (mcrypt_enc_get_iv_size($m),
   → MCRYPT_DEV_RANDOM);
   ```

   Again, this is the same code outlined earlier. Remember that if you are running this script on Windows with an earlier version of PHP, you'll need to change this line to

   ```
   $iv = mcrypt_create_iv(mcrypt_
   → enc_get_iv_size($m),
   → MCRYPT_RAND);
   ```

6. Initialize the encryption:

   ```
   mcrypt_generic_init($m, $key, $iv);
   ```

continues on page 371

```
18  <?php // Encrypt and store the data...
19
20  // Create the key:
21  $key = md5('77 public drop-shadow Java');
22
23  // Data to be encrypted:
24  $data = 'rosebud';
25
26  // Open the cipher:
27  // Using Rijndael 256 in CBC mode.
28  $m = mcrypt_module_open('rijndael-256', '', 'cbc', '');
29
30  // Create the IV:
31  // Use MCRYPT_RAND on Windows instead of MCRYPT_DEV_RANDOM.
32  $iv = mcrypt_create_iv(mcrypt_enc_get_iv_size($m), MCRYPT_DEV_RANDOM);
33
34  // Initialize the encryption:
35  mcrypt_generic_init($m, $key, $iv);
36
37  // Encrypt the data:
38  $data = mcrypt_generic($m, $data);
39
40  // Close the encryption handler:
41  mcrypt_generic_deinit($m);
42
43  // Close the cipher:
44  mcrypt_module_close($m);
45
46  // Store the data:
47  $_SESSION['thing1'] = base64_encode($data);
48  $_SESSION['thing2'] = base64_encode($iv);
49
50  // Print the encrypted format of the data:
51  echo '<p>The data has been stored. Its value is ' . base64_encode($data) . '.</p>';
52
53  ?>
54  </body>
55  </html>
```

7. Encrypt the data:

```
$data = mcrypt_generic($m, $data);
```

If you were to print the value of **$data** now, you'd see something like ◆◆◆□"T◆◆◆□+P◆`L□W%.M □□◆◆k◆, which is how the browser would display binary data.

8. Perform the necessary cleanup:

```
mcrypt_generic_deinit($m);

mcrypt_module_close($m);
```

9. Store the data in the session:

```
$_SESSION['thing1'] =
→ base64_encode($data);

$_SESSION['thing2'] =
→ base64_encode($iv);
```

For the session names, I'm using meaningless values. You certainly wouldn't want to use, say, *IV*, as a session name! For the session data itself, you have to run it through **base64_encode()** to make it safe to store in a plain text file. This applies to both the encrypted data and the IV (which is also in binary format).

If the data were going to be stored in a binary file or in a database (in a **BLOB** column), you *wouldn't* need to use **base64_encode()**.

10. Print a message, including the encoded, encrypted version of the data:

```
echo '<p>The data has been
→ stored. Its value is ' .
→ base64_encode($data) . '.</p>';

?>
```

I'm doing this mostly so that the page shows something **D**, but also so that you can see the value stored in the session. If you were to open the session text file from the server, you'd see the same value.

11. Complete the page:

```
</body>

</html>
```

12. Save the file as **set_mcrypt.php**, place it in your Web directory, and test in your Web browser.

> **TIP** There's an argument to be made that you *shouldn't* apply the MD5() function to the key because it actually decreases the security of the key. I've used it here regardless, but it's the kind of issue that legitimate cryptographers think about.

> **TIP** If you want to determine the length of the key on the fly, use the mcrypt_end_get_key_size() function:
>
> ```
> $ks = mcrypt_end_get_key_size($m);
> ```

D The result of running the page.

Decrypting data

When it's time to decrypt encrypted data, most of the process is the same as it is for encryption. To start:

```
$m = mcrypt_module_open
→ ('rijndael-256', '', 'cbc', '');
mcrypt_generic_init($m, $key, $iv);
```

At this point, instead of using `mcrypt_generic()`, you'll use `mdecrypt_generic()`:

```
$data = mdecrypt_generic($m,
→ $encrypted);
```

Note, and this is very important, that to successfully decrypt the data, you'll need the *exact same key and IV* used to encrypt it.

Once decryption has taken place, you can close up your resources:

```
mcrypt_generic_deinit($m);
mcrypt_module_close($m);
```

Finally, you'll likely want to apply the `rtrim()` function to the decrypted data, as the encryption process may add white space as padding to the end of the data.

To decrypt data:

1. Begin a new PHP script in your text editor or IDE, to be named **read_mcrypt.php** (Script 11.4):

```
<?php # Script 11.4 -
→ read_mcrypt.php
session_start(); ?>
```

Before any HMTL is sent, the session is begun, as in the previous script.

2. Add the opening HTML:

```
<!doctype html>
<html lang="en">
<head>
  <meta charset="utf-8">
  <title>A More Secure Session
  → </title>
</head>
<body>
```

3. Check that the session data exists:

```
<?php
if (isset($_SESSION['thing1'],
→ $_SESSION['thing2'])) {
```

There's no point in trying to decrypt the data if the page can't access it!

4. Create the key:

```
$key = md5('77 public drop-shadow
→ Java');
```

Not to belabor the point, but again, this must be the exact same key used to encrypt the data. This is another reason why you might want to store the key outside of these scripts.

5. Open the cipher:

```
$m = mcrypt_module_open
→ ('rijndael-256', '', 'cbc', '');
```

This should also match the encryption code (you have to use the same cipher and mode for both encryption and decryption).

continues on page 374

Script 11.4 This script uses MCrypt to decrypt previously stored session data.

```php
1   <?php # Script 11.4 - read_mcrypt.php
2
3   /* This page uses the MCrypt library
4    * to decrypt data stored in the session.
5    */
6
7   session_start(); ?>
8   <!doctype html>
9   <html lang="en">
10  <head>
11    <meta charset="utf-8">
12    <title>A More Secure Session</title>
13  </head>
14  <body>
15  <?php
16  // Make sure the session data exists:
17  if (isset($_SESSION['thing1'], $_SESSION['thing2'])) {
18
19      // Create the key:
20      $key = md5('77 public drop-shadow Java');
21
22      // Open the cipher...
23      // Using Rijndael 256 in CBC mode:
24      $m = mcrypt_module_open('rijndael-256', '', 'cbc', '');
25
26      // Decode the IV:
27      $iv = base64_decode($_SESSION['thing2']);
28
29      // Initialize the encryption:
30      mcrypt_generic_init($m, $key, $iv);
31
32      // Decrypt the data:
33      $data = mdecrypt_generic($m, base64_decode($_SESSION['thing1']));
34
35      // Close the encryption handler:
36      mcrypt_generic_deinit($m);
37
38      // Close the cipher:
39      mcrypt_module_close($m);
40
41      // Print the data:
42      echo '<p>The session has been read. Its value is "' . trim($data) . '".</p>';
43
44  } else { // No data!
45      echo '<p>There\'s nothing to see here.</p>';
46  }
47  ?>
48  </body>
49  </html>
```

6. Decode the IV:

```
$iv = base64_decode
→ ($_SESSION['thing2']);
```

The IV isn't being generated here; it's being retrieved from the session (because it has to be the same IV as was used to encrypt the data). The `base64_decode()` function will return the IV to its binary form.

7. Initialize the decryption:

```
mcrypt_generic_init($m, $key, $iv);
```

8. Decrypt the data:

```
$data = mdecrypt_generic($m,
→ base64_decode($_SESSION
→ ['thing1']));
```

The `mdecrypt_generic()` function will decrypt the data. The data is coming from the session and must be decoded first.

9. Wrap up the MCrypt code:

```
mcrypt_generic_deinit($m);

mcrypt_module_close($m);
```

10. Print the data:

```
echo '<p>The session has been
→ read. Its value is "' . trim
→ ($data) . '".</p>';
```

Running Server Commands

Another server-related topic not discussed in this chapter is how to run commands on the server. Whether you ever have the need to or not depends on your server OS and site needs, but you might have to, for example, tap into the ImageMagick library to do some image manipulation, or run a Perl script.

There are many PHP functions available for executing server commands. For starters, there is **exec()**:

```
exec(command, $output);
```

This function takes a command and assigns to **$output** an array where each element is a line of the generated output.

Also available is **system()**, which just returns the output (so that it could be immediately sent to the Web browser):

```
system(command);
```

The **passthru()** function is similar, but it can also return binary output:

```
passthru(command);
```

Finally, you could use **shell_exec()** or the backticks, both of which just return the output:

```
$var = shell_exec(command);

$var = `command`;
```

For security purposes, you should use **escapeshellarg()** or **escapeshellcmd()** to sanctify any command that isn't hard-coded.

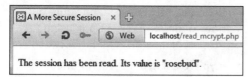

E The session data has been successfully decrypted.

11. Complete the page:

```
} else { // No data!

    echo '<p>There\'s nothing to see
→ here.</p>';

}

?>

</body>

</html>
```

The **else** clause applies if the two cookies were not accessible to the script.

12. Save the file as **read_mcrypt.php**, place it in your Web directory, and test in your Web browser **E**.

TIP If you rerun the first script, you'll see that the encrypted version of the data is different each time, even though the data itself is always the same. This is because the IV will be different each time. Still, the decryption will always work, as the IV is stored in a session.

Review and Pursue

If you have any problems with these sections, either in answering the questions or pursuing your own endeavors, turn to the book's supporting forum (**www.Larry Ullman.com/forums/**).

Review

- How do you write data to a compressed file? (See page 354.)

- How do you read data from a compressed file? (See page 354.)

- What is **cron**? How do you create new cronjobs? (See page 363.)

- What security concerns surround session data? (See page 366.)

- Why are the **base64_encode()** and **base64_decode()** functions used in the encryption examples? (See page 366.)

Pursue

- Modify **db_backup.php** to confirm that the **backups** directory is writable prior to attempting to create the subdirectory.

- Check out the PHP manual's pages on zlib to learn how to have it compress PHP output.

- If you have the need to create ZIP archives, check out PHP's ZIP extension.

- For security purposes, you'd likely want to place the **backups** folder outside of the Web directory (considering its open permissions.)

- To see the effect that compression has on your file, rewrite **backup_db.php** to use **fopen()**, **fwrite()**, and **fclose()** instead.

- Read the next chapter and figure out how to run **db_backups.php** using PHP's Command-Line Interface (CLI).

- If you're using a *nix server or computer, including Mac OS X, read more about **cron** by typing **man cron** or **man crontab** within the command line.

- If you're using Windows and want to automate the execution of a PHP script on that computer, look into creating a scheduled task.

- Improve the security of the MCrypt examples by storing the key in a more secure manner (e.g., in an included file stored in a secure location).

- Change the data being stored in the session just to confirm that it works. Try using, for example, a fake credit card number.

- If you have the inclination, convert any of this chapter's examples to object-based versions.

- Read up on security. A lot!

PHP's Command-Line Interface

PHP is known and loved as one of the best technologies for generating dynamic Web sites. But through the PHP command-line interface (CLI), you can also perform *shell scripting* (command-line programming) using your favorite language, PHP.

PHP CLI lets you run PHP scripts and even snippets of PHP code outside of a Web browser. On Windows, the action takes place within a DOS prompt (aka a console or command window). On Unix and Mac OS X, you'll use the Terminal (or a similar program). In this chapter, I'll cover what you need to know to accomplish these tasks. An understanding of PHP itself is assumed, so the focus will be on the fundamentals of using this alternative interface.

In This Chapter

Testing Your Installation

To get the ball rolling, the first thing you'll need to do is confirm that you have an available PHP CLI and to see what version you have (see the sidebar "CLI vs. CGI"). Hopefully, this is just a matter of following these steps:

1. Open a command-line interface.

2. Type **php -v** and press Return or Enter.

If the CLI version of PHP is installed and is in your *PATH* (a list of locations on your computer where the operating system can find executable files), this should work. Worst-case scenario—assuming PHP CLI is installed, you'll need to use the full path to the CLI executable or move into the PHP directory first.

Along with the **-v** option, there are three others to point out up front:

- **-i** reveals information about the PHP installation.

- **-h** accesses the help file.

- **-m** lists the modules compiled into this PHP installation.

I'll run through these steps for both Windows and Unix/Mac OS X users.

CLI vs. CGI

There are two versions of PHP that can be used for command-line scripting. The older version is the CGI (Common Gateway Interface). It's intended for Web pages but can also be used for shell scripts. The only drawback is that the CGI version needs to be told to behave differently or it's likely to clutter up the command-line interface.

The CLI version is really a pared-down CGI, lacking GET and POST variables. It also does not send out Multipurpose Internet Mail Extensions (MIME) headers, which are needed for Web pages but not for consoles. And the CLI version does not use HTML in its errors or have a maximum execution time.

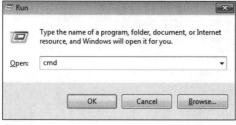

A The Run prompt.

To test your installation on Windows 7:

1. With the desktop showing, press Command+R to bring up the Run prompt.

This works in Windows 7. In earlier versions of Windows, you may have to click Start and then select Run.

2. At the Run prompt, type **cmd** **A** and click OK (or press Enter).

This should bring up a DOS or console window.

3. In the console window, type **php -v** and press Enter **B**.

This should show you the PHP and CLI versions installed. Note that the specifics of what is shown beyond the version will depend on the PHP installation. For example, my results **B** reflect the version of PHP installed as part of the Zend Server Community Edition (**www.zend.com**), which has lots of extra features.

continues on next page

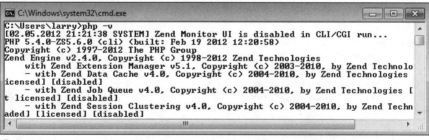

B The command **php -v** shows the version of PHP CLI installed.

4. Still in the console window, type **php -i** and press Enter to learn more about the installation.

   This is the equivalent of running a **phpinfo()** script within a Web browser. There's a ton of information available here, although you'll need to scroll back to view it all (and possibly increase the console's buffer size before running this command).

5. (Having not left the console window...) Type **php -m** and press Enter to see what modules are installed 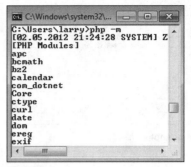.

   This command lists the extensions that the PHP installation supports. This is important should you want to, for example, interact with MySQL using the CLI.

6. (Where else but...) In the console window, type **php -h** and press Enter to see the help menu.

   The help menu, should you need...um... help, is mostly just a listing of the few basic options.

7. In the console window, type **exit** and press Enter to close the window.

C The list of modules built into this PHP CLI installation.

TIP My Windows console window may not look like yours, so don't be alarmed. I've tried to "pretty it up" by changing from the default colors to black text on a white background. To do so, click the icon in the upper-left corner, and then click *Properties*.

TIP Another customization I often make in my console window is that I change the prompt from the default (which is the current directory followed by >) to a simple colon. To do so, type prompt X and press Enter, where *X* is whatever you want the prompt to be.

To test your installation on Unix and Mac OS X:

1. Open your Terminal application.

   Most flavors of Unix that I'm familiar with as well as Mac OS X provide an application called Terminal, which is used for command-line operations. It's likely present in your Applications or Utilities folder, or wherever your OS keeps its programs.

2. In the console window, type **php -v** and press Enter **D**.

   This should show you the PHP and CLI versions installed.

3. Still in the console window, type **php -i** and press Enter to learn more about the installation.

   This is the equivalent of running a **phpinfo()** script within a Web browser. There's a ton of information available here, although you'll need to scroll back to catch it all (and possibly increase the console's buffer size).

4. (Having not left the console window...) Type **php -m** and press Enter to see what modules are installed.

   This lists the extensions that the PHP installation supports. This is important should you want to, for example, interact with MySQL using the CLI.

   continues on next page

: php -v
PHP 5.4.0 (cli) (built: Mar 3 2012 08:58:34)
Copyright (c) 1997-2012 The PHP Group
Zend Engine v2.4.0, Copyright (c) 1998-2012 Zend Technologies
:

D The command **php -v** shows the version of PHP CLI installed.

5. (Where else but...) In the console window, type **php -h** and press Enter to
   see the help menu **E**.

   The help menu, should you need...um...
   help, is mostly just a listing of the few
   basic options.

6. In the console window, type **exit** and
   press Enter to close the window.

TIP There is, on Unix and Mac OS X, a manual page installed for the PHP CLI. To access it,
type man php **F**.

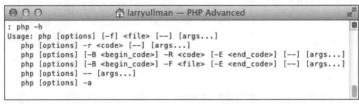

E The PHP CLI help options.

F The PHP CLI man page, quite similar to the help file **E**.

Executing Bits of Code

One of the first uses I find for PHP CLI is to be able to test snippets of code without going through the process of:

1. Writing a formal PHP script

2. Placing it in a Web directory

3. Enabling my Web server, if it's not already on

4. Running the PHP script in a Web browser

Instead of doing all of that, you can test small sections of code with PHP CLI using this syntax:

```
php -r 'php_code_here'
```

For a predictable example:

```
php -r 'echo "Hello, world!";'
```

A couple of things to remember with this syntax: First, using PHP tags will cause parse errors **A**. Second, you may need to experiment to determine whether you should use single or double quotes around the code block. For example, using PHP 5.4 on my Mac, double quotes cause errors when there are variables within the code **B**. However, on Windows 7, PHP 5.4 complained of errors any time I used single quotes but did not complain about using double quotes, with or without variables.

Finally, you should end each statement in PHP with a semicolon, just as you would in a script.

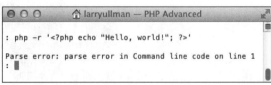

```
: php -r '<?php echo "Hello, world!"; ?>'

Parse error: parse error in Command line code on line 1
:
```

A Do not use PHP tags with the **php -r** option.

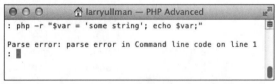

```
: php -r "$var = 'some string'; echo $var;"

Parse error: parse error in Command line code on line 1
:
```

B In some environments, using double quotation marks around your PHP code that contains variables might create parse errors.

To use PHP CLI for code blocks:

1. Follow the steps in the first section of this chapter to access PHP CLI. Open a Terminal application (Mac OS X and Unix), bring up a DOS prompt (Windows), or connect to your remote server.

2. Test an **echo()** statement 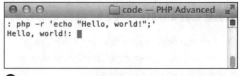:

   ```
   php -r 'echo "Hello, world!\n";'
   ```

   The PHP code being tested is

   ```
   echo "Hello, world!";
   ```

   This code is wrapped within single quotes and placed after **php -r** to execute it. Again, on Windows or other platforms you may need to swap the single and double quotes (if you get a parse error).

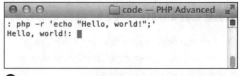

```
: php -r 'echo "Hello, world!";'
Hello, world!: ▮
```

C Among its many benefits, PHP CLI provides yet another way to say *Hello, world!*

Using a Remote Server

If you want to work with PHP CLI on a remote server instead of a local one, that may also be an option. To do so, you must first make sure that the server's administrator—be it an ISP, hosting company, or whoever—allows remote logins. If so, they should provide you with a username and password.

Next, you need an SSH application to connect to that server (SSH provides a secure connection between two computers). If running Unix or Mac OS X, you can use SSH within a Terminal, typing

```
ssh -l username address
```

After the lowercase "L", enter your username. For the address, this can be either a URL—**www.example.com**—or an IP address (123.123.123.123). You'll then be prompted for the password.

For Windows users, I recommend PuTTY (search the Web for the current URL). This simple and free application provides a graphical interface along with the SSH and Telnet clients.

Once connected to the remote server, you can follow the other steps in this chapter.

```
: php -r '$ts = filemtime("states.txt");
echo date("F j Y H:i:s", $ts);'
May 3 2012 15:32:56: █
```

D Using two lines of PHP code, I can print a formatted version of a file's last modification date.

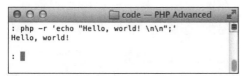

```
: php -r 'echo "Hello, world! \n\n";'
Hello, world!

: █
```

E Thanks to the printed newlines, the command prompt no longer appears immediately after the result of the code (compare with **C**).

3. Print the modification date of a file **D**:

```
php -r '$ts = filemtime("/path/to/
→ somefile.txt");
echo date("F j Y H:clear:s", $ts);'
```

Here, I'm actually executing two lines of PHP code. In the first line, the **$ts** variable is assigned the timestamp value of the last time the **somefile.txt** file was modified. Obviously, you'll need to change the path and name of the file so that it's appropriate for a file—any file—on your server.

In the second line, that timestamp is formatted using the **date()** function and printed. Because of the single quotes surrounding the entire PHP code block, I can enter this code over multiple lines (see the figure).

4. Add a newline or two to the printed result **E**:

```
php -r 'echo "Hello, world! \n\n";'
```

By printing newline characters, I can add spacing to the output.

Interactive PHP CLI

As of PHP 5.1, if PHP is compiled with the Readline extension, you can run PHP in an interactive shell. The interactive shell is simply a continually running version of PHP CLI that allows you to enter commands to be executed.

To invoke the interactive shell, use the -a flag:

```
php -a
```

If your PHP installation is set up to be used as an interactive shell, you should see something like Ⓐ. If you see *Interactive mode enabled* Ⓑ, your PHP is not configured to be used in this manner.

To use the interactive shell:

1. Follow the steps in the first section of this chapter so that you can access PHP CLI.

2. Enter interactive mode:

   ```
   php -a
   ```

3. Type a simple bit of PHP code and press Enter/Return to execute it Ⓒ:

   ```
   echo 'Hello, world!';
   ```

   You'll notice that PHP will execute the code and then show another prompt for you to enter more code. The prompt also nicely appears on the next line, without needing to print a newline character.

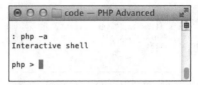

Ⓐ The interactive shell interface, with the *php* prompt.

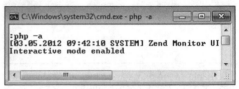

Ⓑ This response means that the Readline extension is not enabled, and the interactive shell cannot be used.

Ⓒ Executing a simple line of code.

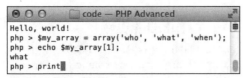

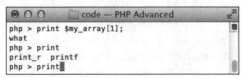

D Variables can be created and used within the interactive shell.

E The interactive shell comes with tab completion and suggestion, such as the names of functions here.

4. Create a variable:

`$my_array = array('who', 'what',`
`→'when');`

`echo $my_array[1];`

You can create, and later reference, variables, constants, and functions in a session.

5. Type *pri* and press Tab to invoke the autocomplete **D**.

Thanks to the Readline extension, the interactive shell includes many useful features, including tab completion and history (via the up and down array keys). As you can see in the figure, the tab completion turns *pri* into *print*.

6. Type *pri* and press Tab twice to see the list of possible autocompletions **E**.

This is an easy way to ensure that you're getting the names of functions right.

7. Type **exit** and press Enter/Return to exit the session.

TIP In theory, autocompletion works with the names of variables, functions, and constants defined in the current session, too. However, in my experience, I find support for all types of autocompletion to be inconsistent.

Creating a Command-Line Script

Being able to test little bits of PHP code from the command line is nice, but it won't take you far. What you'll often want to do is run entire PHP scripts from the command-line interface. Such scripts could perform file or database maintenance, run updates for your Web sites, and more.

A PHP script to be used by PHP CLI is different from a Web script in three ways:

1. It shouldn't use or create any HTML.

2. It doesn't need to use the **.php** extension (although it's fine if it does).

3. The very first line of the script will be

   ```
   #!/usr/bin/php
   ```

There's no harm in using HTML, but it'll just clutter up the result in the console window. As for the file's extension, how the script is run will change (covered in the next section of the chapter), so you could literally use anything. But **.php** is still a fine idea. Or you could use a different extension to distinguish your Web PHP scripts from the command-line ones (or no extension at all!). But of the three rules, only the last one matters (and, frankly, it only matters on Unix and Mac OS X).

That line of code is called the *shebang* line. It tells the operating system where to find the executable that should be used to run this script. For Unix and Mac OS X, that executable should have been installed in **/usr/bin**. If you know that PHP CLI was installed elsewhere, change the shebang line accordingly. For Windows, this line is ignored, but you should keep it in there for cross-platform reliability.

The CLI php.ini

Most PHP installations will end up with two or more usable command-line versions of PHP. The one I'm focusing on in this chapter is CLI. But there are probably other PHPs lingering on your server, like the one used by Apache or IIS for handling Web pages.

An interesting point about PHP CLI is that it uses a different **php.ini** file than the Web PHP module. This file, of course, is where you dictate how PHP behaves. Hence, PHP CLI may run differently than you're used to. For that matter, your PHP CLI installation may support different modules than your Web installation.

You can, when invoking PHP CLI, use options to change the **php.ini** behavior:

- **-c** tells PHP CLI where to look for a **php.ini** file.

- **-n** tells PHP CLI not to use a **php.ini**.

- **-d** sets a **php.ini** value for PHP CLI.

For example, it is recommended that you set **ignore_user_abort** to true when using the CLI. Doing so will allow a command-line script to continue running even after the user aborts the connection. To do that, you could set this when invoking the CLI:

```
php scriptname.php -d
→ ignore_user_abort=1
```

A Text outside of the PHP tags is revealed in the console.

Script 12.1 This PHP script will be run from the command line. It reads in a text file and prints it out, line by line, with the lines numbered.

```
1    #!/usr/bin/php
2    <?php # Script 12.1 - number.php
3
4    /*  This page reads in a file.
5     *  It then reprints the file,
         → numbering the lines.
6     *  This script is meant to be used with
         → PHP CLI.
7     */
8
9    // The file to number:
10   $file = 'states.txt';
11
12   // Print an intro message:
13   echo "\nNumbering the file named
        → '$file'...
14   ------------------\n\n";
15
16   // Read in the file:
17   $data = file($file);
18
19   // Line number counter:
20   $n = 1;
21
22   // Print each line:
23   foreach ($data as $line) {
24
25       // Print number and line:
26       echo "$n $line";
27
28       // Increment line number:
29       $n++;
30
31   } // End of FOREACH loop.
32
33   echo "\n------------------
34   End of file '$file'.\n";
35   ?>
```

After that line, all PHP code goes within the normal PHP tags. Anything outside of the PHP tags is sent to the standard output just like Web-based PHP scripts **A**:

#!/usr/bin/php

<?php

// Do whatever.

?>

This text is also displayed.

<?php

// Do whatever.

?>

For the first implementation of this concept, I'll create a script that reads in a text file and reprints it, numbering the lines along the way.

To create a command-line script:

1. Create a new PHP script in your text editor or IDE, to be named **number.php**, beginning with the shebang line (**Script 12.1**):

   #!/usr/bin/php

   <?php # Script 12.1 - number.php

   Remember that the first line is the most important and that you might need to change it if PHP CLI was installed in a place other than **/usr/bin**. And although Windows users can skip this line, it's best to leave it in there (allowing you to use it on another computer down the road).

   Finally, you still need to use the PHP tags.

continues on next page

2. Identify what file will be numbered:

```php
$file = 'states.txt';
```

Later in the chapter, you'll see how to write this script so that the file information can be assigned when the script is run. For this first example, I'm just going to use a simple plain text file that lists the US states. You can use any plain text file, including even another PHP script from the book.

3. Print an introductory message:

```php
echo "\nNumbering the file named
→ '$file'...
------------------\n\n";
```

4. Read in the file:

```php
$data = file($file);
```

The **file()** function reads an entire file into an array. Each line becomes one array element. You could use **fopen()** and the other file functions instead, if you prefer.

5. Print each line with its number:

```php
$n = 1;
foreach ($data as $line) {
    echo "$n $line";
    $n++;
}
```

To start, a counter is initialized so that the first line is numbered at 1. Then a **foreach** loop goes through the array. Within the loop, each line is printed, prefixed by the line number and a couple of spaces. You do not need to print a newline here, because the line read in from the original file retained that newline. Finally, the counter is incremented.

6. Print a closing message:

```php
echo "\n------------------
End of file '$file'.\n";
```

7. Complete the PHP script:

```php
?>
```

8. Save the file as **number.php**.

Running a Command-Line Script

Now that you've written a script especially meant for a command-line execution (and wasn't it nice not to mess with all that pesky HTML?), it's time to learn how to run it. There are two ways of doing so.

The first option is to directly invoke PHP CLI, as you did when executing a bit of code, this time providing it with the name of a script to execute:

```
php scriptname.php
```

You'll also see the **-f** flag used. It stands for *file*, and whether you use it or not makes no difference on the end result:

```
php -f scriptname.php
```

This method should work just fine, as long as **php** is in your *PATH* and you are in the same directory as **scriptname.php**. Variations to circumvent these limitations might be

```
/usr/bin/php scriptname.php
```

```
php /path/to/scriptname.php
```

```
C:\php\php.exe scriptname.php
```

The second method for executing PHP scripts is to treat the script as if it were an application in its own right:

```
scriptname.php (Windows)
```

```
./scriptname.php (Unix and Mac OS X)
```

This method, which is preferred, can have some tricks to it, so I'll run through the details in the following steps.

To run a command-line script in Windows:

1. Use the instructions outlined earlier in the chapter to access a DOS prompt.

2. Move into the directory where **number. php** was saved **A**:

   ```
   cd C:\path\to\directory
   ```

   continues on next page

A Start by moving into the same directory where the PHP script you want to execute is located.

3. Run the file using the **php scriptname.php** syntax **B**:

php number.php

Hopefully, this should work for you. If you get an error message, it's most likely because **php** is not in your *PATH*. If you don't know how to change your *PATH*, either search the Web for tutorials or turn to my support forums (**www.LarryUllman.com/forums/**).

4. Run the file using the alternative syntax:

number.php

If this doesn't immediately work, it's because you'll need to tell Windows what program to use for running **.php** scripts. To do so (these instructions are for Windows 7, but should be similar on other versions of Windows):

a. Select **number.php** in the Windows Explorer.

b. Control+click or right-click and choose *Open with > Choose default program*.

c. Click Browse in the Open with dialog **C**.

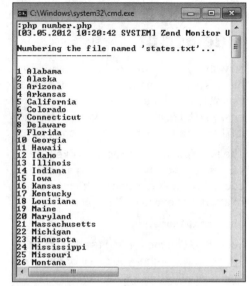

B The execution of the **number.php** script.

C You may need to tell Windows what application to use for your scripts. The **php** executable will not likely come up as an option.

d. Find and select the **php** executable 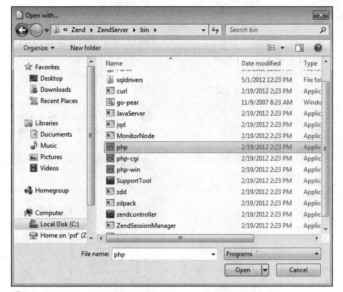, and then click Open.

e. Click OK in the Open with dialog.

From here on out, all **.php** scripts will run just fine from the command-line interface (assuming that you kept the *Always use the selected program to open this kind of file* box checked ⓒ).

ⓓ Find the installed **php** executable to finish the association.

To run a command-line script in Unix and Mac OS X:

1. Use the instructions outlined earlier in the chapter to access a command-line prompt.

2. Move into the directory where **number. php** was saved:

   cd /path/to/directory

3. Run the file using the **php scriptname. php** syntax :

   php number.php

   Hopefully, this should work for you. If you get an error message, it's most likely because **php** is not in your *PATH*. If you don't know how to change your *PATH*, either search the Web for tutorials or turn to my support forums (**www.LarryUllman.com/forums/**).

4. Make the file executable:

   chmod +x number.php

   If you're not familiar with **chmod**, it's a utility for changing the properties of files and directories. The **+x** code says to add executable status to **number.php**.

5. Run the file using the *./scriptname. php* syntax :

   ./number.php

> **TIP** You can use **php -l scriptname.php** to have PHP check a script's syntax without actually running it. The only caveats are that this doesn't work with the **-r** option (for testing bits of code) and it doesn't check for fatal errors.

E The first method for running the PHP script, showing the end of the output.

```
: chmod +x number.php
: ./number.php

Numbering the file named 'states.txt'...
--------------------

1 Alabama
2 Alaska
3 Arizona
4 Arkansas
5 California
6 Colorado
7 Connecticut
8 Delaware
9 Florida
10 Georgia
11 Hawaii
12 Idaho
13 Illinois
14 Indiana
15 Iowa
16 Kansas
17 Kentucky
```

F Executables can be run using the *./ executable* syntax, assuming you are in the same directory as the program to be run.

Working with Command-Line Arguments

The **number.php** example (Script 12.1) is a reasonable-enough application of PHP CLI. The script provides a valuable service but has one limitation: the file to be numbered is hard-coded into the script. It'd be better to set that value when the application is used. This can be easily achieved by rewriting the script so that it uses command-line arguments.

Command-line arguments are values passed to an application when it is run. For example, the PHP CLI takes several configuration options, the name of a script to be run, or some code to be executed. Arguments are passed to the invoked application by adding them after the application's name:

scriptname.php *arg1 arg2...*

In your PHP script, you can then access these arguments by referring to **$argv** and **$argc** (or the more formal **$_SERVER['argv']** and **$_SERVER['argc']**). The **$argv** array stores every argument provided; **$argc** stores the number of items in **$argv**. The only catch to using these is that the name of the script itself is the first listed argument (**$_SERVER['argv'][0]**) **Ⓐ**:

```
#!/usr/bin/php

<?php

echo "\n{$_SERVER['argc']} arguments
→ received. They are...\n";

foreach ($_SERVER['argv'] as $k =>
→ $v) {

    echo "$k: $v\n";

}

?>
```

Let's write a new **number.php** script so that it accepts an argument: the name of the script to number.

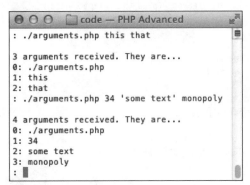

```
● ○ ○    code — PHP Advanced
: ./arguments.php this that

3 arguments received. They are...
0: ./arguments.php
1: this
2: that
: ./arguments.php 34 'some text' monopoly

4 arguments received. They are...
0: ./arguments.php
1: 34
2: some text
3: monopoly
:
```

Ⓐ The **arguments.php** script just prints out the number and values of the arguments used when calling it. Notice that the script name itself is always the first received argument.

To use command-line arguments:

1. Create a new PHP script in your text editor or IDE, to be named **number2. php**, beginning with the shebang line (**Script 12.2**).

   #!/usr/bin/php

   <?php # Script 12.2 - number2.php

2. Check that a filename was provided:

   if ($_SERVER['argc'] == 2) {

   Since the script will receive the script's name as its first argument, **$_SERVER['argc']** must be equal to 2 to indicate proper usage (because the script name itself will count, too). This conditional checks for that.

3. Make sure that the file exists:

   $file = $_SERVER['argv'][1];

   if (file_exists($file) &&
   → is_file($file)) {

   First, the name of the file is identified as the second argument provided (the arguments list being an array, the indexing begins at 0). Then two conditionals confirm that the given file does exist and is a file (because a directory would pass the first test). You'd likely want to add code restricting the files to a certain directory for security purposes.

Script 12.2 This PHP script expects to receive the name of the file to number as a command-line argument.

```
1    #!/usr/bin/php
2    <?php # Script 12.2 - number2.php
3
4    /*  This page reads in a file.
5     *  It then reprints the file, numbering the lines.
6     *  This script is meant to be used with PHP CLI.
7     *  This script expects one argument (plus the script's name):
8     *  the name of the file to number.
9     */
10
11   // Check that a filename was provided:
12   if ($_SERVER['argc'] == 2) {
13
14      // Get the name of the file:
15      $file = $_SERVER['argv'][1];
16
17      // Make sure the file exists and is a file:
18      if (file_exists($file) && is_file($file)) {
19
20         // Read in the file:
21         if ($data = file($file)) {
22
23            // Print an intro message:
24            echo "\nNumbering the file named '$file'...\n------------------\n\n";
25
```

script continues on next page

```
26          // Line number counter:
27          $n = 1;
28
29          // Print each line:
30          foreach ($data as $line) {
31
32              // Print number and line:
33              echo "$n  $line";
34
35              // Increment line number:
36              $n++;
37
38          } // End of FOREACH loop.
39
40          echo "\n-------------------\nEnd
            → of file '$file'.\n";
41          exit(0);
42
43      } else {
44          echo "The file could not be
            → read.\n";
45          exit(1);
46      }
47
48  } else {
49      echo "The file does not exist.\n";
50      exit(1);
51  }
52
53 } else {
54
55      // Print the usage:
56      echo "\nUsage: number2.php
        → <filename>\n\n";
57
58      // Kill the script, indicate error:
59      exit(1);
60 }
61
62 ?>
```

4. Read in the file and print each line:

```
if ($data = file($file)) {
    echo "\nNumbering the file
→ named '$file'...\n
→ -------------------\n\n";
    $n = 1;
    foreach ($data as $line) {
        echo "$n  $line";
        $n++;
    } // End of FOREACH loop.
    echo "\n-------------------\nEnd
→ of file '$file'.\n";
```

This code matches that in **number.php**, except for reading the file's contents as a conditional.

5. Return 0 to indicate proper execution of the application:

```
exit(0);
```

Command-line applications are often written to return a number indicating the successful use of that application (see the sidebar "Creating an Interface" later in this chapter). Typically, 0 represents no problems and a nonzero number represents an error of some sort. Here, the **exit()** function (or language construct) will terminate the execution of the script, and the value provided as an argument to **exit()** will be returned by the script.

continues on next page

6. Complete the conditional started in Step 4:

```
} else {
    echo "The file could not be
    ⇀ read.\n";
    exit(1);
}
```

If the file couldn't be read for some reason, likely a permissions issue, a message should be printed. The **exit(1)** line is used to indicate a problem. Returning a nonzero number when a problem occurs is a convention for command-line applications.

7. Complete the conditional started in Step 3:

```
} else {
    echo "The file does not
    ⇀ exist.\n";
    exit(1);
}
```

8. Complete the conditional started in Step 2:

```
} else {
    echo "\nUsage: number2.php
    ⇀ <filename>\n\n";
    exit(1);
}
```

If the script was not invoked with the proper number of arguments, how it should be used is indicated **B**. This is a command-line convention, also discussed in the "Creating an Interface" sidebar.

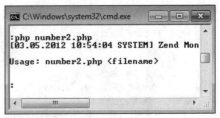

B If no filename is provided, the utility's proper usage is shown.

C The **states.txt** script is numbered by **number2.php**.

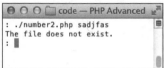

D If the script cannot find the given file, an error is displayed.

9. Complete the PHP script:

   ```
   ?>
   ```

10. Save the file as **number2.php**.

11. Run the script **C**.

    Note that on Windows, you'll need to use this syntax:

    ```
    php number2.php filename
    ```

    If you use

    ```
    number2.php filename
    ```

    the script will only recognize one argument (with a value of *number2.php*).

12. To fully test the script, provide an invalid file-name **D**.

> **TIP** To get really professional with your command-line arguments, check out the various console-related **PEAR (PHP Extension and Application Repository)** packages. For example, Console_Color2 lets you use ANSI colors in the output, and several PEAR packages assist in the reading of command-line arguments.

Creating an Interface

Using PHP in a command-line situation opens up a whole new world that PHP for Web development doesn't have: the user interface. Sure, presentation and usage of Web pages is a vitally important HTML issue, but on the command line it's a different beast.

For starters, most command-line applications indicate how the command is to be used, should it be used incorrectly. Type **php -varmit** and you'll see what I mean. The **number2.php** script does this a little bit (showing the usage) but commands normally do more, like offer help if *commandname* **-h** or *commandname* **--help** is entered.

Finally, command-line applications often return a code indicating how successful the operation was. The number 0 is returned to indicate no problems, and some nonzero number otherwise. In **number2.php**, the integer 1 is returned when things go wrong.

An alternative to using command-line arguments is to request input from the user (although you could use both techniques in combination). By doing so, you can create an interactive application, where it prompts the user for information and does something with what is entered.

Taking Input

Strange as it may seem, taking input in a command-line application is exactly like reading in data from a file. But in this case, instead of using a file handle (a pointer to an opened file), you'll use a special constant, **STDIN**. This stands for *standard input*, which would be the keyboard by default. One easy way to read in standard input would be to use the **fgets()** function:

```
echo 'Tell me something: ';
$input = fgets(STDIN);
```

That line of code creates a prompt 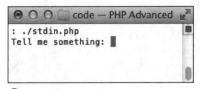. Anything typed there by the user will be assigned to **$input**.

To be more precise with input, I like to use the **fscanf()** function. Like **printf()** and **sprintf()**, discussed in Chapter 1, "Advanced PHP Techniques," this function takes formatting parameters to handle specific types of data. By using this function, instead of a more generic one, you ensure that some basic validation as to the type of data read in can take place. In the next example, **fscanf()** will be used to create an application that converts temperatures between degrees Fahrenheit and Celsius (in either direction).

To take user input:

1. Begin a new PHP script in your text editor or IDE, to be named **temperature. php**, starting with the shebang line (**Script 12.3**):

```
#!/usr/bin/php

<?php # Script 12.3 -
→ temperature.php
```

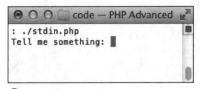

A Any function that attempts to read from the standard input will create a prompt where the user can type.

continues on page 402

Script 12.3 User input is requested when this script runs. The input is read in from **STDIN** and validated; if proper, a temperature conversion occurs.

```php
1   #!/usr/bin/php
2   <?php # Script 12.3 - temperature.php
3
4   /*  This page convers temperatures between
5    *  Fahrenheit and Celsius.
6    *  This script is meant to be used with PHP CLI.
7    *  This script requests input from the user.
8    */
9
10  // Prompt the user:
11  echo "\nEnter a temperature and indicate if it's Fahrenheit or Celsius [##.# C/F]: ";
12
13  // Read the input as a conditional:
14  if (fscanf (STDIN, '%f %s', $temp_i, $which_i) == 2) {
15
16      // Assume invalid output:
17      $which_o = FALSE;
18
19      // Make the conversion based upon $which_i:
20      switch (trim($which_i)) {
21
22          // Celsius, convert to Fahrenheit:
23          case 'C':
24          case 'c':
25              $temp_o = ($temp_i * (9.0/5.0)) + 32;
26              $which_o = 'F';
27              $which_i = 'C';
28              break;
29
30          // Fahrenheit, convert to Celsius:
31          case 'F':
32          case 'f':
33              $temp_o = ($temp_i - 32) * (5.0/9.0);
34              $which_o = 'C';
35              $which_i = 'F';
36              break;
37
38      } // End of SWITCH.
39
40      // Print the results:
41      if ($which_o) {
42          printf ("%0.1f %s is %0.1f %s.\n", $temp_i, $which_i, $temp_o, $which_o);
43      } else {
44          echo "You failed to enter C or F to indicate the current temperature type.\n";
45      }
46
47  } else { // Didn't enter the right input.
48
49      echo "You failed to use the proper syntax.\n";
50
51  } // End of main IF.
52  ?>
```

2. Prompt the user for the input:

```
echo "\nEnter a temperature and
→indicate if it's Fahrenheit or
→Celsius [##.# C/F]: ";
```

The prompt clearly indicates to the user what information is expected and in what format **B**. Because there is no newline character printed at the end of this text, the user will be able to type immediately after the colon.

3. Read in a floating-point number and a string:

```
if (fscanf (STDIN, '%f %s',
→$temp_i, $which_i) == 2) {
```

There's a lot going on in this one line. First, the **fscanf()** function will attempt to read in, from the standard input, one floating-point number and one string. These should match up to the temperature (e.g., 72.3) and the indicator as to the current temperature type (*C* or *F*). There is no "character" format with **fscanf()**, so the **%s** for string will have to do. If **fscanf()** can read in exactly these two data types in that order, they'll be assigned to the variables **$temp_i** and **$which_i**.

The last bit of trickery is that the **fscanf()** function will return the number of values it assigned to variables. So if it reads in two values, assigned to **$temp_i** and **$which_i**, the conditional knows that the proper data was entered.

4. Set a variable to false:

```
$which_o = FALSE;
```

This variable will store the converted temperature (the output). It's initially set to false and will be assigned a proper value in Step 5.

5. Perform the appropriate conversion:

```
switch (trim($which_i)) {
    case 'C':
    case 'c':
        $temp_o = ($temp_i *
        →(9.0/5.0)) + 32;
        $which_o = 'F';
        $which_i = 'C';
        break;
    case 'F':
    case 'f':
        $temp_o = ($temp_i - 32) *
        →(5.0/9.0);
        $which_o = 'C';
        $which_i = 'F';
        break;
} // End of SWITCH.
```

The **switch** checks to see if degrees Celsius is being converted to Fahrenheit or vice versa. If the second piece of input submitted is not *C*, *c*, *F*, or *f*, no conversion takes place.

```
⊙ ○ ○  ☐ code — PHP Advanced        ⬚
: chmod +x temperature.php              ▤
: ./temperature.php

Enter a temperature and indicate if it's
Fahrenheit or Celsius [##.# C/F]: █
```

B The initial prompt.

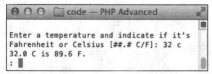

Enter a temperature and indicate if it's
Fahrenheit or Celsius [##.# C/F]: 32 c
32.0 C is 89.6 F.
:

C The result of the calculation is printed as a floating-point number with one decimal.

```
Enter a temperature and indicate if it's Fahrenheit
or Celsius [##.# C/F]: 240.1 M
You failed to enter C or F to indicate the current
temperature type.
:
```

D One of the possible error messages if the script is not used properly.

6. Print the results:

```php
if ($which_o) {
    printf ("%0.1f %s is %0.1f
    →%s.\n", $temp_i, $which_i,
    → $temp_o, $which_o);
} else {
    echo "You failed to enter C or
    → F to indicate the current
    → temperature type.\n";
}
```

If **$which_o** is equal to *C* or *F*, then the conditional is true and the conversion is printed, using the **printf()** function to handle the formatting **C**. Otherwise, a default message is printed **D**.

continues on next page

Taking CLI Further

This chapter covers what you need to know about running PHP code from a command-line interface. For the most part this just means that you'll take what you already know how to do with PHP and execute it in a non-Web interface. That alone is perfect for many automated tasks that you might want to do.

On a more sophisticated level, PHP CLI can be used to interact with the operating system on a low level. One thing to look into is the **pcntl** (process control) extension. The extension, which isn't available when using PHP for Web pages, lets you *fork* your processes (split them off). From there you can go on to the concept of signals. If you don't know what these things are, that's fine: you probably shouldn't be messing with them in PHP anyway. But if you do understand these concepts, knowing that you can work with them in PHP is a welcome bit of news.

Finally, with PHP CLI you can use the backticks, **exec()**, **system()**, and similar functions to call system utilities. Using these functions with PHP CLI doesn't differ from using them in a Web script, but your need to use them might increase.

7. Complete the conditional started in Step 3:

```
} else {
    echo "You failed to use the
 → proper syntax.\n";
} // End of main IF.
```

This **else** clause applies if the **fscanf()** function does not return the number 2, meaning it didn't read in two values 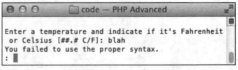. In neither this case nor the **else** clause in Step 6 does the script return a number indicating a problem, but that could be added.

8. Complete the PHP script:

```
?>
```

9. Save the file as **temperature.php**.

10. Run the script 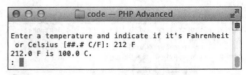.

TIP This script could have been written to take the temperature and the temperature type as two separate inputs. But doing so would have been far less cool than using just one prompt and showing off what **fscanf()** can do.

TIP Any of PHP's file functions can be used on STDIN. This means, for example, that you could use **fgetc()** to retrieve just a single character or **fgetcsv()** to retrieve and parse an entire line.

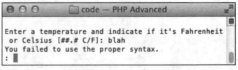

E The second of the possible error messages for misuse.

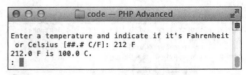

F Successfully converting from Fahrenheit to Celsius.

Built-In Server

An addition to the CLI in PHP 5.4 is a built-in Web server. Using it, you can test PHP scripts in a Web browser without installing and running a Web server application such as Apache. To be absolutely clear, this is not a production-grade Web server, but it can be used to quickly test PHP scripts in browsers.

To use the built-in Web server:

1. Follow the steps in the first section of this chapter so that you can access PHP CLI.

2. Enter the following command to confirm the availability of the Web server **A**:

   `php -h`

   The **-h** flag brings up the help documentation. If the documentation includes the **-S** (it must be a capital letter S) and **-t** options, then the built-in server is supported.

3. Navigate to the directory that contains the PHP script(s) you'd like to test:

   `cd /path/to/directory`

   By default, the Web server will use the directory in which the server was started as the Web root directory, so you should navigate there first.

continues on next page

A The PHP help menu will show you what options are available.

4. Start the server **B**:

```
php -S localhost:8000
```

To start the Web server, use the **-S** flag, followed by the hostname and port to use. On your own computer, *localhost* is a logical and common hostname. For the port, I would recommend 8000 or 8080, which are common alternatives to the default Apache port of 80. Using one of these ports prevents possible conflicts if you already have another Web server running.

You can also use an IP address, if you'd rather:

```
php -S 127.0.0.1:8000
```

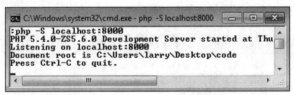

B The Web server has been started.

5. Load **http://localhost:8080/ scriptname.php** in your Web browser **C**.

As you load pages in the Web browser using the CLI server, you'll notice that the console or Terminal window will reflect the history of requests **D**.

6. Press Control+C in the console or Terminal window to stop the Web server.

TIP To use a different Web root directory, regardless of where the Web server is started, use the -t option:

php -S localhost:8000 -t /path/to/
↪ directory

TIP Keep in mind that this Web server will use the PHP CLI configuration, which, again, may run differently and include different modules than your standard PHP installation associated with Apache or IIS.

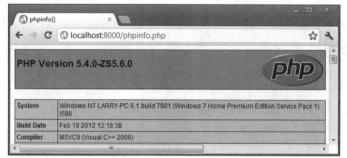

C This PHP script is running through PHP's built-in Web server.

```
⊖ ⊙ ○                          📁 code — PHP Advanced
Listening on localhost:8000
Document root is /Users/larryullman/Documents/Writing/PHP Advanced VQP 3ed/Ch 12/code
Press Ctrl-C to quit.
[Thu May  3 11:13:24 2012] ::1:60207 [200]: /phpinfo.php
[Thu May  3 11:13:24 2012] ::1:60208 [200]: /phpinfo.php?=PHPE9568F34-D428-11d2-A769-00AA001ACF42
[Thu May  3 11:13:24 2012] ::1:60209 [200]: /phpinfo.php?=PHPE9568F35-D428-11d2-A769-00AA001ACF42
[Thu May  3 11:13:24 2012] ::1:60213 [404]: /favicon.ico - No such file or directory
[Thu May  3 11:13:24 2012] ::1:60214 [404]: /favicon.ico - No such file or directory
[Thu May  3 11:13:25 2012] ::1:60225 [404]: /favicon.ico - No such file or directory
[Thu May  3 11:13:25 2012] ::1:60226 [404]: /favicon.ico - No such file or directory
```

D A log of server requests is shown in the window where the server was started.

Review and Pursue

If you have any problems with these sections, either in answering the questions or pursuing your own endeavors, turn to the book's supporting forum (**www.Larry Ullman.com/forums/**).

Review

- How do you access a DOS console or terminal window on your computer? (See pages 379 through 382.)

- What are some good uses of the CLI? (See page 378.)

- How do you confirm the version of PHP you have? (See page 378.)

- How do you execute a line or two of code using CLI? (See page 383.)

- How do you enter the CLI interactive shell? How do you exit it? (See page 386.)

- If you want to execute a PHP script from the command line, what should the first line of code in that script be? What is that line called? (See page 388.)

- How do you run a PHP script using PHP CLI? (See page 391.)

- Through what variable do you access arguments passed when running a script through PHP CLI? What will the first item in that variable reference be? (See page 395.)

- How do you take input from the user? What are some of the ways you can validate the user's input by type? (See pages 400 through 402.)

- How do you use PHP CLI to test a script in your Web browser? How do you change the Web root directory used by the PHP CLI server? (See page 405.)

Pursue

- Create a new version of **temperature.php** that takes the temperature and temperature type as two separate inputs.

- Modify **number2.php** so that it creates a numbered version of the text file as a new file on the server (as opposed to outputting it to the screen).

- If you like the CLI and think it might be useful to you, practice! Try creating new utilities and interactive scripts.

13

XML and PHP

XML, the Extensible Markup Language, is one of the most important technologies in computing. With a range of uses, from sharing data between computers to storing data for a single application, XML provides a format for representing not just information but also information about the information (aka meta-information). XML, like HTML, is based on Standard Generalized Markup Language (SGML), which means that you'll see numerous similarities between the two.

This chapter begins with a basic introduction to XML: what it is, the proper XML syntax, and how to make your own XML document. From there, PHP will take over, both for reading and creating XML documents. You'll learn about and use the two primary XML handling methods. The chapter wraps up with a demonstration of creating RSS (Really Simple Syndication) feeds, an increasingly popular feature of Web sites.

In This Chapter

What Is XML?

XML, which is governed by the World Wide Web Consortium (W3C), was created with several goals in mind:

- To be a regulated standard, not the proprietary technology of any one company
- To act as a highly flexible way to store nearly any type of information
- To be easily readable by humans and still usable by computers
- To be able to check itself for validity and integrity

While XML itself is not actually a markup language—despite its name—it provides a foundation for you to manufacture your own markup language. A *markup language* is used to help define or describe pieces of information. For example, the HTML code `<strong>Giant</strong>` indicates that the word *Giant* should be displayed in such a way as to suggest strong importance.

With XML you use tags to encapsulate pieces of information in defined chunks. XML tags (or *elements* as they are formally called) are the opposite of HTML tags in that *they define what something is* but do not suggest how that something should be displayed. Whereas the purpose of HTML is to *present* information, the purpose of XML is to *identify* information.

XML and...

Because XML is all about providing an independent way to store and transmit data, it's often intertwined with other networking technologies. You'll see other acronyms, like RPC (Remote Procedure Calls), SOAP (which used to be an acronym but technically isn't anymore), WSDL (Web Services Description Language), and REST (Representational State Transfer). All of these technologies help create *Web services*: where part of the content of one Web site is based on data requested from another Web site. Google, eBay, PayPal, Amazon, Yahoo!, and others all offer ways to use their data in your applications.

Every book having its limitations, you won't find examples of these here. Sadly, this chapter alone can only offer a mere introduction to XML. But that knowledge—basic XML—is critical to implementing Web services in your own site when you're ready. If you take the knowledge covered in this chapter, and add that to the discussion of Web services in Chapter 10, "Networking with PHP," you'll have the fundamental tools to use network-provided XML in your Web applications.

The power of XML is that you are not limited to any predetermined set of tags; you can actually use XML to come up with your own. Once you have created your markup language (your own definition of elements), you can begin to store data formatted within the newly defined tags.

XML documents can be created in any text editor or IDE. And although most of today's Web browsers can display XML data Ⓐ, you'll normally want to use another technology, such as PHP, to render the XML data into a more user-friendly format, as you'll see by chapter's end.

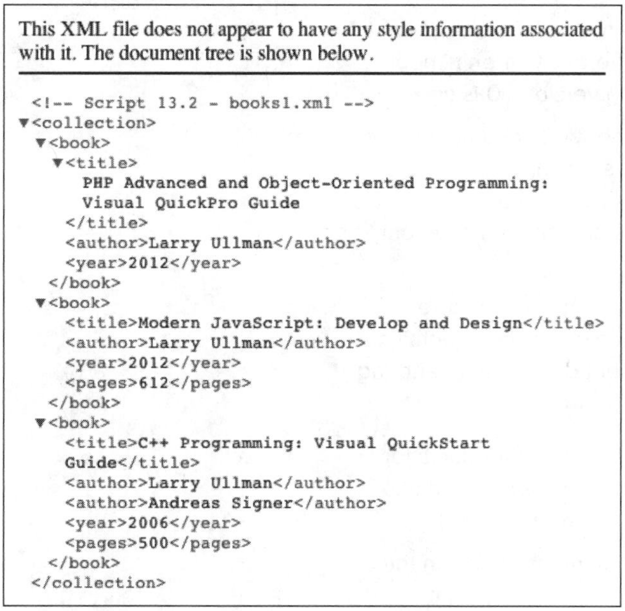

This **XML** file does not appear to have any style information associated with it. The document tree is shown below.

```
<!-- Script 13.2 - books1.xml -->
▼<collection>
  ▼<book>
    ▼<title>
        PHP Advanced and Object-Oriented Programming:
        Visual QuickPro Guide
      </title>
      <author>Larry Ullman</author>
      <year>2012</year>
    </book>
  ▼<book>
      <title>Modern JavaScript: Develop and Design</title>
      <author>Larry Ullman</author>
      <year>2012</year>
      <pages>612</pages>
    </book>
  ▼<book>
      <title>C++ Programming: Visual QuickStart
      Guide</title>
      <author>Larry Ullman</author>
      <author>Andreas Signer</author>
      <year>2006</year>
      <pages>500</pages>
    </book>
</collection>
```

Ⓐ Google Chrome (here, on Macintosh) automatically parses an XML document to display it in a more meaningful form.

XML Syntax

Before doing anything with XML, you must understand how XML documents are structured. An XML document contains two parts:

- The prolog or XML declaration
- The data

The XML prolog is the first line of every XML file and should be in the form

`<?xml version="1.0"?>`

The prolog indicates the XML version and, sometimes, the text encoding or similar attributes:

`<?xml version="1.0" encoding="utf-8"?>`

There are actually two versions of XML—1.0 and 1.1—but the differences aren't important here and using version 1.0 is fine.

The main part of the XML document is the content itself. This section, like an HTML page, begins and ends with a *root* element. Each XML document can have only one root.

Within that root element will be more nested elements. Each element contains a start tag, the element data, and an end tag:

`<tag>data</tag>`

One example might involve products for an e-commerce store (**Script 13.1**). In this example, **store** is the root element.

The XML rules for elements insist on the following:

- XML tags must be balanced in that they open and close (for every **<tag>** there must be a **</tag>**).
- Elements can be nested but not intertwined. HTML will let you get away with a construct like **<strong><em> Soul Mining</strong></em>**, but XML will not.

Script 13.1 An XML document representing two products in a virtual store.

```
1   <?xml version="1.0" encoding="utf-8"?>
2   <!-- Script 13.1 - store.xml -->
3   <!DOCTYPE store SYSTEM "store.dtd">
4   <store>
5       <product>
6           <name>T-Shirt</name>
7           <size>XL</size>
8           <color>White</color>
9           <price>12.00</price>
10      </product>
11      <product>
12          <name>Sweater</name>
13          <size>M</size>
14          <color>Blue</color>
15          <price>25.50</price>
16          <picture filename="sweater.png" />
17      </product>
18  </store>
```

As for the tag names, they are case-sensitive. You can use letters, numbers, and some other characters, but tag names cannot contain spaces or begin with the letters *xml*. They can only begin with either a letter or the underscore.

Before getting into an example, there are two more things to know. First, it is safe to use white space outside of elements but not within the tags (XML, unlike PHP or HTML, is generally sensitive to white space). Second, you can place comments within an XML file—for your own use, not for any technical purposes—by using the same syntax as HTML:

```
<!-- This is my comment. -->
```

To start down the XML path, you'll hand-code an XML document: a partial listing of the books I've written (with apologies for the self-centeredness of the example).

To write XML:

1. Begin a new XML document in your text editor or IDE, to be named **books1.xml** (Script 13.2);

   ```
   <?xml version="1.0"
   → encoding="utf-8"?>

   <!-- Script 13.2 - books1.xml -->
   ```

2. Open with the root element:

   ```
   <collection>
   ```

   For a file to be proper XML, it must use a root element. All of the data will be stored between the opening and closing tags of this element. You will make up the name of this element, as is the case with all of your elements.

   continues on next page

Script 13.2 This is a basic XML document containing information about three books.

```
1   <?xml version="1.0" encoding="utf-8"?>
2   <!-- Script 13.2 - books1.xml -->
3   <collection>
4   <book>
5   <title>PHP Advanced and Object-Oriented Programming: Visual QuickPro Guide</title>
6   <author>Larry Ullman</author>
7   <year>2012</year>
8   </book>
9   <book>
10  <title>Modern JavaScript: Develop and Design</title>
11  <author>Larry Ullman</author>
12  <year>2012</year>
13  <pages>612</pages>
14  </book>
15  <book>
16  <title>C++ Programming: Visual QuickStart Guide</title>
17  <author>Larry Ullman</author>
18  <author>Andreas Signer</author>
19  <year>2006</year>
20  <pages>500</pages>
21  </book>
22  </collection>
```

3. Add a book to the file:

```
<book>
<title>PHP Advanced and
→ Object-Oriented Programming:
→ Visual QuickPro Guide</title>
<author>Larry Ullman</author>
<year>2012</year>
</book>
```

This book is represented by one element, **book**, with three nested elements: **title**, **author**, and **year**.

4. Add another book:

```
<book>
<title>Modern JavaScript:
→ Develop and Design</title>
<author>Larry Ullman</author>
<year>2012</year>
<pages>612</pages>
</book>
```

This book has a fourth nested element: **pages**. It is perfectly acceptable, even common, for similar elements to have different subelements.

5. Add a third and final book:

```
<book>
<title>C++ Programming:
→ Visual QuickStart Guide</title>
<author>Larry Ullman</author>
<author>Andreas Signer</author>
<year>2006</year>
<pages>500</pages>
</book>
```

This record is different from the others in that it has two authors. Each piece of author data (the name) is placed within its own **author** element (rather than putting both names within one element).

6. Complete the XML document:

```
</collection>
```

This closes the root element.

7. Save this file as **books1.xml**.

If you want, view it in a Web browser **A**.

> **TIP** As you can see in Script 13.2, I've not used any indentations or extraneous spaces between tags. You can add those if you want to make the data more human readable.

```
<?xml version="1.0" encoding="UTF-8"?>
<!-- Script 13.2 - books1.xml -->
- <collection>
    - <book>
        <title>PHP Advanced and Object-Oriented
        <author>Larry Ullman</author>
        <year>2012</year>
    </book>
    - <book>
        <title>Modern JavaScript: Develop and D
        <author>Larry Ullman</author>
        <year>2012</year>
        <pages>612</pages>
    </book>
    - <book>
        <title>C++ Programming: Visual QuickSt
        <author>Larry Ullman</author>
        <author>Andreas Signer</author>
        <year>2006</year>
        <pages>500</pages>
    </book>
</collection>
```

A How Internet Explorer 9 displays the **books1.xml** file.

Attributes, Empty Elements, and Entities

The preceding section of the chapter and the **books1.xml** file demonstrate the basic syntax of an XML document. There are three more concepts to cover before learning how to handle XML with PHP.

An element, as already described, has both *tags* and *data*. This is also true in HTML:

`<p>some text here</p>`

Also like HTML, XML elements can have *attributes*:

`<tag attribute_name="value">data</tag>`

`<p class="highlight">some text here`
→ `</p>`

TABLE 13.1 XML Entities

Entity	Meaning
&	&
<	<
>	>
'	'
"	"

XML elements can have an unlimited number of attributes; the only restriction is that each attribute must have a value. You could not do

`<p citation>some text here</p>`

You can use either single or double quotes for quoting your attribute values, but you must use quotes and you should be consistent about which type you use.

Attributes are often used with *empty* elements. An empty element is one that doesn't encapsulate any data. As an HTML example, `<img />` is an empty element. Just as XHTML requires the space and the slash at the end of an empty element, so does XML:

`<tag attribute_name="value" />`

For example, you might have this:

`<picture image_name="me.jpg" />`

The last little idea to throw out here is the *entity*. Some characters cannot be used in XML data, as they cause conflicts. Instead, a character combination is used, known as the entity version of the problematic character. Entities always start with the ampersand (**&**) and end with the semicolon (**;**). **Table 13.1** lists the five most common predeclared XML entities; there are many others.

To use attributes, empty elements, and entities:

1. Open **books1.xml** in your text editor or IDE, if it is not already open.

2. Add an edition number to the first book (**Script 13.3**):

   ```
   <title edition="3">PHP Advanced
   → and Object-Oriented Programming:
   → Visual QuickPro Guide</title>
   ```

   To indicate that this title is a third edition, an attribute is added to its **title** element, with values of 3. The other two books, which are both in their first editions, won't have this attribute, although you could add it with a value of 1.

3. Add a couple chapters to the first book:

   ```
   <chapter number="12">PHP&apos;
   → s Command-Line Interface
   → </chapter>

   <chapter number="13">XML and
   → PHP</chapter>

   <chapter number="14">Debugging,
   → Testing, and Performance
   → </chapter>
   ```

   Three chapters are added, each having an attribute of **number**, with a value of the chapter's number. Chapter 12, whose name is *PHP's Command-Line Interface*, requires the apostrophe entity (**'**).

4. Add a couple chapters to the second book:

   ```
   <chapter number="1" pages="24">
   → (Re-)Introducing JavaScript
   → </chapter>

   <chapter number="2" pages="32">
   → JavaScript in Action</chapter>

   <chapter number="3" pages="34">
   → Tools of the Trade</chapter>
   ```

   To demonstrate multiple attributes, these chapters contain information about their number and page count. It is not a problem that the XML file contains both *elements* called **pages** and *attributes* with the same name.

5. Add a chapter to the third book:

   ```
   <chapter number="12">Namespaces
   → &amp; Modularization</chapter>
   ```

   I'm entering just this one chapter, to demonstrate the ampersand entity.

continues on page 418

Script 13.3 Attributes, empty elements, and entities have been added to the XML document to better describe the data.

```
1   <?xml version="1.0" encoding="utf-8"?>
2   <!-- Script 13.3 - books2.xml -->
3   <collection>
4   <book>
5   <title edition="3">PHP Advanced and Object-Oriented Programming: Visual QuickPro
    ⇥ Guide</title>
6   <author>Larry Ullman</author>
7   <year>2012</year>
8   <chapter number="12">PHP&apos;s Command-Line Interface</chapter>
9   <chapter number="13">XML and PHP</chapter>
10  <chapter number="14">Debugging, Testing, and Performance</chapter>
11  <cover filename="phpvqp3.jpg" />
12  </book>
13  <book>
14  <title>Modern JavaScript: Develop and Design</title>
15  <author>Larry Ullman</author>
16  <year>2012</year>
17  <pages>612</pages>
18  <chapter number="1" pages="24">(Re-)Introducing JavaScript</chapter>
19  <chapter number="2" pages="32">JavaScript in Action</chapter>
20  <chapter number="3" pages="34">Tools of the Trade</chapter>
21  </book>
22  <book>
23  <title>C++ Programming: Visual QuickStart Guide</title>
24  <author>Larry Ullman</author>
25  <author>Andreas Signer</author>
26  <year>2006</year>
27  <pages>500</pages>
28  <chapter number="12">Namespaces &amp; Modularization</chapter>
29  </book>
30  </collection>
```

6. Add an empty element to the first book:

```
<cover filename="phpvqp3.jpg" />
```

The **cover** element contains no data but does have an attribute, whose value is the name of the cover image file.

7. Save this file as **books2.xml**.

If you want, view it in a Web browser Ⓐ.

> **TIP** HTML has dozens upon dozens of pre-declared entities, including the five listed in Table 13.1.

> **TIP** You can also create your own entities in a Document Type Definition file, discussed next in the chapter.

> **TIP** Whether you use a nested element or an attribute is often a matter of choice. The first book in could also be reflected as (omitting a couple elements for brevity):

```
<book>

<title>PHP Advanced and
→ Object-Oriented Programming:
→ Visual QuickPro Guide</title>

<edition>3</edition>

<chapter>

<number>12</number>

<name>PHP&apos;s Command-Line
→ Interface</name>

</chapter>

<cover>php5adv.jpg</cover>

</book>
```

```
This XML file does not appear to have any style information associated with it. The document
tree is shown below.

<!-- Script 13.3 - books2.xml -->
▼<collection>
  ▼<book>
    ▼<title edition="3">
        PHP Advanced and Object-Oriented Programming: Visual QuickPro Guide
      </title>
      <author>Larry Ullman</author>
      <year>2012</year>
      <chapter number="12">PHP's Command-Line Interface</chapter>
      <chapter number="13">XML and PHP</chapter>
      <chapter number="14">Debugging, Testing, and Performance</chapter>
      <cover filename="phpvqp3.jpg"/>
    </book>
  ▼<book>
      <title>Modern JavaScript: Develop and Design</title>
      <author>Larry Ullman</author>
      <year>2012</year>
      <pages>612</pages>
      <chapter number="1" pages="24">(Re-)Introducing JavaScript</chapter>
      <chapter number="2" pages="32">JavaScript in Action</chapter>
      <chapter number="3" pages="34">Tools of the Trade</chapter>
    </book>
  ▼<book>
      <title>C++ Programming: Visual QuickStart Guide</title>
      <author>Larry Ullman</author>
      <author>Andreas Signer</author>
      <year>2006</year>
      <pages>500</pages>
      <chapter number="12">Namespaces & Modularization</chapter>
    </book>
</collection>
```

Ⓐ The updated **books2.xml** in Safari.

Defining XML Schemas

XML files primarily contain data, as you've already seen in the first three scripts. That data can also be associated with a *schema*, which is a guide for the XML document's contents. Schemas are optional, but if provided, can be used to ensure that the XML data is valid.

A schema can be represented using two approaches:

- DTD, a Document Type Definition
- XML Schema

DTD is the older, more accessible approach, and I'll discuss it first. XML Schema is a newer method that allows for mapping of XML data to specific types (instead of general data categories, as you'll see with DTD). I'll discuss XML Schema second.

Incorporating the DTD

To associate a DTD with an XML file, a reference line is placed after the prolog but before the data itself:

```
<?xml version="1.0" encoding="utf-8"?>
```

```
<!DOCTYPE rootelement [definition]>
```

The syntax begins **<!DOCTYPE** *rootelement*. This is similar to HTML documents that begin with **<!DOCTYPE** **html**, stating that the root element of the data is the **html** tag. Within the document type declaration, between the opening and closing square brackets, you can define the elements to be allowed in this XML data.

If you'd rather define the allowed elements in a separate file, your document type declaration would be

```
<!DOCTYPE rootelement SYSTEM
→"/path/to/filename.dtd">
```

where **filename.dtd** is the included file and **/path/to** is a Uniform Resource Indicator, or URI, pinpointing where that file is on the server.

There are two primary benefits to using an external DTD:

- The DTD information will only need to be transmitted once, regardless of how many XML documents that use it are transmitted (when using XML between networked computers).

- External documents are generally easier to edit.

Now that the XML file references the DTD, that file must be created. This process is called *document modeling*, because you are creating a paradigm for how your XML data should be organized.

Defining elements

A DTD defines every element and attribute that's to be used in your markup language. The syntax for defining an element is

```
<!ELEMENT name TYPE>
```

where *name* is the name of the new tag and it will contain content of type *TYPE*.

Table 13.2 lists the four primary element types and their meanings.

If you apply these rules to the e-commerce XML (Script 13.1), you could define some of the elements like so:

```
<!ELEMENT name (#PCDATA)>
```

```
<!ELEMENT size (#PCDATA)>
```

```
<!ELEMENT price (#PCDATA)>
```

```
<!ELEMENT picture EMPTY>
```

The last element, **picture**, is of type **EMPTY** because it has no content (it has an attribute of **filename**).

The rules just defined seem to cover the XML in Script 13.1, but there are still a couple of missing pieces. First, there's another element used, that of **product**, which contains all of the other elements. To define it:

```
<!ELEMENT product (name, size, price,
→picture)>
```

This states that **product** contains four other elements in the order of **name**, **size**, **price**, and **picture**. Definitions can be more flexible by using regular expression–like syntax:

```
<!ELEMENT product (name, size*,
→price, picture?)>
```

TABLE 13.2 Element Types

Type	Association
(#PCDATA)	Generally text (specifically parsed-character data)
(#CDATA)	Generally text (specifically non-parsed-character data)
EMPTY	Nothing
ANY	Anything

TABLE 13.3 Element Type Symbols

Symbol	Meaning
?	Optional (zero or one)
+	At least one
*	Zero or more
|	Or

TABLE 13.4 Element Attribute Types

Type	Meaning	Example
CDATA	Character data	General text
NMTOKEN	Name token	String (without white space)
NMTOKENS	Several name tokens	**NMTOKENS** separated by white spaces (e.g., "Jessica Zoe Sam")
ID	Unique Identifier	Text or numerical, but it must be unique for each element

That line indicates that **product** can contain up to four elements. One element, **size**, can be listed anywhere from zero to multiple times. Another element, **picture**, is entirely optional, but if present, there can be only one. **Table 13.3** lists the pertinent characters for defining elements.

You can extend this even further by dictating that an element contain other elements, parsed-character data, or nothing, using the **OR** character:

```
<!ELEMENT thing (other_element |
→ #PCDATA | EMPTY)>
```

Defining attributes

The second problem with the current model for Script 13.1 is that it doesn't reflect the **picture** element's attribute (the **filename**). To allow elements to have attributes, make an attribute list within the DTD. This can be done only after defining the elements (or at least, the attributes of an element must be defined after the element itself has been defined).

```
<!ATTLIST element_name

attr_name attr_type attr_description

>
```

The **attribute_name** field is simply a text string like *color* or *alignment*. The **attribute_type** indicates the format of the attribute. **Table 13.4** lists the possibilities.

Another possibility is for an attribute to be an enumerated list of possible values:

```
<!ATTLIST element_name

attr_name (value1 | value2) "value1"

>
```

The preceding code says that **element_name** takes an attribute of **attr_name** with possible values of **value1** or **value2**, the former being the default.

The third parameter for an attribute—the attribute's description—allows you to further define how it will function. Possibilities include **#REQUIRED**, meaning that an element must use that attribute; **#IMPLIED**, which means that the attribute is optional; and **#FIXED**, indicating that the attribute will always have the same value. To round out the definition of the **picture** element for Script 13.1, an attribute should be added:

<!ATTLIST picture

filename NMTOKEN #REQUIRED

>

Now that you've seen the foundation of defining elements, you can write a Document Type Definition that corresponds to the books XML.

To write a Document Type Definition:

1. Create a new document in your text editor or IDE, to be named **collection. dtd** (Script 13.4).

```
<!-- Script 13.4 -
→ collection.dtd -->
```

2. Define the **collection** element:

```
<!ELEMENT collection (book+)>
```

The first element to be declared is the root element, **collection**. It consists only of one or more **book** elements.

Note that the separate DTD file does not begin with **<!DOCTYPE**, because that goes within the XML file itself.

Script 13.4 The DTD file will establish all the rules by which the book XML pages must abide.

```
1    <!-- Script 13.4 - collection.dtd -->
2
3    <!ELEMENT collection (book+)>
4
5    <!ELEMENT book (title, author+, year,
     → pages?, chapter*, cover?)>
6
7    <!ELEMENT title (#PCDATA)>
8    <!ELEMENT author (#PCDATA)>
9    <!ELEMENT year (#PCDATA)>
10   <!ELEMENT pages (#PCDATA)>
11   <!ELEMENT chapter (#PCDATA)>
12   <!ELEMENT cover EMPTY>
13
14   <!ATTLIST title
15   edition NMTOKEN #IMPLIED
16   >
17
18   <!ATTLIST chapter
19   number NMTOKEN #IMPLIED
20   pages NMTOKEN #IMPLIED
21   >
22
23   <!ATTLIST cover
24   filename NMTOKEN #REQUIRED
25   >
```

3. Define the **book** element:

```
<!ELEMENT book (title, author+,
→year, pages?, chapter*, cover?)>
```

This tag will contain up to six other tags: **title**, **author**, and **year**, which are required; **chapter**, which is optional and can be listed numerous times; and **pages** and **cover_image**, both of which are optional but can occur only once. The **author** is also flagged as being allowed multiple times.

4. Define the **title**, **author**, **year**, **pages**, and **chapter** elements:

```
<!ELEMENT title (#PCDATA)>
<!ELEMENT author (#PCDATA)>
<!ELEMENT year (#PCDATA)>
<!ELEMENT pages (#PCDATA)>
<!ELEMENT chapter (#PCDATA)>
```

Each of these elements contains only character data. I'm specifically treating them each as parsed-character data, but some people prefer to use unparsed-character data (CDATA) instead.

5. Define the **cover** element:

```
<!ELEMENT cover EMPTY>
```

This one item is different from the others because the element will always be empty. The information for this element will be stored in the attribute.

6. Define the attributes for **title** and **chapter**:

```
<!ATTLIST title
edition NMTOKEN #IMPLIED
>
<!ATTLIST chapter
number NMTOKEN #IMPLIED
pages NMTOKEN #IMPLIED
>
```

The **title** element has one optional attribute, the **edition**. The **chapter** element has two attributes—**number** and **pages**—both of which are optional.

7. Define the attribute for **cover**:

```
<!ATTLIST cover
filename NMTOKEN #REQUIRED
>
```

The **cover** element will take one mandatory attribute, the **filename** of type **NMTOKEN**, which means it will be a string (e.g., *image.jpg*). Keep in mind that the element itself is not required, as defined in the **book** tag. So the XML file should either include **cover** with a **filename** attribute or not include it at all.

8. Save this file as **collection.dtd**.

Now that the document modeling is done, the DTD needs to be linked to the XML file.

9. Open **books2.xml** (Script 13.3) in your text editor or IDE.

continues on next page

10. After the prolog but before the root element, add the doctype declaration (Script 13.5):

`<!DOCTYPE collection SYSTEM`
`→ "collection.dtd">`

As written, this does assume that the XML file and the DTD will be stored in the same directory.

11. Save the file with these new changes (I've also changed its name to **books3. xml**). Place this file and **collection. dtd** in your Web directory (in the same folder), and test in your Web browser, if you want.

> **TIP** One of the great things about XML is that you can write your own DTDs or make use of document models created by others, which are freely available online. Developers have already written models for books, recipes, and more.

Script 13.5 The books file now references the corresponding DTD (Script 13.4).

```
1   <?xml version="1.0" encoding="utf-8"?>
2   <!-- Script 13.5 - books3.xml -->
3   <!DOCTYPE collection SYSTEM "collection.dtd">
4   <collection>
5   <book>
6   <title edition="3">PHP Advanced and Object-Oriented Programming: Visual QuickPro Guide</title>
7   <author>Larry Ullman</author>
8   <year>2012</year>
9   <chapter number="12">PHP&apos;s Command-Line Interface</chapter>
10  <chapter number="13">XML and PHP</chapter>
11  <chapter number="14">Debugging, Testing, and Performance</chapter>
12  <cover filename="phpvqp3.jpg" />
13  </book>
14  <book>
15  <title>Modern JavaScript: Develop and Design</title>
16  <author>Larry Ullman</author>
17  <year>2012</year>
18  <pages>612</pages>
19  <chapter number="1" pages="24">(Re-)Introducing JavaScript</chapter>
20  <chapter number="2" pages="32">JavaScript in Action</chapter>
21  <chapter number="3" pages="34">Tools of the Trade</chapter>
22  </book>
23  <book>
24  <title>C++ Programming: Visual QuickStart Guide</title>
25  <author>Larry Ullman</author>
26  <author>Andreas Signer</author>
27  <year>2006</year>
28  <pages>500</pages>
29  <chapter number="12">Namespaces &amp; Modularization</chapter>
30  </book>
31  </collection>
```

Using XML Schema

XML Schema is a more powerful and complex tool for defining what constitutes acceptable XML data. For example, whereas DTD is vague as to an element's type—most come down to character data of some sort—XML Schema can require that an element contain an integer, a string, a decimal, a valid country code, and more.

XML Schema (note the capital "S" in Schema) was first formalized in 2001, although it is just one of many possible XML schema languages. Since that time, and to avoid confusion with general schema languages, the proper label is now XML Schema Document (XSD). Version 1.1 of XSD just became a W3C recommendation in 2012, although the differences between it and version 1.0 are insignificant to the scope of this chapter.

Incorporating XSD

Unlike DTD, XSD is written in XML. To add XSD to an XML file, use the **schema** element (again, after the XML prolog but before the data):

```
<xs:schema xmlns:xs="http://www.
→w3.org/2001/XMLSchema">

  <!-- Schema Information Here -->

</xs:schema>

<!-- Start XML Data -->
```

There's a bit of extra stuff here in that **schema** is prefaced by *xs*. This is a *namespace* reference, with the opening **schema** tag indicating where the namespace definition comes from.

To use an external XSD document, you'll want to first create the file, giving it an **.xsd** extension. To tie the XSD file to your XML, you have to reference that file in the XML document's root tag. For the e-commerce example, which uses **store** as the root element, you would start with

```
<?xml version="1.0" encoding="utf-8"?>

<store   xmlns:xsi="http://www.
→w3.org/2001/XMLSchema-instance"

xsi:noNamespaceSchemaLocation=
→"somefile.xsd">
```

The first attribute, **xmlns**, identifies the XML namespace for XML Schema instances (*xsi*). That code is used without modification, regardless of your server setup. Next, the **xsi:noNamespaceSchemaLocation** property gets assigned the path to the XSD file. You'll need to make sure this is correct for each XML and XSD combination. Note that the XSD file, being XML, must start with its own prolog and use **schema** as the root element. You'll see this in action momentarily.

But whether you place the schema definition inline, or in an external file, you'll need to know how to define elements in XSD.

Defining elements

Elements are defined within XSD using the format

```
<xs:element name="some_name"
→ type="some_type"/>
```

Each element must have a name. This is how you establish valid element names to use in the corresponding XML. Note that the *xs* identifies the namespace wherein the **element** definition can be found.

The types can be a predefined type, which include:

- **xs:string**
- **xs:integer**
- **xs:boolean**
- **xs:decimal**
- **xs:date**

The meanings of these types are obvious, and you can find the full list of possible types online. There are 19 standard types, and a couple dozen derived types, already defined for you.

With this in mind, the **name** element in the e-commerce example would be defined as

```
<xs:element name="name"
→ type="xs:string"/>
```

Many elements will be of a user-defined type, such as in the books and e-commerce examples. In XSD, these types are represented as **xs:simple** or **xs:complexType**, and I'll return to this topic momentarily.

You can customize the elements by using the attributes of the **element** tag. There is **default**, which declares the default value, and **fixed**, which indicates the only value the element can have. For example, if the **edition** element (for books) were to have a default value of 1, that would look like

```
<xs:element name="edition"
→ type="xs:integer" default="1"/>
```

As with DTD, you can create limits for how many times an element can appear within its context. This is done using the **minOccurs** and **maxOccurs** attributes. These are inclusive:

```
<xs:element name="size"
→ type="xs:string" minOccurs="1"
→ maxOccurs="10"/>
```

That code says that the **size** element has to exist at least once but can be present up to 10 times. This definition would invalidate any XML that contained a product without at least one size.

An important aspect of XSD is that the **minOccurs** and **maxOccurs** attributes have default values of 1, meaning that if these attributes are not stated, the corresponding element will have to exist exactly one time.

To allow for any number of occurrences, you would use 0 as the **minOccurs** value and *unbounded* as the **maxOccurs**:

```
<xs:element name="picture"
→ type="xs:string" minOccurs="0"
→ maxOccurs="unbounded"/>
```

Simple and complex types

Earlier, I said that you could use **xs:simpleType** or **xs:complexType** to create user-defined types. A simple type is a variation on the other default types. For example, you could define your own simple type that is a number between 0 and 10.

Complex types are user-defined types composed of other types. The syntax is trickier:

```
<xs:element name="product">
  <xs:complexType>
    <xs:sequence>
    <!-- Subtypes -->
    </xs:sequence>
  </xs:complexType>
</xs:element>
```

When defining a complex type, you must indicate how the type is composed. Here are the options:

- *Sequence*, the child elements must appear in the given order
- *Choice*, only one of the child elements can appear
- *All*, any or all of the child elements can appear in any order

An alternative way to create a complex type is to define it outside of any individual element, give it a **name** attribute, and then use that new type where needed. This would make sense in situations with repeating custom data types, such as an address or person's full name. You'll see an example in the subsequent set of steps.

As you can tell, writing XSD is verbose and quickly becomes a challenge, but XSD is much more demanding than DTD for validating XML, which can be a good thing.

Creating attributes

Finally, attributes are declared for elements using **xs:attribute**, providing the name and type:

```
<xs:attribute name="price"
→ type="xs:decimal" />
```

The **attribute** element has a **use** property, whose possible values are *optional* and *required* (optional is the default).

One last little hiccup is in situations where an element has both a value and one or more attributes, such as a **title** element that can have an **edition** attribute. To allow for both a value and one or more attributes, you have to use this syntax:

```
<xs:complexType name="titleType">
  <xs:simpleContent>
    <xs:extension base="xs:string">
      <xs:attribute name="edition"
      → type="xs:int" />
    </xs:extension>
  </xs:simpleContent>
</xs:complexType>
```

That code indicates that the base content for the **titleType** element is a string but that it also has an integer attribute for the **edition**.

Whew! Let's now take all this information about XSD to write the proper XSD for the book collection XML file.

To write an XML Schema Definition:

1. Create a new document in your text editor or IDE, to be named **collection.xsd** (Script 13.6):

```
<?xml version="1.0"
→ encoding="utf-8"?>

<!-- Script 13.6 -
→ collection.xsd -->

<xs:schema xmlns:xs="http://www.
→ w3.org/2001/XMLSchema">
```

Again, this is an XML document, so it must begin with the prolog. The root element of the page is schema, which associates the schema definition with the *xs* namespace.

2. Define the **collection** element:

```
<xs:element name="collection">

  <xs:complexType>

    <xs:sequence>

      <xs:element name="book"
→ type="bookType"
→ maxOccurs="unbounded" />

    </xs:sequence>

  </xs:complexType>

</xs:element>
```

The first element to be declared is the root element, **collection**. It consists only of one or more **book** elements. The **book** element type will be of type **bookType**, to be defined next.

3. Define the **book** element:

```
<xs:complexType name="bookType">

  <xs:sequence>

    <xs:element name="title"
→ type="titleType" />

    <xs:element name="author"
→ type="xs:string"
→ minOccurs="1"
→ maxOccurs="unbounded" />

    <xs:element name="year"
→ type="xs:int" />

    <xs:element name="pages"
→ type="xs:int" minOccurs="0"
→ maxOccurs="1" />

    <xs:element name="chapter"
→ type="chapterType"
→ minOccurs="0"
→ maxOccurs="unbounded"/>

    <xs:element name="cover"
→ type="coverType"
→ minOccurs="0"
→ maxOccurs="1" />

  </xs:sequence>

</xs:complexType>
```

The **bookType** of complex element is a bit more complicated. It can contain any or all of the following elements: **title**, **author**, **year**, **pages**, **chapter**, and **cover**. Of these, **author**, **year**, and **pages** are simple types. The **chapter**, **title**, and **cover** elements will be user-defined complex types.

The default is that exactly one of each element is required, which is fine for the **title** and **year**. The **author** is allowed any number from 1 to infinity. The **chapter** element can be present any number of times, including 0. And the **pages** and **cover** are both optional but can appear only once.

continues on page 430

Script 13.6 This XSD file establishes specific rules by which the book XML data must abide.

```
1   <?xml version="1.0" encoding="utf-8"?>
2   <!-- Script 13.6 - collection.xsd -->
3   <xs:schema xmlns:xs="http://www.w3.org/2001/XMLSchema">
4
5   <xs:element name="collection">
6       <xs:complexType>
7           <xs:sequence>
8               <xs:element name="book" type="bookType" maxOccurs="unbounded"/>
9           </xs:sequence>
10      </xs:complexType>
11  </xs:element>
12
13  <xs:complexType name="bookType">
14      <xs:sequence>
15          <xs:element name="title" type="titleType" />
16          <xs:element name="author" type="xs:string" minOccurs="1" maxOccurs="unbounded" />
17          <xs:element name="year" type="xs:int" />
18          <xs:element name="pages" type="xs:int" minOccurs="0" maxOccurs="1" />
19          <xs:element name="chapter" type="chapterType" minOccurs="0" maxOccurs="unbounded"/>
20          <xs:element name="cover" type="coverType" minOccurs="0" maxOccurs="1" />
21      </xs:sequence>
22  </xs:complexType>
23
24  <xs:complexType name="coverType">
25      <xs:attribute name="filename" type="xs:string" />
26  </xs:complexType>
27
28  <xs:complexType name="chapterType">
29      <xs:simpleContent>
30          <xs:extension base="xs:string">
31              <xs:attribute name="number" type="xs:int" />
32              <xs:attribute name="pages" type="xs:int" />
33          </xs:extension>
34      </xs:simpleContent>
35  </xs:complexType>
36
37  <xs:complexType name="titleType">
38      <xs:simpleContent>
39          <xs:extension base="xs:string">
40              <xs:attribute name="edition" type="xs:int" />
41          </xs:extension>
42      </xs:simpleContent>
43  </xs:complexType>
44
45  </xs:schema>
```

4. Define the **coverType** element:

```
<xs:complexType name="coverType">
    <xs:attribute name="filename"
    → type="xs:string" />
</xs:complexType>
```

The **coverType** element has only a **filename** attribute, which would have a string value.

5. Define the **chapterType** element:

```
<xs:complexType name="chapterType">
    <xs:simpleContent>
        <xs:extension base="xs:string">
            <xs:attribute name="number"
            → type="xs:int" />
            <xs:attribute name="pages"
            → type="xs:int" />
        </xs:extension>
    </xs:simpleContent>
</xs:complexType>
```

The **chapterType** element has both a value, which is a string (i.e., the chapter name), and two attributes: number and pages, both of which are integers.

6. Define the **titleType** element:

```
<xs:complexType name="titleType">
    <xs:simpleContent>
        <xs:extension base="xs:string">
            <xs:attribute name="edition"
            → type="xs:int" />
        </xs:extension>
    </xs:simpleContent>
</xs:complexType>
```

Similar to the **chapterType** element, **titleType** has both a value and an attribute.

7. Close the **schema** element:

```
</xs:schema>
```

8. Save this file as **collection.xsd**.

Now that the document modeling is done, the DTD needs to be linked to the XML file.

9. Open **books2.xml** (Script 13.3) in your text editor or IDE.

10. Change the root element to reference the XSD file (**Script 13.7**):

```
<collection xmlns:xsi="http://www.
→ w3.org/2001/XMLSchema-instance"
xsi:noNamespaceSchemaLocation=
→ "collection.xsd">
```

As written, this does assume that the XML file and the DTD will be stored in the same directory.

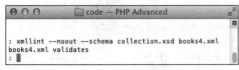

```
000          code — PHP Advanced
: xmllint --noout --schema collection.xsd books4.xml
books4.xml validates
: █
```

A The command-line **xmllint** utility shows that the XML is valid, per the XSD definition.

11. Save the file with these new changes (I've also changed its name to **books4.xml**).

12. If you want, use an online or command-line **A** validation tool to text the XML against the XSD.

TIP XSD supports the mixed attribute on elements, which allows those elements to contain both subelements and data. This would allow you to, for example, use HTML within an XML element.

Script 13.7 The books file now references the corresponding XSD (Script 13.6).

```
1    <?xml version="1.0" encoding="utf-8"?>
2    <!-- Script 13.7- books4.xml -->
3    <collection xmlns:xsi="http://www.w3.org/2001/XMLSchema-instance"
4    xsi:noNamespaceSchemaLocation="collection.xsd">
5    <book>
6    <title edition="3">PHP Advanced and Object-Oriented Programming: Visual QuickPro Guide</title>
7    <author>Larry Ullman</author>
8    <year>2012</year>
9    <chapter number="12">PHP&apos;s Command-Line Interface</chapter>
10   <chapter number="13">XML and PHP</chapter>
11   <chapter number="14">Debugging, Testing, and Performance</chapter>
12   <cover filename="phpvqp3.jpg" />
13   </book>
14   <book>
15   <title>Modern JavaScript: Develop and Design</title>
16   <author>Larry Ullman</author>
17   <year>2012</year>
18   <pages>612</pages>
19   <chapter number="1" pages="24">(Re-)Introducing JavaScript</chapter>
20   <chapter number="2" pages="32">JavaScript in Action</chapter>
21   <chapter number="3" pages="34">Tools of the Trade</chapter>
22   </book>
23   <book>
24   <title>C++ Programming: Visual QuickStart Guide</title>
25   <author>Larry Ullman</author>
26   <author>Andreas Signer</author>
27   <year>2006</year>
28   <pages>500</pages>
29   <chapter number="12">Namespaces &amp; Modularization</chapter>
30   </book>
31   </collection>
```

Parsing XML

There's more to XML than just composing XML documents, DTD files, and XML schemas in text editors, although those steps are the basis of XML. Once XML data exists, applications can then *parse* it. Parsing XML is a matter of using an application or library to read XML files and...

- Check if they are well formed
- Check if they are valid
- Make use of the stored data

A parser, in short, takes XML files and breaks them down into their various pieces. As an example, the code **<artist>Air</artist>** consists of the opening tag (**<artist>**), the content (*Air*), and the closing tag (**</artist>**). While this distinction is obvious to the human eye, the ability of a computer to pull meaning out of a string of characters is the power of XML.

There are two types of XML parsers: event-based and tree-based. The former goes into action when an event occurs. An example of an event would be encountering an opening tag in an XML file. By reading an entire file and doing things at each event, this type of parser—also called a SAX (Simple API for XML)—manages the entire XML document. Expat, to be demonstrated next, is an event-based parser.

The second parser type views an XML file and creates a tree-like representation of the entire thing that can then be manipulated **Ⓐ**. These are primarily DOM (Document Object Model) systems. Later in the chapter, you'll see how to use SimpleXML, which is a DOM parser.

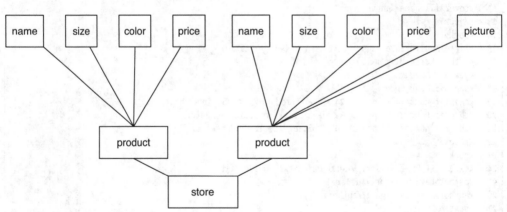

Ⓐ A DOM, or tree, representation of the store XML file (Script 13.1).

Parsing XML with Expat

Using Expat with PHP is a four-step process:

1. Create a new parser.
2. Identify the functions to use for handling events.
3. Parse the file.
4. Free up the resources used by the parser.

The first step is accomplished using `xml_parser_create()`:

```
$p = xml_parser_create();
```

The second step is the most important. Because Expat is an event-based parser, it makes use of callback functions when events occur. The primary events that will occur when parsing XML consist of discovering:

- An opening tag
- The content between tags
- A closing tag

You need to tell PHP what user-defined functions should be called when each of these events occurs. For the opening and closing tags, use the `xml_set_element_handler()` function:

```
xml_set_element_handler($p, 'open_
→ element_fx', 'close_element_fx');
```

For the element content, use `xml_set_character_data_handler()` to name the callback function:

```
xml_set_character_data_handler($p,
→ 'data_fx');
```

Now, when the parser encounters the different events, it will automatically send that content to the proper function.

Parsing the file requires the use of the `xml_parse()` function, which takes two arguments (and an optional third):

```
xml_parse($p, $data, $stop);
```

This function is first fed the pointer or reference to the parser, and then the information to be parsed. The third argument tells the parser when to stop working.

Finally, you should free up the resources used by the parser:

```
xml_parser_free($);
```

Just one use of PHP and XML is to turn XML documents into formatted HTML so that the information can be displayed in the browser. As an example, I'll write a PHP script that uses Expat to make a legible Web page from an XML file.

To parse XML with PHP:

1. Create a new document in your text editor or IDE, to be named **expat.php**, beginning with the standard HTML (**Script 13.8**):

```
<!doctype html>
<html lang="en">
<head>
   <meta charset="utf-8">
   <title>XML Expat Parser</title>
   <link rel="stylesheet"
   → href="style.css">
</head>
<body>
<?php # Script 14.7 - expat.php
```

This script is going to use a bit of CSS, placed in an external file. You can download that from **LarryUllman.com**.

2. Begin the function for handling opening tags:

```
function handle_open_element($p,
→ $element, $attributes) {
```

This function will be called whenever an opening tag is encountered by the parser. This function will receive from the parser the parser reference, the name of the element, and an associative array of any attributes that element contains. As an example, the **chapter** element can have both **number** and **pages** attributes. Upon encountering that tag, the parser will send this function the values **$p** (for the parser), **chapter** (the name of the element), and an array that could be defined like so:

```
$attributes = array ('NUMBER' =>
→ 1, 'PAGES' => '34');
```

continues on page 437

Script 13.8 This script uses PHP in conjunction with the Expat library to parse XML documents, turning them into an HTML page.

```
1    <!doctype html>
2    <html lang="en">
3    <head>
4      <meta charset="utf-8">
5      <title>XML Expat Parser</title>
6      <link rel="stylesheet" href="style.css">
7    </head>
8    <body>
9    <?php # Script 13.8 - expat.php
10
11   /*  This script will parse an XML file.
12    *  It uses the Expat library, an event-based parser.
13    */
14
15   // Function for handling the open tag:
16   function handle_open_element($p, $element, $attributes) {
17
18      // Do different things based upon the element:
19      switch ($element) {
20
```

script continues on next page

```
21        // Need to address: book, title, author, year, chapter, and pages!
22
23        case 'BOOK': // Books are DIV's:
24            echo '<div>';
25            break;
26
27        case 'CHAPTER': // Chapters are Ps:
28            echo "<p>Chapter {$attributes['NUMBER']}: ";
29            break;
30
31        case 'COVER': // Show the image...
32
33            // Get the image info:
34            $image = @getimagesize($attributes['FILENAME']);
35
36            // Make the image HTML:
37            echo "<img src=\"{$attributes['FILENAME']}\" $image[3] border=\"0\"><br>";
38            break;
39
40        case 'TITLE': // Titles are H2s:
41            echo '<h2>';
42            break;
43
44        // Everything else is just displayed:
45        case 'YEAR':
46        case 'AUTHOR':
47        case 'PAGES':
48            echo '<span class="label">' . $element . '</span>: ';
49            break;
50
51    } // End of switch.
52
53 } // End of handle_open_element() function.
54
55 // Function for handling the closing tag:
56 function handle_close_element($p, $element) {
57
58    // Do different things based upon the element:
59    switch ($element) {
60
61        // Close up HTML tags...
62
63        case 'BOOK': // Books are DIV's:
64            echo '</div>';
65            break;
66
67        case 'CHAPTER': // Chapters are Ps:
68            echo '</p>';
69            break;
```

script continues on next page

```
70
71       case 'TITLE': // Titles are H2s:
72           echo '</h2>';
73           break;
74
75       // Add a break to the others:
76       case 'YEAR':
77       case 'AUTHOR':
78       case 'PAGES':
79           echo '<br>';
80           break;
81
82    } // End of switch.
83
84  } // End of handle_close_element() function.
85
86  // Function for printing the content:
87  function handle_character_data($p, $cdata) {
88      echo $cdata;
89  }
90
91  # --------------------
92  # End of the functions.
93  # --------------------
94
95  // Create the parser:
96  $p = xml_parser_create();
97
98  // Set the handling functions:
99  xml_set_element_handler($p, 'handle_open_element', 'handle_close_element');
100 xml_set_character_data_handler($p, 'handle_character_data');
101
102 // Read the file:
103 $file = 'books4.xml';
104 $fp = @fopen($file, 'r') or die("<p>Could not open a file called '$file'.</p></body></html>");
105 while ($data = fread($fp, 4096)) {
106     xml_parse($p, $data, feof($fp));
107 }
108
109 // Free up the parser:
110 xml_parser_free($p);
111 ?>
112 </body>
113 </html>
```

3. Begin a **switch** for handling the different elements:

```
switch ($element) {
  case 'BOOK':
    echo '<div>';
    break;
```

Depending on the element received, the function will do different things. Each book will be wrapped within **DIV** tags, and so when the opening **book** element is encountered, the opening **DIV** element is created.

One thing to be aware of with Expat is that every element and attribute name is received in all-uppercase letters, thanks to something called *case-folding*. Thus, even though the XML data uses *book*, it must be *BOOK* here to match.

4. Add a case for **chapter** elements:

```
case 'CHAPTER':
  echo "<p>Chapter {$attributes
→ ['NUMBER']}: ";
  break;
```

For the **chapter** element, I'll want to create a paragraph that begins with the chapter's number. That value is available through the **$attributes** array, again using all capital letters.

5. Add a case for **cover** elements:

```
case 'COVER':
  $image = @getimagesize
→ ($attributes['FILENAME']);
  echo "<img src=\"{$attributes
→ ['FILENAME']}\" $image[3]
→ border=\"0\"><br>";
  break;
```

If the element is the **cover**, I'll place the image itself in the page in lieu of referring to the textual name of the element or its attributes.

6. Complete the **switch** and the function:

```
    case 'TITLE':
      echo '<h2>';
      break;
    case 'YEAR':
    case 'AUTHOR':
    case 'PAGES':
      echo '<span
→ class="label">' .
→ $element . '</span>: ';
      break;
  } // End of switch.

} // End of handle_open_element()
→ function.
```

The book title will be placed within H2 tags. The year, author, and pages are just written using the syntax

```
<span class="label">YEAR</span>:
→ 2012
```

That code is begun here, with the value to follow.

continues on next page

7. Begin defining the function for handling any closing elements:

```
function handle_close_element($p,
↪$element) {
   switch ($element) {
      case 'BOOK':
         echo '</div>';
         break;
      case 'CHAPTER':
         echo '</p>';
         break;
      case 'TITLE':
         echo '</h2>';
         break;
```

This function is more straightforward than its predecessor. All this does is close the proper HTML tag for each XML element.

8. Complete the function:

```
      case 'YEAR':
      case 'AUTHOR':
      case 'PAGES':
         echo '<br>';
         break;
   } // End of switch.
} // End of handle_close_element()
function.
```

For the year, author, and pages, a break is added. Nothing needs to be done for cover elements.

9. Add the final function:

```
function handle_character_data($p,
↪$cdata) {
   echo $cdata;
}
```

The `handle_character_data()` function will be used for the information between the opening and closing tags—in other words, the data. In this case, all this function has to do is print the received data. With different types of XML data, other steps may be required.

10. Create a new parser and identify the functions to use:

```
$p = xml_parser_create();

xml_set_element_handler($p,
↪'handle_open_element',
↪'handle_close_element');

xml_set_character_data_handler($p,
↪'handle_character_data');
```

11. Read and parse the XML file:

```
$file = 'books4.xml';

$fp = @fopen($file, 'r') or
↪die("<p>Could not open a file
↪called '$file'.</p></body>
↪</html>");
while ($data = fread($fp, 4096)) {
   xml_parse($p, $data, feof($fp));
}
```

To parse the file, I first try to open it using **fopen()**. Then I loop through the file and send the retrieved data to the parser. The main loop stops once the entire file has been read, and the parser is told to stop once the end of the file has been reached.

12. Free up the parser and complete the page:

```php
xml_parser_free($p);

?>

</body>

</html>
```

13. Save the file as **expat.php**, place it in your Web directory, along with **books4.xml** (Script 13.7), **collection. dtd** (Script 13.6), and the **phpvqp3.jpg** image file (downloadable from the book's Web site, **LarryUllman.com**).

14. Test in your Web browser **B**.

TIP Remember when working with XML to always use formal PHP tags (<?php and ?>). The informal PHP tags (<? and ?>) will conflict with XML tags.

TIP For more on the Expat functions, see www.php.net/xml.

TIP The Expat library can read an XML document, but it cannot validate one.

TIP You can change the case-folding using xml_parser_set_option().

PHP Advanced and Object-Oriented Programming:

AUTHOR: Larry Ullman
YEAR: 2012

Chapter 12: PHP's Command-Line Interface

Chapter 13: XML and PHP

Chapter 14: Debugging, Testing, and Performance

Modern JavaScript: Develop and Design

AUTHOR: Larry Ullman

B Running **books4.xml** through the PHP-Expat parser generates this HTML page, viewable in any browser.

Using SimpleXML

Expat provides an acceptable way to process XML, but it's not without its negatives. For example, attributes are only available when Expat encounters the opening tag. In the previous example, it would not be easy, for example, to show the number of pages after a chapter's name or the edition after a book title. Fortunately, as with almost everything in programming, there is an alternative approach.

Added in PHP 5 is a great tool for working with XML documents, called SimpleXML. While not as elaborate as other DOM-based parsers, SimpleXML is terrifically easy to use, with several nice built-in features.

To start the process off, use the `simplexml_load_file()` function to load an XML file into an object:

```
$xml = simplexml_load_
file('filename.xml');
```

Alternatively, you could use `simplexml_load_string()` if you had a bunch of XML stored in a string.

From there, there are many ways you could access the XML data. To refer to specific elements, use the format `$xml->`*`elementname`*. If there are multiple items of the same element, you could treat them like arrays:

```
echo $xml->elementname[0];
```

Looking at the DOM represented by the tree in Ⓐ, you could use `$xml->product[0]` and `$xml->product[1]`.

For nested elements, just continue this syntax:

```
echo $xml->product[0]->name;
```

```
echo $xml->product[1]->price;
```

Using a **foreach** loop, it's easy to access every element in a tree:

```
foreach ($xml->product as $product) {
    // Do something with:
    // $product->name
    // $product->size
    // etc.
}
```

Attributes are easy to access as well, by referring to them like an array:

```
$xml->elementname['attribute'];
```

With just this bit of information in mind, let's parse the **books4.xml** file using SimpleXML this time. The output will start by matching that created using Expat, but with a little more information and flair.

Modifying XML

The SimpleXML library also makes it easy to modify the loaded XML data. The **addChild()** and **addAttribute()** methods let you add new elements and attributes. You can also change the value in an element by using the assignment operator:

```
$xml->product->name =
→ 'Heavy T-Shirt';
```

To use SimpleXML:

1. Create a new document in your text editor or IDE, to be named **simplexml. php**, beginning with the standard HTML (Script 13.9):

```
<!doctype html>
<html lang="en">
<head>
  <meta charset="utf-8">
  <title>SimpleXML Parser</title>
  <link rel="stylesheet"
→ href="style.css">
</head>
<body>
<?php # Script 13.9 - simplexml.php
```

continues on page 443

Script 13.9 The SimpleXML library provides an easy, DOM-based way to access all of the data in an XML file.

```
1    <!doctype html>
2    <html lang="en">
3    <head>
4      <meta charset="utf-8">
5      <title>SimpleXML Parser</title>
6      <link rel="stylesheet" href="style.css">
7    </head>
8    <body>
9    <?php # Script 13.9 - simplexml.php
10
11   /*  This script will parse an XML file.
12    *  It uses the simpleXML library, a DOM parser.
13    */
14
15   // Read the file:
16   $xml = simplexml_load_file('books4.xml');
17
18   // Iterate through each book:
19   foreach ($xml->book as $book) {
20
21       // Print the title:
22       echo "<div><h2>$book->title";
23
```

script continues on next page

```
24      // Check for an edition:
25      if (isset($book->title['edition'])) {
26          echo " (Edition {$book->title['edition']})";
27      }
28
29      echo '</h2>';
30
31      // Print the author(s):
32      foreach ($book->author as $author) {
33          echo "<span class=\"label\">Author</span>: $author<br>";
34      }
35
36      // Print the other book info:
37      echo "<span class=\"label\">Published:</span> $book->year<br>";
38
39      if (isset($book->pages)) {
40          echo "<span class=\"label\">Pages:</span> $book->pages<br>";
41      }
42
43      // Print each chapter:
44      if (isset($book->chapter)) {
45          echo 'Table of Contents<ul>';
46          foreach ($book->chapter as $chapter) {
47
48              echo '<li>';
49
50              if (isset($chapter['number'])) {
51                  echo "Chapter {$chapter['number']}: ";
52              }
53
54              echo $chapter;
55
56              if (isset($chapter['pages'])) {
57                  echo " ({$chapter['pages']} Pages)";
58              }
59
60              echo '</li>';
61
62          }
63          echo '</ul>';
64      }
65
66      // Handle the cover:
67      if (isset($book->cover)) {
68
69          // Get the image info:
70          $image = @getimagesize
            → ($book->cover['filename']);
71
```

script continues on next page

```
72          // Make the image HTML:
73          echo "<img src=\"{$book->cover
         → ['filename']}\" $image[3]
         → border=\"0\" /><br>";
74
75      }
76
77      // Close the book's DIV tag:
78      echo '</div>';
79
80  } // End of foreach loop.
81  ?>
82  </body>
83  </html>
```

2. Read the file:

   **$xml = simplexml_load_file
   → ('books3.xml');**

   This one line is all you need to read in the entire XML document.

3. Create a loop that iterates through each **book** element:

   foreach ($xml->book as $book) {

   The XML file contains several **book** elements. With each iteration of this loop, another of the **book** elements will be assigned (as an object) to the **$book** variable. If the XML file is represented as a tree **C**, then **$book** at this point is one of the branches of the tree.

   continues on next page

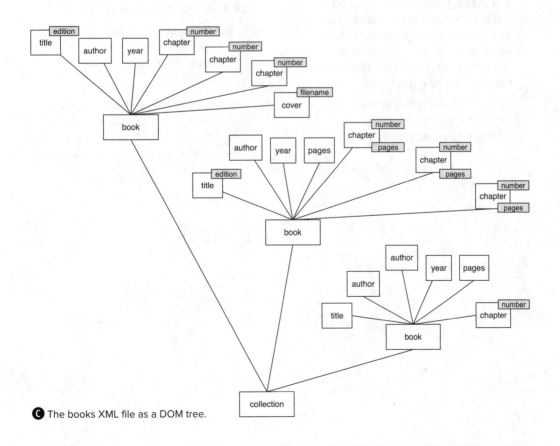

C The books XML file as a DOM tree.

4. Print the book's title:

```
echo "<div><h2>$book->title";
```

Referring to a subelement is this easy. For the first iteration of the loop, this is the equivalent of directly referring to **$xml->book[0]->title**.

The title will be printed within **H2** tags, which are started here, as is the **DIV** that surrounds each book.

5. Print the book's edition, if applicable:

```
if (isset($book->title['edition'])) {

    echo " (Edition {$book->title
    →['edition']})";

}
echo '</h2>';
```

The **isset()** function can be used to test if an element or attribute exists, as if it were any other variable. If the **edition** attribute exists, it'll be printed in parentheses: **(Edition *X*)**. Then the title's closing **H2** tag is printed.

As you can see, unlike in the Expat example, it's quite easy to access element attributes whenever you want.

6. Print the author(s):

```
foreach ($book->author as $author) {

    echo "<span
class=\"label\">Author</span>:
→ $author<br>";

}
```

Another **foreach** loop can iterate through all the authors. Remember that, by definition in the **collection. xsd** file, each book element has at least one author subelement, but it can also have multiple.

7. Print the year and the page count:

```
echo "<span class=\"label\">
→ Published:</span>
→ $book->year<br>";

if (isset($book->pages)) {

    echo "<span class=\"label\">
    → Pages:</span>
    → $book->pages<br>";

}
```

Most of this output will exactly match that of the Expat example, with some little differences such as easily being able to use *Pages* instead of *PAGES*.

8. Begin the process of printing each chapter:

```php
if (isset($book->chapter)) {
    echo 'Table of Contents<ul>';
    foreach ($book->chapter as
      →$chapter) {
```

A book may or may not have any chapter elements in it but could have several. The **isset()** checks if any exist. If so, the chapters will be printed as an unordered list. Another **foreach** loop will access each chapter.

9. Print the chapter information:

```php
echo '<li>';
if (isset($chapter['number'])) {
    echo "Chapter {$chapter
      →['number']}: ";
}
echo $chapter;
if (isset($chapter['pages'])) {
    echo " ({$chapter['pages']}
      →Pages)";
}
echo '</li>';
```

The chapter's name will be printed within **LI** tags. If the chapter has a **number** or **pages** attribute, that information should be printed as well.

10. Complete the chapter's **foreach** loop and conditional:

```php
    }
      echo '</ul>';
}
```

11. Handle the book's cover:

```php
if (isset($book->cover)) {
    $image = @getimagesize
      →($book->cover['filename']);
    echo "<img src=\"{$book->cover
      →['filename']}\" $image[3]
      →border=\"0\" /><br>";
}
```

If a cover element exists, the image's information is gathered from the file on the server and the appropriate HTML **img** tag is generated.

12. Close the **DIV** tag for this book and complete the page:

```php
    echo '</div>';
} // End of foreach loop.
?>
</body>
</html>
```

continues on next page

13. Save the file as **simplexml.php**, place it in your Web directory, along with **books4.xml** (Script 13.7), **collection. xsd** (Script 13.6), and the **phpvqp3. jpg** image file (downloadable from the book's Web site, **LarryUllman.com**.

14. Test in your Web browser **D**.

TIP The asXML() method returns the loaded XML data as an XML string.

TIP Because PHP treats elements and attributes as objects, you'll need to cast them to strings if you want to use them for comparison or in any standard string functions.

TIP SimpleXML also supports *XPath*, a language used to perform queries (search for data) within XML.

TIP The DOM parsers, like SimpleXML, will require more memory on the server than SAX parsers because they load the entire XML data into a variable.

PHP Advanced and Object-Oriented Programming:

Author: Larry Ullman
Published: 2012
Table of Contents
- Chapter 12: PHP's Command-Line Interface
- Chapter 13: XML and PHP
- Chapter 14: Debugging, Testing, and Performance

Modern JavaScript: Develop and Design

Author: Larry Ullman

D The beginning of the book's output.

Creating an RSS Feed

RSS, which stands for Really Simple Syndication (it used to mean Rich Site Summary or RDF Site Summary), is a way for Web sites to provide listings of the site's content. Normally, this list contains at least the titles of articles, plus their descriptions (and by "article," think of any type of content that a site might offer). Users access these feeds using an RSS client (many Web browsers support RSS as well). If a user wants to read more of an article, there's a link to click, which takes them to the full Web page. RSS is a great convenience and has become popular for good reasons.

RSS feeds are just XML files that have already-established tags. RSS documents begin with the **rss** root element, with a mandatory attribute called **version**. You'll want to use the latest version of RSS for that value, which is 2.0 as of this writing. So an RSS document starts with

```
<?xml version="1.0" encoding="utf-8"?>
<rss version="2.0">
```

After that, all RSS files contain a single **channel** element. Nested within this element are others, like **title**, **description**, and **link**, all of which describe the RSS feed.

```
<channel>
<title>Name of the RSS Feed</title>
<description>Description of the RSS
→ Feed</description>
<link>Link to the Web site</link>
```

Those three elements are required within **channel**. There are many optional ones, too, like **language** (e.g., *en-us*), **copyright**, **managingEditor** (an email address), **webMaster** (also an email address), and so on. See the formal specifications at **www.rssboard.org/rss-specification** for more.

The **channel** also contains multiple **item** elements, each item being a piece of content (an article). The **item** elements also have **title**, **description**, **link**, and other nested elements.

```
<item>
<title>Article Title</title>
<description>Article
→ Desc</description>
<link>Link to this article</link>
</item>
```

None of the item subelements are required, except that either a **title** or **description** must be present. You might also use **author** (an email address) and **pubDate** (the article's publication date). This last one is tricky because its value must be in the RFC 822–specified format. If you don't know what that is offhand, it's *Wed, 01 Nov 2012 16:45:23 GMT*.

That's really all there is to it! Remember, RSS is just formatted XML. If you understand XML, you can create RSS.

For this example, I'll create a pseudo-RSS feed of some blog postings. Naturally, most blogging software is capable of creating its own RSS feed, but it's a good use of the concept and will be easy enough for you to alter for your own needs.

To create an RSS feed:

1. Begin a new document in your text editor or IDE, to be named **rss.php** (Script 13.10).

   `<?php # Script 13.10 - rss.php`

   This is not a Web page to be viewed in the browser, so it creates no HTML, just XML.

2. Send the Content-type header:

   header('Content-type: text/xml');

   This page will have a **.php** extension, because it's a PHP page that must be properly handled by the Web server. But to create an XML page, a header should be sent with the proper *Content-type*.

Script 13.10 This PHP script uses an array to generate an RSS feed.

```
1    <?php # Script 13.10 - rss.php
2
3    /* This script will create an RSS feed.
4     * The feed content will be based upon an array.
5     */
6
7    // Send the Content-type header:
8    header('Content-type: text/xml');
9
10   // Create the initial RSS code:
11   echo '<?xml version="1.0" encoding="utf-8"?>
12   <rss version="2.0">
13   <channel>
14   <title>Larry Ullman&apos;s Important Things</title>
15   <description>The most recent things Larry has been writing about.</description>
16   <link>http://LarryUllman.com/</link>
17   ';
18
19   // Manufacture the data:
20   $data = array(
21       0 => array('title' => 'SSH Key Authentication', 'description' => 'The wonderful hosting
         �→ company that I use', 'link' => 'http://www.larryullman.com/2012/05/25/
         �→ ssh-key-authentication/', 'pubDate' => '1337930580'),
22       1 => array('title' => 'What It Means to Be a Writer, Part 1', 'description' => 'A little while
         �→ back, I had a series of emails', 'link' => 'http://www.larryullman.com/2012/05/23/
         �→ what-it-means-to-be-a-writer-part-1-defining-your-book/', 'pubDate' => '1337683425'),
23       2 => array('title' => 'Learn to Write', 'description' => 'There was a recent posting by',
         �→ 'link' => 'http://www.larryullman.com/2012/05/18/learn-to-write/', 'pubDate' => '133733103')
24   );
25
26   // Loop through the data:
27   foreach ($data as $item) {
28
29       // Print each record as an item:
30       echo '<item>
```

script continues on next page

```
31      <title>' . htmlentities($item['title']) .
        → '</title>
32      <description>' . htmlentities($item
        → ['description']) . '...</description>
33      <link>' . $item['link'] . '</link>
34      <guid>' . $item['link'] . '</guid>
35      <pubDate>' . date('r', $item
        → ['pubDate']) . '</pubDate>
36      </item>
37      ';
38
39 }
40
41 // Complete the channel and rss
   → elements:
42 echo '</channel>
43 </rss>
44 ';
```

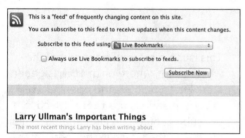

A Firefox, which supports RSS, shows the **channel** element's **title** and **description** values at the top of the page.

3. Create the initial RSS code:

```
echo '<?xml version="1.0"
→ encoding="utf-8"?>

<rss version="2.0">

<channel>

<title>Larry Ullman&apos;s
→ Important Things</title>

<description>The most recent
→ things Larry has been writing
→ about.</description>

<link>http://LarryUllman.com/
→ </link>

';
```

These lines of XML get the ball rolling. To start, there's the XML prolog, required in all XML documents. Next is the **rss** element and the opening **channel** tag. Within the **channel**, three tags are used to help describe this feed **A**.

continues on next page

4. Define the data to use for the feed:

```
$data = array(
    0 => array('title' =>
    'SSH Key Authentication',
    'description' =>
    'The wonderful hosting
    company that I use', 'link' =>
    'http://www.larryullman.com/
    2012/05/25/ssh-key-
    authentication/', 'pubDate' =>
    '1337930580'),

    1 => array('title' => 'What It
    Means to Be a Writer, Part 1',
    'description' => 'A little
    while back, I had a series
    of emails', 'link' => 'http://
    www.larryullman.com/2012/05/
    23/what-it-means-to-be-a-
    writer-part-1-defining-your-
    book/', 'pubDate' =>
    '1337683425'),

    2 => array('title' => 'Learn to
    Write', 'description' =>
    'There was a recent posting
    by', 'link' => 'http://www.
    larryullman.com/2012/05/18/
    learn-to-write/', 'pubDate' =>
    '133733103')

);
```

This data would normally be derived from a database, but this array is simple enough to use to demonstrate the core concepts.

5. Print each record as an item:

```
foreach ($data as $item) {
    echo '<item>
    <title>' . htmlentities($item
    ['title']) . '</title>
    <description>' . htmlentities
    ($item['description']) .
    '...</description>
    <link>' . $item['link'] .
    '</link>
    <guid>' . $item['link'] .
    '</guid>
    <pubDate>' . date('r', $item
    ['pubDate']) . '</pubDate>
    </item>
    ';
}
```

This is the most important part of the whole script, where each **item** is generated. First, you have the opening **item** tag. Then, there's the **title**, which is the subject of the posting and becomes the title of the article in the feed. After that is the **description**, which is what will be printed in the feed describing the article. For both the **title** and the **description**, the retrieved value is run through the **htmlentities()** function because XML does not allow many characters that might appear in those values.

Next is the **link** element, which is a link to the actual "article" online. After that is an element called a **guid**, which isn't required but is a good idea. This is a unique identifier for each item. The URL, which will be unique for each item, can be used here as well.

Finally, there's the **pubDate**, which needs to be in an exact format. Fortunately, PHP's **date()** function has a shortcut for this: *r*. This makes the formatting a lot easier!

6. Complete the **channel** and **rss** elements:

```
echo '</channel>

</rss>
';
```

7. Save the file as **rss.php**, place it in your Web directory, and load it in an application that supports RSS feeds 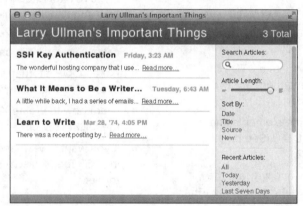.

Not all browsers support RSS natively; look online for RSS reading applications you can use, too.

TIP If you want to confirm that you've generated a valid RSS feed, check out http:// feedvalidator.org.

TIP Because of some perceived issues with RSS, an offshoot format called Atom was created. Meant to define a better standard for feeds, Atom is an open standard (unlike RSS, which is both closed and frozen from further development). Although Atom is worth considering, many of the largest Web sites still use RSS 2.0 for their feeds.

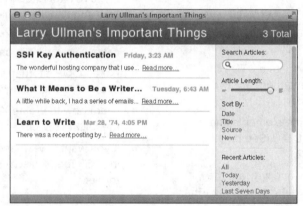

B Viewing the RSS feed in Safari.

Review and Pursue

If you have any problems with these sections, either in answering the questions or pursuing your own endeavors, turn to the book's supporting forum (**www.Larry Ullman.com/forums/**).

Review

- What does XML stand for? What is it used for? (See pages 409 and 410.)

- What line does XML data begin with? (See page 412.)

- What are the rules for XML tags? Is XML case-sensitive or case-insensitive? (See pages 412 and 413.)

- What are the rules for attributes? (See page 415.)

- If an element does not require a closing tag, what can you do instead? (See page 415.)

- How do you associate a DTD with an XML document (there are two answers)? (See page 419.)

- How do you define elements and attributes using DTD? (See pages 420 through 422.)

- What are entities and why are they required in XML data? (See page 415.)

- How does XSD differ from DTD? (See pages 425 through 427.)

- How do you associate an XSD with an XML document (again, two answers)? (See page 425.)

- What are the two types of XML parsers demonstrated in this chapter? How do they differ? (See page 432.)

- What are RSS feeds? How are they created using PHP? (See page 447.)

Pursue

- If you're unfamiliar with the HTML entities, research the topic online.

- Check online for existing DTDs that might be useful to you.

- If you want, rewrite **books3.xml** to use an inline DTD.

- If you think you'll want to use XSD more, search online for further tutorials and information. You'll also want to research the possible element types, beyond the basic ones.

- If you want, rewrite **books4.xml** to use an inline XSD.

- Check out the command-line **xmllint** (if your system has it) or an online XSD validation tool.

- If you're interested in XML, learn about how you can use namespaces.

- Check out possible XML editing applications that will run on your computer.

- For an OOP alternative to Expat, look into PHP's **XMLReader** class.

- Learn how to create XML in PHP using the **XMLWriter** class.

- If you want to learn more about creating RSS feeds, also research the Atom format.

Debugging, Testing, and Performance

To conclude this book, I want to discuss three concepts you'll most likely want to begin implementing as you go forward. By now you're certainly comfortable with debugging, and so, first, it's time to learn how to use third-party tools to make debugging easier. Second, there's the concept of *unit testing*, which can greatly change how you write, and test, software. Finally, there is the subject of profiling and performance enhancing.

Note that most of this chapter's material will require that you're able to install software on your server. This can—and often should—be your own development computer, though.

In This Chapter

Debugging Tools

When you first start programming, learning how to debug effectively is difficult. This is unfortunately ironic, because when you're just starting, you're doing *a lot* of debugging. Over time, however, you will pick up basic debugging skills and better understand the common causes of errors. And, hopefully, you'll become a better programmer who writes code with fewer errors in the first place.

As you start doing more sophisticated programming, particularly that involving objects, the basic debugging approaches may no longer suffice. At some point, it becomes time to pick up a third-party debugging tool that will offer you more bang for your proverbial buck. The three most common PHP debugging tools are:

- Advanced PHP Debugger (APD; `www.php.net/apd/`)
- DBG (`www.php-debugger.com/dbg/`)
- Xdebug (`www.xdebug.org`)

All are reasonably good choices, but in this chapter, I want to discuss Xdebug. It has the features you'll need and is well maintained (it was created by one of the core PHP developers, Derick Rethans). I'll first explain how to install Xdebug, and then introduce some of its basic usage.

That being said, if you're using a particular text editor or IDE for your PHP development, you ought to see if it supports Xdebug or another debugging tool. If so, you should enable and learn that debugger. By using a debugger enabled in your programming application, you will likely get other useful debugging features, such as the ability to create breakpoints and debug a PHP script as it runs.

Installing Xdebug

In order for you to use Xdebug, it must be installed and enabled in PHP. I'll explain how to do that in the next sequence of steps. As with the installation of pretty much any software, the particulars will vary depending on the operating system in use. In the steps, I'll explain how to install Xdebug on Windows. If you're using a version of *nix, including Mac OS X, see the sidebar.

Installing Xdebug on *nix

Installing Xdebug on *nix systems, including Linux and Mac OS X, can either be stunningly easy or painfully hard, depending on many factors. In any case, you'll need command-line access and the ability to execute commands as the super user. If you don't already know what these mean, installing Xdebug on your system may not be for you.

Xdebug can be installed on *nix systems using PECL (`http://pecl.php.net`). Assuming you have PECL installed, then it's just a matter of executing

```
pecl install xdebug
```

or

```
sudo pecl install xdebug
```

In theory, this will work. However, on my Mac, I had to take many, many steps to get this to work properly (largely because the tools PECL needs to work were not installed already).

If you also have problems, I'd recommend searching the Web or using my support forums for assistance.

To install Xdebug on Windows:

1. Run a **phpinfo()** script to confirm that Xdebug is not already installed.

    Xdebug is not likely to be installed, but it's best to check nonetheless. The rest of the steps assume Xdebug is not already installed.

2. Check if the Xdebug extension already exists on your computer.

    For example, if you installed XAMPP (**www.apachefriends.org**), the **php_xdebug.dll** file can be found in your **<XAMPP install directory>\php\ext** directory (e.g., **C:\xamppp\php\ext**).

    If that DLL file or another usable Xdebug DLL file *does* exist on your computer, skip to Step 5.

3. If the Xdebug extension does not already exist on your computer, download it from **www.xdebug.org**.

    Prebuilt Windows extensions are available in several flavors from the downloads page **A**. If you're unsure which variant you should download, see the custom installation instructions page. On that page, you can paste the output from a **phpinfo()** script, and it will tell you precisely which file to download.

4. Move the downloaded file into a logical directory on your computer.

    It'd make the most sense to place it in the same directory as your other PHP extensions.

5. Open your PHP configuration file in a text editor or IDE.

    If you don't know what your active PHP configuration file is, check the output from a **phpinfo()** script.

continues on next page

RELEASES

The Windows binaries generally work for every mini release for the mentioned PHP version, although the extension is built against the most current PHP version at that time. The VC*x* marker tells with which compiler the extension was built, and Non-thread-safe whether ZTS was disabled. Those qualifiers need to match the PHP version you're using. If you don't know which one you need, please refer to the custom installation instructions.

Xdebug 2.2.1
Release date: 2012-07-14

* source (MD5: 5e5c467e920240c20f165687d7ac3709)
* Windows binaries:
    PHP 5.2 VC9 (32 bit) (MD5: fc20a8709283cb867b88a267e88eba29)
    PHP 5.2 VC9 TS (32 bit) (MD5: e12b84fbf9ad73c0ea28c18c07e5f355)
    PHP 5.3 VC9 (64 bit) (MD5: 0d63405c057efac6a53dc7d3d5c26b88)
    PHP 5.3 VC9 (32 bit) (MD5: ec6924d1912a2917006dbfa8eacbe2a0)
    PHP 5.3 VC9 TS (64 bit) (MD5: 466ed4527988320e093071614b1464c2)
    PHP 5.3 VC9 TS (32 bit) (MD5: fc5a776b3b9a007b9520d863b447e89d)
    PHP 5.4 VC9 (64 bit) (MD5: 5ef86c46d386c50079c721c0e336e303)
    PHP 5.4 VC9 (32 bit) (MD5: 303539c59286941f236ce12c78f87105)
    PHP 5.4 VC9 TS (64 bit) (MD5: 81cacc87168c99c7f65ba202dc12c4b2)
    PHP 5.4 VC9 TS (32 bit) (MD5: 0004d5a52f012c25123efa950f2ccfce)

A Download a prebuilt version of Xdebug that matches your Web server configuration.

6. Enable the Xdebug extension by adding this line:

```
zend_extension = "C:\xampp\php\
→ ext\php_xdebug.dll"
```

You should first search the file to see if Xdebug isn't already referenced. For example, using XAMPP, that line already exists but is commented out (i.e., it's prefaced by a semicolon). In that case, enabling the extension is just a matter of removing the semicolon.

If Xdebug is not referenced, you need to add that line.

In any case, make sure that the path to the DLL file is accurate for your system.

7. Save the PHP configuration file.

8. Restart your Web server.

9. Rerun a `phpinfo()` script to confirm that Xdebug is enabled **B**.

TIP Xdebug will conflict with some other PHP extensions and can adversely affect performance of scripts and the Web server. For these reasons, I recommend that you *not* install Xdebug on a production server.

TIP Although Xdebug is open source, and therefore free, "support agreements" are available. These are essentially donations to Derick Rethans for the work he has done creating and supporting Xdebug.

xdebug

xdebug support	enabled
Version	2.1.0rc1

Supported protocols	Revision
DBGp - Common DeBuGger Protocol	$Revision: 1.145 $

Directive	Local Value	Master Value
xdebug.auto_trace	Off	Off
xdebug.collect_assignments	Off	Off
xdebug.collect_includes	On	On
xdebug.collect_params	0	0

B Xdebug is now enabled!

Using Xdebug

Once you've successfully installed Xdebug, you can start using it in your scripts. There's really not much to that—Xdebug does all the heavy lifting for you. The following will explain how to use the new features Xdebug adds to your PHP installation.

To use Xdebug:

- Use **var_dump()** to learn more about any particular variable **C**.

  The first feature that Xdebug adds that you should take advantage of is a more useful and attractive **var_dump()** output:

  ```
  # Iterator.php - Script 9.9
  // other code
  var_dump($hr);
  ```

  Presumably, you're already using **var_dump()** as a debugging tool, and now it's just better.

- If you're specifically interested in the values of any global variables, invoke the **xdebug_dump_superglobals()** function **D**:

  ```
  xdebug_dump_superglobals();
  ```

- To adjust what specific global variables are shown, change how Xdebug runs:

  ```
  ini_set('xdebug.dump.SERVER', '*');
  ini_set('xdebug.dump.GET',
  → 'something');
  ```

  Xdebug can be configured in a couple of ways (see the sidebar), but using **ini_set()** within the script is simple and direct. The previous two lines of code say that you want to see all of the **$_SERVER** values but only **$_GET['something']**.

  To be clear, those lines need to be added before the **xdebug_dump_superglobals()** function call.

  continues on next page

```
object(Department)[1]
  private '_name' => string 'Human Resources' (length=15)
  private '_employees' =>
    array
      0 =>
        object(Employee)[2]
          private '_name' => string 'Jane Doe' (length=8)
      1 =>
        object(Employee)[3]
          private '_name' => string 'John Doe' (length=8)
  private '_position' => int 0
```

C Xdebug makes the **var_dump()** output more information and easier to use.

```
Dump $_SERVER
$_SERVER['MIBDIRS']          =string 'C:/xampp/php/extras/mibs' (length=24)
$_SERVER['MYSQL_HOME']       =string '\xampp\mysql\bin' (length=16)
$_SERVER['OPENSSL_CONF']     =string 'C:/xampp/apache/bin/openssl.cnf' (length=31)
$_SERVER['PHP_PEAR_SYSCONF_DIR'] =string '\xampp\php' (length=10)
$_SERVER['PHPRC']            =string '\xampp\php' (length=10)
$_SERVER['TMP']              =string '\xampp\tmp' (length=10)
$_SERVER['HTTP_HOST']        =string 'localhost' (length=9)
```

D A pretty display of the global variables and values received by a page.

- To show undefined values, too, add this code:

  ```
  ini_set('xdebug.dump.undefined',
  → 'on');
  ```

  By default, the **xdebug_dump_superglobals()** function does not show undefined values. To change that behavior, turn that setting on.

- To see what else Xdebug does for you, manually create a (non-parse) error and rerun the script **E**.

Another benefit of using Xdebug arises without adding any extra code to a script. When an error occurs, Xdebug will automatically output a very useful stack trace **E**. This is equivalent to invoking **debug_print_backtrace()**, plus some HTML formatting.

There are a couple of caveats about this, however. Xdebug will not print stack traces if the following is true:

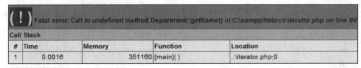

#	Time	Memory	Function	Location
1	0.0016	351160	{main}( )	..\iterator.php:0

(Fatal error: Call to undefined method Department::getName() in C:\xampp\htdocs\iterator.php on line 90)

Call Stack

E Error messages are now displayed in a prettier, and slightly more informative, format.

Customizing Xdebug

You can customize how Xdebug runs in one of two ways. The first is to use the **ini_set()** function. This function can be used to change many different PHP settings, including those in Xdebug. Alternatively, you can directly edit the PHP configuration file.

The arguments for doing the latter are first, that you only have to make changes once and they'll apply to all scripts. Second, the changes will apply even if the script has a parse error. The negatives are that you have to have permission to edit the PHP configuration file—and be comfortable doing so, and that you have to restart the Web server with every change.

It's easier to use **ini_set()**, but you have to add the necessary code to every file, or create an includable file that does the same. Invocations of **ini_set()** also have no effect if the PHP script has a parse error.

However you decide to customize Xdebug's behavior, see the Xdebug documentation for all of the possible options.

- The **display_errors** setting is disabled (which should not be the case on a development server anyway).

- You're using your own custom error handler.

- Exceptions are thrown.

  The next two bullets explain how to circumvent these last two issues.

- To use Xdebug output in your own error handler, call

  xdebug_get_function_stack();

  This function returns the Xdebug output for you.

- To enable Xdebug handling of exceptions, use this **F**:

  ini_set('xdebug.show_exception_
  →trace', 'on');

- To have Xdebug report on the values passed to functions, use this **G**:

  ini_set('xdebug.collect_params',
  →'4');

  There are other possible values, from the default of 0 (if you do not want to show those values) to 4, which shows the most amount of information.

- For even more information about function calls, have Xdebug show the value of local variables:

  ini_set('xdebug.show_local_vars',
  →'on');

TIP An alternative way to use Xdebug is to have it write all the data to a trace log. This is a separate file that you would then need to review.

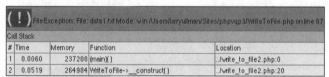

F Xdebug's stack trace for a thrown exception.

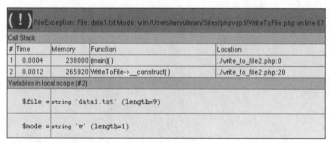

G Xdebug's more detailed information about a specific function call **F**.

Unit Testing

Unit testing is a relative newcomer to programming, but it is an approach that many developers have embraced. The premise of unit testing is that you define tests to confirm that particular bits of code work as needed.

Here are a few of the benefits of unit testing:

- Tests will minimize bugs (this is the most obvious benefit).

- Tests can help you improve your design.

- Tests can assist in creating documentation for your code.

- You are less likely to break code and introduce errors as you make changes down the line.

Learning how to implement unit testing involves syntax and theory. I'll introduce both in this chapter.

As for unit testing theory, unit tests should

- Be easy to write, read, and execute.

- Be as atomic as possible (i.e., specific and small).

- Check that code works as intended.

- *Not* be used to validate user input.

- *Not* be used to handle problems that could possibly arise during the live execution of a site.

To put these ideas in context, remember that error and exception handling in your code should watch for *bad things that could possibly happen*. This might be poor user input or an inability to open a file. Unit testing, as a comparison, should test for *what absolutely should happen and what absolutely shouldn't*. You'll see specific examples shortly.

As the scope of the application increases, and as you add and modify the code, you continue to write tests for the new code, while still checking all of the original code against the existing tests, too. By doing this, you ensure that the introduction of new and modified code doesn't break something that was previously working.

The best way to implement unit testing is to use one of the many libraries available for the purpose. The de facto standard is PHPUnit (**www.phpunit.de**). Over the next several pages, I'll explain how to define tests and run your code against them.

TIP A popular alternative to PHPUnit is Simpletest (**www.simpletest.org**).

Test-Driven Development

In this chapter, the focus is on writing unit tests to validate existing code. Another approach is called *test-driven development* (TDD). It takes the opposite stance: you define your tests and then write code that passes those tests.

Although this approach may be counterintuitive, there's a lot to be said for it. Besides the unit-testing benefits already outlined, TDD also means:

- You won't end up writing tests to match the code (which, therefore, defeats the purpose of testing).

- You have targets to shoot for, in terms of features needed and what isn't required.

- You know when the code is done, because all the tests pass.

- You're less likely to experience "coder's block," because you'll have a running list of what to code next.

TDD is related to the concept of *extreme programming*, which, as you might imagine, is an entirely different way of creating software.

Installing PHPUnit

In order to use PHPUnit, you must first install it. It's available through PEAR (http://pear.php.net). If you haven't used PEAR before, check out the PEAR manual (or search the Web, or ask in my support forums) for more instructions.

To install PHPUnit:

1. Access your computer via a command-line interface.

    If you're not accustomed to using the command line, these steps may be a bit advanced for you.

2. Upgrade PEAR 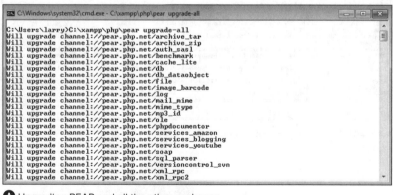:

    ```
    pear upgrade-all
    ```

    PHPUnit recommends that you upgrade PEAR before installing PHPUnit. This command will upgrade all the PEAR packages (including PEAR itself).

    Note that on non-Windows operating systems, you may need to preface this command with **sudo**:

    ```
    sudo pear upgrade-all
    ```

continues on next page

A Upgrading PEAR and all the other packages.

You may also need to provide a full path to PEAR:

```
sudo /path/to/pear upgrade-all
```

Or (on Windows with XAMPP):

```
C:\xampp\php\pear upgrade-all
```

Again, search online or use the support forums if you have difficulty with this.

3. Install PHPUnit **B**:

```
pear config-set auto_discover 1
```

```
pear install pear.phpunit.de/
→ PHPUnit
```

PHPUnit does not reside in the normal PEAR locations (aka, *channels*), so the first command is necessary in order to download PHPUnit from the PHPUnit.de Web site.

Again, you may need to preface these commands with **sudo** and/or the full path to PEAR.

You should see a message **B** upon successful completion.

Defining tests

Unit tests are defined using *assertions*. An assertion is a programming concept that simply says: confirm that this is the case.

In theory, you could define your own assertion functions, but one of the benefits of a unit-testing framework such as PHPUnit is the number of assertion functions it defines for you:

- `assertContains()`
- `assertCount()`
- `assertEquals()`
- `assertFalse()`
- `assertFileExists()`
- `assertGreaterThanOrEqual()`
- `assertNull()`
- `assertRegExp()`
- `assertSame()`
- `assertTrue()`

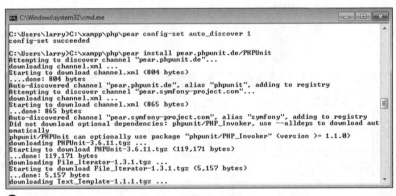

B PHPUnit has been successfully installed.

That's just a smattering of the assertion functions that exist. For a full listing, and to see how each is used, see the PHPUnit manual.

To create a unit test, you need to match an assertion function with the goal of the particular test. For example, the following code would assert that **$needle** is found in **$haystack**:

```
assertContains($needle, $haystack);
```

Because this is an assertion, this test would fail if the needle is *not* found within the haystack. This is functionally equivalent to

```
if (!in_array($needle, $haystack)) {
    echo 'The test has failed!';
}
```

As another example, this code asserts that **$var** equals *PHPUnit*:

```
assertEquals('PHPUnit', $var);
```

Using code examples from this book, the **check_urls.php** file (Script 11.2) has a **check_url()** function that is supposed to return an array containing two elements. You can test for that:

```
$results = check_url($url);
```

```
assertCount(2, $results);
```

Or, as another example, the **getName()** method of the **Employee** class (used in various formats in various chapters) should return the given **Employee** object's name. Here's that test:

```
$e = new Employee('Chuck');
```

```
assertEquals('Chuck', $e->getName());
```

This may seem a bit silly and redundant, but that's kind of the point: let's confirm that the code does exactly—and only— what it's supposed to do.

Assertions are at the heart of unit testing: what is it that must be the case. In theory, each test should assert one specific idea, although sometimes a test may assert a couple of very similar ideas.

TIP PHPUnit is also capable of validating output (what would be printed) via PHP's output buffering. See the PHPUnit manual for details.

TIP Most PHP errors will also equate to a test failure in PHPUnit.

Creating test cases

Tests in PHPUnit get grouped together in a suite of *test cases*. Normally, one suite of test cases would be created for each class you've defined. Understand that unit testing is *not* specific to object-oriented programming but is more commonly used with OOP than with procedural programming, particularly when frameworks are involved.

With PHPUnit installed, you create a test suite by extending the **PHPUnit_Framework_TestCase** class:

```
class SomeClassTest extends PHPUnit_
→ Framework_TestCase {
}
```

Conventionally, you'll name the new class a combination of the name of the class being tested, followed by *Test*.

Within this class, create one new public method for each test. Each method's name should start with *test*:

```
function testSomething() {
    // Actual test.
}
```

There won't be a one-to-one correlation between the number of test methods defined and the number of methods in the class being tested. This is because class methods may be complex and do multiple things, whereas unit tests are intended to be small and specific.

The last thing to know before getting into an example is that you must invoke all the assertion methods via **$this**:

```
function testSomething() {
    $this->assertTrue($var);
}
```

Using the **$this** object is necessary because when PHPUnit goes to run the tests, it will create an object of the class type. Through that object, the tests will be run, and the assertion functions will be accessible via **$this**.

To demonstrate unit testing, let's create some unit tests for the **Rectangle** class, first introduced in Chapter 4, "Basic Object-Oriented Programming." In this next sequence of steps, you'll create just a single test and then learn how to run that. Subsequently, you'll create all the requisite tests.

To create a test case:

1. Begin a new PHP script in your text editor or IDE, to be named **RectangleTest. php** (Script 14.1):

   ```
   <?php # RectangleTest.php -
   → Script 14.1
   ```

2. Include the **Rectangle** class:

   ```
   require('Rectangle.php');
   ```

   In order to actually test the class, this class will need to make objects of that

Script 14.1 This shell defines one unit test.

```
1    <?php # RectangleTest.php - Script 14.1
2    // This page defines the RectangleTest
     → class.
3
4    // Need the Rectangle class in order
     → to work:
5    require('Rectangle.php');
6
7    // Define the class:
8    class RectangleTest extends
     → PHPUnit_Framework_TestCase {
9
10       // Test the getArea() method:
11       function testGetArea() {
12
13           // Need a Rectangle:
14           $r = new Rectangle(8,9);
15
16           // The assertion tests the math:
17           $this->assertEquals
             → (72, $r->getArea());
18
19       } // End of testGetArea() method.
20
21   } // End of RectangleTest class.
```

class type. Therefore, this page must also include that class definition.

3. Begin defining the test class:

```
class RectangleTest extends
→ PHPUnit_Framework_TestCase {
```

This class inherits from the **PHPUnit_Framework_TestCase** class.

4. Start defining the **getArea()** test method:

```
function testGetArea() {
```

This test will verify that the **Rectangle** class's **getArea()** method works as it should. Remember that all tests must begin with the word *test*.

5. Create a **Rectangle** object:

```
$r = new Rectangle(8,9);
```

The test needs this object in order to access the method being tested.

6. Define the assertion:

```
$this->assertEquals(72,
→ $r->getArea());
```

The **getArea()** method of the **Rectangle** class should return the value of the rectangle's height times its width. With dimensions of 8 and 9, that value should be 72. This assertion says that

it's expected that 72 is the result of the **getArea()** call.

7. Complete the method and the class:

```
} // End of testGetArea()
→ method.

} // End of RectangleTest class.
```

8. Save the file as **RectangleTest.php**.

As you're about to see, the tests themselves will be run from the command line, so the file does not need to be saved to your Web directory.

9. Save a copy of **Rectangle.php** in the same directory as **RectangleTest.php**.

TIP Xdebug supports the ability to check the amount of *code coverage*: how much of the written code is covered by unit testing. See the Xdebug manual for details.

Running tests

Once you've created a suite of tests, they can be run. This is normally done through the command line by executing the **phpunit** command:

```
phpunit SomeTest
```

This code will run the tests defined in **SimpleTest.php** and output the results. That's all there is to it! Note that you don't have to include the **.php** extension, as long as the test name is the same as the file it's in.

To run your tests:

1. Access your computer via a command-line interface.

2. Move to the directory where you stored **RectangleTest.php**:

   cd /path/to/dir

   Obviously, you'll need to change this to be correct for your system.

3. Run the tests 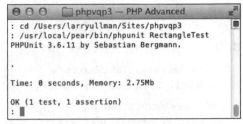:

   phpunit RectangleTest

   Again, depending on your computer, you may need to provide a full path to the PHPUnit utility.

4. Fix your code until it passes every test.

   In the output, a period indicates success and an *F* indicates failure 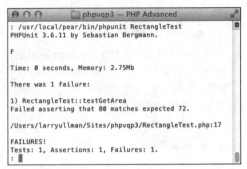.
   E means error and *I* means incomplete, or not yet implemented.

5. Celebrate!

TIP There are ways to run PHPUnit tests using code in your Web browser. Search online for examples.

TIP Although it may seem like a pain to run tests through the command line (as opposed to the Web browser), you can easily automate the process. When you have a lot of tests to run for a lot of classes, this is a much easier option.

TIP Depending on the operating system and the PHPUnit configuration, you may or may not need to include the class definition of the class being tested.

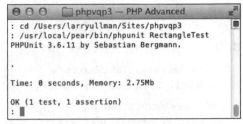

 The one test successfully passed!

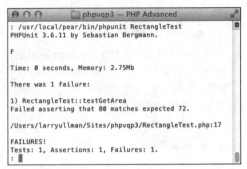

 If there was a bug in the code, the test would have failed.

Script 14.2 How you might use a **setUp()** method to help test the **WriteToFile** class from Chapter 8.

```php
1   <?php # WriteToFileTest.php - Script 14.2
2   // This page defines the WriteToFileTest
    → class.
3
4   // Need the WriteToFile class in order
    → to work:
5   require('WriteToFile.php');
6
7   // Define the class:
8   class WriteToFileTest extends
    → PHPUnit_Framework_TestCase {
9
10      // Need this information:
11      private $_fp = NULL;
12      private $_file = 'somefile.txt';
13      private $_data = 'test data';
14
15      // Open the file for writing:
16      function setUp() {
17          $this->_fp = fopen($this->_file, 'w');
18      }
19
20      // Write and test:
21      function testWrite() {
22          fwrite($this->_fp, $this->_data);
23          $this->assertEquals($this->_data,
              → file_get_contents($this->_file));
24      }
25
26      // Close the file:
27      function tearDown() {
28          fclose($this->_fp);
29      }
30
31  } // End of class.
```

Setting up tests

One of the hardest aspects of unit testing is accurately replicating how the code will be used in the real world. For example, almost always, *something* will have to happen before an assertion can be made, even something as simple as the creation of an object in order to test its methods. You can see an example of this in the **RectangleTest** suite. Those things you need in order to perform a test are called "fixtures" in unit-testing parlance.

In theory, you could create your fixtures in the testing method, as in the **testGetArea()** example. But if multiple tests all require the same fixture, there's a better alternative: define a **setUp()** method:

```
function setUp() {

    // Create object or whatever.

}
```

The **setUp()** method will automatically be called before each test is run. There is a corresponding **tearDown()** method that will be called after each test is run. For example, the **setUp()** method might open a file for writing, the test will confirm that the file can be written to successfully, and **tearDown()** would close the file (**Script 14.2**).

Note that you won't need **tearDown()** methods as often as you will **setUp()**. Also, each of these methods will be called before and after each individual test, not at the beginning and end of the entire test suite.

Let's complete the **Rectangle** class suite by adding a **setUp()** method and more tests.

To use a setUp() method:

1. Open **RectangleTest.php** (Script 14.1) in your text editor or IDE, if it is not already.

2. Add an attribute that will store a **Rectangle** object (**Script 14.3**):

   ```
   protected $r;
   ```

   This variable will be instantiated in the **setUp()** method.

3. Define the **setUp()** method:

   ```
   function setUp() {
      $this->r = new Rectangle(8,9);
   }
   ```

   This method creates a new object and assigns it to the attribute. To make this class even easier to read and use, you could place the width and height dimensions in class attributes, too.

4. Change the **testGetArea()** method so that it uses the attribute:

   ```
   function testGetArea() {
      $this->assertEquals(72,
      → $this->r->getArea());
   }
   ```

   Now this method can refer to the class attribute, instead of creating its own object.

5. Define the **getPerimeter()** test:

   ```
   function testGetPerimeter() {
      $this->assertEquals(34,
      → $this->r->getPerimeter());
   }
   ```

   This is similar to the **getArea()** test, but the math is different.

6. Define the **isSquare()** test:

   ```
   function testIsSquare() {
      $this->assertFalse($this->
      → r->isSquare());
      $this->r->setSize(5,5);
      $this->assertTrue($this->
      → r->isSquare());
   }
   ```

   The original rectangle object will not be a square, and the first assertion confirms that. To test that the method works properly when it should be a square, the rectangle is first resized.

continues on page 470

Script 14.3 The complete suite of tests for the **Rectangle** class.

```php
1   <?php # RectangleTest.php - Script 14.3 #2
2   // This page defines the RectangleTest class.
3
4   // Need the Rectangle class in order to work:
5   require('Rectangle.php');
6
7   // Define the class:
8   class RectangleTest extends PHPUnit_Framework_TestCase {
9
10      // For storing the Rectangle object:
11      protected $r;
12
13      // Create an object to use:
14      function setUp() {
15          $this->r = new Rectangle(8,9);
16      }
17
18      // Test the getArea() method:
19      function testGetArea() {
20          $this->assertEquals(72, $this->r->getArea());
21      }
22
23      // Test the getPerimeter() method:
24      function testGetPerimeter() {
25          $this->assertEquals(34, $this->r->getPerimeter());
26      }
27
28      // Test the isSquare() method:
29      function testIsSquare() {
30
31          // Should not be a square in this case!
32          $this->assertFalse($this->r->isSquare());
33
34          // Make it a square and test again:
35          $this->r->setSize(5,5);
36          $this->assertTrue($this->r->isSquare());
37
38      }
39
40      // Test the setSize() method:
41      function testSetSize() {
42          $w = 5;
43          $h = 8;
44          $this->r->setSize($w, $h);
45          $this->assertEquals($w, $this->r->width);
46          $this->assertEquals($h, $this->r->height);
47      }
48
49   } // End of RectangleTest class.
```

7. Define the **setSize()** test:

```
function testSetSize() {
    $w = 5;
    $h = 8;
    $this->r->setSize($w, $h);
    $this->assertEquals($w,
    ↪ $this->r->width);
    $this->assertEquals($h,
    ↪ $this->r->height);
}
```

You don't want to just assume that any method, including something as simple as **setSize()**, works properly. So this test first changes the rectangle's size and then confirms the results.

8. Save the file and run the tests **E**.

TIP Unit testing involving databases requires a fair amount of extra knowledge. See the PHPUnit manual for specifics and examples.

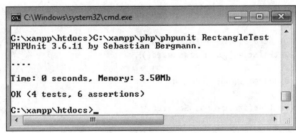

E All of the new tests have been run and successfully passed.

Profiling Scripts

Moving on from debugging and testing, a more advanced skill to pick up is *profiling* your scripts. Profiling is the process of analyzing a script to see where there may be performance problems: slow bits of code and process bottlenecks. Once you've got a script completely working, profiling in order to make performance improvements is a prudent next step.

There are several profiling tools available for PHP, starting with the debugging utilities already mentioned: APD, DBG, and Xdebug. Since I've already explained how to install Xdebug, let's use it.

However, profiling in Xdebug requires that you install another tool. Xdebug outputs its profiling data in a "cachegrind" format. Historically, this was readable by utilities such as KCacheGrind, originally written for Linux. While there are other utilities now available, it may be easiest to install webgrind (**https://github.com/jokkedk/webgrind**).

The next sequence will explain how to configure Xdebug to perform profiling, and how to install webgrind. In the following section of the chapter, you'll learn what to do with the results.

To use Xdebug with webgrind:

1. Download webgrind.

   The webgrind package is hosted at Github. You can download it from there, using the URL already mentioned.

2. Unzip webgrind.

   Webgrind comes as a zip file that must be expanded.

3. Move the resulting webgrind folder into your Web server directory.

   Webgrind is written in PHP, which means it needs to be on a PHP-enabled server and accessed through a Web browser.

4. Open your **php.ini** file in a text editor or IDE.

   The next step is to enable Xdebug in your PHP configuration file.

continues on next page

5. Add these lines of code **Ⓐ**:

```
xdebug.profiler_enable = 1
xdebug.profiler_output_name =
→ cachegrind.out.%t.%p
```

The first line turns the profiler on. The second line specifies the filename format for the profiling output. The filename will be *cachegrind.out* followed by a timestamp, followed by the process id.

You may also need to set the **profiler_output_dir** to a writable temporary directory **Ⓐ**.

6. Save the **php.ini** file.

7. Restart your Web server.

8. Run any PHP script to have Xdebug profile it.

TIP There's a strong argument for profiling your scripts as they run on the production server. But after doing so, be sure to disable Xdebug for better overall performance.

TIP Profile data files can get quite large. You'll want to watch the profiling output directory to clear those out once they're no longer needed.

TIP Xdebug can be configured to only profile a script if a certain value is passed in the URL or a cookie, which is a good idea.

TIP You probably won't need to configure how webgrind itself works, as it uses Xdebug's configuration by default. But if you do, just open the webgrind **config.php** file.

```
2105   ; xdebug.profiler_enable
2106   ; Type: integer, Default value: 0
2107   ; Enables Xdebug's profiler which creates files in the profile output directory. Those files can be
2108   ; read by KCacheGrind to visualize your data. This setting can not be set in your script with ini_set
2109   ; ().
2110   xdebug.profiler_enable = 1
2111
2112   ; xdebug.profiler_enable_trigger
2113   ; Type: integer, Default value: 0
2114   ; When this setting is set to 1, you can trigger the generation of profiler files by using the
2115   ; XDEBUG_PROFILE GET/POST parameter. This will then write the profiler data to defined directory.
2116   xdebug.profiler_enable_trigger = 0
2117
2118   ; xdebug.profiler_output_dir
2119   ; Type: string, Default value: /tmp
2120   ; The directory where the profiler output will be written to, make sure that the user who the PHP
2121   ; will be running as has write permissions to that directory. This setting can not be set in your
2122   ; script with ini_set().
2123   xdebug.profiler_output_dir = "C:\xampp\tmp"
2124
2125   ; xdebug.profiler_output_name
2126   ; Type: string, Default value: cachegrind.out.%p
2127   ;
2128   ; This setting determines the name of the file that is used to dump traces into. The setting
2129   ; specifies the format with format specifiers, very similar to sprintf() and strftime(). There are
2130   ; several format specifiers that can be used to format the file name.
2131   ;
2132   ; See the xdebug.trace_output_name documentation for the supported specifiers.
2133   xdebug.profiler_output_name = "cachegrind.out.%t.%p"
```

Ⓐ The relevant Xdebug configuration area of the **php.ini** file.

Improving Performance

Once you've started profiling your Web applications and scripts, you'll start to see how you can improve their performance. In looking at the profiling output, you can identify where the bottlenecks are. I'll explain the simple steps for viewing the profiling output in a moment, but first I'll explain what you should be watching for in the profiling results.

Start by looking at two possible indicators of inefficiency:

- Processes that take disproportionately more time than the others

- Processes that take disproportionately more time than they should

You should not focus on the specific amount of time different bits of code require to execute. Those times are unlikely to be that accurate. At the very least, the mere act of profiling a script is going to drag down its performance. Instead, look at the time a process takes relative to the whole script. There will be processes that you would expect to take a lot of time, but there will also be those that shouldn't. Look at the first category in hopes of making significant gains; look at the second because something may be amiss.

Implementing Server Caches

A great, but more advanced, way to improve the performance of your script is to implement *server-side caching*. Just as browsers cache resources so they don't have to be re-downloaded, you can have a server cache different Web components so that they don't have to be re-executed.

There are several types of caches you can implement. To start, you can cache the output of a script, which is to say the generated HTML. Once cached, the server can provide the static HTML file upon request, rather than rerun the underlying PHP script.

Second, you can implement *opcode caching*. PHP is an interpreted language. This means that at runtime—when a user requests a page, the server must read the PHP code and compile it into another code format, which is then executed. Opcode caching stores a version of the compiled code in server memory. This stored version can then be executed upon subsequent requests, saving the time and processing required to perform the compilation.

Depending on your database application, you may have *query caching*, too. There are variations on this, starting with having the database store the results of a query so that the query does not need to be executed again. Similarly, many database applications can "remember" or internally optimize queries. In such cases, the queries will still need to be executed, but they can be executed more efficiently.

For many of these caches, good PEAR classes and PECL extensions are available, such as the Alternative PHP Cache (APC). You can also see the documentation for your database application and look online for other tutorials.

Over time, by profiling and tweaking your code, you'll begin to pick up patterns. In particular, input/output operations will normally be the most expensive:

- Working with files
- Interacting with databases
- Networking (i.e., communicating with other servers)
- Interacting with the server (this includes working with files and databases, of course, as well as sending emails, calling other utilities, and so forth)

Your code is probably not *unnecessarily* doing any of these things, but they're worth investigating to see if you can't minimize or optimize those interactions.

You'll also find that user-defined functions can have a significant performance impact. In the profiling data, take a look at the *function call counts*: how many times a function is called. Then look into optimizing those that are called most frequently.

Other bottlenecks will arise from loops and working with large sets of data, such as XML or a big array.

Most importantly, make sure you don't introduce bugs as you make optimization tweaks. Of course, having unit testing in place will guard against doing so!

Just like you (hopefully) make fewer mistakes the longer you've been programming, in time you should be writing more efficient code after you've been profiling for a while.

To view the profile log in webgrind:

1. Load webgrind in your browser.

   This should be just a matter of going to `http://<domain>/<webgrind dir>`.

   (The downloaded file from Github has a longer name, but I rename the directory *webgrind*.)

2. Use the form at the time of the page to select what profile you want to view Ⓐ.

   At first, you'll probably want to view 100% of the profile data. Use the second select menu to choose the script being profiled. Then make sure you're viewing information in percent, as already explained.

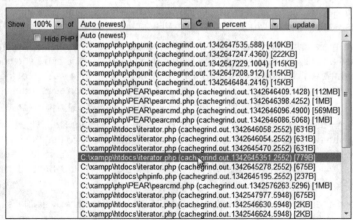

Ⓐ The webgrind interface for choosing a script profile data to view.

3. Use the columns at the top of the table to sort by different criteria 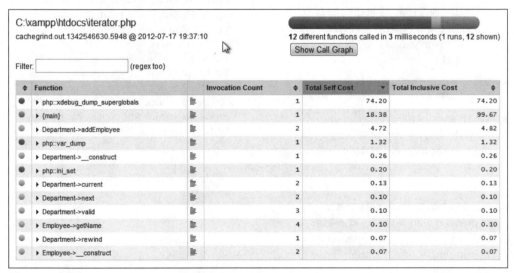**B**.

Start by looking at the *total self cost*. This is the time required to execute a given function, not counting any function calls that function may make. The *total inclusive cost* also reflects the time taken to execute functions that are called.

Next, look at the *invocation count*. A high invocation count with a low total self cost is good; the opposite may be a problem.

4. Click the arrow next to a function reference to see more information.

You'll see that the format presents PHP's own functions using the syntax *php::function_name*. Class methods are presented using *ClassName->method Name*. The code outside of any function or class is listed under *{main}*.

For a comparison of self cost vs. inclusive cost, you'll see that {main} will have a total cost of nearly 100%, which makes sense, because {main} represents all of the code being executed. However, the self cost for {main} will be much lower, as the primary code invokes lots of other functions and methods.

5. Find a potential problem, attempt to optimize the code, and re-profile.

6. Repeat Step 5!

TIP You can normally make the biggest performance difference by throwing money at the problem. This includes buying new hardware (e.g., multiple servers) or upgrading the hardware you have. That's not always feasible, however.

C:\xampp\htdocs\iterator.php
cachegrind.out.1342546630.5948 @ 2012-07-17 19:37:10

12 different functions called in 3 milliseconds (1 runs, **12** shown)
Show Call Graph

Filter: _____ (regex too)

Function	Invocation Count	Total Self Cost	Total Inclusive Cost
▸ php::xdebug_dump_superglobals	1	74.20	74.20
▸ {main}	1	18.38	99.67
▸ Department->addEmployee	2	4.72	4.82
▸ php::var_dump	1	1.32	1.32
▸ Department->__construct	1	0.26	0.26
▸ php::ini_set	1	0.20	0.20
▸ Department->current	2	0.13	0.13
▸ Department->next	2	0.10	0.10
▸ Department->valid	3	0.10	0.10
▸ Employee->getName	4	0.10	0.10
▸ Department->rewind	1	0.07	0.07
▸ Employee->__construct	2	0.07	0.07

B The profile data for the `iterator.php` script, run while using Xdebug.

Review and Pursue

If you have any problems with these sections, either in answering the questions or pursuing your own endeavors, turn to the book's supporting forum (**www.Larry Ullman.com/forums/**).

Review

- What is *Xdebug*? What useful features does it provide? (See pages 457 through 459.)

- What is *unit testing*? What are the benefits of unit testing? (See page 460.)

- What are some of the properties that unit tests should exhibit? (See page 460.)

- What is *TDD*? (See page 461.)

- What are *assertions*? How do you invoke the assertion methods within the test class? (See page 462.)

- How do you create a test case (a suite of tests) using PHPUnit? How do you create an individual test? (See pages 463–464.)

- What is *profiling*? What is *webgrind*? (See page 471.)

- What kinds of things should you be watching for in profile data? (See pages 473 and 474.)

Pursue

- If you're not entirely satisfied or impressed with Xdebug, consider installing and trying an alternative debugging or profiling tool.

- Begin using Xdebug as you develop new projects.

- Do more research on unit testing.

- Do more research on PHPUnit.

- Apply unit testing to as many script examples as you want from this book, or to your own code.

- If you like the concept of unit testing, look into TDD.

- Profile some of your own scripts and see what improvements can be made.

- Look into server-side caching.

More Application Testing

There are many ways of testing a script or application's performance, from benchmarking (simple timing of a script) to profiling to *load testing*. Load testing is where you emulate multiple concurrent users to see how the whole server responds.

Many utilities are available to help you perform load testing, including ab (ApacheBench), httperf, and siege. On the other side of the equation, I recommend using a utility such as YSlow! (this is a Firefox Web browser extension) to analyze the HTML and other resources the browser is required to download for your site. Many online sites can also run performance tests on a single page request and make decent recommendations on the results.

Index

B

b type specifier, meaning of, 37

backing up database, 356–357

backtrace, printing, 50

behavioral patterns

    explained, 215

    using, 233

books1.xml document, beginning, 413

books1.xml file, opening, 416

bootstrap file

    confirming module file, 60

    creating, 57–60

    header file, 60

    main page, 57–60

    purpose, 57

    switch conditional, 59–60

    validating, 59

browser cache, affecting, 75–79

C

c type specifier, meaning of, 37

cache header types, 75

cache-control directives, 75

Cache-Control header type, 75, 79

caching. *See also* server caches

    affecting, 76–79

    pages, 75

CGI (Common Gateway Interface), versus CLI (command-line interface), 378

check_urls.php document, creating, 334

class attributes, accessing, 127–132

class constants versus static attributes, 176

class design, benefits, 140

class versus object names, case-sensitivity, 126

classes. *See also* inheritance; OOP (object-oriented programming)

    versus abstract classes, 184

    attributes in, 121

    autoloading, 136

    components, 140

    creating objects from, 156

    defining for CMS with OOP example, 299–303

    defining in OOP, 121–123

    deriving from parents, 153–156

    designing with UML, 140–142

    functions in, 121

    get and **set** methods, 132

    inheriting, 152–156

    inheriting from, 153–156

    instanceof keyword, 152

    loosely coupled, 209

    methods, 121

    in OOP, 120

    relationship between, 203

    switch statement, 123

    using quotation (") marks with, 152

    variables in, 121

ClassName, destructor's name for, 139

ClassName::methodName() syntax, explained, 175

CLI (command-line interface). *See also* interactive PHP CLI

    backticks, 403

    built-in Web server, 405–407

    versus CGI (Common Gateway Interface), 378

    code blocks, 384–385

    command-line arguments, 395–399

    creating command-line script, 388–390

    creating interface, 399

    exec() backtick, 403

    executing bits of code, 383–385

    fscanf() function for input, 400

    -h option, 378

    -i option, 378

    -m option, 378

    pcntl (process control) extension, 403

    php.ini, 388

    remote server, 384

    running command-line script, 391–394

    system() backtick, 403

    taking user input, 400–404

    testing installation, 378

    using, 378

    -v option, 378

    verifying version of, 381